CISTERCIAN STUDIES SERIES: NUMBER SEVENTY-ONE

Medieval Religious Women I

Distant Echoes

MEDIEVAL RELIGIOUS WOMEN

CISTERCIAN STUDIES SERIES: NUMBER SEVENTY-ONE

Medieval Religious Women

Volume One

DISTANT ECHOES

Edited by
John A. Nichols and Lillian Thomas Shank

Cistercian Publications Inc.
1984

The work of Cistercian Publications
is made possible in part
by support from Western Michigan University.

Available in Britain and Europe from
A.R. Mowbray & Co Ltd
St Thomas House Becket Street
Oxford OX 1 1SJ

in all other areas from

Cistercian Publications
WMU Station
Kalamazoo, Michigan 49008

Typeset by the Carmelites of Indianapolis

Library of Congress Cataloging in Publication Data

Main entry under title:
Medieval religious women.
(Cistercian studies series; no. 71)
Contents: v. 1 Distant echoes.
1. Monastic and religious life of women—History—Middle
Ages, 600–1500—Addresses, essays, lectures. 2. Monasticism
and religious orders for women—History—Middle Ages,
600–1500—Addresses, essays, lectures.
I. Nichols, John, 1939–   II. Shank, M. Thomas.   III. Series
 BX4210.M345 1983   271'.9'000902   83–2111
ISBN 0-87907-871-5

Table of Contents

Foreword

THE SEEDS OF THIS VOLUME were first sown in 1980. What began as a sharing of enthusiasm for the history and spirituality of women between two secular scholars and a cistercian nun has gradually grown into an international collaboration between Cistercians and scholars and is now yielding a harvest of, not just one but, three volumes on medieval women religious. Men and women, academic scholars and contemplative religious who have a common bond of interest in women's position in the world today and in the past have worked together for over three years to bring this about. They shared a deep inner desire (I like to think, the movement of the Holy Spirit) to stir things up. They accepted the challenge of working side by side, motivated by the conviction that insight into woman's search for feminine identity, man's desire to understand his feminine pole, and their mutual need to explore interior spiritual values could be furthered by a study of women's history and a specifically feminine spirituality.

Providentially, the initial seed of interest sprouted and took root. The three enthusiasts—Dr Thomas Renna of Saginaw Valley State College, Michigan, Dr Rozanne Elder, editor of Cistercian Publications, and Sister Lillian Thomas Shank of Our Lady of the Mississippi Abbey in Iowa, saw grow up a team of editors which included Abbot Aidan Carr of Mepkin Abbey, South Carolina, Abbot Thomas Davis of New Clairvaux Abbey in California, Dr John Nichols, professor of history at Slippery Rock University in Pennsylvania, and cistercian sisters from Mount St Mary's Abbey in Massachusetts and Mississippi Abbey in Iowa. Dr Elder and Fr Chrysogonous Waddell of Gethsemani Abbey (Kentucky) were our faithful consulting editors and offered their wise advice at all stages of the venture.

In the autumn of 1980 we sent out a first Call for Papers on 'The Monastic Woman of the Medieval Period'. As contributions came in and as the editors began pruning to foster the growth of each into a cohesive whole, trying to meet the needs of both scholarly and monastic disciplines, we found ourselves with rich fruit.

THE THREE VOLUMES

The first volume, *Distant Echoes*, presents from an historical frame of reference the variety of lifestyles open to religious women from the fourth to the fifteenth centuries. It considers such important factors as economy, enclosure, relationship to bishops, and the reasons behind the evident lack of information about these nuns. Our contact with them is like a distant echo, often a barely audible reverberation sounding through the writings of and about men. This volume hopes to make those echoes clearer.

The second volume, *Peace-Weavers*, will focus more on individual women and their spiritualities, experiences, and values. They were indeed peaceweavers who drew together into an harmonious whole all peoples by their total choice of the nonviolent Christ in living their consecrated lives. They speak their messages of peace by this living witness, or, as Dr Jo Ann McNamara phrases it, by being 'living sermons' of the gospel message. They speak of devotion to the crucified Christ and an intensity of womanly love. Often referred to as the 'handmaidens of Christ' and as *sponsae Christi* (brides of Christ), they identified with the poor Christ in purity and simplicity. Called to weave peace by their lives of prayer, in the strong weakness of true humility and in an abounding charity, they challenge us to live, whether in the world or in the cloister, this peace in our time. These articles give valuable information on the lives of medieval religious women and express for us today the values they embodied.

The third volume, *The Cistercian Monastic Woman: Hidden Springs*, will deal specifically with the nuns of the Order of Cîteaux. Few studies of them exist in English. St Lutgard, Beatrice of Nazareth, Ida of Leau, Alice of Schaerbeek, St Gertrude and St Mechtild are vessels of living waters whose lives and writings put us in touch with that ultimate spring and source, the Holy Spirit. By their paths of hidden holiness they sought union with God and within this lived union a solidarity with their brothers and sisters. Viewing cistercian women from the twelfth to the seventeenth centuries, contributors to this volume also seek to lay the groundwork of historical and methodological studies. We hope that this beginning will invite even more studies on these fruitful yet hidden springs.

Each volume follows a chronological sequence, and because of the diversity of disciplines and subjects, each contains an epilogue chosen by the editors as focussing the studies therein.

CLOISTER AND CLASSROOM

This collaboration between monks and the academic scholars has been a pioneer endeavor. Challenging and rewarding, it has made both expand their horizons and helped each to be open to the other's discipline without betraying her own. We have learned much from each other. It has also been frustrating and at times discouraging, involving long hours of reading and discerning, consulting and recasting. We all nevertheless felt that this work is important in providing not only a solid scholarly assessment of medieval religious women, but also a portrayal of real women from the past. We wanted to find out what was important to them, to seek clues to their motivations, and to draw into focus their material and spiritual contribution to our christian tradition.

Ideally, the editors wanted articles that presented the whole woman, not merely the historical figure set in her religious institution—whether double monastery, anchorhold, or abbey—but the living woman, her sense of mission, her self-concept, her way to God as a *woman* religious. To condense this whole perspective into one article proved almost impossible. To view women across a thousand years in one volume proved equally difficult and the editors were obliged in Volume I to concentrate on historical circumstances and events and in Volume II on the personality and spirituality of individual women, the *monachae* of the Middle Ages. *These two volumes are meant to complement each other*; they represent two aspects of a single experience. This collaboration has also provided a beautiful experience of men and women cooperating—listening to each other, working together and sharing their unique gifts and insights.

The editors would like to encourage all readers to expand with us; we ask the academic scholars in their studies to be aware of the deeply human, and often deeply spiritual, experiences they analyse, and monastics to draw from the scholarly insistence on accurate content and objectivity a means to deepened insight into their own religious values. The lived monastic experience offers scholars a chance to draw into wholeness their data and analytical objectivity. Academic scholars offer the benefit of their broad experience and the gift of their unique personal visions developed in their own lifestyle. In these three volumes we have then the first fruits of this collaboration. We hope, in years to come, to see an abundant harvest.

ACKNOWLEDGEMENTS

Many were the laborers involved in sowing and cultivating these seeds. Mother Angela Norton, Abbess of Mount St Mary's Abbey had written to Cistercian Publications some years earlier to ask for studies on our cistercian nuns. Her support and encouragement has been constant throughout, as has that of Mother Columba Guare and Mother Gail Fitzpatrick, former and present abbesses of Mississippi Abbey. Other initial support came from the enthusiastic encouragement of Dr Renna and Abbot Thomas Davis. Abbot Thomas later became one of our editors and has done much to advance the project by his solid comments. Abbot Aidan Carr, with his lively remarks and wise suggestions, lightened the burden of much correspondence. Enlisting Dr John Nichols, professor of history at Slippery Rock University proved a significant step in the growth of our project, for he quickly became a tireless co-editor and efficient co-organizer. After years of personal research on medieval english cistercian nuns, his scholarly expertise has complemented the interest in spirituality of the monastic editors. He cannot be thanked enough for his generosity and his willingness to listen and frankly dialogue. To these men, working through some fifty articles, amid their professional and abbatial responsibilities, we owe much gratitude!

Alongside them are our sisters at Mount St Mary's Abbey, especially Sisters Agnes Day, Gertrude Ballew and Colman O'Dell, who read and commented on every article. Several sisters did translating and literary editing, and still others contributed articles. At Mississippi Abbey Sr Thomas Shank acted as coordinator of the project, handling most of the correspondence; Sister Mary Ann Sullivan helped by her careful reading and wise suggestions, as have Sisters Regina Keating, Rosemary Durcan, Kathy Lyzotte and Joanna Daly. We have learned many lessons and lived through many tensions in the production of these volumes; we have also enjoyed the adventure thoroughly.

We cannot forget our cistercian brothers who assisted wholeheartedly, some through letters of encouragement, some by doing literary editing and translating. Especially to be thanked are Brothers Stephen Veberst and Gerard McDonough of New Melleray Abbey in Dubuque, who did most of the copying work. Our contact with these men always showed an esteem for womanhood and feminine values and an eagerness to promote studies which would make these values known.

Our literary editors were Sister Beverly Aitkens of Santa Rita Abbey in Arizona, Sister Colman O'Dell of Mount St Mary's, Father Joseph Bauwens of New Melleray Abbey, and Sister Mary Adorita Hart, BVM of Clarke College in Dubuque, Iowa, who did excellent editing with great interest and generosity.

Last, but certainly not least, we owe a special debt of gratitude to all our contributors. We were impressed with their unfailing cooperation, their humble acceptance of readers' and editors' suggestions, and their unflagging encouragement to us. We had a sense of working together to make three really good volumes. Dr Penny Gold, Dr JoAnn McNamara and Dr Mary Skinner showed an active interest in the project by their suggestions and corrections. Especially insightful were the suggestions of Dr JoAnn McNamara on the material to be included in the introductions.

It has been a unique privilege for us to come into contact with all of you either personally, by letter, or through your articles. It is our prayer that Our Lady, the loveliest of women, may bless you all!

L.T.S. for
The Editors

Introduction

John A. Nichols

GIVEN THE LENGTH of the Middle Ages and the varieties of religious life experienced by women who lived in that era, the history of medieval religious women in western Europe is a topic enormous in scope. Current research in women's studies has proven that it is essential to study the activities and achievements of women in the past because those women can be an inspiration for persons who live in the present and their accomplishments can give guidance to those who plan for the future. The growing realization that women have made and continue to make important contributions to all aspects of human experience has produced a reading audience eager to learn more about women who were heretofore unknown or little known to students of the past. This volume on *Medieval Religious Women: Distant Echoes* is not only evidence of persons interested in writing and reading about a select group of women who lived in an important era in history, but it is also an attempt to expand our awareness of the activities and achievements of women who made significant contributions to their own age.

At the outset, the reader should be aware that the life of a medieval religious woman differed considerably from that of most of her modern counterpart. The teaching, nursing, missionary, and community work so commonly associated with modern religious women were insignificant or secondary responsibilities for the nuns of the Middle Ages. The primary purpose of the medieval religious woman was to do the work of God or the *opus Dei*; nuns spent much of their time in prayer and the divine offices. Medieval society recognized the importance of prayer and religious women charged with that responsibility were held in great respect.

The cloister was the ideal environment for the nuns to fulfill their spiritual obligations. The separation of the monastery from the world was considered necessary so that the nuns, like monks, could have a prayerful intimate relationship with God. The physical size of a nunnery to a large degree determined the number of women who could practise the religious life. Even though a great number of monasteries were founded for women during the Middle Ages, there were still more women who aspired to be nuns than

1

physical space allowed. As a consequence, only a select few were permitted
to join the ranks of religious women and it is on these women that this
volume focuses.

The importance of medieval monastic women was established as early as
eighty-seven years ago when, in 1896, Lina Eckenstein wrote an historical
overview of religious women in the Middle Ages for her *Woman Under Mo-
nasticisim*.[1] Her monumental work was followed in 1922 by Eileen Power,
whose study of *Medieval English Nunneries, c. 1275 to 1535* focused on a
geographic and chronological dimension for women in religious life.[2] Articles
and books in English since that time, such as Catherine Boyd's *A Cistercian
Nunnery in Medieval Italy*[3] or more recent works such as Brenda Bolton's
'*Mulieres Sanctae*'[4], Christopher J. Holdsworth's 'Christina of Markyate'[5], or
Eleanor McLaughlin's 'Women, Power and the Pursuit of Holiness in
Medieval Christianity'[6], are studies less comprehensive and more specific
than the earlier works. In addition to articles specifically on women,[7] one
can find reference to women in the histories of religious orders. These histories, however, always center on the activities of men and give the male
religious nearly all the credit for the achievements of their Order.

One such example of imbalance between the men and women within one
Order can be found in the very important book by Louis F. Lekai, *The Cistercians: Ideals and Reality*, published in 1977 by Kent State University Press.[8]
Lekai divided his book into two parts. The first is a history of the order
from the ecclesiastical reform of the eleventh century and the foundation of
Citeaux in 1098 to the White Monks of the twentieth century (pp. 1–224).
This half of the book details the activities of the most famous Cistercians,
such as St Bernard of Clairvaux, or the role of the abbots or their monasteries
in the growth and success of the Order. The second half of the book (pp.
227–399) relates specific topics of particular interest to the Cistercians, such
as the liturgy, *conversi* or laybrotherhood, economy, and art. It is in this half
of the book that there can be found a single chapter on the cistercian nuns
(pp. 347–363). While Lekai does a credible job of summarizing the part
women had in the Order, one can see from an analysis of his book that
women were assigned a very small part of the Order's total history. In specific terms, only seventeen pages out of 399, or less than five percent of
Lekai's total history, focused on the nuns of the Cistercian Order.

Why such inequality? Why have women not received greater attention
from historians? Male bias or misogynism aside, the difficulty of writing
about female religious stems from the lack of extant information on them as
compared to their better known, more fully documented male counterparts.
In medieval England and Wales, for example, there were over 700 monasteries of men who followed either the benedictine or augustinian Rules.
Their total population in the early thirteenth century has been placed at

14,000 religious, or nearly twenty monks per monastery.[9] There were, however, only 150 houses of women, with an estimated population of 3,000.[10] Even though these nuns and canonesses followed the same benedictine and augustinian rules as the monks and canons and had the same average twenty religious per convent, only 17.5 percent of all medieval monasteries in England and Wales were houses of women. 'Further, the male monasteries were nearly always larger [in physical size] and better [financially] endowed. Many nunneries existed on the edge of penury.' As a result, not only were there fewer nuns than monks but the smaller, poorer nunneries also left fewer records for historians.[12]

This imbalance between the relative wealth and the number of monasteries for men compared to women has not only led to the writing of men's history but it has distorted women's history. For example, two recent books on medieval monasticism state that the life of the nuns was the same as the monks, yet neither author could prove his statement or for that matter cite his source.[13] This is a device too frequently used to describe women's activities, namely, if the men did something, then it follows that women must have done the same thing. This reasoning is flawed because it does not take into account the institutional, biological, societal, and psychological limitations imposed on women.

Such limitations in the Middle Ages produced a number of factors which made the nunneries and the lives of women within them quite unlike life in monasteries for men. Some monks became ordained priests who administered to the sacramental needs of their brothers. Nuns, on the other hand, were denied ordination so they needed to hire a priest to celebrate Mass for the community and to hear the nuns' confessions. Many of the new religious Orders of the High Middle Ages, like the Cistercians, Franciscans, and Dominicans, were exempt from episcopal jurisdiction because they had their own internal visitation system. Nearly all nunneries, however, were subject to their local bishops and were thereby denied advantages the male houses enjoyed. Male religious could and did go to universities; women religious could not. Women found it much more difficult to egress from their convents to conduct business associated with their temporal affairs; monks were not nearly so restricted. These are not the only differences between the male and female religious, but the awareness that nuns had specific limitations imposed on them which were not applicable to monks proves that the religious life of the nuns was not the same as that of the monks.

Persons who write about the history of medieval religious women have come to realize that nothing can be taken for granted. Most of the time, one must start from scratch and reconstruct women's history from the extant documents. In many ways, *Medieval Religious Women: Distant Echoes* has done just that. Not only is this the first collection of essays to focus exclusively on women in religious life during the Middle Ages but it is also a volume that uses new sources or looks at well-known sources in a new way to discern the part that women played in history.

An excellent example of using well-known sources in a new way is our lead article 'Muffled Voices: The Lives of Consecrated Women in the Fourth Century' by Jo Ann McNamara. She found that when she studied the writings of male authors like Jerome, Ambrose, and Gregory of Nyssa she was able to extract information about women's lives which had been overlooked by others well-acquainted with the works of these saintly writers. Since no written work survives by any of the women McNamara identifies, she feels their story is 'muffled' because they speak not for themselves but through 'the writings of the most famous men of the age.' Her article sets the tone for the volume: the study of women's achievements has been curbed by lack of records, disinterest on the part of historians, and the inability of these women to speak out on their own behalf. As a result, the voices of these medieval women are like distant echoes which are hard to hear and difficult to interpret. McNamara's essay also sets the chronology for the volume. Her article deals with religious women in the fourth century, the earliest the editors felt reflected the forces which created the civilization known as the Middle Ages.

The next article by Dorothy de F. Abrahamse, 'Byzantine Asceticism and Women's Monasteries in Early Medieval Italy' continues themes introduced by McNamara. For one thing, Abrahamse focuses her study on the Early Middle Ages. For another, she admits that the dearth of sources makes it difficult fully to evaluate the role women had in monastic communities. Yet, within these limitations, Abrahamse scours all the sources available to students of this subject and produces a scholarly paper on female ascetic life as it was probably practised in byzantine convents of Rome and southern Italy between the seventh and tenth centuries.

The third paper in this collection is 'Strict Active Enclosure and Its Effects on the Female Monastic Experience (ca. 500–1100)' by Jane T. Schulenburg. It is well-known that during the Middle Ages both nuns and monks were enclosed within a monastery. Schulenburg explains how claustration separated the religious from the distractions of the world and produced an atmosphere conducive to prayer. Yet while both monks and nuns were believed to be equal in the eyes of God, Schulenburg found by her examination of sources that Carolingian reform councils established a precise, uniform, and rigorous policy of claustration for all nuns but not for all monks. Such reform produced different monastic ideals and expectations for women, and in time it affected all levels of their religious life, including in some cases the very survival of a community itself.

This notion is documented in the next article by Mary Skinner, 'Benedictine Life for Women in Central France 850-1100: A Feminist Revival.' She found that many monasteries for women did not survive the Carolingian period because they were either destroyed or were given over to monks or canons. When political conditions started to stabilize in the late tenth and early eleventh centuries, however, nunneries began to be founded and women were important in this revival. Skinner proves by the examination of the extant charters that women were active as both founders of and donors to women's monasteries, and that competition to enter was so keen that admittance to one benedictine monastery in central France was limited to women of at least the lesser aristocracy.

While Skinner does not survey the life-style of the nuns, the next article on 'Humility and Power: Anglo-Saxon Nuns in Anglo-Norman Hagiography' by Susan Millinger does. Her study is an analysis of the lives of two late tenth-century nun saints, Edith of Wilton and Wulfilda of Barking. The lives of these women not only show why they chose the monastic life but also narrate their deeds of charity, acts of humility, and workings of miracles. Both were excellent examples of how, by strong will and sustained faith, women were able to live a committed and successful religious life.

SUMMARY OF ARTICLES: HIGH MIDDLE AGES

Sally Thompson's paper, 'Why English Nunneries had No History: A Study of the Problems of the English Nunneries Founded After the Conquest,' marks the transition in the volume from the Early to the High Middle Ages. Yet while the eleventh century saw the flowering of medieval civilization, similar difficulties face authors who write about its women religious as hamper students of the Early Middle Ages; the 'very scarcity of documents' make it appear as if some nunneries 'had no history.' After surveying the relatively few primary sources available for English convents founded after 1066, Thompson goes on to explain why she feels the documents for recovering their story are so surprisingly meager.

The twelfth century witnessed a tidal wave of spiritual intensity which swept a revolution into religious life. New experiments in monastic living were attempted and the next two articles show examples of men and women working together to create a viable religious experience. Penny Gold's 'Male/Female Cooperation: The Example of Fontevrault' and Sharon Elkins' 'All Ages, Every Condition, and Both Sexes: The Emergence of A Gilbertine Identity' deal with new Orders founded by charismatic men but receptive to

the spiritual needs of women. Both Robert of Arbrissel, founder of Fontevrault, and Gilbert of Sempringham, founder of the Gilbertines, had women
followers right from the start, but the two articles demonstrate the different
relationships betwen the nuns and the canons or monks in the two Orders.
Gold proves by an examination of Fontevrault's early history that Robert of
Arbrissel successfully institutionalized an arrangement in which 'the women
were the focus of the community, with the men there to serve the women.'
Elkins establishes, on the other hand, that Gilbert of Sempringham had
difficulty organizing his vision for a religious life and it passed to others after
his death to justify the Order's existence and to determine the role women
were to play in it.

When new Orders would not accept females or there were not enough
abbeys to meet the needs of women, a phenomenon occurred during the
late twelfth and early thirteenth centuries in the urban centers of the Low
Countries as a result of this rejection. Dennis Devlin's 'An Example of
Feminine Lay Piety in the High Middle Ages: the Beguines' details both the
origin of this 'women's movement' and the success women had in practising
a form of religious lay piety. By examination of the lives of some of the more
prominent beguines, like Mary of Oignies, Devlin is able to show not only
the areas—such as eucharistic devotion—in which these women excelled but
also explains how their piety influenced the medieval Church and society.

'The Nun as Anchoress: England 1100–1500' by Ann K. Warren takes
Devlin's themes one step further by showing how the ecclesiastical establishment legitimatized female devotion. To be an anchoress, a woman had to
make up her mind to become a recluse and willingly remain a recluse for the
duration of her life. She had also to find sufficient financial support and a
suitable location for her cell or *reclusorium*. When ready, she applied to a
bishop and if he found her worthy he performed the rites of reclusion.
While Warren's paper does not elaborate on the type of spiritual life practised by the anchoress, she does prove that such a life was not only possible
for women but a calling highly respected by the institutions and peoples of
her day.

SUMMARY OF ARTICLES: THE CISTERCIAN CONNECTION

The issue of financing the *reclusorium* introduces the next article by Coburn
V. Graves, 'Stixwould in the Market Place: The Economy of an English-
Cistercian Nunnery'. It would be naïve for anyone to think that monasteries
of women could exist without an economic base. In order to live a religious
life nuns needed lands and income which would produce sufficient monies
to meet their expenses. Graves' insightful paper on the revenues of Stix-

would Priory not only documents the modest prosperity the nuns enjoyed but also demonstrates that between the date of their foundation and the advent of the Black Death in 1349, the women successfully managed extensive holdings throughout the diocese of Lincoln.

In addition to fiscal matters, a nunnery also had to contend with the supervision of male superiors charged with the care of the nuns. My article on 'Medieval Cistercian Nunneries and English Bishops' examines the relationship between the twenty-seven English Cistercian women's houses and the Church hierarchy. Episcopal jurisdiction over nunneries consisted of two types. First, the bishops had the right to confirm action initiated by the nuns, such as the election of an abbess or the appointment of a chaplain. Second, the nunneries were visited by the diocesan who examined their temporal and spiritual condition and ordered reform in areas found wanting. While problems certainly existed, a healthy religious life seems on the whole to have been practised by the nuns in these English houses.

The last article in the collection and the third consecutive paper on women and the cistercian Order is by Elizabeth Connor, 'Ten Centuries of Growth: The Cistercian Abbey of Soleilmont'. This house was founded in the Low Countries in 1088 as a benedictine nunnery but the nuns sought and secured affiliation with the cistercian Order in 1237. The difference between Connor's article and those which precede it is that hers does not limit itself to the Middle Ages but traces the history of the nuns of Soleilmont from the date of their abbey's establishment to the present. So often students feel that a topic in history has little or no meaning on their lives because the events occurred in the remote past. In the case of Connor's study, however, we learn not only about the medieval nuns of Soleilmont but about the religious lives of the women who live in that same community today and are therefore direct successors of, and affected by, a tradition which is still alive after nearly nine hundred years.

EPILOGUE

What remains to be said? The epilogue for this volume is written by Jean Leclercq as a question: 'Does St Bernard Have a Specific Message for Nuns?' In reading it, we discover that Leclercq does not think that Bernard, the famous cistercian abbot of Clairvaux, had a specific message for nuns. Rather the message Bernard imparted was not sex-specific but applicable to all persons, women and men, regardless of whether they lived in the Middle Ages, dwell in the present, or will exist in the future. In other words, Bernard's works, like those of other great authors, were written in the past but his ideas can still inspire those of any age who pause long enough to read them.

In like manner, this volume on medieval religious women is addressed not just to the medieval historian, the religious, or the student of women's studies. It is a volume written for those interested in expanding their awareness about themselves. By reading about what women did in the medieval past, we can come to an appreciation of their contributions and attainments. In hearing the distant echoes of what they did and how they influenced the world in which they lived, we can by association, faith, and work make a similar contribution. Taken in that light, *Medieval Religious Women: Distant Echoes* is not only a testament to the religious women who lived in the Middle Ages, but also an inspiration for us who live in the present.

Slippery Rock University
Slippery Rock, Pennsylvania

NOTES

1. Lina Eckenstein, *Woman under Monasticism* (New York: Russell and Russell, 1896).
2. Eileen E. Power, *Medieval English Nunneries, c. 1275 to 1535* (New York: Biblo and Tannen, 1922).
3. Catherine E. Boyd, *A Cistercian Nunnery in Medieval Italy: The Story of Rifreddo in Saluzzo, 1220–1300* (Cambridge: Harvard University Press, 1943).
4. Brenda M. Bolton, 'Mulieres Sanctae', *Women in Medieval Society* ed. Susan M. Stuard (Phil.: Pennsylvania Press, 1976) 141–158.
5. Christopher J. Holdsworth, 'Christina of Markyate', *Medieval Women*, ed. Derek Baker (Oxford: Blackwell, 1978) 185–204.
6. Eleanor McLaughlin, 'Women, Power and the Pursuit of Holiness in Medieval Christianity', *Women of Spirit: Female Leadership in the Jewish and Christian Tradition*, edd. Rosemary Ruether and Eleanor McLaughlin (New York: Simon and Schuster, 1979) 99–130.
7. In addition to citations in the works given above, a bibliography on women in religious life can be found in Giles Constable, *Medieval Monasticism: A Select Bibliography* (Toronto: University of Toronto Press, 1976) 56–61.
8. Louis J. Lekai, *The Cistercians: Ideals and Reality* (Kent: Kent State Univeristy Press, 1977).
9. The best souce for the names and numbers of religious establishments is David Knowles and R. Neville Hadcock, *Medieval Religious Houses England and Wales* (New York: St Martin's Press, 1971). For the sake of this comparison, I am omitting the mendicant Orders and the double-housed Gilbertines, and am dealing only with a community large enough to follow the regular observance of its monastic Rule. The monasteries by Order and number are augustinian canons (218), benedictine monks (292), bonshommes brethern (2), carthusian monks (9), cistercian monks (80), cluniac monks (32), grandmontine brethern (3), premonstratensian canons (38) and tironensian monks (4); in all 708. See Roy Midmer, *English Mediaeval Monasteries 1066–1540* (Athens: Georgia Press, 1979) 3–10.
10. The monasteries by Order and number for the women are augustinian canonesses (23), benedictine nuns (92), bridgettine nuns (1), cistercian nuns (29), cluniac nuns (2), premonstratensian canonesses (3); in all 150. See Midmer, *Monasteries*, pp. 3–10.

11. Frances and Joseph Gies, *Women in the Middle Ages* (New York: Barnes and Noble, 1978) p. 64.

12. Compare for example the cartularies, or legal documents, of the monasteries as given in Godfrey R.C. Davis, *Medieval Cartularies of Great Britain* (London, 1958). Only three of the twenty-nine cistercian nunneries, for example, had cartularies that have been preserved.

13. 'The early regulations of the nuns have not survived, but there is no reason to doubt that their ascetic standards and daily *borarium* were the same as the monks'', Lekai, *Cistericans*, p. 348. 'The spiritual lives of the nuns differed little from those of the monks', Midmer, *Monasteries*, p. 5.

Muffled Voices:
The Lives of
Consecrated Women
in the Fourth Century

Jo Ann McNamara

BY THE FOURTH CENTURY, roman women of the upper classes had achieved a position of unparalleled freedom and scope. Roman law had developed steadily in the direction of greater individual control over property and greater freedom within the context of the family for both wives and daughters. Concurrently, roman law had gradually gained preeminence over local custom in most areas of the vast Empire. Finally, the christian Emperor Constantine rescinded Augustan marriage laws and allowed every unmarried woman of twenty-five or more unlimited control of her own person and property.[1] During the century that followed, many wealthy and influential women began to experiment with the ascetic life. They plunged wholeheartedly into the absorbing world of religious fellowship and controversy whose members sought to challenge and renew the old patterns of society. Their detractors called them mad. Their admirers called them 'virile' souls, who had burst the confines of their own sex to fly unfettered to the very apex of the society of the City of God.[2]

Macrina, Mary, and two Melanias; Marcellina, Marcella, Paula, and Eustochium: the heroines of our study were memorialized in the writings of the most famous men of the age. They were presented as exemplars, models, dear companions, supporters and collaborators. They live for us as reflections of their eulogists. Their voices, energetic but muffled, echo through this unparalleled body of literature. Macrina speaks through the account of her brother, Gregory of Nyssa, and Marcellina in the reflections of her brother,

11

Ambrose. The history of Palladius and the threnodies of Jerome summon up a whole company of women. The letters written to and about these women by all the important Fathers of the Church have been lovingly preserved through a millenium and a half. But not a single epistle has survived from anyone in that society of literate and highly educated women.

Still, half a conversation is better than none. The purpose of this paper is to try to discern something of the voices of these women in the writings of the men they knew and supported. Can we, for example, hear the voices of real women in the theological tracts praising the virgin life? Were there living prototypes for the ten legendary virgins who met at a banquet to discuss the philosophic aspects of virginity in imitation of the gentlemen of ancient Athens?[3] Every writer who described the lives of the aristocratic ascetics of the period agreed that they were learned and well-educated women who together conducted regular seminars at which they discussed religious subjects. It is, therefore, very likely that in his story of the philosophic banquet Methodius was repeating ideas that passed commonly among the women of his acquaintance.

The vivid contrast between the bondage of married life and the freedom of virginity was a favored topic of Jerome, Augustine, Ambrose, and other promoters of asceticism. The theme was first stated by Paul, who observed that those who married must be concerned with the things of the world.[4] But fourth-century writers were often very detailed in their description of what 'the world' was like. Was it Ambrose or his virgin sister Marcellina who first described the horrors of courtship for women?

> How miserable is she who, to find a husband, is, as it were, put up for sale, so that the one who offers the highest bribe obtains her. Slaves are sold for better terms, for they often choose their masters; if a virgin chooses her husband it is an offence, but if she is not chosen it is an insult. And though she is fair and beautiful, she both fears and wishes to be seen lest the very fact of her being seen should not be fitting. What fears and suspicions she experiences as to how her suitors will turn out! She is afraid that a poor man may trick her or a noble one despise her.[5]

Was it Jerome or the widowed mother Paula who complained of the exhausting distractions of the happiest married life?

> The married woman had paint laid on before her mirror and, to the insult of her Maker, strives to acquire something more than her natural beauty. Then comes the prattling of infants, the noisy household, children watching for her word and waiting for her kiss, the reckoning up of expenses, the preparation to meet the outlay. On one side, you will see a company of cooks, girded for onslaught and attacking the meat; there you may hear

the hum of a multitude of weavers. Meanwhile a message is delivered that the husband and his friends have arrived. The wife, like a swallow, flies all over the house. She has to see to everything. Is the couch smooth? Is the pavement swept? Are there flowers in the cups? Is dinner ready? Tell me, pray, where amid all this is there room for the thought of God?[6]

There is a strong message here for women seeking a new way of life that might enable them to exercise other talents and capacities. The women whose names and histories we know seem to speak to us almost clearly in passages such as these. There was, however, another group of anonymous women engaged in shaping radical new lifestyles and they are represented only in the admonitory sermons and homilies of their critics. The followers of men convicted of heresy and the companions of renegade monks, freelance preachers and other persons of dubious orthodoxy and respectability appear only dimly. The ascetic movement was not widely popular among the ordinary laity or the clerical hierarchy of the fourth century. Its episcopal proponents, like Ambrose and Augustine, were always careful to avoid association with the more radical ascetics and to caution their own followers to discretion and modesty. Female ascetics, particularly, were continually urged to be humble, to avoid offending their matronly peers. They were warned against even the most discreet associations with men. Even so, they are all too often obscured by scandal fed by envy for their free and untrammeled lives.

In brief, though evidence available to us concerning the women who engaged in the early ascetic movement is plentiful, it is fraught with difficulties and obscurities. It is probable that we will never be able to speak with any confidence about their interior lives and motivations. We can, however, draw from the surviving documents a very vivid description of the public lives they lived in the last century of the Roman Empire in the west.

TYPES OF CONSECRATED WOMEN

Who were these women whose lives were so novel and innovative that they were likened to angels, to self-selected martyrs? Who were the athletes of God, the brides of Christ? First among them, by unanimous acclaim, were the virgins. While the year 271 AD, when Antony fled into the desert, is commonly taken to be the beginning of the monastic movement, his impulses to deny the demands of his body and seek for perfect purity had long been anticipated by women in the christian community. Like nearly all of the great male monastic leaders, Antony had a sister. At the death of his parents when he was about eighteen, her welfare became his responsibility and his first consideration. Indeed, even after he had parted from her he counted his continuing anxiety for her welfare among the strongest of the temptations to which he was subjected in his retreat. He had originally kept back some goods in order to provide for her support in a *parthenion*, a community of virgins.[7]

In his anxiety to hasten on to the experiences of his hero in the desert, Antony's biographer never paused to provide us with the name of his sister or any account of that female community in which she lived. How did Antony intend her to spend her future? By the late third century, the consecrated virgin was already a well-established member of the christian community and 'virginity' had already come to mean a permanent and special state, not an ephemeral condition preceding marriage. Those who chose the life were ready to die a painful death in defiance of the Augustan marriage laws. Indeed, Antony's sister might easily have lived to become one of those virgins targeted especially by Diocletian's persecutions. These women, like Ambrose's ancestress Soteria or the semi-legendary Agnes, were subjected to torture and threatened or real rape to force them to break their vows. By the first decade of the fourth century, Antony's sister would not yet have been old enough to be numbered among the seven virgins of Ancyra who were forcibly placed in a brothel. Those women escaped rape and went to their deaths intact because they could repell their would-be rapists with references to the age and dessication of their bodies.[8]

Antony's biography makes no reference, however, to the attitude of his sister. He settled her with the virgins as matter of factly as he might have settled her with a husband. Already in the fourth century we have accounts of virgins who were consecrated, not by their own initiative, but by that of their parents. Possibly the removal of these women from the marriage market was even seen as a christian alternative to female infanticide. This may have been the motive for Asella's father, who dedicated her to virginity from childhood.[9] Brotherly responsibility for a sister may also have partially motivated Jerome to settle his sister under the spiritual direction of a friend, to the indignation of his aunt and other relatives.[10] In other cases, girls were apparently consecrated to the virgin life at the initiative of their mothers, perhaps to save them from marital experiences that their mothers regretted. The most famous of these were Eustochium, the daughter of Paula, and Paula II, daughter of Paula's only son and his wife Laeta, who had apparently entered into a chaste marriage after the baby's birth.[11] Eustochium was trained by her widowed mother and her ascetic friends from earliest childhood. Jerome later interested himself enthusiastically in the pedagogical challenge of raising a perfectly pure woman, uncontaminated by worldly influence. Eustochium accompanied her mother on her flight from Rome to a monastic life in Bethlehem and later the whole community welcomed the opportunity of raising the infant Paula II in even more controlled conditions. A prominent feature of the education of both girls was their isolation from all companions who might expose them to a worldly point of view, including married women and unconsecrated widows. Their purity of mind was similarly to be totally unsullied by the classical education which so distinguished their mentors.[12] The lives of the second generation of virgins were clearly being shaped toward a far more cloistered and silent life than that of their predecessors.

It was clearly much more difficult for those young women who wished to take the initiative themselves in dedicating their lives to Christ. Financial independence was an absolute necessity for the female ascetic, since any effort to be self-supporting in the ancient world would almost inevitably involve some degree of prostitution. Hagiographic literature supplies many examples of heroic women who braved poverty and solitude in order to remain unmarried against the will of their parents. But most women bowed to parental authority and married if they could not persuade their parents or guardians to support their higher aspirations. The sympathy of her family and the active support of her brother Ambrose lay behind Marcellina's success as one of the first exemplars of virginity in Rome.[13]

The best-known of the self-consecrated virgins was Macrina, sister of the two great Capadoccian fathers, Basil and Gregory of Nyssa. Gregory wrote an account of her life and a philosophical dialogue purporting to record her reflections during her last days.[14] Macrina's desire to remain a virgin received the sympathetic support of her mother, Emilia. But their combined pleas made no impression on her father, who was determined that she would be suitably married. Like so many of her contemporaries, Macrina ultimately bowed to his will and accepted betrothal to a young man who unexpectedly died before the marriage could be completed. This extraordinary circumstance enabled the sharp-witted young woman to argue that, since betrothal was legally held to be as binding as marriage, she was not a maiden but a widow, bound to remain faithful to a husband who was only transported to another world. Popular christian feeling of the day tended to look with disfavor upon second marriages, as did pagan sentiment.[15] In any case, this argument seems to have borne more weight with her father than had her initial pleas. As a virgin, Macrina lived with her parents and, after her father's death, she and her mother made their home into an ascetic community. Gregory credited her with drawing him and his brother into the ascetic movement. Though Basil had initially been inclined, in the first flush of youth, to be puffed up with his own intellect, he became one of the most influential theorists of monasticism in the eastern church.

Demetrias was also a consecrated virgin of the early fifth century. Augustine rejoiced at her ability to turn the pre-eminent Anician family from

its resistance to the ascetic movement by persuading her grandmother Proba
to release her from her betrothal.[16] The family had only recently fled to
Africa in the wake of the Visigothic sack of Rome which may have shocked
Proba out of her more worldly preoccupations or shaken the convictions of
the male members of the family enough to allow the women to have their
way. They may even have considered a community of virgins a safer refuge
for a young girl than her own household. The barbarians were, after all,
Christians themselves and claimed to respect religious establishments. As
Jerome testified, they spared the virginity of Principia, companion of his old
friend, the widow Marcella, and after an initial impulse to abuse the two
women, escorted them to a church where they might be protected from
other marauders.[17]

A second group of consecrated women are somewhat more ambiguous in
their social status since they lived with men. Some of them were virgins, the
sub-introductae or *agapetae* who lived as a group in clerical households or as
individuals in houses with male virgins.[18] Others were virgin wives who had
married but whose marriages were not consummated. Among these belonged the unnamed wife of Amoun, founder of the monastic community
of Nitria in Egypt.[19] He was a young man whose desire to retain his virginity
was frustrated by his parents' insistence that he marry. On his wedding
night, however, he succeeded in persuading his bride that consummation
would be a sin because the priest had mistakenly performed the ritual for
consecration of virgins rather than a nuptial blessing. She agreed to forego
the conjugal act in exchange for his agreement that they would continue to
live in the same house. At the end of eighteen years, she suggested that he
leave her so that he might receive the admiration of the world for his un-
stained virginity. He agreed with alacrity, left her established in their joint
home, and went to found his famous desert monastery.

Among this group we must also number those women who married and
lived ordinary conjugal lives but eventually persuaded their husbands to
forego their sexual rights. Her biographer claimed that by many artful ma-
noeuvers Melania the Younger 'seduced' her husband to the ascetic life.[20]
Her original effort on their wedding night to persuade him to virginity failed,
but after she had borne two children in painful circumstances, and lost them
both to death, he finally agreed to join her in vows of continence. They
travelled around the Mediterranean world together for some years before
they finally entered separate monastic establishments.

Paulinus of Nola and his wife, Therasia, had similarly started life together
as a normally wedded couple. At some point, she bore and lost a child. He
became a priest and ultimately a bishop. Some combination of these circumstances convinced them to take vows of continence and embark upon a
rich life of mutual spiritual endeavor. Nor were they unusual. Paulinus' letters

illuminate a world of similarly dedicated couples stretching from Italy to Spain, Gaul, and Africa and including the rather exotic example of Sulpicius Severus who, after his wife's death, continued to live with her mother under mutual vows of continence. To Paulinus, Augustine wrote:

> Your wife is also made visible to your readers, not as one leading her husband into luxury, but rather as leading him back to strength in his innermost being. We salute her, also, with the greetings owed to your holiness alone, because she is joined in close union with you, and is attached to you by spiritual bonds which are as strong as they are chaste. There the cedars of Lebanon are laid on the ground; there they are joined by the thongs of charity to be the material of the Ark and are incorruptibly floated on the waters of this world; there, glory is despised that it may be acquired and the world given up that it may be held; there, the infants or even the growing children of Babylon are dashed against a stone, that is, the vices of disorder and worldly pride.[21]

A third group of dedicated women were not virgins in body though they were often classed as 'honorary' virgins by their admirers. As Augustine pointed out, every female is born a virgin in body but it requires dedication to make a virgin soul.[22] Jerome doubted publicly whether a virgin spirit could survive the contamination of the market place, however intact the body.[23] The virgins who frequented the baths, went to banquets, participated in the social round of the great imperial cities were rarely included among the 'true virgins.'

On the other hand, loss of the physical seal of virginity might sometimes be excused and held not to impair a woman's claim to the title. This was automatically applied to virgins whom persecutors had molested in the course of their final torment. In general, forcible rape of any sort was considered not to affect the virginity of someone who steadfastly resisted any consent of her own will or mind. The ephemeral accidents of the body, therefore, were often separated from the enduring realities of the virgin will.

As we have seen, the extension of the classification of virgin to married women who were reputed to live chastely with their husbands already made the title somewhat ambiguous. Jerome, among others, showed a tendency to attempt to extend it even further to Paula who, he claimed, had submitted to her husband only to satisfy his desire for children.[24] A similar claim, as we have seen, was made for Melania the Younger.[25] Women who lost their husbands to death and determined to devote their widowhoods to the ascetic life were then entered into the ranks of the consecrated women and indeed they make up the majority of the women whose lives are open to us.

Widows were, of course, free of the authority of their husbands and, after Constantine, free of the authority of their fathers as well as regards marriage.

They were of relatively mature age and experience and had generally acquired the habit of commanding their households. They were in control of some portion of their own or their husband's estates and therefore more financially independent than other women. Some of them, like Emilia, may have wished initially to dedicate themselves as virgins. Others may have been brought to asceticism through the grief of their loss, like Paula's daughter Blaesilla, who gave up a life of frivolity for excesses of mortification that eventually led to her death.[26] Many others, like Melania the Elder and Marcella, are presented to us only after their lives were well-established and we do not know what led them to the decision to become ascetics.

All the virgins, chaste wives, and consecrated widows whom we have named were members of the wealthy upper classes of the Empire. There were, however, thousands of less spectacular women who lived in their circles and who can only be seen dimly within the community.

Ideally, the consecrated woman lived in total seclusion and the theoretical literature abounds with references to virgins shut up in their chambers or enclosed in desert solitudes. More concretely, biographies and correspondence indicate that they did indeed live in their own homes without meeting the demands of an elaborate social life. Some women were even rather dramatically reclusive. Palladius makes reference to one woman in Rome who shut herself away and was said to have spoken to no one for many years. When a famous monk from the east, dressed only in a loincloth, visited her, however, she received him readily, boasting that she had become quite dead to the world. She received a lesson in humility when he made her admit that she was not quite dead enough to walk naked in public through the market place, as he did.[27] A woman named Alexandra who had 'entombed herself' for years with a veil, hiding the face that had once driven a man mad for love, appears, however, to have been readily accessible to converse with Melania the Elder.[28] Alexandra also regularly saw women who supplied food through the window in her tomb.

A virgin with living parents who supported her aspirations could probably spend a fair amount of her time in isolation and prayer while her parents ran the household and provided her with the necessities of life. But even these women were not lost to all society. Asella, who had been consecrated from childhood and was reputed to be very reclusive, was a regular member of the ascetic society associated with the house of Marcella.[29] She received, and presumably answered, letters from Jerome. Melania visited the baths with her maids, even though she rather ostentatiously limited her contact with water to bathing her eyes—probably in literal obedience to her parents' command that she wash.[30] Other virgins were not so strict. Not only did they bathe but they did so, to the scandal of their detractors, in the fashionable morning hours popular with young men about town.[31] Those who had no servants to do their marketing and other business would have had to have done it for themselves despite the contaminating influences of the marketplace.[32]

Servants were not lacking to the wealthy virgins and widows who enjoyed regular visiting. Indeed, these households were apparently quite populous, deserving of Jerome's appellation, *domestica ecclesia*.[33] When bishops Epiphanius and Paulinus, with the young Jerome in their company, visited Rome, Epiphanius stayed in Paula's house, presumably with his retinue.[34] Jerome was always reticent about that Roman sojourn, but it is probable that he was one of the guests on that occasion. With his employer, he visited regularly with Marcella, Asella, Lea, and other women zealously engaged in introducing the ascetic life to Rome. Similar hospitality was extended by Marcellina, Ambrose's sister, to a virgin of Verona, Indicia, on some occasion when Ambrose was absent. Marcellina later testified to her brother in defense of the modesty and propriety of her deportment on that occasion.[35]

Indicia's need for a character witness arose from difficulties with her own living arrangements. Apparently she was orphaned and, quite naturally, sought a home with her sister. Her brother-in-law went to the trouble and expense of cutting a separate entrance into the wall of his house to ensure the privacy of her apartments. Perhaps he also wished to assure his own privacy from her. Ambrose suggests that the renovation was designed to separate the sisters from one another. Certainly, Indicia's habit of secluding herself in her chamber at some point laid her open to scandal, causing Ambrose to write an outraged letter attempting to save her from a threatened physical examination by the local midwives of Verona.

Most consecrated women, for this very reason, had at least one chaperone, if not a house full of them. Macrina persuaded her mother to join her in establishing a household retreat. Gregory of Nyssa gives the superficial impression that his mother and sister lived a life of complete poverty and seclusion. But then he notes the testimony of a visitor to their establishment that they entertained him and his wife (and their retinue) generously, if temperately, installing them in separate quarters according to sex. The couple were delighted enough with the uplifting atmosphere of the household that they exchanged notes through the servants agreeing to lengthen their stay.[36]

In short, where fortune allowed it, the consecrated woman of the fourth century, virgin or widow, who lived in her own home was usually accompanied by relatives and a fairly large number of servants. In addition, she might add one or more ascetic companions to her *familia*, which may well have provided a much-needed refuge for religious women without the fortune to support independent establishments. When Marcella was attacked by the Visigoths in Rome, she was sharing her household with her friend Principia.[37] The slandered Indicia had both a companion and a 'free-born nurse' in addition to Marcellina to testify to her habits.[38] When Paula went to the Holy Land with her daughter, Eustochium, she was attended by a 'flock of virgins' who intended to settle with her in the desert. Though Jerome says specifically that she refused the hospitality of the bishop's palace, he does not explain how she housed the retinue of dependents in the humble cottage she chose.[39] Once installed in Bethlehem the party numbered about fifty women, but it probably grew in size after its arrival.

Who were these women found in the retinues of the wealthy, consecrated like them to the godly life? Jerome tells us that the women of Paula's community were divided into three social classes reflecting their rank in life, though all dressed alike and shared the hardships of the communal life. The opportunities for women without male support to make their own way in the roman world were severely limited. Even the familiar role of domestic servant would have been difficult to obtain in so extensive a slave-holding society. Indeed, in the course of her lengthy effort to divest herself of her wealth, Melania the Younger is said to have disposed in one way or another of 80,000 slaves, many of whom she placed in monasteries. Many she sold to other masters because they expressed a desire not to be freed, and apparently were also not willing to enter into the severer discipline of Melania's houses. At Thagaste, for example, she kept a narrow wooden cage for mortifying the too insistent flesh.

Roman women were not independently eligible for the dole, and the private charities dispensed by the christian communities seem to have been somewhat unsystematic in nature. Consecrated women are said to have earned money by spinning, making cloth and occasionally copying manuscripts. But again Jerome amply testifies to their constant need for supplemental support from the wealthy. A woman alone and without fortune was therefore in very sad straits and would often have found herself with little choice between starvation and prostitution. Many of the women who joined the retinue of Melania the Younger apparently had such histories. She stiffened their resolve by bringing them with her to attend difficult childbirths.[40]

Women from the poorest classes may thus have benefitted most readily from the generosity of wealthy ascetics, finding shelter and a livelihood from the bounty of the consecrated rich. If so, this real move in the direction of regenerating society on this earth has not often been noticed in the history of the movement. Other women, perhaps of a humbler, middling social sphere, apparently had homes of their own in which to pursue their religious callings but were not wealthy enough to have establishments accommodating separate quarters for men or to support dependent women in the unimpeachable demeanor of the rich. At least some of the virgins who took consecrated men into their households to secure physical and material support, seem to have belonged to this group. According to the fiercely sarcastic John Chrysostom, they gained protection from the outer world at the expense of more terrible domestic dangers from their own impulses and of scandal to their neighbors.[41]

The final solution to the problem of finding suitable living arrangements for ascetically inclined women was provided by communities of anchorites or cenobites. At the end of the third century, Antony's contemporary, Pachomius, was, tradition records, called out of his cave in the Egyptian desert by an angel with tablets of bronze upon which were engraved the first monastic rule.[42] Following the instructions of the angel, he gathered together a series of communities of thousands of men and, separately, women who would combine the virtues of the communal life—shared living quarters, meals, and manual labor—with the solitaries' experiences of prayer, silence, and contemplation. Throughout the fourth century, these communities drew a generation of seekers after perfection into the desert.

Like Antony, Pachomius had a sister. Her name was Mary and his biographer tells us that she went to the desert originally to look for her brother whom she had thought dead. He refused to break his solitude to see her but told her that if she wished to follow him in the ascetic life he would send some of the brothers to build her a house. The biographer does not tell us how word of her presence there may have spread or who the other women were who were drawn to join her in the desert under the direction of a monk delegated by Pachomius to give the sisters instruction. He does say, however, that the sisters followed the same rule that Pachomius had devised for the brothers and that the women were apparently related to the brothers who occasionally visited with them under the monk's supervision. By the latter half of the fourth century, when Palladius observed the community, it numbered about four hundred women and had two offspring. In comparison with the brotherhoods, these were relatively small communities. Nor did they rival the establishments of thousands attributed to Melania and others active in more urban environments. Moreover, the regular communication between the women and the men that seems to have charaterized the original group had apparently ceased.[43]

Palladius tells several anecdotes intended to underline the principle of isolation from men. Indeed he went so far as to say that the only men who ever entered the female community were the priest and his deacons who went over on Sundays for services. The single exception—if exception it might be called—were the monks who went across the river on a signal from the sisters to collect their dead for burial in the common cemetery. Only in death, did they believe the barriers of different sexes could be overcome. Palladius also notes however, that the brothers provided the sisters with a number of material goods from the excess supplied by their own labor. He says nothing about what the sisters may have done in exchange.

Occasionally, however, male visitors did enter these female precincts. On one occasion, a hermit was admitted because an angel had instructed him to seek out a particular sister who could give him a needed lesson in humility. He found her in the kitchen, living off scraps, the object of considerable harrassment from other members of the community because she had been feigning madness.[44] Palladius himself much admired a woman named Amma Talis who headed a community in Antinoë of sixty young women. He claimed that she was so loved by her sisters that they held themselves in check without the need for a lock on the door as was found in other monasteries[45].

From these small scraps of information, it is clear that these primeval communities of monastic women were already subjected to two important deviations from the rule written on bronze by angelic hands. The annals of male monasticism are filled with accounts of men for whom retreat into the desert was a temporary experience. Even the men who stayed for most of their lives in their communities were prone to move regularly back and forth into nearby cities. They showed up on a variety of errands, exchanging their handicrafts for money and supplies, preaching and delivering messages that had come to them from their meditative silences. Mobs of monks sometimes arrived in Alexandria or other cities of the east to demonstrate in favor of some theological position being disputed by their clerical colleagues. Monastic women, however, were apparently expected to remain in their communities for the rest of their lives. There is no evidence that they conducted business in the cities or joined the demonstrations of their brethern. Palladius seems to suggest that they were generally locked in to prevent that kind of wandering.

The second deviation is related to the first. The nuns depended on the monks for at least part of their sustenance and were prohibited from carrying on business in the cities. Instead they received fabricated goods from the monks without any stipulated exchange. This limitation on their liberty and the resulting burden on the resources of the male community may explain why female communities were much smaller. It is very probable that the numbers of women who could settle in the desert was severely limited by economic restrictions that had nothing to do with their pious impulses. Poor women, unsupported women, women driven solely by desire for God, may have found that there was in fact no place for them in these desert communities. A few women may have paid their way by doing the heavy work of the community, as did a woman feigning madness, but ultimately they too would have to be given a share of whatever was being provided to the sisters from the male community or from outside sources.

Conversely, these women raise for us the same problem as does Antony's sister. Were they there on their own initiative or not? This question may throw some light on a grim anecdote relayed by Palladius. A sister was approached by a man who had stumbled unawares upon their community and offered her his services as a tailor. Quite properly, she responded, 'We have our own tailors', and sent him on his way. But this paltry incident proved to be a spark in a powderkeg of jealousy and discontent. Another sister accused her of breaking the rule by speaking with a man. Factions formed in the community and the sister was driven by their harrassment to drown herself in the Nile. The accuser then hanged herself in remorse. Both women were denied christian burial and the accusing faction was excommunicated for seven years (but apparently kept in a penitential state within the community).[46] It is a tale depressingly reminiscent of tales told of women in medieval communities where social status, dowry and family influence were the major qualifications for entry.

There is, of course, no reason to suppose that all the women of the Tabenisi were the unwilling sacrifices of their brothers' devotions. Some of them may have followed their menfolk into the desert willingly, converted by them to the ascetic life and equally dedicated to its pursuit.[47] Others, like their better-known urban sisters, may have been the original instigators of the move, drawing their brothers, fathers, or spouses after them into the wilderness. Even so, it appears possible that the more formal monasticism of the desert did not welcome large numbers of women without masculine protection or financial independence. Indeed, women who did enjoy financial independence appear to have preferred, like Paula and Melania the Elder, to set up their own communities rather than live in the shadow of the great male monasteries of the desert.

Finally, fourth and fifth century hagiography is rich in tales of young women who, for the sake of virginity, fled from the homes of recalcitrant parents and the protestations of insistent suitors. In many cases, they are said to have disguised themselves as men and lived either as hermits in lonely places or in communities of monks. Sometimes their sex remained undiscovered until they died. In others, they appear to have drawn scandal upon themselves by associating with women. Indeed, some of these romantic persons appear to have courted scandal by appearing to have engaged in improper relationships in order to increase their own humility. Many of these stories are of disputed authenticity but they are not so inherently improbable as they may sound.[47a] The desert ascetics lived as solitaries. Even when grouped in communities they often had individual cells where they devoted themselves to prayer, fasting, and other bodily mortifications. They shunned bathing and never undressed publicly. They spoke little, gathering only intermittently for common prayer or perhaps for meals eaten in silence. When they worked together in fields or small factories, they again observed silence. There is, clearly, no compelling reason to reject the possibility that an emaciated woman, clothed in monkish robes, silent and prayerful, passed for years as one of such a company.

OCCUPATIONS OF THE CONSECRATED

Devoted as they were to prayer, fasting and meditation, all fourth century ascetics were painfully aware that idleness is the devil's workshop. Even the entombed Alexandra told Melania the Elder that she spun flax hour after hour while praying and repenting of her sins.[48] The ascetic women who lived in their own homes or in monasteries had many things to occupy their time and distract them from the idle thoughts that led to *accidia*, spiritual sloth. Despite the claims of their male admirers, they were far from free of the burdens of worldly affairs. To be sure, they were spared the time-consuming vanities of painting, primping, hair styling, and dressing which polemicists would have us believe preoccupied most of the married women of roman society. The virgins were also relieved of the burdens of child care, but the widows were not. Indeed, not the least of their merits, we are repeatedly told, was the devotion with which they nursed their own infants and personally educated them in the christian life as they grew. Even after Paula's own children were grown she was not entirely free of these preoccupations. She and her virgin daughter, Eustochium, eagerly anticipated the arrival of the infant Paula II, destined to be raised in their monastic society. The aged Jerome promised her mother, Laeta, that she would not lack for family life and affection with a doting grandmother, a loving aunt and the aged Jerome himself to dandle her from his shoulders and help her with her studies.[49]

In their community at Bethlehem, Paula and Eustochium did many of the menial tasks of housekeeping, cooking, and cleaning. Moreover, they entertained pilgrims and visitors on a broad scale, as did Macrina and Emilia, Melania the Elder and other heads of great establishments. With so much hospitality to proffer and so many dependents to provide for materially, administratively, and spiritually, we may wonder when they found time for God.

Nor were the less well-known members of the community idle. Paula's establishment was divided into three communities for women of different classes. This may have been a general practice. Certainly clusters of about fifty women each in female establishments are common to most of the literature. Each group needed supervision and spiritual guidance, presumably from deputies of the foundress. In addition, daily tasks of domestic maintenance were supplemented by handwork, particularly spinning.

The building and decoration of churches, chapels, and monuments outside their own foundations preoccupied many of these women. Though Augustine had advised her to avoid such preoccupations, even charity, we glimpse the older Demetrias as an active church builder in Rome.[50]

Charity of all sorts was viewed from the earliest christian centuries as a particularly feminine activity. Augustine's mother, Monica, was in the habit of making the daily round of churches carrying food and drink to share with the poor who frequented the sacred premises.[51] One woman was given a penance because she became impatient with an enterprising pauper who kept reappearing in the line and she rebuked him for seeking more than his share. The wealthy Fabiola, in association with Paula's widowed son-in-law, Pammachius, established a large hospice for the sick and poor as well as travellers in Ostia and visited it regularly.[52] Humbler women living in the cities on a more modest level pursued an endless round of church-going; there they met their fellow devotees daily. They went in and out visiting the sick, carrying alms and food to the needy, exhorting the weak and giving spiritual counsel to the unhappy.

For the wealthy and their companions, this round of church-going and visiting became far more extensive. In the fourth century, pilgrimage was already a popular practice. Paula and the two Melanias are but the best-known of the women who travelled exhaustively around the sacred sites of the Holy Land. Despite Jerome's touching picture of his heroine riding humbly on the back of an ass, forsaking her accustomed litter even in the dead of winter,[53] Paula was not travelling alone and her retinue seems to have been extensive. Melania the Younger took advantage of aristocratic privilege to use the facilities of the imperial post to lighten the expenses of her travels around the Mediterranean world, divesting herself of her vast fortune as she went, re-settling her slaves in new occupations, under new masters, or in religious communities. She was accompanied by her husband—which would have doubled the number of their necessary attendants,[54] accounted among the humble travellers by our informants. Jerome noted that shortly before his arrival, the Holy Land had been scandalized by the wealth, luxury and open-handed hospitality of another female pilgrim. Was this predecessor of the Wife of Bath the pious widow Egeria who left us a first hand account of her own travels?[55] Probably not.[56] Egeria, Paula, and the two Melanias were surely not the only women to combine a love of travel with their pious instincts.

These busy active women moving in and out, through cities and the world at large, in fact, offended many writers. They were accused of scandal-mongering, gossiping, tale-bearing, and idle frivolity, and told that they would be better off immured at home than scurrying through the market place. More than one resentful clergyman remarked that women who could not live in modest seclusion would be better off to marry and devote themselves to proper housekeeping. Chrysostom inveighed against virgins who required a procession of 'wise women' going in and out of their houses to assure their physical integrity.[57] Ambrose railed vehemently against those who offered the same insult to Indicia.[58] Even his defense, however, betrays the uneasiness which these unsupervised women provoked.

Moreover, many of them used their wealth, their influence, and their learning to interfere directly in the affairs of a church increasingly dominated by a professional male clergy not uniformly friendly to the competition of lay ascetics. Study of the Bible and other religious activities formed a basic part of the daily occupation of consecrated women. Among her other tasks, Paula undertook to supervise the instruction of all her community in memorizing and understanding Scripture. In addition, she and Eustochium learned Hebrew the better to assist Jerome in his great life's work of biblical translation and exegesis.[59] Indeed, Jerome's critic Palladius comdemned him for subverting the intelligence of 'that genius of a woman' to his own ends.[60] Jerome's other great friend Marcella, who remained in Rome amidst her own circle until her death in the wake of the Visigothic invasion, held regular meetings in her home for study and discussion. She amazed Jerome with the eagerness and acuity with which she questioned and challenged him. He admitted that, in fact, he had often entrusted her with exegetical answers to his correspondents in his name.[61] Melania the Elder apparently instructed Rufinus on many of the finer points of exegesis. Jerome accused her of having exposed him to the seductive heresies of Origen and she did not deny it.[62]

Nor were these women abashed or timid about entering the great theological battles of the age. The involvement of the Empress Justina in support of the Arians is well known from the bitter denunciations of Ambrose.[63] In Egypt the elder Melania stood as the great bulwark against the Arian bishop of Alexandria. She even braved arrest and physical abuse in her championship of the Nicene orthodoxy, though she was not backward in using her aristocratic background and family influence against the governor who threatened her.[64] Later in her life, Melania used all her power to protect Rufinus and the Origenists and to promote the cause of Origen among her peers in Rome against the organized opposition of Marcella and her circle.[65] Her granddaughter, Melania the Younger, was similarly energetic in the great quarrels in Constantinople involving the patriarch, John Chrysostom, and the Empress, Eudoxia. Both Jerome and Augustine worked hard to turn Proba, Demetrias, and their circle away from the heresies of Pelagius.[66]

CONCLUSION

During the fifth century, the women of the christian ascetic world become increasingly obscure to our view. We know that the monastic movement continued to grow and spread in the world of the barbarian invaders as it had in the beleaguered roman world we have been observing. But the broader, less formalized life of the independent virgin or widow seems to have been lost. In part, this is probably a problem of sources. The fifth century, particularly in the west, was an age of war and disaster, not an ideal time for the leisurely writing of letters and tracts in praise of virgins and virginity. As we have noted, the letters of our fourth century heroines were not preserved and we are dependent on the indirect evidence of their more famous brothers and friends for our knowledge of them. There are several reasons why women of the fifth century may not have shared this advantage.

They may have lost their fortunes. The vast wealth that supported Paula, the Melanias, and their contemporaries had largely been dissipated even before the onslaught of the barbarians. Afterwards, we find a much poorer, more restricted world which was less likely to support such generous patronesses. Many consecrated women may have continued living in modest privacy without the wealth or influence to attract the attention of such literary lionizers as Jerome, Ambrose, and Augustine.

The independent female ascetic, like her male counterparts, may have been less admired than she had formerly been. The fifth century saw a period of rapprochement between the great aristocratic families of Rome and the ecclesiastical hierarchy of Christianity.[67] The imperial establishment in Constantinople moved increasingly to control and restrict the disruptive monastic elements of the east while the growing power of the papacy in the west was gradually being extended to comprehend and control the unbridled enthusiasm of its ascetic population.

The cloister became a well-established alternative to marriage for women of the early middle ages and, as such, provided a popular refuge. The history of monasticism in the fifth century, however, is the growing story of rules and formal houses. Like his predecessors, Cassian had a sister for whom he established a female community. But an increasingly stricter division of the sexes and cloistering of women could only tend toward misogyny among influential men directed toward women who made themselves conspicuous, even in virtue. At the end of our period, in the first rule specifically directed toward monastic women, Caesarius of Arles provided that his sister and her community be permanently cloistered, dependent on male monks for every outside service and dependent on their private resources to support them in an environment where self-support was made impossible.

Hunter College
Institute for Research in History

NOTES

1. Previously, I have traced the history of this development in 'Wives and Widows in Early Christian Thought', *International Journal of Women's Studies* 2, 6 (1979) 575–92.

2. J. McNamara, 'Sexual Equality and the Cult of Virginity in Early Christian Thought', *Feminist Studies* 3 3–4 (1976) 145–58.

3. Methodius, *Symposium; Sources Chrétiennes* [SCh] 95.

4. 1 Corinthians 7:38.

5. *De virginibus* 1.56; PL 16: 215.

6. *Adversus Helvidium: Liber de perpetua virginitate B. Mariae* 17; PL 23: 193.

7. Athanasius, *Life of Antony* 2–3; *Nicene and Post-Nicene Fathers* [NPF] 4: 189.

8. *Acta Sanctorum* May 18:147.

9. Jerome, *Epistola 24: Ad Marcellam*; PL 22: 427. For a detailed account of Jerome's relations with these women see J.N.D. Kelly, *Jerome: His life, writings and controversies* (London: Duckworth, 1975). For a good general discussion of their place in the introduction of asceticism to the west, see R. Lorenz, 'Die Anfänge des abendländischen Monchtums im 4 Jahrhundert', *Zeitschrift für Kirchengeschichte* 77 (1966) 1–61.

10. *Epistola* 6; PL 22: 338.

11. *Epistola* 107; PL 22: 818.

12. *Epistola* 22, 16; PL 22: 403.

13. Ambrose, *De virginitate* 5.6–7; PL 16: 184. See also Paulinus of Nola, *Vita Ambrosii* 4; PL 14: 30. For a modern account of Ambrose's life, see A. Paredi, *Saint Ambrose, His Life and Times* (South Bend: University of Notre Dame Press, 1964).

14. Gregory of Nyssa, *Vie de Sainte Macrine* SCh 178: 135–67. *Dialogue on the Soul and Resurrection*, tr. V.W. Callahan, *Ascetical Works* (Washington: Catholic University Press, 1966) 161–94.

15. See Marjorie Lightman and William Zeisel, 'Univira', *Church History* 46, 1 (1977) 19–32.

16. Augustine, *Epistola* 150; PL 33: 145. Peter Brown, 'Aspects of the Christianization of the Roman Aristocracy', *Religion and Society in the Age of Augustine* (London: Faber and Faber, 1972) 161–82, suggests that this shift on the part of the Anicii was a part of a general move toward reconciliation of the old roman aristocracy with the christian hierarchy in the fifth century.

17. *Epistola* 127, 13; PL 22: 1092.

18. The condition of these women has drawn the attention of a number of modern writers, particularly H. Achelis, *Virgines subintroductae* (Leipzig, 1902), H. Koch, *Virgines Christi. De Gelübde der gottgewichten Jungfrauen in den ersten drei Jahrbunderten* (Tübingen, 1907) and P. de Labriolle, 'Le mariage spirituel dans l'antiquité chrétienne', *Revue historique* 137 (1921) 204–25.

19. Palladius, *Lausiac History* 8; ACW 34.

20. *La Vie de sainte Mélanie* 8, ed. D. Gorce, SCh 90, 143 .

21. *Epistola* 27; PL 33: 107.

22. Augustine, *De sancta virginitate* 10; CSEL 41: 243.

23. *Adversus Helvidium* 21; PL 23: 250.

24. *Epistola* 108, 4; PL 22: 871.

25. *Vie de sainte Mélanie*, 1; Gorce, SCh 90:132.

26. Jerome, *Epistola* 39; PL 22: 415.

27. Palladius, *Lausiac History*, 37. 12–16; ACW 00.

28. *Ibid.*, 5

29. Jerome, *Epistola* 24; PL 22: 427.

30. *Vie de Sainte Mélanie*, 1. In the *Lausiac History*, Palladius describes her redoubtable grandmother, Melania the Elder, as boasting that water had not touched her feet or face for many years to correct a self-indulgent young man who washed hands and face in cold water on a hot day.

31. This is a constant complaint first noted by Cyprian, *De habitu virginum* 19; CSEL 3: 201.

32. Chrysostom, *Les cohabitations suspects*, 9; ed. J. Dumortier, *Nouvelle Collection de Textes et Documents* (Paris: Société de Guillaume Budé, 1955) 75.

33. *Epistola* 30. 4; PL 22: 443.

34. *Epistola* 108. 6; PL 22: 881.

35. Ambrose, *Epistola* 5; PL 16: 939.

36. *Vie de sainte Macrine* 170–71 and 183.

37. Jerome, *Epistola* 127; PL 22: 1095.

38. Ambrose, *Epistola* 5; PL 16: 929.

39. *Epistola* 108. 14; PL 22: 890.

40. *Vie de Sainte Mélanie.*

41. *Cohabitations suspects*, 6–7.

42. Palladius, *Lausiac History*, 32; See Vielleux, *Pachomian Koinonia* II (Kalamazoo: Cistercian Publications, 1981) 125 For detailed discussion of pachomian monasticism, see P. Ladeuze, *Etude sur le cénobitisme Pakhomien pendant le IVe siècle et la première moitié du Ve* (Minerva: Frankfurt am Main, 1961), and Veilleux, *Pachomian Koinonia* I-III.

43. *The Bohairic Life of Pachomius* 27, trans. Armand Veilleux, *Pachomian Koinonia* I (Kalamazoo, 1980) 49–50. cf. Palladius' sketchy account, *Lausiac History*, 194.

44. *Lausiac History*, 34. The anonymous life of Pachomius, *Vita Prima Graeca*, 32, adds that monks "who had not yet reached perfection" could visit their female relatives in the women's monastery by appointment with Mary. See the translations of A.N. Athanassakis, *The Life of Pachomius* (Missoula, MT: Scholars Press, 1975) and of Armand Veilleux, *Pachomian Koinonia* I (Kalamazoo, 1980).

45. Palladius, *Lausiac History*, 59.

46. *Lausiac History*, 33; Third Greek Life of Pachomius, 44 (inserted into the *Vita Pima Graeca* by Athanassakis, p.47.)

47. This is the implication of the *Vita Prima Graeca* 32 and 37.

47.^a See John Anson, 'The Female Transvestite in Early Monasticism: The Origin and Development of a Motif', *Viator* S(1974) 1–32.

48. Palladius, *Lausiac History*, 5.

49. Jerome, *Epistola* 107, 13; PL 22: 000.

50. Brown, 'Christianization of the Roman Aristocracy', 180.

51. *Confessions*, 6, 2.

52. Jerome, *Epistola* 77; PL 22: 697.

53. *Epistola* 108. 7; PL 22: 882.

54. *Vie de Sainte Mélanie*, 21.

55. *Journal de Voyage*, SCh 21.

56. Kelly, 191, reviews the literature regarding this controversy.

57. *Cohabitations suspects* 3.

58. *Epistola* 5; PL 16: 929.

59. *Epistola* 108. 26; PL 22: 902.

60. *Lausiac History*, 41.

61. *Epistola* 127. 7; PL 22: 1091.

62. *Epistola* 33. 7; PL 22: 447.

63. *Epistola* 20 describes his resistance to his sister Marcellina (PL 16: 1034).

64. *Lausiac History*, 46.

65. P. Courcelle, 'Paulin de Nole et Saint Jérôme', *Revue des études latines* 25 (1947) 250–80.

66. P. Brown, 'The Patrons of Pelagius', *Religion and Society in the Age of Augustine*, 208–26.

67. Brown, 'Christianization of the Roman Aristocracy', *Religion and Society in the Age of Augustine* (London, 1972) 84–94.

Byzantine Asceticism and Women's Monasteries in Early Medieval Italy

Dorothy de F. Abrahamse

THE OLD, but, alas, still standard histories of medieval women's monasticism are largely accounts of Frankish and Anglo-Saxon foundations. In spite of the importance of Italy in the history of early monasticism in the west, there has been no specific study of the development of feminine monastic institutions and ascetic ideals of the age between Benedict and Gregory VII. In part, this fact is not surprising, for there are no saints' lives or letters to provide a picture of women ascetics as there are of the great early medieval abbesses of the north. But from chronicles, papal documents, and other sources we know of the existence of women's monasteries in major Italian centers throughout the period. Moreover, the history of monasticism in Italy is of particular interest, not only as the home of Benedict, and Cassiodorus, and the site of Bobbio and Subiaco, but as a unique cultural meeting point between roman, northern (lombardic), and greek traditions of asceticism. This paper will examine evidence for women's role in the last of these traditions, in the italo-greek monasteries of Rome and southern Italy, and offer some comparisons with what is known of the latin female communities of the era.[1]

BACKGROUND AND PROBLEMS OF EVIDENCE

Let me begin with the reminder that southern Italy, byzantine until the end of the tenth century, gave rise in the final two centuries of byzantine rule to a greek monastic culture that was to develop under norman domination in the eleventh and twelfth centuries and survive to the end of the middle ages.[2] The origins of italo-greek asceticism are shrouded in obscurity and controversy (was it the product of native greek-speaking populations or of Constantinian exiles?), but scholars can agree that the main features of its development in the ninth and tenth centuries are illuminated by a remarkable series of hagiographic texts describing the lives of peripatetic saints whose eremitic asceticism coexisted with the establishment of cenobitic foundations and semi-eremitic *lavras*.[3] The interchange between the monastic worlds of Italy and the east was constant, with ascetic developments paralleling those of the other great monastic centers in Greece and Asia Minor, and the *scriptoria* of italian monasteries served as important centers for the copying of byzantine religious manuscripts in the west.[4] Beyond the bounds of byzantine Italy proper, important meeting points for greek and latin monasticism existed in Italy between the seventh and tenth centuries. The greek monastic population of Rome in the seventh and eighth centuries is well-attested, and the translations of texts, calendars, cults, and relics that can be traced there testify to its importance in greek cultural transmission.[5] We know of no greek monasteries in Ravenna, but chronicles and saints' dedications indicate that in lombard Italy byzantine asceticism was admired and imitated to some degree.[6] Characterized by the rigorous ascetic practices of its saints in their grottoes and by the fluid interchange between eremitic and communal life, eastern asceticism was a potent force in early medieval Italy.

What part of this life was open to women ascetics? We must begin by examining the nature of the sources that establish their existence. In a sparsely documented age, nuns and their monasteries are frequently invisible in both greek and latin sources. No literature addressed specifically to women religious (rules, foundation *typika*, lives of contemporary abbesses) survives from the Italy of this period, and women's absence from the public life of the Church means that feminine foundations do not appear on the council lists by which male communities are known. In consequence, incidental references to women's monasteries are scattered and hard to evaluate. Latin monastic evidence begins with an extraordinary source—the register of Gregory the Great (590–604).[7] Gregory's correspondence supported and encouraged monastic communities throughout the west, and included references to a large number of female foundations. The letters provide a valuable picture of these establishments, but their limitations as evidence are important to bear in mind. The pope's monastic correspondents were emphatically latin, and this would seem to indicate that by the early seventh century greek monasteries had not yet been established. But recent scholars have warned that this should be seen as a reflection of Gregory's own policies and circle of correspondents; other evidence suggests the continuing importance of a greek church and population, in Sicily in particular, during this age.[8] Secondly, the *registrum* is isolated; its detailed evidence is not matched in any subsequent papal registers or other documents. The fact that most of the foundations known from Gregory's letters are never heard of again, then, cannot be taken as conclusive evidence for discontinuity or destruction.

Latin female communities in subsequent centuries in Rome and southern Italy are known primarily through chronicles and documentary sources. Local monastic histories from this area recorded foundations for women and, especially from the tenth century, some surviving charters and inventories, as well as papal correspondence, demonstrate the establishment of female communities.[9] Problems with the material are evident; the authenticity of many early charters is questionable, and some chronicle information is equally suspect. But evidence generally accepted provides names, dates, and a record of continued patronage to and endowment of monasteries for women. Other limitations should be mentioned: Sicily and much of southern Italy, under byzantine jurisdiction, were not included in the papal and ecclesiastical records that contain much of our information, even though some of these regions contained latin monasteries. The material cited above offers little evidence for ascetic practices or contemporary attitudes toward female religious life. Basic questions remain to be investigated by western monastic historians: the influence of Montecassino and its adaptation to female asceticism; the models followed by early Lombard founders; and the relationship between men's and women's communities.

Byzantine monastic life between the seventh and tenth centuries is reflected through an entirely different literature. Although archeology and other material evidence may eventually change our assessment, the history of the italo-greek monasteries of Sicily and Calabria is still written on the basis of two series of hagiographic texts: a group of biographies and passions composed probably in the seventh and eighth centuries to justify the origins of episcopal sees in sicilian cities, and the mostly contemporary biographies of late ninth, tenth, and eleventh century ascetic heroes.[10] None of these works is devoted to the life of a woman ascetic, but nuns and their monasteries sometimes appear in incidental roles. Hagiographers considered them a standard part of monastic landscape they described. A distinctive attitude towards women in general colors many of the *vitae*, and its consequences for the role of the nun will be explored. In addition, contemporary sources from other parts of the Empire, often copied in tenth century italian *scriptoria*, may provide fuller information for some basic features of women's participation in the byzantine monastic world. Hagiographic evidence has obvious limitations: Although its episodes can offer vivid insights into ascetic beliefs and the social roles of monks and nuns, these texts provide little specific evidence for the foundation, endowment, or organization of women's communities. Saints' lives, by nature, describe the extraordinary rather than the commonplace and contemporary works must be read as religious rather than historical documents. Italian texts present particular problems, for in spite of their vivid portrayal of eremitic life, many *vitae* are known only in latin translations and paraphrases, others remain still unedited, and most lack modern critical editions.[11] Any comparisons between byzantine and latin female asceticism must, in consequence, be very tentative, and must be made in full recognition of the difficulties of evaluating disparate kinds of evidence. We will attempt, first, to demonstrate that communities for women existed in both greek and latin Italy in the early middle ages, and that such communities were often established in geographical proximity to each other. Then we will evaluate some of the characteristics which the byzantine tradition would have brought to any encounter between the two.

LATIN COMMUNITIES FOR WOMEN

The female foundations which can be identified from Gregory's correspondence in Rome and southern Italy were surprisingly numerous, but they appear to have been generally small, often new, and usually in need of papal protection and endowment.[12] Following late roman custom, many were established in houses or estates (*in domo, in villa*) by aristocratic women or, on occasion, on similar property belonging to the papacy.[13] Gregory's letters ordered support for indigent communities from the papal patrimony, regulated claims of family members over property donations, and suppressed abuses of custom and dress.[14] But what is most noteworthy is the role Gregory afforded to the abbess. His correspondence was often directly with women superiors, and bishops were called in more often to protect women's communities against abuses from outside than to regulate them. None of these monasteries appear to have been under the jurisdiction of a masculine community, nor does Gregory ever refer to presbyters or other masculine overseers in any of the letters. Rather, in letters to nunneries in Gaul, he guarantees the autonomy of the abbess in conducting affairs of the house, and the freedom of feminine communities from outside interference from patrons, church or lay officials.[15] Invasions had already begun to disrupt these monasteries by Gregory's time, and it is perhaps not surprising that even in Rome no continued existence for these small foundations can be documented. But the number of otherwise unknown communities revealed by his letters is clear testimony of the persistent popularity of ascetic life for women in late sixth century provincial Italy.

For the next two centuries the latin foundations of southern Italy and Rome are known from references in chronicles and papal lists. It is not surprising that the role of the patrons and compilers of these works—the lombard dukes and the community of Montecassino—looms large, and that evidence of women's monasteries is largely restricted to their initial establishment. Thus, a series of female foundations by the lombard dukes of Benevento and their wives is recorded for the late seventh and eighth centuries, beginning with the establishment of the monastery of St Peter *maioras foras muros* in Benevento by Theodorata, wife of Duke Romuald, in 675, and continuing with three mid-eighth century ducal foundations (Hagia Sophia in Benevento, 768; S. Salvator at Alife; S. Maria de Plumariola, 745).[16] A women's community is also known to have existed within the confines of the ducal palace in Benevento during the eighth century. Hagia Sophia, established by Duke Arichis with his sister as abbess, became the repository for the translated relics of St Mercurios and was described as a sanctuary of some magnificence (*opulentissimum ac decentissimum*). Its existence is of particular interest, for contemporary chroniclers recognized the duke's conscious imitation of Justinian's church, even to the point of using Greek letters for its name. But we do not know whether the Duke's imitations of byzantine splendor went beyond architecture.[17] In the course of the eighth century the growing influence of Montecassino can be seen in the subjection of female communities to benedictine male monasteries: S. Maria in Plumariola and S. Sophia were placed under benedictine monks' jurisdiction in the late eighth century, and another benedictine foundation (S. Maria *ad portam summam*) is recorded in the same period. A papal charter of exemption to Montecassino from the mid-ninth century includes four women's monasteries—S. Maria in Plumbariola, S. Maria in Cingla, S. Sophia in Benevento, S. Maria in Cosentia—while another—S. Salvatori at Alife—was placed under the jurisdiction of the benedictine monks of S. Vincent of Voltura by its founder.[18] Thus, in the late seventh and eighth centuries, two powerful forces—the lombard dukes and benedictine monks—promoted the establishment of ascetic life for women.

Not much is known of roman convents in these centuries. The *Liber Pontificalis* records two instances of papal establishment of women's monasteries in deserted churches for liturgical purposes, and a list of roman monasteries from 806 includes several female foundations unknown in earlier sources; but the continued existence of earlier foundations as women's communities is often questionable.[19] However, it is here, in the increasingly greek ascetic atmosphere of seventh and early eighth century Rome, that a meeting between greek and latin ascetic traditions for women must have taken place, for by the end of the seventh century greek women had certainly entered some of the monasteries in Rome, partly as a result of the flight of eastern monastic communities from the Arab and Persian invasions. Hagiography and foundation traditions suggest the identity of some of the communities affected by the migration. One of the miracles recorded for the translated relics of Anastasius of Persia was the cure in 713 of the demon-possessed daughter of a Bishop Syros, recently arrived from Constantinople.[20] Syros, according to the story, had placed his daughter in the monastery of Cassianos for training in psalmody, hymns, chant, and readings. Cassianos, known from a letter of Gregory I, is located by Dom Ferrari in the large complex of St Laurence *foris muros*, and had probably housed a community of consecrated virgins since late roman times.[21] Another saint's life with strong ties to seventh-century Rome, the greek *Vita* of Gregory of Agrigentum, describes the penance and tonsure of a converted sicilian prostitute by the 'deaconess of St Cecilia', and her subsequent life in the cloister. Although the biography's legendary nature is well known, it has been demonstrated that the work was probably written in the eighth century by someone at St Sabas in Rome.[22] Independent evidence suggests the existence of a convent adjoining the basilica of St Cecilia in the late sixth century.[23] Two later foundation traditions may show the greek origins of other women's houses. S. Maria in Campo Martis claimed in the tenth century that it had been granted by the mid-eighth century pope, Zacharias, to constantinopolitan nuns from St Anastasia fleeing with their relic of Gregory Nazianzen. The assertion is dubious; in byzantine sources the church of Anastasia and its relics were still flourishing in tenth century Constantinople, but there may be evidence for greek nuns at Campo Martis.[24] S. Maria in Tempuli associated its development with a byzantine icon of the Virgin.[25] This evidence is suggestive rather than decisive. It is unlikely that many whole communities of nuns fled Persians, Arabs, or Iconoclasts to re-establish themselves in Rome. But the story of Bishop Syros' daughter does suggest a plausible situation. In the context of the burgeoning greek monastic culture of seventh and eighth century Rome, the appearance of greek communities for the sisters, daughters, and widows of immigrants could certainly be expected. They probably did not last long; St Laurence and St Agatha and Cecilia, like several latin women's communities, had become men's monasteries by the early ninth century, and few greek monasteries retained greek rites into the tenth century.[26] When a group of greek nuns from Calabria arrived at Rome in the tenth century, there was reportedly no existing greek community, and they were established in a latin foundation with their superior serving as prioress under a latin abbess.[27] But even though these Greek communities for women were evidently small and ephemeral, they do demonstrate that one meeting point for eastern and western ideas on female asceticism certainly existed in the early middle ages.

During the tenth century the endowment of monasteries for women became a popular aristocratic benefaction. Bernard Hamilton has demonstrated how the house of Theophylact promoted female asceticism in tenth century Rome, and a similar impulse may be seen in surviving charters from southern Italy. Documents from Salerno record the donation by a Susanna *sanctimonialis* of a church and property for the construction of a monastery for women, and of another foundation by a couple known as Guido and Aloaria.[28] In Capua documents from the monastery of St John the Baptist record its initial foundation by Landolf, son of Landenolf, in return for perpetual prayers, and the subsequent donation of lands inherited from her mother by Sichelperba, one of the nuns of the community.[29] Similar foundations may be found in charters surviving from Amalfi, Ravello, Scala, and Benevento.[30] The analysis of these foundations is a subject of a separate study, but a few features are pertinent here. Patrons expressed their desire for the perpetual prayers of the community, implying that liturgical functions were of primary interest and that women's communities were considered efficacious performers of monastic ritual.[31] Some charters reflect widows' donations of their own inherited property, but in other documents no immediate family tie between donor and community members is apparent. The role of benedictine communities in the area continues to be notable; in many of the surviving charters a community of benedictine monks appoints a *praepositus* for the nuns, and the charter contains guarantees that the freedom of the community to elect its own abbess will be respected.[32] Finally, it should be noted that these charters, with detailed descriptions of property and legal rights, show little interest in the liturgical or ascetic life of the community. Local landowners promoted monastic life for women, but it is difficult for us to tell what kind of life was established. The time of their foundation coincided with the flight of greek ascetics north from Calabria to these provinces where, as Bernard Hamilton has shown, they were received and protected by local rulers.[33]

WOMEN ASCETICS IN ITALO-GREEK TRADITION

The overlapping greek world saw women ascetics through very different eyes. Two series of hagiographical texts provide almost all the extant evidence for italo-greek asceticism before the eleventh century and occasionally mention women ascetics in specific situations. Mothers and sisters of saints are frequently portrayed as entering religious life; as Gregory of Agrigentum's mother was associated with the canonessess of the city, the mother of Sabas entered a monastery, as did the sister of Nilus the Younger. Ascetics sometimes were described as founding monasteries for their female relatives, as did Luke of Demenna and Phantinos the Younger. Women religious also appear as the beneficiaries of cures: Philippos of Agira's miracles included the cure of a nun of a monastery of Sergios and Bacchos in Sicily; and the *vita* of Gregentius of Tafar describes his benefits to a nun and a canoness, and his visit to a women's monastery near Akragas. The relics of Phantinos the Elder were associated with a convent near Taureano in the ninth century, and several pieces in honor of the saint refer to the nuns' care of the shrine.[34] The evidence shows in a general way that female asceticism was a constant part of the hagiographer's world. Several references also establish the existence of tenth century foundations for women in Calabria, otherwise unknown,[35] and one or two offer vivid insights into existing communities. But the most significant evidence for women religious in these biographies lies in the general views of women expressed here and the influence of these views on female asceticism.

Far more than texts from other provinces of the middle byzantine empire, these hagiographies view women as seductive threats to monks. The theme of attempted seduction, a commonplace of the desert fathers' tradition, appears frequently. The life of Gregory of Agrigentum centers around an accusation of fornication made against the saint by a prostitute; Elias the Younger's life includes a seduction attempt by the wife of a Christian to whom the young Elias had been sold as a captive; and biography of Elias the Speliot includes a very similar seduction attempt by the wife of his aristocratic host.[36] The Elias the Younger episode, where the cosmetics and statagems of the would-be seductress are described in loving detail, has been shown to be derived from the story of Potiphar's wife, making probable use of descriptions of John Chrysostom and Theodoret.[37] All three episodes are certainly hagiographical *topoi* added to stress the chastity of the ascetic in the most imaginative sections of the biographies.

Women seeking cures, especially aristocratic women, were also viewed as seductive, impudent, and polluted. The biography of Zosimos includes the story of a patrician woman oppressed by 'savage weakness' who came to demand a cure from the saint with what the biographer described as the customary evil of *temerariae feminae*, eliciting an appearance from the martyr Lucia to eject *foetidam hanc impudentemque mulierem*.[38] A similar story is told of the tomb of Elias the Speliot, which a patrician woman entered in a state of uncleanness and polluted. The biographer of Sabas describes the appearance of women seeking help from the saint in a time of famine as 'lacking in their customary shame'.[39] This attitude was certainly not unique to italian hagiographers, nor does it dominate most texts. But its persistence suggests how deeply the fear of sexual temptation, especially in encounters with stong-minded women, must have colored any role women might have played in ascetic life.

In the life of the most influential of all italo-greek saints, Nilus the Younger of Grottaferrata, however, *gynaikophobia* was indeed a dominant, almost obsessive feature. Nilus made it his custom never to eat with women. He perferred talking with a serpent to a woman, and by the end of his life he avoided the sight of women completely, claiming that the mere sight of a female made the devil appear and torment him.[40] The saint's worst temptation from the devil was the vision of an enormous Alemanni woman, and when a nun he encountered on the road attempted to show reverence to him, Nilus, 'recognizing a trick of Satan', beat her violently with his stick and subsequently ordered that his monks never leave the monastery unaccompanied. So sensitive to the presence of women was the saint, according to his biographer, that after a week's journey he sensed that a girl, ignorant of his prohibitions, had wandered into his community's chapel to pray in his absence.[41] The intensity of the theme is of particular significance in this *vita*, for it was through Nilus, most austere of the ascetics, that the latin world had its closest contact with greek asceticism in the eleventh century, and his influence at Montecassino, Capua, and Rome has frequently been described. An episode describing the saint's horror at the presence of a young presbyter in a capuan convent may reflect a specifically greek response to more relaxed latin regulation of nunneries.[42]

If Nilus's prohibitions were extreme, fear of female pollution certainly had practical consequences. The exclusion of women from monasteries of men meant that they might be barred from relics housed in masculine communities. Bishop Syros in eighth-century Rome was unable to take his daughter to the shrine of Anastasius and had to beg a detachable tooth[43]; Elias the Speliot's body became the center of a healing cult after his death, and although female relatives of the saint were evidently able to visit the shrine, access for other women was limited. The biography describes a monk dressing his niece in men's clothing to bring her to the relics, and a layman was given the loan of a sandal belonging to the saint 'on condition that it not be touched by a married man'; the relic was dipped in water which affected the cure of three women.[44] Such prohibitions were clearly not universally observed, and they did not mean that convents were not founded in ascetic centers, as Luke of Demenna's and Phantinos the Younger's foundations for their female relatives demonstrate. But it does bespeak a significant separation from much of ascetic life—its relics and liturgical centers—for nuns as for other women.

Italo-greek asceticism for men was characterized by its emphasis on eremetism combined with cenobitism, but there is no good evidence that women participated in this life in Italy or in other provinces in the middle byzantine period. A popular tradition of romantic fiction in Byzantium dominated the biographies of women saints of the fifth and sixth centuries— the legend of the disguised female ascetic living as a desert hermit. The stories have been shown to be the products of desert monks' imaginations,[45] with no basis in real tradition, but they clearly captured the interest of eastern and western hagiographers. The legends of Maria of Egypt and Theodora of Alexandria were among the most popular hagiographical transplants to the west, and were copied and translated in Italy during the eighth and ninth centuries.⁴⁶ The only known biography of a sicilian female saint, Marina of Sicily, turns out on inspection to be a retelling of the theme, and is interesting only for its use of vernacular Greek.⁴⁷ Like its tenth-century byzantine counterparts, the story provides no reason to believe that a real tradition lay behind it. Yet another reference to a female hermit is equally unreliable. A twelfth-century description of the cult of Nicander included the name of a woman, Elizabeth, among a group of hermits whose relics were venerated in the church, but the legend has not been considered reliable.⁴⁸ Unless these tales can be documented by better evidence, women's ascetic life in Greek Italy should be considered conventual.

Although hagiographical sources from the eighth and ninth centuries can do little more than establish the existence of women's communities, they can be used to characterize various kinds of communities founded in the tenth century. The foundation of monasteries for the female relatives of a holy man is notable, for it reflects a pattern common in other byzantine provinces. In spite of the standard hagiographic rhetoric describing the ascetic's decision at the outset of his career to turn his back on earthly ties, families were rarely forgotten by byzantine saints.⁴⁹ Luke of Demenna gave the habit to his widowed sister and her sons, and made her abbess of a community of nuns, where she became, according to his biographer, an example of virtue 'not unlike her brother'.⁵⁰ In doing this, he followed the example of the ninth-century byzantine holy men Peter of Atroa, Euthymius the Younger of Thessalonica, and Theodore of Studion, whose *vitae* all document the establishment of communities under the direction of mothers and sisters.⁵¹ Like the brothers and nephews of ascetics who frequently appear as their successors in directing monastic complexes, female relatives were supported in the perpetuation of family interests in a dynastic world.

At least one abbess is described as a respected figure in her own right. Despite his strong misogynist views, Nilus the Younger maintained a special admiration for an aged abbess who had lived a severe monastic life from a young age and had acted as a spiritual guide to the saint from his youth. Her reputation was regarded as unique in Rossano by Nilus' hagiographer, and her small community of nuns was probably not wealthy.⁵¹ It must have presented a contrast in the same town to the convent of Anastasia, whose troubles also appear in the *vita* of Nilus. This was the foundation of an imperial official who had endowed the community with property and left it in the care of a monk on his return to Constantinople; at the approach of death, the monastic caretaker sensed that the nuns would fall prey to the greed of the town's rulers and placed the community in the hands of Nilus. The hagiographer's description of the saint's action offers a significant insight into the functions of this kind of guardianship: collecting its dispersed property, reconstituting the community, and appointing an abbess, the saint argued to the town elders that the foundation was worthy of their support 'for if any of you should die, and his wife wish to live in holiness, and, having nowhere to go, be associated with another man, the fault will be yours for not taking care that such a city should have a monastery'.[52] The meaning is clear in the light of greek ecclesiastical marriage legislation, for byzantine tradition allowed second marriages only with a penance, considered third marriages 'moderated fornication', and outlawed any successive marriages completely.[53] Thus, the provision of access to a monastery for one's widow as a religious duty as well as a means of preserving property intact suggests a practical motivation for the apparent predominance of widows in 'communities of virgins'. Local, devoted to prosaic ends, such communities would have embraced a life far different from the spectacular practices of ascetic heroes.

BYZANTINE VIEWS OF FEMALE ASCETICISM

The italian hagiographic evidence thus establishes the continued presence of female ascetic groups in the monastic landscape, suggests a variety of intensity and endowment in such communities, and, above all, emphasizes the deep contradictions and constraints under which women religious lived in their dual role as women and ascetics. But in order to learn something of the organization of women's communities and of the ideals preached directly to female ascetics, we must turn to eastern Byzantine sources of the same age. Official church concerns, recorded in the canons of early medieval councils, echoed the fear of the violation of nuns, further attempts to enclose them, and the outlawing of customs smacking of paganism.[54] The closest thing to a 'rule' for nuns from the eastern empire probably derives from these centuries.[55] Its author warns his readers to remember the presence of death, not to pray in anger, to avoid pride and to practise virtues. Some specifics of monastic life are enjoined: the nun is to sleep on wood, to remain alone at night, to keep vigil and meditate after the evening psalmody for the greater part of the night. Practical advice is included—words to say when hunger or drowsiness strikes and warnings to guard one's ears and eyes and to keep one's hands from touching the body of another. A page on manual labor in the garden is addressed to monks rather than nuns, and has raised the questions about the specifically female intention of the whole work. Clearly missing is any reference to obedience to an abbess or other members of the community; these rules are precepts for the individual to turn her mind to Christ through ritual, but it is hard to imagine that they were ever intended to guide a community. Theodore of Studion, a late eighth century monastic reformer whose works were read and copied widely

in Italy, left letters to a circle of women correspondents which indicate the
diversity of ascetic orders for women surviving in his age: the recipients of
his advice included deaconesses, canonesses, abbesses, and recluses. The
rhetorical tradition of byzantine correspondence meant that he offered little
specific advice, but his monastic imagery is strikingly consistent with the
sentiments of italian hagiography. Nuns are urged to avoid the sight of men,
to be dirty, and to break the chains of sexual desire by remembering the
bridal couches to be readied for them as brides of Christ.[56]

The most important insights into female ascetic life are contained in the
lives of women saints of seventh, ninth, and tenth century Greece and Constantinople. These include the *vitae* of three abbesses and a nun whose relics
became the centers of popular healing cults, and although the works make
use of hagiographical *topoi* and are not written by contemporaries of their
heroes, they all exhibit direct knowledge of the nunneries in which the
saints' traditions were preserved.[57] The fact of their existence is in itself
significant; in contrast to the distant virgin martyrs or legendary 'disguised
females' of early byzantine hagiography, these were very real members of
religious houses, commemorated by their communities and relatives, whose
bodies were believed to work miracles after death. The ascetic practices
described are in some cases quite specific. One text, difficult to date, in-
corporates a detailed account of the establishment of a women's monastery,
including the charter from the donor, the appointment of a deacon as its administrator, the founding abbess's oath of faith to him on behalf of the community, and the festal liturgy that celebrated its establishment. The same
text describes the building of a three-storied chapel and a cemetery and the
wall that provided its enclosure.[58] In all these works, the liturgical life of the
nuns is portrayed, and although these sections are particularly likely to be
rhetorical, they emphasize the centrality of psalmody, chanted as the nuns
stood unsupported, sometimes with arms outstretched, vigils lasting the
greater part of the night, and offices repeated at the third, sixth, and ninth
hours. Tears, a feature of all eastern saints' lives, are particularly prominent
marks of the female ascetic. Holy women practised the ascetic rigors of
fasting, sleeping upright, and keeping vigils. Like their male counterparts,
they ate no meat.[59] In short, despite their views of feminine weaknesses,
byzantine hagiographers saw nothing to distinguish women's ascetic practices from those of their masculine contemporaries except one thing: no
matter how rigorous the regime, women ascetics remained in their communities rather than following the masculine pattern of combining cenobitic life
with periods of eremitic isolation. Within their communities, women were
considered capable of carrying out the strenuous regime without significant
alteration.

Masculine directors—generally deacons or presbyters—are constant figures in these works. They were usually more than administrators; one biography describes the community's expectation that its presbyters' tombs would work miracles, and another includes an excursus on the deeds of its director. They do not, however, overshadow the commanding figure of the abbess even when she is not the heroine of the *vita*—it is clearly she who was responsible for the spiritual life of its members.[60] Finally, we should note that the women in these biographies, like Luke of Demenna's sister and the community reorganized by Nilus, most often entered their communities as widows.[61]

The *vitae* do not survive in many manuscripts and they were not incorporated into standard *menologia*, so we cannot know where they were read. One biography, the life of Athanasia of Aegina, survives only in a south italian manuscript of the early tenth century and in a latin translation that must have its origin there.[62] Her biography had elements that could represent a model for the greek female ascetic in Italy. As a young widow, Athanasia joined a community, and led it to a more secluded site under the direction of a presbyter. In addition to the perpetuation of her ascetic regime, she was responsible for the building of three churches, lived in Constantinople in a monastery of nuns for seven years, and on returning died near the tomb of a famous saint. Anastasia's relics, guarded by the community, began early to work the miracles that proved her sanctity for the benefit of suffering women and children; her memory was celebrated in public *panegyreis* at the tomb.[63] It is not a dramatic life; it can in no way compare with the ascetic feats or public encounters of the hermit saints or northern abbesses, and it is not clear that this essentially private asceticism could have influenced latin institutions in the way that the more spectacular eremitic tradition did. But until the end of the middle ages when the greek rite monasteries were finally dissolved, women's communities remained a constant, if silent, part of the ascetic landscape of southern Italy alongside their latin counterparts.[64] Despite the limitations imposed on them, some of these women offered important testimony to the possibilities of female participation in a rigorous ascetic regime. As the development of latin female asceticism in early medieval Italy begins to be uncovered, the presence and possible influence of the coexisting greek tradition for women must not be forgotten.

California State University
Long Beach

TABLE OF ABBREVIATIONS

AA SS	*Acta Sanctorum*, Antwerp and Brussels, 1643–
BHG	*Bibliotheca Hagiographica Graeca*, 3rd. edition, (*Subsidia Hagiographica*, 8a) Brussels, 1957.
exc.	excerpted
ep.	*episcopus*
MGH	*Monumenta Germaniae historica: Scriptores rerum langobardicarum*, Hanover, 1878.
Mir. Anast. Rom.	Miracula Anastàsii romani, ed. H. Usener, *Acta M. Anastasii Persae*, Bonn, 1894, pp. 14-20.
PG	J. P. Migne, *Patrologiae Cursus Completus, series Graeca*, Paris, 1857-1866. '
summ.	summary
trans.	translation
V. Christ. et Macar.	*Vita Christophori et Macarii* (Life of Christopher and Macarius) ed. I. Cozza-Luzi, *Historia et laudes S. Sabae et Macarii juniorum e Sicilia*. Rome, 1893.
V. Elias Spel.	*Vita Elia Spelaeotes* (Life of Elias the Speliote) AA SS Sept. 3: 848- 87.
V. Elias jun.	*Vita Elia junioris* (Life of Elias the Younger), ed. G. Rossi Taibbi, *Vita di Sant'Elia il Giovane*. Palermo, 1962.
V. Greg. Agrig.	*Vita Gregorii Agrigentini* (Life of Gregory of Agrigentum) PG 98: 549-716.
V. Greg. Taph.	*Vita Gregentii Tapharis* (Life of Gregentius of Tafar) ed. A. Vasiliev in *Vizantijski Vremenik* 14 (1907) 39-46 (excerpts)
V. Luc.	*Vita Luca Demennae* (Life of Luke of Demenna) AA SS Oct. 6: 337-41.
V. Nil. jun.	*Vita Nili junioris* (Life of Nilus the Younger), PG 127: 476-97.
V. Phil. Agir.	*Vita Philippi Agirae* (Life of Philip of Agira) AA SS Mai 3: 1*-7*.
V. Sabae	*Vitae Sabae* (Life of Sabas), ed. I. Cozza-Luzzi, *Historia et laudes S. Sabae et Macarii juniorum e Sicilia*. Rome, 1893.
V. Zos.	*Vita Zosimi* (Life of Zosimus) AA SS Mart. 3: 839-43 (Latin summary)

NOTES

1. Lina Eckenstein, *Women under Monasticism: Chapters on Saint-Lore and Convent Life Between AD 500 and 1500* (Cambridge, 1896), and Philibert Schmitz, *Histoire de l'ordre de Saint-Benoît* (Maredsous, 1958-56), Vol. VII are still the standard surveys of the subject. Neither work treats women's monasteries in Italy in the early middle ages. For general bibliography on the subject, see Giles Constable, *Medieval Monasticism: A Select Bibliography* (Toronto, 1976), Susan Mosher Stuard, ed., *Women in Medieval Society* (Pennsylvania, 1976), and Jane Tibbetts Schulenburg, 'Sexism and the Celectial Gynaeceum – from 500 to 1200', *Journal of Medieval History* 4 (1978) 117-33.

2. Recent surveys of italo-greek monasticism include Silvano Borsari, *Il monachesimo bizantino nella Sicilia e nell' Italia meridionale prenormanne* (Instituto italiano per

gli studi storici in Napoli 14; Naples, 1963); Andre Guillou, 'Grecs d'Italie du Sud et de Sicile au Moyen Age: les moines', *Mélanges d'Archéologie et d'Histoire* 75, (Paris, 1963) 79–110 (reprinted in *Studies on Byzantine Italy*, London: Variorum, 1970); Evelyne Patlagaean, 'Recherches recentes et perspectives sur l'histoire du monachisme italo-grec', *Revista di storia della chiesa in Italia* 22 (1968) 146–66.

3. The argument over the impact of greek refugees on the native population of Sicily and Calabria, and the extent of an existing hellenic population in these areas is examined by Borsari, *Il monachesimo*, 7–22, who argues for a significant greek population and ascetic tradition in Sicily before the seventh century, and by Guillou *Les moines*, pp. 82–84.

4. Pertusi, 'Bisanzio e l'irradiazione della sua civilta in Occidente nell'Alto Medio Evo'. *XXI Settimani di Studi sull'alto Medio Evo*, (Spoleto, 1964) 75–134; id., 'Aspetti organizzativi e culturali dell'ambiente monacale greco dell'Italia meridionale', *Eremitismo in Occidente nei secoli XI e XII*, Miscellanea del Centro de Studi Medievali IV (Milan: Pubblicazione Università Cattolica Sacro Cuore, 1965) 382–426; id., 'Rapporti tra il monachesimo italo-greco ed il monachesimo bizantino nell'alto Medio Evo', *Italia Sacra* 21 (1972) 473–520, T. Minusci, 'Riflessi studitani nel monachesimo italo-greco', *Il Monachesimo Orientale*, Orientalia Christiana Analecta 162 (Rome, 1958) 215–33.

5. On greek monasteries in Rome: G. Ferrari, *Early Roman Monasteries and Convents from the Vth through the Xth century* (Vatican City 1957)—a register of known foundations and sources; on relics and the cult of saints: E. Follieri, 'Il Culto dei santi nell'Italia greca', *Italia Sacra* 21 (1972) 553–572, E. Patlagaean, 'Les moines grecs d'Italie et l'apologie des thèses pontificales (VIII–IX siècles)', *Studi Medievali* n.s. 5 (1964) 579–602; on architecture and liturgy (general): E. Krautheimer, *Rome: Profile of a City* (Princeton, 1980) 89–109.

6. Ravenna: A. Guillou, *Regionalisme et indépendance dans l'Empire byzantin au VII siècle*, *Studi Storici LXXV–LXXVI* (Rome; Institut storico italiano per il Medio Evo, 1969). Lombard evidence is discussed by *Bernard Hamilton* (see note 33) For the influence of later Greek eremetism on northern monasticism, see the papers collected in *Eremetismo in Occidente* (above, n. 4).

7. *Gregory I Registrum epistularum; MGH Epistolae* VI, ed. P. Ewald & L. Hartmann (Berlin, 1891).

8. Borsari, *Il monachesimo*, 28–35.

9. A recent index of sources for latin monasteries is to be found in Kehr-Holtzman, *Italia Pontifica* VIII, IX, X (Berlin, 1961–75); although the work treats papal records, it includes bibliography for monasteries not documented papally in each diocese.

10. Sicilian cycle: Patlagean, 'Les Moines grecs d'Italie' (above, n. 5), and *Studi Medievali* n.s. 6 (1965) p. 305. Saints' lives included in the cycle are: *Vita Gregorii Agrigentini* (BHG 707), ed. Migne, PG 98: 549–716; *Vita Pancratii Taormina* (BHG 1410–1410a), by Veselovski, *Sbornik otedeleni russkie jazyka* 40.2 (St Petersburg, 1886), 73–110; Marcianus ep. Syracus (BHG 1030) *Acta Sanctorum* June 2 (1698) 788–795; Alphios and the martyrs of Lentini (BHG 57–62), *Acta Sanctorum* May 2 (1680) 772–78, 528–48; Philippos of Agira (BHG 1531), *Acta Sanctorum* May 3 (1680) 1*–7*; Stephenus of Rhegium (BHG 1668), *Acta Sanctorum* July 2 (1721) 220; Gregentius of Tafar (BHG 705), exc. A. Vesilovsky in *Vizantijski Vremenik* 14 (1907) 39–66. Ninth and tenth century biographies: Leo of Catania (BHG 981–981e), ed. B. Latysev, *Hagiographica graeca inedita*, Memoires de l'Academie imp. de St. Petersburg VIII serie, XII.2 (1914) 12–28;Nicander, Gregorius, Petrus, Demetrius and Elizabeth of Messina (BHG 1329), Latin transl. *Acta Sanctorum* September 6 (1757) 88–91; Elias of Enna (†903), (BHG 580), ed. G. Rossi Taibbi, *Vita di Sant'Elia il Giovane* (Palermo, 1962); Elias Spelaeotes (†960), (BHG 581), *Acta Sanctorum* September 3 (1750) 848–87; Philaretus the Younger (†1070), (BHG 1513), Latin trans. *Acta Sactorum* April 1 (1675) 606–18; Phantinus of Taurianos (BHG 1508), Latin trans. *Acta Sanctorum* July 5 (1727) 556–67; Zosimus, ep. Siracuse,

Latin summ., *Acta Sanctorum* ch 3, 839–43; Leoluke of Corleone, Latin trans., *Acta Sanctorum* ch 1, 98–102; Luke of Demenna, Latin trans., *Acta Santorum* October 6, 337–41; Sabas (BHG 1611), ed. Cozza-Luzzi, *Historia et laudes SS Sabas et Macarii iunioris* (Rome, 1893 [not seen]), excerpt Pitra, *Analecta sacra* I (Paris, 1876) 306–13; Christophorus and Macarius, ed. Cozza-Luzzi, *Historia et laudes*, 71–96, 143–44; Vitalus, *Acta Sanctorum* ch 2, pp. 26–34; Nilus (BHG 1370), ed. Migne, PG 127, 476 –97; Nicademos of Kellarana, ed. Magri, *Testi e Studi Bizantino-Neoellenici* III (Rome, 1969); summary of selected *vitae* in G. da Costa-Louillet, 'Saints de Sicile et d'Italie Meridionale', *Byzantion* 29–30 (1959–60) 89–172.

11. Criticism and commentary on editions and recent scholarship in G. Schiro, 'Per l'esumazione di alcuni testi agiografici siculo-italo-greci,' *Bizantino-Sicula*, Quaderni dell' Instituto Siciliano di studi bizantini e neoellenici 2, (1966), 85–103, and E. Patlagean, 'Recherches recentes' (above, n. 2). Most of the *vitae* in the *Acta Sanctorum* are reprints of the seventeenth-century latin translations and paraphrases of Gaetani.

12. Gregory I, *Reg* 9; 23 (Nola), 42 (Monostheo); 46, 69; II, 38; III, 36; IV, 11, 61, 34; V, 4; VII, 12, 23; VIII, 34; IX, 54, 84, 86, 114, 137, 197, 224; 223, 207; XI, 13, XIII, 6; XIV, 2.

13. Gregory I, *Reg.* I, 23: *ancillas Dei quasdam Nolanae civitatis in Arboridana domo commanentes.* XIV, 2 . . . *de monasterio sancti Hermae, quod in domo Pomponianae religiosae feminae constructum est.* . . . II, 38: *monasterium ancillarum, quod est in Monostheo fundo, ab ecclesia nostra de Villa nova fundo.* . . . II, 10: *Hortum Felicianie quondam presbyteri.* . . .

14. Gregory I, *Reg.* 23, IX, 86; XII, 6, V, 4; IX, 197, IX, 207.

15. Gregory I, *Reg.* XIII, 11,12;VII, 17.

16. Kehr, *Italia Pontifica* IX: 105–7 (St Petri Maioria foras Muros); 78–82 (St Sophiae); 115–16 (S Salvator); VIII, 195 (S Mariae de Plumbariola).

17. Kehr, *Iralia Pontifica* IX: 101. Erchempert, *Historia Langobardum Beneventanorum*; MGH, *Scriptores Rerum Langobardicarum* 3: p. 243: *Infra Beneventi autem moeniam templum Domino opulentissimum ac decentissimum condidit, quod Grego vocabulo Agian Sophian, id est sanctam sapienteam, nominavit; dotatumque amplissimis prediis et variis opibus sanctimoniale coenobium statuens, idque sub iure beati Benedicti in perpetuum tradidit permanendum.*

18. Kehr, *Italia Pontifica* VIII: 195, 125. A charter of Nicholas I conceding exemption to the monastery of Benedict *et quatuor monasteriis puellarum, s. Mariae in Plumariola, s. Mariae in Cingla, s. Sophiae infra civ. Beneventana, s. Mariae in civ. Cosentia*; IX, 103, 115. (s. Salvatori Alife).

19. S. Eugenia, *Liber Pontificalis*, 2 ed. Duchesne (Paris, 1955–57) I: 510. Corsarum, *Liber Pontificalis* II:112, and a list from 806: *Liber Pontificalis* II: 22–25. For a register of roman monasteries with citations of sources and bibliography, see Dom Guy Ferrari, *Early Roman Monasteries* (Vatican City, 1957).

20. Anastasii Persa, *Miracula Romana*, ed. H. Usener, *Acta M. Anastasii Persae* (Bonn, 1894) 14–20. For a commentary on greek flight to the west, see C. Mango. 'La culture grecque et l'occident au viiie siècle', *Settimani di Studi Sull' Alto Medioevo XX* (Spoleto, 1973) 683–721.

21. Ferrari, *Early Roman Monasteries*, 185.

22. *Vita Gregorii Agrigentini A. Leontio Heg. S. Sabae*; Migne, PG 98: 74. Commentary arguing for the dating: Patlagean, 'Les moines grecs,' 579–80; 596–602.

23. Ferrari, *Early Roman Monasteries*, 23–25.

24. Ferraril, *Early Roman Monasteries* 207–9. Ferrari cites references in unpublished documents of the monastery which suggest greek members of the community. On Gregory's relics in Constantinople; see R. Janin, *Géographie Ecclésiastique de L'Empire byzantin, 5/3, Constantinople: les églises et les monastères* (Paris, 1953) p 26–29. See also Bernard Hamilton, 'Monastic Revival in Tenth-century Rome', *Studia Monastica* 4 (Barcelona) 35–68, 43; idem, 'The House of Theophylact and the Promotion of Religious Life among Women in Tenth Century Rome', *Studia Monastica* 12,

(1970) 195-217, esp. 208-13, where earlier bibliography is cited. Both studies are reprinted in *Monastic Reform, Catharism and the Crusades* (London: Variorum, 1979). The community was certainly latin in the tenth century; Hamilton regards the legend of its Greek foundation as possible but unproven.

25. Ferrari, *Early Roman Monasteries*, 225. Hamilton, 'Monastic Revival' 43-44, 'House of Theophylact' 196-201. The icon of the Virgin, restored in the twentieth century, has been attributed by its restorer to a byzantine craftsman of the eighth or ninth century.

26. Hamilton, 'The City of Rome and the Eastern Churches in the Tenth Century', *Orientalia Christiana Periodica* 27 (Rome, 1961) 5-26, (*Monastic Reform, Catharism and the Crusades, Chapter 3*).

27. Hamilton, 'City of Rome', 11-12.

28. A. Campagna and G. Crisci, *Salerno Sacra* (Salerno, 1962) 411-16.

29. J. Mazzoleni, ed. *Le Pergamene di Capua* (Naples, 1957) Vol. 1, documents 1, 3.

30. Kehr, *Italia Pontifica* VIII: 381-88; 395, 401-2, 9: 100, 102. Amalfi: R. F. Candida, *Codice Diplomatico Amalfitano*, R. Archivio di Stato di Napoli I, (Naples, 1917), 28-30.

31. *Pergamene di Capua* 1; doc. 1: *socere sue que est in eodem monasterio die noctuque laus omnipotentis Dei et oratio pro eo. . . .*

32. *Pergamene di Capua* 1, doc. 1, Scala, Amalfi S. Laurence (Kehr, VIII 387, 395).

33. B. Hamilton, 'Orientale lumen et magistra latinitas: Greek Influences on Western Monasticism (900-1100)' *Le millénaire de Mont Athos, 963-1963*, Études et mélanges 1 (Chevetogne, 1963) 181-216, esp. 181-89. (*Monastic Reform, Catharism & Crusades, Chapter 5*).

34. *Vita Greg. Agrig.* 49, *V. Christ. et Macar.* 7, 17-18; *V. Nil. Jun.* 28.

35. *V. Luc.* 15. On Phantinos; see Follieri, *Vita inedita* p. 26. *V. Phil. Agir., AA SS* May 1, p. *7; *V. Greg. Taph.*, Vesilovsky, pp. 49-52. For Phantinos the Elder; see canons in *Acta Sanctorum* July 5 (Note 10): on the Taureano convent, Folliere, 'Un Canone di Giuseppe Innografo per S. Fantino "Il Vecchio" de Tauriana', *Revue des Études Byzantines* 19 (1961) 130-51, p. 135. Other convents known from hagiographical evidence are Arenario (Nilus, 28), Anastasia in Rossano (Nilus, 45), see also B. Capelli, *Monachesimo Basiliano ai confini calabro-lucani* (Naples, 1961) 95.

36. *V. Greg. Agrig.* 53-55; *V. Elias Spel.* 23; *V. Elias Jun.* 11-12.

37. G. Rossi-Taibbi, *Vita di S. Elia il Giovane, Commentary*, pp. 134-35.

38. *V. Zos.* 5.

39. *V. Elias Spel.* 93; *V. Sabas* 14.

40. *V. Nil. Jun.* 39, 42, 88.

41. *V. Nil. Jun.* 19, 39, 67.

42. *V. Nil. Jun.* 79. For the influence of Nilus on Montecassino, Capua, and Rome, see Bernard Hamilton, 'Orientale Lumen' (n. 33 above).

43. *Mir. Anast. Romani.*

44. *V. Elias Spel.* 82, (niece brought in disguise); 86, wife of 'spiritual son' of saint; 93, female child brought secretly; 96, daughter of 'nephew in the flesh' of saint.

45. Analysis of these texts in the context of byzantine hagiographical tradition may be found in E. Patlagean, 'L'histoire de la femme déguisée en moine et l'évolution de la sainteté féminine à Byzance', *Studi Medievali*, Series 3, vol. 17 (1976) 597-623. The imaginary nature of the legends is argued by J. Anson, 'The Female Transvestite in Early Monasticism: The Origin and Development of a Motif,' *Viator* 5 (1974) 1-32.

46. A. Siegmund, *Die Überlieferung der griechischen christlichen Literatur in der lateinischen Kirche bis zum zwölften Jahrhundert* (Munich, 1949) 256-69.

47. G. Rossi-Taibbi, ed., *Martirio di Sant Lucia, Vita di Santa Maria*, Instituto Siciliano di Studi Bizantini e Neogreci: Testi, 6 (Palermo, 1959), introduction to *Vita of Maria*, pp. 75-77.

48. A latin version of the legend is published in *Acta Sanctorum* September 5: 88-91; the greek legend, still unpublished, is included in the early fourteenth-century

menologion of Messina (Codex Messanus Graecus 30). For an evaluation of its dubious historical value, see the entry in *Bibliotheca Sanctorum* (Vatican, 1961–71) Vol. 9, p. 851. The inclusion of a female ascetic is not specifically commented on.

49. For an examination of the family connections of saints in the ninth century, see the unpublished dissertation of K. Ringrose, 'Saints, Holy Men and Byzantine Society, 726–843', (Rutgers, 1976), and that of S. Stavrakis, 'The Provincial Elite: A Study in Social Relationships During the Ninth and Tenth Centuries', (University of Chicago, 1978). I plan to analyze this material in a monastic context in a forthcoming article on byzantine provincial monasticism.

50. *V. Luc. Demenna* 14.

51. *Vita Petri Atroae*, ed. V. Laurent, *La vie merveilleuse de St. Pierre d'Atroa*, Subsidia Hagiographica 29 (Brussels, 1956) 43, *Vita Retractata Petri Atroa*, ed. V. Laurent, *La Vita Retractata et les miracles posthumes de St. Pierre d'Atroa*, Subsidia Hagiographica, 31 (Brussels, 1958), 1: 104, *Vita Euthymii Junioris*, ed. L. Petit, 'Vie et office de St. Euthyme le jeune', *Bibliothèque Hagiographique Orientale* 5 (Paris, 1904) 14–50 (reprinted from *Revue de l'Orient chrétien* 8 [1903] 168–205), 3, 37; Theodore of Studion, *Oratio funebris ob matrem suam*, PG 99: 884–902, *et passim*.

52. *V. Nil. Jun.* 45–46.

53. The theological issues are discussed briefly by J. Meyendorff, *Byzantine Theology* (New York, 1979) 196–99, with further bibliography. The legislation has received considerable discussion because of the controversy occasioned by the successive marriages of the tenth-century emperor Leo VI 'the Wise'.

54. *Concilium in Trullo* (692) 4, 45, 46, ed. P-P. Joannou, *La Discipline Générale Antique; Pontifica commissione per la redazione del codice di diritto canonico orientale. Fonti*, 9 (Rome, 1962).

55. *Didascalia Monazouson*, in J. Pitra, *Spicilegium Solesmense* (Paris, 1852–58) 4: 416–35. The *Didascalia*, like other collections of Byzantine canon law attributed to the Patriarch John IV Nesteutes (582–95) is now believed to have been compiled between the eighth and tenth centuries. See H.-G. Beck, *Kirche und Theologische Literatur im Byzantinischen Reich*, (Munich, 1959) 423–24.

56. Theodore of Studion, *Epistolae* II. 19, 43, 52, 104, 124, 150; ed. Migne, PG 99: 904–1669.

57. Abbesses: Irene of Chrysobalantos, abbess of a constantinopolitan convent, whose biography was probably written in the late tenth century (*Vita Irenes* [BHG 952], *Acta Sanctorum* July 6: 602–34); Athanasia of Aegina, the ninth-century abbess whose life is described below (*Vita Athanasiae Aeginae*, BHG 180, *Acta Sanctorum* August 3: 170–75); Matrona of Constantinople, an abbess of the sixth century, whose biography is dated to that century by its editor (*Vita Matronae*, BHG 1221, *Acta Sanctorum* November 3: 790–813); Theodora of Thessalonica, a late ninth-century nun, was the subject of two biographies and a miracle account: 1) *Vita Theodorae*, BHG 1737, ed. Arsenij, *Zitie i podvigi sv. Theodory Solunskoj* (Jurjev, 1899); 2) E. Kurtz, *Mémoires de l'Acadamie imp. de Saint-Petersbourg*, 8ᵉ Série, VI, 1 (1902) 1–36; 3) Kurtz, *Ibid.*, 37–49.

58. *V. Matronae* 36: 'Antiocha [the donor] making these gifts to the blessed Matrona and writing them down gave the charter to her. According to law she appointed the deacon Marcellus as the representative (*eis prosopon*) of the saint, . . . and swearing faith to the deacon on behalf of the community, she went away strengthened in mind and body. She established a spiritual flock, which until the present has struggled unbendingly according to the rule [*kanon*] given to her'.

59. See the *V. Irenes. Chrysobal.* 13 (devotion to scriptures, *stasis* with outstretched arms), 14 (clothing, diet of bread, water, vegetables), 50 (tears), (stasis, lenten diet). *V. Athan. Aeg.* 3 (diet, fish on Easter, bread and vegetables, sleeping, tears), 5 (clothes, psalm-singing regime), 22 (vigils, tears). *V. Theod. Thess.* 22, 26 (service to monks and manual labor). *V. Matronae* 41 (description of regime taught to entering member).

60. *V. Theod. Thess.* 13–19 (speech of Antonios), *V. Ath. Aeg.* 7–8 (Matthew

presbyter, miracles, drowning 'deprives of relics', successor Ignatius presbyter, tomb works miracles after death). *V. Matronae* 36 (oath to Marcellus,). The care of appointed presbyters and their authority is demonstrated throughout, but Matrona's final authority on the entrance of a new member (40–42) is significant. The life of Irene has no reference to a masculine overseer. In the life of Theodora of Thessalonica the abbess ('the great one') is represented as an unrivalled spiritual authority in the community and over the life of Theodora, despite the presence of an overseer for external decisions and the proximity of a nearby men's monastery.

61. *V. Ath. Aeg.* 3; *V. Theod. Thess* 19.

62. The *vita* survives in a Greek codex of the tenth century which has been identified as Italo-Greek, and in a Latin codex described as identical by its editors in the *Acta Sanctorum*. A palimpsest of the 9–10th century of Grottaferrata has a saint's life identified by Ehrhard as that of Athanasia. A. Ehrhard, *Überlieferung und Bestand der hagiographischen und homiletischen Literatur der griechischen Kirche (Texte und Übersuchungen 50–52)*, Leipzig 1937–52, I, 610; I, 1, 3, 926.

63. *V. Ath. Aeg.* 14–17 (miracles).

64. For bibliography and an account of women's monasteries at the end of the middle ages, see V. H. Laurent, A. Guillou, *Le 'Liber Visitationis' d' Athanase Chalkéopoulos, Studi e Testi*, 206 (Vatican, 1960), the edition of a visitation with full bibliography for monasteries mentioned.

Strict Active Enclosure and Its Effects on the Female Monastic Experience (ca. 500–1100)

Jane Tibbetts Schulenburg

HISTORICALLY FASCINATING as well as timely and controversial is the issue of the enclosure of women religious. Cloister (*claustrum*), meaning 'that by which anything is shut up or closed, a lock, bar, bolt', was originally associated with the idea of incarceration.[1] Jean Leclercq says of it:

> It is only in the course of the Middle Ages that *clausura* enters into the juridical vocabulary of the Church; it designates there: (1) the material obstacle which marks the bounds of property; (2) the space reserved to those who enter there or who live there; (3) the body of ecclesiastical laws relative to this obstacle and to this space.[2]

In general, rules of cloister govern egress and ingress of the enclosure;[3] they regulate what is called 'active cloister', i.e. leaving the monastery; and 'passive cloister', the introduction of strangers into the monastery.[4]

Enclosure has always been part of the monastic life of both monks and nuns. Monasticism requires a certain separation from the world and therefore infrequent contact with outsiders. Chapter sixty-six of the Rule of St Benedict states that 'there is no necessity for the monks to go about outside of it, since that is not at all profitable for their souls'.[5]

Although enclosure is required of both monks and nuns, an unequal emphasis has been placed over the years on the ideal of strict, unbroken claustration for women. Thus the obligations resulting from the prescriptions of enclosure are sex specific. Their application varies in severity according to whether nuns or monks are concerned;[6] and even within feminine monasticism, the degree of enclosure varies according to the nature of the community and its particular mission in the Church.

The first decree of universal enclosure for women (the bull *Periculoso*) was promulgated only in 1298 by Boniface VIII. It had been preceded, however, by a long and significant tradition of cloistering female religious. Indeed, the essential roots of, and rationalizations for, this institution already existed in the early Middle Ages.

This study surveys one aspect of enclosure: the prescriptions of strict *active cloistering*, i.e. the policy and practice in regard to going out of the monastery. It will explore some of the effects of this policy on nuns, especially within the context of the general decline of monasticism for women from, approximately, the late eighth through the late eleventh centuries. Its major focus will be on the developments of enclosure in the general area of medieval France, with references to Germany and England, from approximately 500 to 1100.

THEORY AND RATIONALIZATION FOR THE EARLY ENCLOSURE
OF WOMEN RELIGIOUS

References to the enclosure of women can be found in the writings of the Church Fathers, monastic rules, the canons of the church councils, saints' lives, charters, chronicles, and correspondence. Except for a few saints' lives and letters, these sources come from male ecclesiastical writers and therefore reflect a male perspective on the theory and practice of claustration. Many of our sources are didactic works, directives, or legislation, which often provide warnings or exhortations to female religious on the specific necessity of enclosure. They generally underline the proscriptive or negative aspect of cloistering. Thus the nature and paucity of our sources for this early period leave us ill-informed in regard to the *vox feminae*, and the perspective which medieval women religious might have brought to this essentially female issue.

Claustration to some degree was an integral part of monastic life. The monastic experience required a 'spiritual space' apart from the distractions and diversions of the world. Monastic life assumed an environment which would foster detachment and an atmosphere conducive to prayer. Preparation for the kingdom of heaven required a renunciation of the world.

In this early period, enclosure was also a very practical response to physical realities. This was the age of the viking, the saracen, and the magyar invasions, of political anarchy and local violence. Not infrequently did female religious fall victim to brutality; some were raped, some were forcibly carried off from their monasteries to become slaves of the invaders; still others were abducted and then married off to the local nobility.[7] Monastic enclosure established a protective, physical barrier—consisting in some cases of high, thick walls with few entrances. It also established a type of sacrosanct, inviolable space which added a psychological safeguard to the lives and chastity of these brides of Christ. Enclosure allowed women to live a type of religious life which would have been extremely difficult at the time outside of an established cloister. In the period from ca. 500–1100, however, ecclesiastical assessments of the need for enclosure for women, as well as attempts at its strict application, seem to have experienced a subtle shift.

Some of the earliest references to strict enclosure for women are found in patristic writings. The necessary protective constraints of active enclosure for brides of Christ are stressed, for example, in the correspondence of St Jerome. In his letter to Eustochium (382–84) he warned of the very real dangers to a virgin who leaves her protected environment and ventures outdoors:

> Go not out from home, nor wish to behold the daughters of a strange country . . . Diana went out and was ravished. I would not have you seek a bridegroom in the highways, I would not have you go about the corners of the city. . . . Your Spouse cannot be found in the broad ways. Narrow and strait is the way that leadeth to life. . . . You will be wounded, you will be stripped, and you will say, lamenting: "The keepers that go about the city found me, struck me, wounded me; they took away my veil from me." . . . Jesus is jealous. He does not wish your face to be seen by others . . . unless you avoid the eyes of young men, you shall depart from my bridal chamber and shall feed the goats which shall be placed on the left hand.[8]

Pope Gregory the Great also assumed the need for active enclosure for the 'handmaidens of God'. In a letter to Januarius, Bishop of Cagliari (593–94), he rebuked the bishop for being remiss in his guardianship of the convents in Sardinia. Pope Gregory instructed the bishop carefully to select a man to attend to the needs of the nuns, and

> . . . so assist the inmates of these monasteries that they may no longer be allowed to wander, against rule, for any cause whatever, private or public, beyond their venerable precincts; but that whatever has to be done in their behalf may be transacted reasonably by him whom you shall depute. But let the nuns themselves, rendering praises to God and confining themselves to their monasteries, no longer suggest any evil suspicion to the minds of the faithful.[9]

The need for strict protective cloistering for a community of female religious was first formally articulated by Caesarius of Arles (470–542).[10] In light of the dangers of the time (especially the barbarian invasions), Caesarius stressed the imperative need for nuns to be totally separated and protected from the world. In the *Life* of Caesarius unbroken enclosure is compared to Noah's ark: Caesarius is seen as another Noah who built the ark to shelter Caesaria's daughters from the storms, tempests, and perils of the world. As brides of Christ they were to be concealed from the world within the ark; and none was permitted to leave her shelter until the day of her death. Within this secure environment they were to devote themselves to the contemplative life and await the heavenly kingdom.[11] Caesarius of Arles also described the ideal of enclosure in the letter *Vereor*, written to his nuns:

> She who desires to preserve religion in an immaculate heart and a pure body, ought never, or certainly only for great and unavoidable necessity, go out in public. . . . For a soul chaste and consecrated to God should not have constant association with externs, even with her relatives, either they coming to her or she going to them; lest she hear what is not proper, or say what is not fitting, or see what could be injurious to chastity.[12]

The importance of unbroken claustration and details of its practical application are articulated by Caesarius especially in his *Regula ad virgines* (513), written for his sister Caesaria's convent of St John. Of the seventy-three articles of the rule, some nineteen deal with specific regulations for full cloister. As a modern translator of the work has noted, when compared with St Caesarius' Rule for Nuns, his companion Rule for Monks, 'has by no means the detail and strictness of the nuns' Rule for every aspect of cloister'.[13] The importance Caesarius attached to the strict, unbroken active enclosure of his nuns is underlined by the fact that his first general article deals with this prescription.[14] He warns the nuns:

> If a girl leaving her parents desires to renounce the world and enter the holy fold to escape the jaws of the spiritual wolves by the help of God, she must never, up to the time of her death, go out of the monastery, nor into the basilica, where there is a door.[15]

Article 50 of the *Regula* reiterates this restrictive policy:

> This is what we especially wish to be observed by you without any relaxation, that no one of you up to the time of her death, be permitted to go forth from the monastery or into that basilica in which you have a door, or presume on her own to go out.[16]

In this sixth century rule we can find all the characteristics of modern enclosure.

Caesarius of Arles' *Regula ad virgines*, with its rigorous enclosure, proved very influential in Merovingian Gaul. The rules for nuns written by St Aurelian, Bishop of Arles (546–ca. 555), and Donatus, Bishop of Besançon (ca. 627–58), were based in part on Caesarius' Rule. They, too, adopted policies of strict enclosure for their nuns.[17] Caesarius' program of unbroken cloister for female religious was adopted by Bishop Syagrius of Autun for his nuns at St Mary's, Autun. Under the influence of the Rule of Donatus, the monastery of Chamalières in Auvergne was strictly enclosed.[18] The abbey of St Mary of Soissons was also placed under rigorous claustration. In a charter of privilege (ca. 666) enacted by Drausius, Bishop of Soissons, these nuns—according to the rule appropriate to their sex—were to remain enclosed within their monastery without ever being able to obtain permission to leave.[19] The tenth century house of Regensburg also seems to have come under the influence of the rule of Caesarius of Arles and to have observed a policy of unbroken enclosure.[20]

One of the best-known institutions to adopt the *Regula* of Caesarius was St Radegund's monastery of Holy Cross, Poitiers.[21] Gregory of Tours suggests in his *History of the Franks* that the adoption of this rule was a way to compensate for the lack of spiritual guidance or episcopal patronage, or even to cope with the very real hostility of their local bishop, Maroveus of Poitiers. According to Gregory:

> Down the years Radegund had frequent occasion to seek the help of the Bishop, but she received none, and she and the Mother Superior whom she had appointed were forced to turn instead to Arles. There they received the Rule of Saint Caesarius and the blessed Caesaria. They put themselves under the protection of the King, for they aroused no interest or support in the man who should have been their pastor.[22]

The 'Letter of the Seven Bishops to St Radegund' recognized the adoption of the Rule of Caesarius of Arles by the monastery of Holy Cross. The bishops seemed especially impressed with the innovation of rigorous, unbroken enclosure, for nearly one-third of their letter focuses on this policy.

> . . . if a woman is chosen as an inmate of the monastery of Poitiers, according to the Rule of Caesarius, Bishop of Arles, of blessed memory, she shall never have the right to leave it. . . . If therefore any nun, driven insane by the prompting of a mind diseased, shall seek to bring the shame of such opprobium upon her vows, her glory and her crown, and, at the Devil's urging, like Eve expelled from Paradise, shall venture forth from the cloisters of her convent as if from the Kingdom of Heaven itself, to visit this place and that, to be bustled and trodden under foot in the vile mud of our public streets, she shall be cut off from our communion and shall be stricken with the awful wound of anathema. . . .[23]

In this letter we find for the first time a reference to the use of sanctions, i.e. anathema, for infractions of enclosure.[24]

Although the Rule of Caesarius seemed to exercise little direct influence on the female monastic experience after the seventh century,[25] the spirit of his *regula* seems to have exerted an indirect influence on church legislation of the period.[26] With the carolingian reform movement came increased pressure to place monasteries under episcopal authority. A new emphasis was placed on uniformity of practice and custom, the ordering and consolidation of houses, and the benedictine rule came to be adopted generally by monasteries of nuns and monks. One of the major reform issues of the period was strict, unbroken claustration for female religious, a policy which had in fact been carefully articulated by Caesarius of Arles but little developed by Benedict. In their attempts at organization and reform, carolingian church councils imposed restrictive legislation on all monastic houses, male and female. Although the reform councils did not devote a great deal of attention to women under monasticism, what little legislation there was points to a general consensus on the need for strict, full enclosure for nuns.

Although few previous conciliar decrees had specified active cloistering for nuns,[27] carolingian councils from the mid-eighth to the mid-ninth century issued a proliferation of sex-specific canons stipulating rigorous, unbroken claustration for nuns. Although many reform canons underlined the need for stability among male religious, the regulatory enactments were invariably much stricter for nuns than for monks.

A survey of the most important carolingian reform legislation on the topic of active enclosure for female religious has turned up the following information:

—The Council of Ver (Verneuil), 755, stipulated that if houses of nuns did not observe their rules, the bishop of the diocese must reform them. This council also enumerated the special circumstances under which abbesses would be allowed to leave their cloisters: when forced by war, or once a year when called by the king. In this latter case, the abbess could leave only with the authorization of the bishop. Nuns were absolutely prohibited from leaving their monasteries.[28]

—The National Assembly of Heristal (779) decreed that abbesses were not to absent themselves from their monasteries.[29]

—An edict of 789, the *Duplex legationis edictum*, stipulated that strict cloister (*earum claustra sint bene firmata*) was to be observed by all female religious. The abbess could not leave her monastery without the permission of the king, nor did she have the power to permit her nuns to leave the convent.[30]

—The Council of Friuli (796/97) prescribed severe cloister for all monasteries of women. Abbesses and nuns were prohibited from leaving their monasteries on the pretext of a pilgrimage to Rome or to other 'venerable places',[31] on the grounds that unavoidable interaction betwen nuns and men during these trips might form dangerous relationships.[32]

—The 'Capitulary of Theodulf' (797) specified that all of the faithful were to come together to the church to hear mass and the sermon with the exception of women sanctified to God. For, according to custom, these women were not to go out into the public *sed claustris monasterii contineri*.[33]

—The Councils of Riesbach and Freising (800) forbade abbesses to leave their monasteries without the permission of their bishops. In case of necessity, the bishop was to accord them this permission. Even so, they were to be accompanied by nuns who, on their return, would not relate to the others what they saw in the world.[34]

—The General Council of Aix-la-Chapelle (802) warned that monasteries of women must observe strict enclosure. The abbesses and nuns must equally observe the cloister and were to remain at all times, and with diligence, within the enclosure. They were not to go out without the leave or counsel of the bishop. Abbesses were to ask permission from their bishops when they needed to send nuns outside the monastery or to receive strangers within the house.[35]

—The Council of Tours (813) declared that abbesses, without the leave of their bishop, did not have the authority to go outside of their monasteries unless to meet with the emperor.[36]

—The Council of Mainz (Mayence), also in the year 813, stipulated that abbesses must live with their nuns according to the Rule of St Benedict, if this rule had been adopted, or of a manner which conformed to the canons. However, *all* nuns and canonesses were required to observe enclosure. Abbesses were to stay fixed in their monasteries and were not to go out without the leave and counsel of their bishop.[37]

—In the same year, the Council of Chalon-sur-Saône again distinguished between female religious who lived strictly under the Rule of St Benedict and those who observed canons. The following regulations seem to have been especially addressed to those who observed the canonical regulations. Canon 57 warned that, when the monastery is situated in an episcopal city, the abbess could leave only with the permission of the bishop or his representative, unless by imperial order. If the abbess were allowed to leave the monastery, she was to be accompanied by a few nuns. She was then to watch over them and make sure that they were not given the freedom or occasion for sinning.[38] The abbess was not permitted to make a long trip. Chapter 62 stipulated that nuns must never leave the monastery unless the abbess sent them to act on an urgent problem.[39]

—At the Synod of Aix-la-Chapelle (817) a collection of regulations for women religious was drawn up. Called the *De institutione sanctimonialium*, it was especially aimed at women religious who followed the canonical regulations (canonesses). Canon 18 stipulates that because of the 'fragility' of their sex, these female religious were to be strictly cloistered.[40] Another canon specifies that since they were prohibited from going outside of their monastery, they were not allowed to manage their ecclesiastical or personal property; rather this function was to be delegated to an outsider.[41] (In contrast to this, their male counterparts, the canons, were allowed to manage their own properties.)[42] Another canon warns that abbesses were to remain in their monasteries and were not to make sojourns into the towns.[43] In this legislation we find, too, certain specifications for creating a physical cloister, i.e. how the buildings should be arranged to insure that enclosure be observed.[44]

—The Council of Mainz (847) also demanded rigorous cloister for abbesses and nuns. It repeated earlier regulations that the abbess whose monastery was located in the city was not allowed to leave except by the permission of the bishop or by order of the king. When she did go outside of the monastery, she was to be accompanied by a few of her nuns, for whom she was then responsible, and again none was to be given the freedom or occasion for sinning.[45]

At least a dozen separate pieces of legislation from ca. 750–850, then, require strict, unbroken active claustration for women religious. It should also be noted that these councils showed an equal, perhaps even a greater, concern for passive enclosure. Reform legislation aimed at total enclosure for women. With the carolingian reforms, the issue of claustration had become, for the first time, one of the most important topics of church legislation for women under monasticism. After the carolingian period enclosure became a matter, not of conciliar or episcopal concern, but of monastic or regular emphasis.[46]

A survey of carolingian reform canons directed to monks on issues of enclosure reveals certain discrepancies between them and directives to women. While on the one hand reform councils continually exhorted abbesses and nuns to practice full claustration, abbots and monks were invariably allowed greater latitude in their dealings with the outside world. Although there were conciliar attempts to regulate the monks' external activities, these restrictions were neither as sweeping, nor as strict as the legislation for female religious. Regulations for monks seem to have been directed more toward monastic stability than full claustration. The canons, for example, warn monks not to frequent taverns,[47] go to banquets, enter hostels,[48] take part in worldly festivities,[49] leave the monastery alone,[50] serve as godfathers,[51] embrace a woman,[52] or accept a parish.[53] The legislation condemns vagabond monks who go from province to province, city to city, raising useless questions and causing arguments.[54] Monks were not to go to Rome or elsewhere without being sent on an errand by their abbot.[55] The reform councils also repeatedly forbade monks to leave their monasteries to occupy themselves with temporal affairs, or to be involved in activities for monetary gain.[56] Those who had only recently been admitted to monastic life were not to be sent outside to fulfill a mission on behalf of the house.[57] Several canons stipulate that male religious were not to appear in secular assemblies or meetings.[58] Others warn that monks and abbots must no longer appear in civil tribunals without the bishop's consent. And the abbot himself was not to discuss his disputes/cases before the tribunal; rather he must have his *advocatus* plead and argue his cases.[59]

This brief comparison of enclosure regulations in the legislation of carolingian councils points up some rather sharp discrepancies. These detailed proscriptions which, in effect, outline the activities of monks outside of their cloisters, suggest they lived in a totally different world from that of the nuns: a world which assumed a much greater degree of autonomy and independence than that of the female religious. The very silence, or omission of similar activities in the canons directed to nuns, implies a much more restricted atmosphere, a more rigorous policy of claustration for the female religious. Stricter enclosure is demanded of nuns than monks; essentially a double standard exists. And one of the most crucial differences is that the abbot invariably controls the enclosure of his own community. He maintains the authority to determine when it was necessary for him or for his monks to go outside the monastery for the benefit of the house. Although he has certain limitations on his personal mobility as abbot, these restrictions do not approach the strictness of those imposed on abbesses. In the observance of cloister, as De Clercq observed, 'it is the abbot who gives the monks permission to leave, while it is the bishop who authorizes the abbesses to leave and who is able to decide in which cases the nuns can be sent to the outside'.[60] The reform provisions of strict active enclosure deprived the abbess of autonomy in this area. In her dealings with the 'outside world' she was made dependent on her bishop. Claustration necessarily curtailed her personal involvement in administrative, economic, and judicial affairs. Other source material from the period echoes this growing concern with enclosure.

The *Vita* of Saint Lioba (written in 836) is very informative about the policy of strict enclosure practiced in Anglo-Saxon England. According to this saint's life, the double monastery of Wimborne was a royal house, 'surrounded with high and stout walls, and supplied with a sufficiency of income by a reasonable provision . . . .'[61] From the beginning, both monks and nuns observed strict regulations in regard to passive enclosure.[62] The provisions for active cloister were, however, specifically aimed at women.

> Truly, any woman who renounced the world and wished to be associated with the community, entered it never to go out again, unless a good reason or matter of great expediency sent her out by the advice (of the abbess).

Moreover, the mother of the congregation herself, when she had need to make arrangements or give orders about any outside affairs for the profit of the monastery, spoke through the window, and from there decided whatever expediency required to be arranged or commanded.[63]

Yet although the monastery of Wimborne followed strict, unbroken enclosure, this policy was controlled by the authority of its abbess.

The *Regula monachorum* originally found among the works of St Jerome, but perhaps dating to the ninth century, provides another example of this preoccupation with strict claustration for nuns.[64] It devotes a long and extremely interesting chapter to the need for rigorous, total enclosure for female religious. Chapter 27, 'On Enclosure', begins by underlining the ascetic necessity of strict cloister for nuns. Because of worldly vanities or concerns it warns:

> ...dearest one, let your convent become your tomb: there you will be dead and buried with Christ, until rising with him you will appear in his glory. Finally, the thing that is most frightening to the one lying in a burial mound is the grave robber who sneaks in at night to steal precious treasure. Thieves dig this up, to steal with infinite skill the treasure that is inside. Therefore the tomb is watched over by a bishop whom God installed as the primary guardian in his vineyard. It is guarded by a resident priest who discharges his duty on the premises: so that no one may enter recklessly or try to weaken the tomb.[65]

The Rule then continues with a detailed description of the material protection provided by strict enclosure. It emphasizes high walls and doors with strong locks. The bishop controlled the keys and also determined who entered or exited the monastery.[66]

Unbroken enclosure was of extreme importance in the establishment of the first cluniac monastery for women, founded at Marcigny in 1056. From its inception, Abbot Hugh of Cluny specified that strict cloister was to be observed by the nuns. According to the *Life of St Hugh*, he required that once a woman had freely entered this glorious prison (*gloriosum hunc carcerem*), none would be given leave to go out of the cloister.[67] Leaving the protection of the monastery he viewed as dangerous, for 'in appearing in the world they made others eagerly desire them or they saw in the world things they themselves desired'.[68]

In 1095 Pope Urban II issued a charter for the monastery of Marcigny. He warned that no one was to molest the nuns, so that 'enclosed for the fear of God (*Pro Dei timore clausae*) and dead to the world, secure from all attack and far from worldly oppression, they should ever strive with the strength of their entire mind and soul towards the vision of their eternal spouse'.[69]

Peter the Venerable compared the severity of cloister at Marcigny to a perpetual prison which inmates entered willingly. The nuns were never to leave the monastery of Marcigny for any reason. They were forbidden by the command of the abbot to walk outside their cloister walls, or even outside of the regular houses in which they lived, as did other nuns. Nor could they travel by horse.[70] As he said:

> The world being dead to them, they were dead to the world, and becoming unseen by all, after their vocation they laid over their eyes and faces a thick veil, like a shroud; they wore it until their death, as a symbol that should forever remind them of their latter end and warn them to prepare for it. Enclosed in this cloister of salvation, or rather buried alive in this sepulchre, they waited to change a temporary prison for the freedom of eternity, and to change this burial for resurrection.[72]

St Anselm, a little earlier, had articulated the reform ideal of rigorous enclosure for female religious in a letter to a nun, Mabilia, who was contemplating going out of the cloister to visit her relatives. He warns her not to be involved in dealings with people in the world or in secular conversation, but rather to maintain enclosure. If she wishes to be a nun and a bride of Christ, she should say with St Paul, 'The world is dead to me and I am dead to the world' (Gal. 6:14). And again with St Paul, she should consider all things of this world as fleeting dung (1Ph. 3:8). If her relatives wanted to see her, Anselm suggested, they should come to her, for it was not permitted her to go out of the cloister, except as God bears witness to this necessity.[73]

The reformer Ivo of Chartres also stressed the need for strict enclosure in an early twelfth-century letter to the nuns of St Avit-le Guêpières. He warns:

> The cloister of our monastery has been made in order that those who love the world are not received by you into the camp of those who flee the world; in order that you do not appear in public; that you do not introduce images of the corporal vision of the world into your soul which pollute it; that even if you have allowed your soul to lose its interior virginity, you do not permit your body to be exposed to corruption.[74]

An especially fascinating summary of the growing preoccupation with strict enclosure for nuns can be found in a twelfth-century reform document written by the german cistercian monk, Idung of Prüfening.[75] In this treatise, entitled 'An Argument on Four Questions', the third question deals with the spiritual direction of nuns, specifically, 'whether cloistered nuns and monks, although they keep the one Rule of St Benedict, should also have the same guardianship of the cloister'.[76] This extremely useful work summarizes many of the earlier arguments for female claustration and also discusses the justifications for discrepancies in the application of strict enclosure to monks and nuns.

Idung's rationale for the ascetic necessity of strict claustration for female religious begins with the premise that 'because the feminine sex is weak, it needs greater protection and stricter enclosure'.[77] He then contends that:

> . . . the feminine sex . . . has four formidable and declared enemies. Two are within the sex itself: lust of the flesh and frivolous feminine inquisitiveness. Two are without: the casual lechery of the masculine sex and the wicked envy of the devil. To these are added [the fact] that a woman can lose her virginity by violence—a thing which in the masculine sex nature itself prevents.[78]

Idung then utilizes some of the classical arguments of St Jerome to support this 'necessary' protection for women religious.[79] He writes:

> Reason, authority, precedents, the veiling of the head, the consecration, the betrothal itself . . . what do all these things imply but that the heavenly bride should be protected by enclosure so careful that she be not leered at by an immodest eye, the messenger of a lecherous heart, lest her glory should become her shame by that wretched downfall which the prophet laments.[80]

In the following argument he attempts to justify the necessary discrepancy in the application of enclosure to monks and nuns.

> . . . the protection of enclosure which the Rule of St Benedict requires is unlike and less than that which is due the bride of Christ. St Benedict did not write his rule for consecrated virgins but only for monks. In it a monk is permitted to be sent out on a journey in answer to some call, to sell at the market and buy what the needs and requirements of the monastery demand. Now no one doubts that this is unfitting (and wholly unbecoming) for any reason for the spouse of an earthly king, much less for the bride of the King of heaven. Many other things as well which do not apply to that sex are in that same Rule which was written, all agree, only for monks, because in it there is no mention of virgins.

> If [St Benedict] . . . had written a Rule for them do you really think that he would with dangerous license have allowed that sex to appear in public? It would be contrary to the words and examples of the fathers and contrary to his own example; for he himself visited his own sister St Scholastica, a woman consecrated to a life of holiness, only once a year.[81]

Idung's attitude toward women is especially revealing:

> He [Benedict] wrote no rule for consecrated virgins nor was it necessary to
> write any, because in those times monasteries of virgins existed only under
> the guardianship of abbots. And with good reason! It is not expedient for
> that sex to enjoy the freedom of having its own governance—because of its
> natural fickleness and also because of outside temptations which womanly
> weakness is not strong enough to resist.[82]

He finally concludes his argument:

> The examples of holy monks bear witness, however . . . that the Rule per-
> mits a monk to go to the market for the needs of the monastery . . . . And
> what has been said on the third question can prove (unless the contrary is
> proved) that the protection of an unbroken enclosure is more necessary for
> women than for men, for dedicated holy women than for monks.[83]

We see a great variety of evidence in the sources of this period of growing
concern, even perhaps obsession, with the need for rigorous, unbroken active enclosure for women religious. In concentrated response to the apparent abuses of the time, and in the name of monastic uniformity, legislation
requiring strict claustration for all nuns which appeared for the first time with
the carolingian reform councils, was renewed with perhaps even greater precision and rigor in the monastic regulations of the eleventh and twelfth
centuries.

There remains, however, the problem of discrepancy between *praxis* and
written norm—of knowing how widely these strictures were actually applied, or how closely they were adhered to in reality. Throughout the period there seems to have been some latitude in the observance of strict claustration. On the one hand, as several councils point up, strictly cloistered
houses coexisted with institutions of female religious which followed, with
seemingly less severe regulation, the canons. Furthermore, in some early cloisters, the rule of full claustration was apparently observed only with great difficulty, or was perhaps disregarded or, when necessary, evaded. The constant repetition of canons requiring strict enclosure for female religious
underscores the difficulties of applying these strictures. Nevertheless, it appears that during the early middle ages, many monasteries of women were
expected, and actually attempted, to follow a policy of strict, unbroken
claustration. Only through incidental evidence are we able to catch a glimpse
of the implementation of this policy.

REALITY: THE OBSERVANCE OF STRICT, ACTIVE ENCLOSURE

One of the earliest references to the application of active enclosure occurs in the *Vita* of St Caesarius of Arles. An episode in this saint's life describes how fire broke out in a house near the convent of St John and threatened to engulf everything in the area in flames. The disturbed *ancillae Dei*, who were not permitted to go outside their monastery (*quibus foris exire non licebat*), fled with their books and treasures to the monastery cistern, or water conduits, in which, conveniently at this time, there was little or no water. Warned of fire, Carsarius arrived in the middle of the night at the place where the fire was especially concentrated. He shouted down from the walls to reassure his nuns, 'Do not fear, *benedictae*'. And soon, through his virtue, a miracle occurred: the fire was extinguished.[84]

In his *De excidio Thoringiae* Fortunatus notes St Radegund's elegy to her relative Amalfrid. St Radegund responds that 'If I were not submitted to the holy cloister of the monastery (*sacra monasterii si me non claustra tenerent*), I would come to you, [Amalfrid], immediately'.[85]

Gregory of Tours' *Book of Miracles* provides some fascinating detail of events surrounding the funeral of St Radegund:

> When [the funeral procession] passed under the enclosure walls, the crowd of nuns appeared at the windows of the towers, or mounting even to the crenellations which crowned the wall, they burst out in moans and lamentations; their cries of sorrow and their clapping of hands provoked the tears of all the assistants. . . .[86]

The nun Baudonivia in her *Life of St Radegund*, noted the following very significant detail. Since no one living in the monastery was allowed to go out, the nuns' lamenting took place on the walls above the procession. The noise of their clapping rose above the chants. To reduce the hardship which strict claustration imposed on the nuns, and at their request, the funeral procession halted at the base of the tower within the enclosure.[87]

In a letter written ca. 850–860 to the nuns of St Mary of Soissons, Paschasius Radbertus, abbot of Corbie, who had been brought up and educated in this monastery, praises the discipline of the community and its adherence to unbroken enclosure (*alvearium esse monasticae disciplinae, quo aeterna clausura sanctimoniales illae sese obseraverant. . .*).[88]

Another example of the convergence of theory and legislation is provided by the cluniac monastery of Marcigny. Peter the Venerable has recorded how one night, flames threatened the very cells of the nuns. The Archbishop of Lyons (the papal legate) happened to be staying in the area. After being warned by townspeople of the fire, he immediately went into the cloister, and by his authority and by their obedience' attempted to convince the nuns to leave this extremely perilous place. A nun of the monastery named Gisla responded to his pleas:

> My father, the fear of God and the command of our Abbot keep us enclosed within these limits until we die. Under no pretext, in no circumstances, can we pass the bounds assigned to our penitence, unless he who enclosed us in the name of the Lord should himself permit it. Therefore order us not to do that which is forbidden; but rather command the fire to draw back in the name of our Lord Jesus Christ.[89]

And according to the story, at the legate's prayer, the flames miraculously withdrew.

Despite these examples of rigorous observance, our sources make clear the difficulties of maintaining absolute claustration. One early reference to the type of problem which might be encountered in the practice of strict, active enclosure for nuns again concerns St John's, Arles. The *Vita* of St Rusticula (d. ca. 632) describes how the abbess found herself enmeshed in political troubles and consequently accused of favoring a pretender to the throne. When the king gave orders for her arrest, she protested that she obeyed the king of heaven more than the earthly king; and that she would rather die than transgress the command of the holy father, Caesarius (i.e. than break enclosure.) Despite this, a nobleman, Faraulfus, forced her to leave the monastery. Fortunately the king soon became convinced of her innocence and St Rusticula was allowed to return to her community.[90]

While many female houses attempted to follow a policy of severe, unbroken enclosure, the sources reveal some variety in the observance of claustration. We find evidence of a certain freedom of movement which was allowed, or in many cases simply assumed by, abbesses and nuns. A seventh-century example concerns the nuns of the monastery of St Julian, outside of the walls of Auxerre. The founder, Bishop Palladius (d. ca. 658), in his foundation charter prescribed that the nuns were to go in procession each Thursday to the cathedral.[91] The *Life* of St Frobert, seventh-century abbot of Montier-la-Celle, also incidentally notes another case of deviation. Contrary to her normal habits, the abbess of St Quentin left her monastery, which observed enclosure, to assist at the funeral of her superior and father, St Frobert.[92]

In contrast to their continental sisters, anglo-saxon female religious of this early period seem to have been relatively free of the trend to restrictive cloistering which we have been tracing. Only later would abbesses and nuns in Britain feel the influence of reform ideology with its emphasis on monastic uniformity and strict bishop/abbot controlled enclosure championed by carolingian synods and continental monastic reforms. Although it appears that some early english houses were in fact enclosed, the enclosure seems to have been under the jurisdiction of the abbess (as in the case of Wimborne) and within the framework of the double monastery. In the proceedings of a few anglo-saxon councils, one notes the presence and participation of abbesses. Abbess Ebba, aunt of the king, participated in the deliberations of a northumbrian council of 680–81.[93] Five abbesses were present at the Council of Beccanceld in 694.[94] At the Synod on the Nidd, 706, Abbess Aelfflaed was singled out as the 'best counsellor of the whole province'.[95]

The number of anglo-saxon nuns who went to Germany at St Boniface's request also suggests a certain mobility for female religious. These nuns engaged in missionary activities in Germany; they established monasteries for women and schools among the new converts. St Walburga, a prominent anglo-saxon nun, became abbess of the double monastery of Heidenheim. Her *Life* notes that at least on one occasion she left the monastery to restore to perfect health the dying daughter of a local nobleman.[96]

Another anglo-saxon nun involved in this missionary movement was St Lioba, a relative and great friend of St Boniface and abbess of the monastery of Bischofsheim. In accordance with the wishes of Boniface, Lioba was given the special honor of visiting and praying at the male monastic community of Fulda.[97] As abbess of Bischofsheim, she maintained contact with the temporal rulers of the period, especially Charlemagne and his queen, St Hildegard. Many times she was summoned to the court and laden with gifts by the emperor.[98]

The making of pilgrimages, especially to Rome, also points to a certain freedom of movement for abbesses and nuns. In the correspondence of St Boniface, a letter written by the anglo-saxon abbess Eangyth and her daughter Bugga (719–22) asks Boniface for his advice: 'whether to live on in our native land or go forth upon our pilgrimage'.[99] Abbess Eangyth and Bugga realized the potential conflict of the pilgrimage with monastic stability/cloister:

> We are aware that there are many who disapprove of this ambition and disparage this form of devotion. They support their opinion by the argument that the canons of the councils prescribe that everyone shall remain where he has been placed; and where he has taken his vows, there he shall fulfill them before God.[100]

Boniface's careful advice to them is instructive. He writes that 'I cannot presume either to forbid or to urge strongly upon thee a journey abroad'.[101] If they cannot find in England 'the freedom of a quiet mind' they should, provided they have 'the will and power, seek liberty for contemplation by going abroad, just as did our sister Wiethburga [Wethburg]'.[102] But Boniface warns that they should wait until the dangers of the Saracens had ceased before setting out on their journey. Therefore, when the time was right, the nun Wethburg would send them a letter of invitation. 'And so thou shouldst prepare the necessaries for the journey and accept her advice, and afterwards do what the goodness of God shall enjoin.'[103]

It is then of special interest to compare this early, rather positive, personal response to the nuns' request to go on pilgrimage, with St Boniface's later, rather severe, official 'reform' position, found in his letter to the Archbishop of Canterbury (747). He writes that frankish churchmen are agreed that:

> ...it would be well and favorable for the honor and purity of your church, and provide a certain shield against vice, if your synod and your princes would forbid matrons and veiled women to make these frequent journeys back and forth to Rome. A great part of them perish and few keep their virtue. There are very few towns in Lombardy or Frankland or Gaul where there is not a courtesan or a harlot of English stock. It is a scandal and a disgrace to your whole church.[104]

The *Chronicle* of Hugh of Flavigny mentions the early eleventh-century case of Ava, illustrious abbess of the monastery of St Maur of Verdun. In the reform tradition, Ava wanted to learn more about the regular practices of monasticism. Out of friendship for Abbot Richard, founder of St Maur, St Odilo of Cluny allowed her to come to the great reform center of Cluny to observe monastic life.[105]

These varied examples point to a limited mobility on the part of abbesses and nuns. Most cases involved only a very few, select abbesses, and the trips outside seem to have been undertaken with the approval, if not the explicit permission, of the male church hierarchy. A few other instances in our sources, however, underline the difficulties churchmen experienced in enforcing unbroken enclosure; they depict female religious consciously ignoring and breaking these strictures.[106]

An early and exceptional case concerns a late sixth-century revolt at the monastery of Holy Cross, Poitiers. Under the leadership of a disappointed aspirant for the position of abbess, some forty nuns left the monastery in protest. The sources note that 'at the prompting of the Devil' they 'had escaped from the nunnery of Radegund' and 'had refused to go back inside the walls of their institution'.[107] They were ultimately excommunicated.[108]

Gregory of Tours describes another case of broken enclosure at Holy Cross:

... there lived in the nunnery a certain recluse who a few years
before, had lowered herself from the wall and fled to Saint Hilary's church,
accusing her Mother Superior of many transgressions.... Later on she
had herself pulled up into the nunnery by ropes at the very spot from
which she had previously lowered herself down.[109]

In penance, the nun asked permission to be enclosed in a secret cell where
she would be cut off from any contact with the community.

Two miracle stories in Jonas' *Life* of St Colomban and his disciples (7th c.)
describe the violation of enclosure at the monastery of Faremoutiers. In one
of these cautionary tales, Jonas tells how the devil, through his temptations,
tainted some especially credulous novices by leading them away from the
company of their sisters and making them violate cloister. One night, under
cover of darkness and with the aid of a ladder, the nuns attempted to leave
the cloister. As they did so, however, they were terrified by a flash of lightning and thunderbolt, and wanted desperately to return to the safety of the
abbey. But through the artifices of the devil, they were unable to move: they
had become as heavy as lead. Confused, the nuns recognized their wrong-
doing and on their return to the monastery they related all of this in humble
confession to their abbess.[110]

Perhaps the most interesting case of blatant disregard of strict claustration
occurs in the excommunication of Abbess Switha and two of her nuns. In
the official correspondence of Bishop Lull of Thuringia (755–86) is a letter
excommunicating Switha. According to the letter, Abbess Switha had totally
disregarded enclosure and had allowed two of her nuns to leave the monastery. As Bishop Lull asserted, this action was against canonical regulations,
the discipline of the holy rules, and, very importantly, had happened without
the necessary permission and counsel of her bishop. He argued that through
this ill-conceived action, which permitted her *vagas* and *inoboedientes* nuns to
go to distant regions and experience secular life, the abbess had contributed
to the perdition of their souls. For their conscious perpetration of this act,
and for this kind of 'foolishness' and 'carelessness', the abbess and her nuns
were to be excommunicated. Furthermore, the nuns were not to be received
back into the monastery and were to do penance on bread and water for the
rest of their lives.[111]

As Huyghe has noted, this letter is of special interest in that it is not a
legislative text but it demonstrates that the traditions of enclosure established
by Boniface for Mainz were in effect ca. 780. Huyghe also argues:

> This severity which pushed St Lull to excommunicate the abbess and to
> exclude from monastic life the two nuns who had one day dared to leave
> without his permission, proves that the rule was still well enough observed
> for the bishop to believe that so harsh a sanction would be effective.[112]

This survey of source material points to a variety of observance of enclosure by female religious. One finds examples from severe, full claustration, to a more flexible enclosure with some approved autonomy and mobility (especially for abbesses), to blatant disregard for enclosure. The paucity of material on the nuns' observance of strict claustration might be a function of the historical documentation of the period. References to the quiet, day-to-day preservation of strict claustration are not apt to be recorded. Again, these sources were compiled by male writers and reflect their interests. The moralistic, didactic works of churchmen—such as saints' lives, chronicles, tracts, letters of direction—tend to record cases of abuse and the 'just' punishment meted to nuns for their moral lapse, or to provide women religious with heroic examples of the virtue of maintaining strict enclosure. Most of the evidence we have on the observance of enclosure comes indirectly from incidental references in various sources. It is therefore extremely difficult to know how widespread the actual practice of strict enclosure was in this early period; the silent observance of enclosure likely escaped comment by contemporaries.

This problem of the discrepancy between theory and reality, written norm and *praxis*, has plagued modern scholars in their studies on the existence and significance of female enclosure in the medieval world. J. B. Thiers has attempted to prove that the law of enclosure was in force as early as the fourth century.[113] In his classic study, *La Clôture des moniales des origines à la fin du XIIᵐᵉ siècle*, Gerard Huyghe finds the early legislation on enclosure coincides with the creation of the first religious communities of women. He contends that already at the end of the sixth century the discipline of enclosure exhibited in Gaul a coherent organization and was everywhere assumed without discussion. Religious cloister was imposed with force in the carolingian period, when episcopal legislation was bolstered by imperial intervention.[114] Dom Philibert Schmitz argues that strict enclosure for women did not exist in the High Middle Ages and that as late as the thirteenth century it still depended essentially on the will of the abbess.[115] James R. Cain in 'Cloister and the Apostolate of Religious Women', traces the evolution of enclosure for women, and argues that although in the formative years of religious life cloister was recognized as an essential element in the formation of religious women, it was only with Boniface VIII's *Periculoso* that cloister was imposed by the Holy See as a universal obligation and as a strict policy which allowed no exceptions.[116] Roger Gazeau contends that cloister for nuns was not significant until the eleventh-century reform movement—especially after 1050 and throughout the twelfth century.[117] Jean Leclercq observes that 'In reality, there were some laws from the sixth century, but up to the fourteenth century they were neither universal, nor strict, nor largely observed'.[118] And finally, Peter Anson has singled out the importance of the carolingian period in noting that before the end of the eighth century the general body of nuns was not bound by enclosure legislation.[119]

We have noted, then, varied levels of strictness in the practice of enclosure during the Early Middle Ages. With the carolingian reform movement we found for the first time a major preoccupation with the need for strict female enclosure. There was a concerted effort to establish a precise, uniform and rigorous policy of claustration for *all* nuns. On one level, the proliferation of canons focusing on full claustration for women religious was part of the reform attempt at uniformity in religious practice; its primary purpose seems however to have been restrictive. That is, it was directed toward curbing or remedying a variety of abuses in female communities by sanctions established for infractions of enclosure. This seems to have been a new motivation for this sex-specific proscriptive program.

Since most of the carolingian reform councils and synods were of a local or regional nature, rather than being universal church councils, their initial influence was no doubt limited. Nevertheless the cumulative effect of the consistent repetition of legislation aimed at increasing episcopal authority over monastic life, and specifically at the regulation and control of female enclosure, should not be underestimated. Also carolingian rulers, through their intervention in church councils and their directives to the *missi*, exercised a decisive influence on cloister legislation and its application throughout the realm. With the growing precision and severity of reform legislation, behavioral norms were established for female religious. In turn, these prescriptions became important in the social conditioning of abbesses and nuns. Thus with this reform ideology one can see beginning a shift in the expectations society had of female religious which would become crucial, for example, in regard to the role of the abbess and her potential effectiveness as an administrator. Some of the important responsibilities and privileges which the abbess had previously assumed, or decisions which she had customarily made as head of her community, were, at least theoretically, removed from her authority. With the policy of full, unbroken enclosure a certain element of the abbess' legitimate autonomy shifted from the local female-controlled monastic sphere to men, especially to bishops. Thus we can perhaps see the beginning of an erosion of the public role of the abbess in the increased emphasis on her private role within the enclosure. We can, in general, note that with the carolingian reform ideology and its restrictive enactments of enclosure came a loss of autonomy by, and increase of control over, female religious and a movement toward greater dependency on men.

ENCLOSURE, LOSS OF AUTONOMY, AND ECONOMIC HARDSHIP

Although our limited sources provide evidence that there was variance in the observance of strict, full claustration by female religious, the repercussions of this policy must not be minimized. From the carolingian period on, the policy of strict enclosure which stressed different rights, powers and expectations for monks and nuns, was to play an important role in some of the most basic areas of the female monastic experience.

One of the most fascinating yet enigmatic questions in the study of monasticism is the growing disparity in monastic foundations for women and men between the mid-eighth and the end of the eleventh centuries. The period from ca. 550–750 witnessed a high level of enthusiasm for female monastic life. In the general statistics of monastic foundations in France and England, one finds a high percentage of new houses established for women,[120] as well as a substantial number of large women's communities. A reflection of their success and visibility can be seen in the high percentage during this same era of female saints, almost entirely recruited from among the abbesses and founders of these houses.[121] Women's initial enthusiasm and appreciation for monastic life seems to have waned after the mid-eighth century— the age of invasions, widespread devestation, and immense disorder, as well as church reform. During this era there was a substantial drop in new foundations for women. There appears also to have been a marked decline in the number of female religious. The percentage of female saints plummeted. And the monastic experience of women seems to have remained on this reduced level until the twelfth century. In contrast to the pattern of female establishments, houses for men, after a slow start, seem to have maintained a fairly consistent record for new foundations. In fact, with the tenth and eleventh century reforms, they experienced a period of renewed monastic vitality and immense activity. What are the reasons for this shift? Is there any relationship between carolingian policies of strict enclosure for women and the widespread decline in the foundations and prosperity of women's houses?

In studying these monastic foundations one is struck by the ephemeral aspect of so many of the women's monasteries. Many of them were small proprietary houses and survived only a generation or two. Their untimely demise may have come through a complex of factors which included destruction by invaders, fire, flood, famine, pestilence, usurpation of rights, dissipation or the secularization of patrimonies, indigency; and from the direct and indirect effects of the carolingian reform policies of full enclosure: the consolidation of female houses, the discouragement of double monasteries, and favorable changes in attitudes toward marriage.[123] We also find evidence of incompetence or mismanagement of properties sometimes attributed to young, inexperienced abbesses, lay abbesses, or inept or unjust *advocati.*

The endowments of even the wealthiest and most efficiently run houses often proved in practice to be insufficient to the continued indefinite maintenance of a monastery. Basic economic problems seemed to become aggravated when the number of nuns increased at a rapid rate, often surpassing the house's resources. A number of the carolingian reform councils dealt with the problem of the necessary regulation of numbers of religious in relation to material assets of the monastery. They insisted repeatedly that monasteries not accept more vocations than they were able to feed.[123]

It must, nevertheless, have been tempting to a monastery to try to accommodate as many nuns as possible. According to Baudonivia's *Life*, St Radegund had wanted her new foundation to be able to shelter the greatest possible number of souls consecrated to the 'Husband who does not die'.[124] (And at St Radegund's death the monastery of Holy Cross had approximately two hundred nuns.)[125]

New entrants might, at least temporarily, ease financial woes, for novices would often endow the monastery with their dowries. It was no doubt extremely difficult, if not impossible, in the early stages of a foundation to achieve the necessarily delicate balance between numbers and resources. Nevertheless, if the numbers of nuns exceeded the monastery's resources, very real material poverty would ensue. On the other hand, very small houses would find themselves in an equally precarious situation, for they would be unable to carry out all the spiritual and material functions required of a monastic community. Thus reform councils ordered that these small communities of nuns (*monasteriola*) be consolidated or even eliminated because of the paucity of their numbers.[126] The first chapter of the *Duplex legationis edictum*, for example, specified that small monasteries (*monasteriis minutis*), where nuns lived without a rule, were to be combined into one regular congregation at a place designated by the bishop.[127]

The notorious revolt of the nuns of Holy Cross in Poitiers, although tied to political motives, may nonetheless have been spurred as well by problems of the very real material poverty which these nuns were forced to endure. For, as we have noted, in simply one generation, their numbers had soared to two hundred nuns, not to mention the monks, clerics, and *familia* there. In addition to accusations against the bishop for his incompetent handling of this crisis, the leaders of the revolt complained that 'they could no longer endure the poor food, the lack of clothing and, indeed the harsh treatment'.[128] This may have reflected the imbalance which the house was experiencing, as the numbers of nuns exceeded the monastery's resources. A capitulary issued much later by Louis the Pious (822–24) specifically forbade the monastery of Holy Cross to maintain more than one hundred nuns.[129]

Tied to these problems of numbers and support was the monastic practice of sending out colonies of nuns to found daughter houses. Although this perhaps alleviated the immediate overcrowding of the motherhouse, in the long run it often proved a substantial drain on the monastery's finances and womanpower.[130]

Despite the fact that male houses faced similar economic crises during this period, they were not further hampered by restrictions of full enclosure. Abbots and monks continued to be actively involved in expanding and defending their material interests. There are many cases in our sources (especially in the hagiographic literature) of abbots and monks taking 'business trips' in order to acquire important relics for their foundations. These holy acquisitions were often so crucial to the economy of the community that the possession of a 'high powered' relic might actually determine the ultimate success and longevity of a monastery. While monks enjoyed a certain flexibility and direct involvement in the administration, aggrandizement and defense of their temporal holdings, nuns under the strictures of full enclosure were (according to written norms) made increasingly dependent on their bishop, *advocatus*, or the male personnel who administered their temporal affairs. Unfortunately, this arrangement often set the stage for abuse, for a conflict between administration and exploitation, for the victimization of the dependent house by its supposed protectors.

In the sixth century, Caesarius of Arles had recognized the possible conflict of interest with the bishop and had therefore provided for his nuns' financial independence and their exemption from episcopal jurisdiction.[131] A similar fear of the vulnerability of her enclosed nuns to the potential usurpations of their bishop was registered by St Radegund in her 'Letter of Foundation'. (One of St Radegund's reasons for adopting the *Regula* of Caesarius of Arles was, as we noted earlier, to compensate for their bishop's lack of support and blatant hostility.) From the beginning, Radegund attempted to make her monastery economically independent by deeding over all of the property given her by her former husband, King Lothar.[132] She noted that this endowment was to be carefully guarded so that her nuns would not live to say that she had left them destitute.[133] She also warned:

> If perchance after my death any person whatsoever, either the bishop of this city (listed first), or some representative of the king, or any other individual should attempt, in a spirit of malevolence, or by some legal subterfuge, to disturb the community, or to break the Rule....[134]

Later in this same letter she stated:

> ...or if any person, possibly even the bishop of the diocese, shall wish to claim, by some new-fangled privilege, jurisdiction of any sort over the nunnery, or over the property of the nunnery, beyond that which earlier bishops, or anyone else, have exercised during my lifetime ... may all such persons be shut off from your grace as robbers and despoilers of the poor.[135]

The canons of several church councils of the period hint at basic problems of negligent episcopal behavior and conflicts between bishops and monasteries.[136]

A number of interesting sources underscore the particular vulnerability of some female communities dependent on episcopal and secular protectors. One seventh-century case of abuse of episcopal authority concerns the great monastery of St John of Laon and its abbess, St Anstrudis. According to her *Vita*, the Bishop of Laon, Madelgarius, attempted to appropriate for himself the income of St John's, which Anstrudis' family had built. The abbess, in this case obviously unable to rely on her ecclesiastical superior's support, turned for assistance to the court and Pepin of Landen, who defended her claims against attempted episcopal usurpation and sent his son Grimoald to deal with the unjust prelate.[137]

The *Life* of St Opportuna (d. ca. 770) also demonstrates the precarious situation of women's communities. St Opportuna was abbess of the small monastery of Montreuil which practised regular observance, including enclosure. The community was under the protection of her brother, Bishop Godegrandus. During his absence on an extended pilgrimage to Rome and Palestine, however, his replacement abused this position of authority. He cruelly pillaged church properties and carried off their means of subsistence, not sparing St Opportuna and her house even though she was his bishop's sister.[138]

There is also substantial evidence of the victimization of female religious by their lay protectors, especially their *advocati*. The well-documented case of the Belgian monastery of Moorsel is of special interest. During the norman invasions the nuns of Moorsel fled with the body of their patron saint, Gudula. After the danger of further invasion had subsided, the community returned to Moorsel, and found their monastery completely devastated. They rebuilt on the same spot, only to find themselves in a particularly defenseless position in regard to their apparent lay protector/*advocatus*, the lord of Moorsel. He had appropriated to himself all of the property which had formerly belonged to the monastery. We learn from the *Vita* of St Gudula that by means of privations and injurious treatment he forced the *ancillae Christi* to flee the monastery, and prevented them from filling the vacancies that death had created among them.[139] The *Vita Berlindis* notes that the poverty at this monastery was so great that scarcely six nuns were able to find sufficient bread and water for their sustenance. In fact, because of this poverty, St Berlindis chose to leave the monastery before taking her vows.[140]

Although we are again limited by our source material, we can conjecture that the events at Moorsel were repeated, with some variation, in many of the nunneries of the day. Although many men's houses suffered destruction by invaders, usurpations and the secularization of their properties, the women's houses seem to have been even more vulnerable. This special 'female weakness' is explicitly noted in one charter. A charter of 1045 from the abbey of Ronceray specifically refers to the victimization of this monastery because of its weak, defenseless postion as a *female house*.[141]

The special defenselessness of female communities seems in some cases to have been further exacerbated by the policy of full enclosure. As Catherine Boyd has argued in relation to Cistercian houses of the thirteenth century, 'In the case of small nunneries it [enclosure] entailed serious hardship and inconvenience. Those modern writers who interpret every violation of enclosure as evidence of a moral lapse forget that economic necessity often forced the nuns to go outside their convents.'[142]

We find in the reform canons of this early period, therefore, strong evidence of a type of 'double bind' for nuns: economic necessity requiring active involvement with the world and strictures of unbroken enclosure. The Council of Ver/Verneuil (755), for example, provides telling evidence of this special conflict. One of its canons specified: 'If a monastery [of women] is too poor to keep their observance [for example, *the cloister*], the bishop must make known this situation to the king who will provide for them by charity.'[143] The Second Council of Reims (813) stipulated that 'the Emperor is to be implored mercifully to provide the subsidies whereby the nuns may obtain the sustenance (food, clothes) and [other] necessities from their superiors, and so that both their way of life and their chastity may be preserved—diligently looked after in keeping with the frailty of the sex'.[144] The Second Council of Aix-la-Chapelle (836) was especially outspoken on this problem of poverty and the violation of enclosure. According to *Cap.* 12, (36),

> in some places the monasteries seem to be brothels (*lupanaria*) rather than monasteries; and this because of neglect of revenues or, indeed the negligence of superiors. And so it is demanded that men with proved piety [monk-ecclesiastics] make an initial survey of the situation after which they are to strive to reform such things according to [the norms of] monastic observance.

Cap. 13, (37), warns that 'Abbesses are to provide the necessary food and clothing so that a lack of these may not provide the occasion for the nuns to fall into the devil's snare'.[145]

Small monasteries, or houses where the number of nuns surpassed their resources, must also have found themselves in an especially unenviable position in their attempts to adhere to the norms of enclosure and yet survive. For it seems that one of the basic problems inherent in the strictures of enclosure was that female religious were unable actively to solicit lands or money from potential donors for the essential support of their foundations. Since their very existence depended on endowments, along with the dowries of their nuns, revenues from their landed estates, offerings brought in by their collections of relics, and the general donations of the faithful, it was of prime importance to have sustained contributions from benefactors. In addition to the special restrictions of active enclosure, the enforced isolation of rigorous passive enclosure—for example restrictions against the reception and entertaining of potential donors, prohibitions against educating boys— seems further to have jeopardized the nuns' economic efforts by severely limiting their contacts and visibility. Full enclosure seems to have severely hampered their ability to obtain the 'necessary rewards' from the faithful. Without the continual flow of donations and other outside means of material aggrandizement, many of these early houses found it increasingly difficult, if not impossible, to continue to survive on their endowments alone.

At the same time that the carolingian and subsequent reformers were advocating unbroken enclosure for female religious, the institution of the double monastery was also coming under suspicion and beginning to disappear. The double community had provided a symbiotic relationship wherein nuns and monks aided one another in their spiritual and material lives. The division of labor of a double house is described in the *Vita* of St Gertrude of Nivelles (d.659). The abbess, as head of the community, gave the care of the monastery's external, temporal affairs over to its brothers; and concerns within the monastic enclosure were delegated to a group of her nuns.[146] Monks and nuns worked as equals in a co-ordinated effort. They formed an economic unit or cell, with shared community interests. The presence of an adjacent male community may also have provided an element of protection which lessened the special vulnerability (especially toward invaders and usurpers) an isolated, all-female community might experience. The double house seems to have been particularly well-suited to the rural milieux of England, the north of France, Belgium, and Germany.

The double monastery provided a good solution to the various problems inherent in the policy of strict enclosure: it allowed the nuns' community to *maintain its autonomy* while observing strict enclosure. And indeed, many of the successful enclosed female houses of this early period were double monasteries. However the physical arrangement of the double house, and its close association of male and female religious, came under attack by reformers; and eventually this special experiment in monastic life, which had been extremely favorable to women, disappeared.

CONCLUSIONS

Many factors were involved in the decline of women's monasticism from the mid-eighth to the end of the eleventh century. Because of the complexity of the problem and the paucity of sources, it is impossible to posit any simple cause and effect relationship. One important contributing factor, along with other restrictive reform policies and with the socio-economic components of the age, was definitely the policy of narrow enclosure. Social conditioning, the concerted repetition of restrictive ideological policies of rigorous enclosure, inculcated different monastic ideals and expectations for women than for men. It could affect all levels of their religious lives, including the very survival of their communities. The application of rigorous claustration seems to have had an especially devastating effect on the small, female proprietary houses which were popular during this early period. Enclosure, often linked to the very real poverty of a monastic community, may help explain the apparent decline of interest and the abatement in recruitment in female monasticism from the late eighth/ninth century through the late eleventh century. We no longer see, for example, the enthusiastic rush of royal and noble women to embrace monastic life.[147] Especially in France and England, few new houses were established for noblewomen.

One of the most basic aspects of monastic life affected by this restrictive enclosure legislation was the autonomy of nuns' communities. As the reformer Idung of Prüfening wrote in arguing the need for female enclosure: 'It is not expedient for that sex to enjoy the freedom of having its own governance—because of its natural fickleness and also because of outside temptations which womanly weakness is not strong enough to resist.'[148] Inherent in the ideology of enclosure was a basic assumption of the inability of the abbess and her community to order their lives. Control over the life of the community, privileges and responsibilities which the abbess and her nuns had previously assumed were removed to the authority of the bishop or abbot. By legislating increased dependence on bishops and *advocati*, and in severely restricting interaction with the outside world, strict enclosure encouraged nuns to become economically helpless. It trained them not to assume the often necessary responsibility for decision-making in their own monasteries. By its very definition, strict cloistering insured that many women's communities could no longer be autonomous, independent bodies, but rather parasites and burdens placing a heavy economic strain on the church hierarchy and the 'state'. This problem was already foreseen in the canons of the carolingian councils which made provisions specifically for the alleviation of the poverty of enclosed monasteries of women. (No similar provisions were made for male houses.) Under these strictures, female religious could no longer be viewed as indispensable assets or partners as they had previously been, as in the early double monasteries of anglo-saxon England or merovingian Gaul; rather they became dependents, perpetual minors, and constant liabilities. In some of the houses the indirect effects of observing enclosure seems to have confined them nearly out of existence.

With a loss of autonomy came a similar loss in public influence and general visibility for the abbess and her monastery. As Suzanne Wemple has argued:

> Abbesses of both types of monasteries, for Benedictines and canonesses, lost not only their freedom of movement but also their former influence. Although emperors and kings periodically summoned them, undoubtedly to discuss the disposition of monastic resources, abbesses, unlike abbots, did not participate in reforming assemblies.[149]

In general there appears to have been an erosion of the abbess' former public role; the emphasis now fell on her private role within the enclosure.

Another very important area affected by the policy of narrow claustration was female monastic education. The beginning of a growing disparity between the levels of male and female monastic education can be traced, at least in part, to the policies of strict enclosure. Again, as Suzanne Wemple has observed:

> Flexible monastic structures, such as those which existed in Merovingian times, were more congenial for female creativity than the rigid Carolingian nunneries. The strict cloistering of women religious and the separation of the sexes in the monastic schools of the ninth century were not conducive to the realization of the intellectual potential of women. Rather, they resulted in the exclusion of women religious from the mainstream of education and led to the perpetuation of the misogynistic myth that, compared to men, women had weaker minds.[150]

And finally, it is of interest to note briefly some of the subtle shifts in the ecclesiastical motivations or rationale for the need for and adoption of the policy of narrow enclosure for women. In its early use, for example as articulated by Caesarius of Arles, enclosure seems to have been viewed as essentially an external, physical defense. Its purpose was to protect the nuns and their chastity from barbarian invaders and local violence. Caesarius saw it simply as an integral part of a total monastic policy (along with economic self-sufficiency and exemption from episcopal jurisdiction) which would in turn insure the community's *autonomy* and *spiritual independence* under the authority of its abbesses. Enclosure was viewed as a means to an end—the establishment of a protective environment to encourage the religious life of the nuns.

With the carolingian and late eleventh-twelfth century reforms, however, the policy became a means to remedy abuses found in the female monasteries of the time. In part it aimed at eradicating, or at least severely limiting, the external activities of female religious, such as their 'wanderings', and at eliminating any type of close association of the sexes. At its root this restrictive policy seems to have been based on the clerical reformers' fear of female sexuality and their pervasive distrust of women. It seems to reflect the underlying misogynism which one finds especially during periods of reform. In large part, the basic rationale for narrow enclosure seems to have been the desire of *controlling* woman's sexuality through enforced isolation, not guarding her autonomy. In the reformers' minds, enclosure appears to have been viewed primarily as an internal safeguard which would protect the female religious from the fragility of her sex, and only secondarily to serve as a physical protection from the dangers of the outside world.

The reformers, with their stress on religious uniformity, wanted the policy of narrow claustration to be applied to all female religious. Nuns no longer had a choice between a strict, cloistered life and a more flexible cloister; whether they followed the benedictine Rule or canonical regulations, all female religious were placed under strict enclosure. With the reforms, claustration came to be viewed as the only legitimate way in which monastic women could lead exemplary lives. As Jean Leclercq, has noted, this legislation was always made by men who did not share the life style of enclosed women and did not consult them.[151] Without experiencing its strictures, these carolingian and late eleventh-twelfth century reformers made strict enclosure for female religious nearly an end in itself.[152]

In the final analysis, this sex-specific policy of severe, unbroken claustration was predicated on the reformers' apparently contradictory perception of women. As it developed during the carolingian reforms, the policy of cloister reflected an atmosphere of fear, suspicion, and distrust of women and their sexual weakness, and perhaps a low general esteem for women in religion. Yet at the same time, medieval churchmen attached the highest possible value to virginity, and to those 'fragile vessels' who had chosen to become brides of Christ needed special protection. Idung of Prüfening, in his argument on the need for enclosure for women, summarized these dichotomized views very well:

> When therefore we say . . . 'a consecrated woman', the full meaning will include both [concepts]: namely, the fragile sex and the intention of holy virginity. Virgil describes the one in this way: 'Fickle and forever changeable is a woman.' The apostle describes the other when he says: 'A virgin takes thought for the things of the Lord, that she may be holy in the body and in spirit.' When these two qualities coincide in one person, who can devise a suitable protection by which the fragile sex might persist in its undertaking—which is to be an angel?[153]

NOTES

* This is a revised and expanded version of a paper presented at the Sixteenth International Congress on Medieval Studies, Western Michigan University, Kalamazoo, May 9, 1981. I should like to express my thanks to the National Endowment for the Humanities for a 1981–82 Fellowship which has made this study possible. I am especially grateful to Father Chrysogonus Waddell for his careful and helpful criticism. I should also like to thank Dr Mary Woodward and Sister Thomas Shank for their encouragement and suggestions. I am also indebted to Father Roger de Ganck for his kind assistance in procuring a copy of G. Huyghe's study. However only I am responsible for the approach, methodology, and conclusions presented here.
This study is much indebted to an excellent historical review of the entire issue of enclosure by Emile Jombart and Marcel Viller, 'Clôture', *Dictionnaire de spiritualité, ascétique et mystique, doctrine et histoire* 2 (Paris, 1953) 979–1007, and the classic study by G. Huyghe, *La clôture des moniales des origines à la fin du XIIIme siècle* (Roubaix, 1944). See also F. Cabrol and H. Leclercq, 'Clôture monastique', *Dictionnaire d'archéologie chretienne et de liturgie* 3/2 (Paris, 1914) 2024–34; J. Creusen, 'Clôture', *Dictionnaire de droit canonique* 3 (Paris, 1938) 892–908; B. Dolhagaray, 'Clôture', *Dictionnaire de théologie catholique* 3/1 (Paris, 1923) 244–57; D. C. Lambot, 'Le prototype des monastères cloîtrés de femmes: L'abbaye S. Jean d'Arles', *Revue liturgique et monastique* 23 (1938) 169–74. See also the recent articles by R. Gazeau, 'La clôture des moniales au XIIᵉ siècle en France', *Revue Mabillon* 58 (1974) 289–308; Jean Leclercq, 'La clôture: points de repère historiques', *Collectanea Cisterciensia* 43/4 (1981) 366–76, and 'Le cloître est-il une prison?' *Revue d'ascétique et de mystique* 47 (1971) 407–20. The only extensive work on this topic in English is an excellent overview by Father James R. Cain, 'Cloister and the Apostolate of Religious Women' taken from his doctoral dissertation in canon law, *The Influence of the Cloister on the Apostolate of Congregations of Reigious Women* (Rome, 1965). See *Review for Religious* 27/2 (1968) 243–80; 27/4: 652–71; 27/5: 916–37; and 28/1 (1969) 101–21. I would like to thank the St Benedict Center, Madison, WI, for their kind use of this periodical. See also P. F. Anson, 'Papal Enclosure for Nuns', *Cistercian Studies* 3 (1968) 109–23; 189–206; and V. T. Schaaf, *The Cloister* (Cincinnati, 1921).

1. Charlton T. Lewis and Charles Short, *A Latin Dictionary* (Oxford, 1879, rpt., 1969) 351.

2. Jean Leclercq, 'La clôture: points de repère historiques', *Collectanea Cisterciensia* 43 (1981) 366.

3. W. B. Ryan, 'Cloister, Canonical Rules for', *New Catholic Encyclopedia* (Washington D.C., 1967) 3:957.

4. B. Dolhagaray, 'Clôture', *Dictionnaire de théologie catholique*, 3/1 (Paris, 1923) 246.

5. *St. Benedict's Rule for Monasteries*, trans. Leonard J. Doyle (Collegeville, 1948) 94. The rule also assumed a certain latitude for monks, however. Chapter 67, for example, deals specifically with 'Brethren Who Are Sent on a Journey'. It warns:

> And let no one presume to tell another whatever he may have seen or heard outside of the monastery, because this causes very great harm. But if anyone presumes to do so, let him undergo the punishment of the Rule. And let him be punished likewise who would presume to leave the enclosure of the monastery and go anywhere or do anything, however small, without an order from the Abbot. (p. 95).

6. Dolhagaray, pp. 245, 252.

7. See my forthcoming article, 'Narrow and Strait is the Way that Leadeth to Life: The Heroics of Virginity (ca. 500–1100)' (Publication pending).

8. St Jerome, Letter 22, trans. C. C. Mierow in *Ancient Christian Writers* 33: *The Letters of St. Jerome* (Westminster, 1963) 1: 158–59.

9. St Gregory the Great, Epistle 8, trans. P. Schaff and H. Wace in *A Select Library of Nicene and Post-Nicene Fathers of the Christian Church*, Second Series (New York, 1895) 12: 147.

10. See especially Sr Maria Caritas McCarthy, *The Rule for Nuns of St. Caesarius of Arles: A Translation with a Critical Introduction* (Washington D.C., 1960); R. Naz, 'Césaire d'Arles (règles de saint-)', *Dictionnaire de droit canonique* 3 (Paris, 1938) 260–78; and C. Lambot, 'Le prototype des monastères cloîtrés de femmes: L'abbaye St. Jean d'Arles', *Revue liturgique et monastique* 23 (1938) 169–74.

11. *Vitae Caesarii episcopi Arelatensis libri duo*, cap. 35; *MGH Scriptorum rerum merovingicarum* 3: 470.

12. McCarthy, p. 54. In the context of the letter, *exire in publicum* does not mean going out in public in the sense of leaving the monastery; rather, it refers simply to going out to the apartments of the convent where visitors were permitted.

13. *Ibid.*, 63. McCarthy also notes, 'The Rule for monks merely prohibits the monks from going out, and women from entering the monastery, and forbids the secret reception of mail' p. 63, no. 72.

14. E. Jombart and M. Viller, 'Clôture', *Dictionnaire de spiritualité, ascetique et mystique, doctrine et histoire* 2 (Paris, 1953) 988.

15. McCarthy, p. 171. See also p. 171, note 3, for a possible alternative translation.

16. *Ibid.*, p. 188. Also for an alternate translation see p. 188, note 22. Articles 59 and 73 further stress the need for rigorous enclosure. See pp. 189–90, 204.

17. *Ibid.*, p. 158. The first chapter of Aurelian's *Regula ad virgines* stresses the permanency of the rule and the need for stability, and warns that it is not permitted for the nun, up until her death, to go out from the monastery (PL 68:399). Chapter XII stipulates that if a nun is permitted to leave her monastery, she must be accompanied by the abbess, the provost, or an aged nun. The Rule also warns that the abbess must not remain outside of her monastery (PL 68:401). The Rule for Nuns by St Donatus of Besançon, based on the rules of Caesarius, Benedict, and Columban, stresses that the abbess is able to leave her monastery only if she is ill, or if compelled by some occupation (PL 87:291–92). Hope Mayo has noted that the rule also implies (through its omission of several chapters of the benedictine Rule which referred to activities of the religious outside of the monastery) that Donatus' nuns were subject to a stricter cloister than were benedictine monks. Hope Mayo, 'The Rule for Nuns of Donatus of Besançon', paper presented at the International Symposium, Benedict and Scholastica: Then and Now, St. Benedict Center, Madison, WI, 10 October 1980.

18. McCarthy, p. 161.

19. *S. Mariae Suessionensis privilegium*; J. Mabillon, *Annales Ordinis S. Benedicti* (Lucca, 1739) 1:444. See also G. Huyghe, *La clôture des moniales des orgines à la fin du XIIIᵐᵉ siècle* (Roubaix, 1944) 31.

20. McCarthy, p. 161.

21. *Ibid.*, 159–61. In St Radegund's 'Letter of Foundation' she states, 'I accepted the Rule in accordance with which St Caesaria had lived, and which in his loving care St. Caesarius had drawn up from the writings of the holy fathers to suit her very needs.' Gregory of Tours, *History of the Franks* 9.41, trans. Lewis Thorpe (Harmondsworth, 1974) 535. See also René Aigrain, *Sainte Radegonde* (Paris, 1918) 109–34.

22. Gregory of Tours, 9.40; 550–31. Aigrain, pp. 110–13, 119.

23. Gregory of Tours, 9,39; 528–29. In her letter Radegund also foresaw among the potential problems of the monastery after her death the breaking of enclosure: 'If perchance . . . any nun shall wish to break the Rule and go out into the world . . .' Gregory of Tours 9.42;536.

24. Huyghe, 29.

25. McCarthy, 154.

26. Huyghe (p. 23) notes this influence in the merovingian council of Orleans (549) which gave to the private law of Caesarius a universal validity for all of the frankish church.

27. One of the earliest examples of female enclosure in the West is noted in the

Fifth Council of Orleans (549). Its Canon 19 distinguishes between a one year probation required of girls entering strictly enclosed communities and the three year probation required of candidates for less strictly enclosed communities. Charles Joseph Hefele and Dom H. Leclercq, *Histoire des conciles* 3/1 (Paris, 1909) 163. In the East one finds several early examples of strict enclosure legislation directed specifically toward female religious. See J. Leclercq, 'La clôture', 367–68.

28. Hefele-Leclercq 3/2 (1910) 936.

29. Carlo de Clercq, *La Législation religieuse franque de Clovis à Charlemagne (507–814)* (Louvain/Paris, 1936) 159.

30. Cap. 19; *MGH Capitularia regum francorum* 1:63.

31. Hefele-Leclercq 3/2: 1095.

32. Cap 12; *MGH Concilia aevi karolini* 1: 193–94.

33. Cap. 46; PL 105: 206.

34. Hefele-Leclercq 3/2: 1106.

35. Carlo de Clercq, 197–98.

36. Cap. 30; *MGH Concilia aevi karolini* 1: 290.

37. Cap 13; Hefele-Leclercq 3/2: 1140. *MGH Concilia aevi karolini* 1:264.

38. Clercq, 242. *MGH Concilia aevi karolini* 1:284.

39. *MGH Concilia aevi karolini* 1:285.

40. *Institutione sanctimonialium*, no. 18; *MGH Concilia aevi karolini* 1:449.

41. *Ibid.*, no. 8; 444.

42. Council of Aix-la-Chapelle (816) Cap. 115; *MGH Concilia aevi karolini* 1:397. See also Suzanne F. Wemple, *Women in Frankish Society: Marriage and the Cloister 500–900* (Philadelphia: University of Pennsylvania, 1981) 168.

43. Hefele-Leclercq 4/1 (1911) 14–15.

44. *Ibid.*, 15. Canon 11 argues that the monasteries of women should be surrounded by solid walls of the sort that no one is able to enter or leave except by the door. Within the heavily walled enclosure they were to establish refectories, *cellaria*, dorters, and the other necessary buildings.

45. Cap. 16; *MGH Capitularia regum francorum* 2: 180.

46. Huyghe, 52, 58.

47. Can. 14; Hefele-Leclercq 3/2: 1029; Council of Frankfurt, (794) Can. 19; *Ibid.*, 1058.

48. Council of Reims (813), can. 18, 26; *Ibid.*, 1137.

49. Council of Riesbach (799/803) can. 24; *Ibid.*, 1106.

50. Council of Aix-la-Chapelle (817), can. 15; *Ibid.*, 4/1: 26.

51. *Ibid.* can. 16.

52. *Ibid.* can. 16.

53. Council of Riesbach (799/803) can. 25; *Ibid.*, 3/2:1106.

54. Council of Pavia (850) can. 21; *Ibid.*, 4/1:188.

55. Council of Ver/Verneuil can. 10; *Ibid.*, 3/2:937.

56. Council of Aix-la-Chapelle (789) can. 22; *Ibid.*, 1029. Council of Frankfurt (794) can. 11; *Ibid.*, 1057. Council of Reims (813) can. 25, 29, 30; *Ibid.*, 1137. Council of Mayence (813) can. 10, 12, 14; *Ibid.*, 1140. Council of Mayence (829) can. 28; *Ibid.*, 4/1:65.

57. Council of Aix-la-Chapelle (789) can. 72; *Ibid.*, 3/2:1033.

58. *Ibid.* can. 72; Council of Reims (813) can. 29; *Ibid.*, p. 1137.

59. Council of Mayence (813) can. 12; *Ibid.*, p. 1140; Other councils forbidding the involvement of monks with secular courts and judges include: the Council of Frankfurt (794) can. 11; *Ibid.*, p. 1057; Council of Riesbach (799/803) can. 25; *Ibid.*, p. 1106.

60. Clercq, p. 302.

61. Dorothy Whitelock, ed., *English Historical Documents, c. 500–1042*, 1 (New York, 1955) 719.

62. *Ibid.* '. . . each of them was regulated by that rule of conduct, that neither of them was entered by the opposite sex. For a woman was never permitted to enter

the congregation of men, or any man the house of the nuns, except priests only, who used to enter the churches solely to perform the office of Mass, and when the service was solemnly concluded, immediately to return to their own dwelling'.

63. *Ibid.*

64. Cap. 27. Cited by Jombart-Viller, 989–90. See PL 30; 414–15.

65. Cap. 27; PL 30: 414–15. I would like to thank Sara Richards for her translation of this section of the *Regula*.

66. Cap. 27; *Ibid.*, 415.

67. *Vita S. Hugonis Abbatis Cluniacensis*, in M. Marrier and A. Quercetanus, *Bibliotheca Cluniacensis* (Brussels and Paris, 1815) 455. See also Jean Leclercq, 'Le cloître est-il une prison?' *Revue d'ascétique et de mystique* 47 (1971) 407–20.

68. *Vita S. Hugonis*, p. 455.

69. *Notae ad vitam sancti Hugonis*; Marrier-Quercetanus, p. 87.

70. s. Peter the Venerable, *De Miraculis, Liber primus*, Marrier-Quercetanus 22: 1281.

71. *Ibid.*

72. Joan Evans, *Monastic Life at Cluny, 910–1157* (London, 1931) 29. Citing Peter the Venerable, *De Miraculis* 1. 22.

73. Ep. 127; PL 159: 163–64.

74. Ivo of Chartres, Letter 10; PL 162: 22, cited by Jombart-Viller, pp. 991–92.

75. See J. Leahey's introduction, annotation and, with G. Perigo, translation of 'An Argument Concerning Four Questions by Idung of Prüfening' in *Cistercians and Cluniacs: The Case for Citeaux*, Cistercian Father Series 33 (Kalamazoo, 1977) 143–92.

76. CF33:167–76.

77. *Ibid.*, 168.

78. *Ibid.*

79. *Ibid.*, 168–69, 172.

80. *Ibid.*, 173. He goes on to cite further admonitions from St Jerome's letter to Eustochium on the shame surrounding the loss of virginity. He also uses the Old Testament examples of Uzzah and the ark and Hezekiah's showing the treasury of God to the Assyrians to prove 'that the spouse of Christ, God's most precious treasure, ought to be guarded and enclosed as if under seal, lest the Assyrians, that is the lewd eye, be able to gawk at her'. CF 33:175.

81. *Ibid.*, 175–76.

82. *Ibid.*, 176.

83. *Ibid.*

84. *Vitae Caesarii Episcopi Arelatensis libri duo*; *MGH Scriptorum rerum merovingicarum*, 3:494.

85. Fortunatus, *Appendix Carminum*, I; *MGH Auctorum antiquissimorum* 4/1: 273.

86. *Gregorii episcopi turonensis liber in gloria confessorum* c. 104; *MGH Scriptorum rerum merovingicarum*, 1:815–16. See also Aigrain, 169.

87. *De vita sanctae Radegundis, liber II*, 2.24; *MGH Scriptorum rerum merovingicarum*: 393. Aigrain, 170.

88. Mabillon, *Annales ordinis S. Benedicti*, III, 50. See also Huyghe, p. 49.

89. Peter the Venerable, *De Miraculis*, 1. 22, cited by Evans, pp. 29–30. Three separate episodes of sacrificial self-disfigurement as a defense against rape by barbarian invaders might also be attributed, at least in part, to the ideology of unbroken claustration for nuns. See my forthcoming article, 'Narrow and Strait is the Way'.

90. *Vita Rusticulae sive Marciae Abbatissae Arelatensis* 10; *MGH Scriptorum rerum merovingicarum*, 4:344–45.

91. Bénédictins de Paris, *Vies des saints et des bienheureux selon l'ordre du calendrier avec l'historique des fêtes* (Paris, 1946) 4 (Avril):227–28.

92. *Vita Froberti* 6; *Acta Sanctorum*, January 1:510.

93. Hefele-Leclerq 3/1:539.

94. *Ibid.*, 587–88. The Council of Beccanceld was presided over by the king and included two bishops from Kent, five abbesses, priests and many nobles.

95. *Life of St. Wilfrid* 60; Whitelock, *English Historical Documents* p. 695. During the synod 'the bishops separated from the rest and began to take counsel together; sometimes the archbishop consulted with them and sometimes the prudent virgin Aelfflaed'. (p. 697), cap. LX.

96. *De miraculus sanctae Waldburgis; MGH Scriptorum*, 15/11 540.

97. *Vita Leobae Abbatissae Biscofesheimensis; MGH Scriptorum*, 15/1:129–30.

98. *Ibid.*

99. Ep 6 [14]; *The Letters of Saint Boniface*, trans. E. Emerton, *Columbia University Records of Civilization*, (New York, 1940, 1976) 39.

100. *Ibid.*

101. Ep.27 (ix); *The English Correspondence of St. Boniface*, trans. and ed. E. Kylie (London, 1911) 68.

102. *Ibid.* 68–69.

103. *Ibid.* 69.

104. Ep. 62 [78]; Emerton, p. 140.

105. *Chronicon Hugonis, lib. II*; PL 154:239.

106. It is necessary to emphasize the difference between a temporary breach of enclosure, which we are discussing here, and religious apostasy, i.e. permant renunciation of monastic life.

107. Gregory of Tours, *History of the Franks*, 9.41; 533.

108. *Ibid.* 9.41; 534.

109. *Ibid.* 9.40; 532.

110. *Vitae Columbani abbatis discipulorumque eius, liber II; MGH, Scriptorum rerum merovingicarum* 4:138–39.

111. Ep. 128; *MGH Epistolae merowingici et karolini aevi* 1:415–16.

112. Huyghe, p. 39.

113. Cited by Leclercq, 'La clôture', 367.

114. Huyghe, 3, 32, 51.

115. Philibert Schmitz, 'Bénédictin (ordre), Bénédictines', *Dictionnaire d'histoire et de géographie ecclésiatique* 7(Paris, 1934) 1220. See also Ph. Schmitz, *Histoire de l'Ordre de Saint Benoît: Les Moniales*, 7 (Maredsous, 1956) 232–41.

116. Cited by J.R. Cain, 'Cloister and the Apostolate of Religious Women;, *Review for Religious*, 27, no. 2 (1968), 267.

117. Roger Gazeau, 'La clôture des moniales au XIIe siècle en France', *Revue Mabillon* 58 (1974) 289–308.

118. Leclercq, 'La clôture', 367. He also notes (p. 368): "C'est seulement au cours de VIIIe siècle que la législation se precise et se généralise, en Occident, et selon un processus semblable à celui de l'Orient: même lenteur dans l'évolution, même époque d'aboutissement, même tendance vers une plus grande rigueur, surtout pour les moniales, même intention dominante d'éviter le vagabondage monastique.' See also page 369 for his comments on the importance of the carolingian reform.

119. P.F. Anson, 'Papal Enclosure for Nuns', *Cistercian Studies* 3 (1968) 110, 115.

120. Rough statistical information for a comparative study on monastic foundations has been gathered from L.-H. Cottineau, *Répertoire topo-bibliographique des abbayes et prieurés*, 2 vols. (Mâcon, 1935–37), and from David Knowles and R. Neville Hadcock, *Medieval Religious Houses: England and Wales* (London, 1971). I have studied this in a paper, 'Women and Monasticism: Crises of Invasion and Reform', presented at the Fourteenth International Congress on Medieval Studies, Western Michigan University, Kalamazoo, May 4, 1979.

121. See my article, 'Sexism and the Celestial Gynaecum—from 500 to 1200', *Journal of Medieval History* 4 (1978) 117–33.

122. On the importance of carolingian marriage reforms for women, see Jo Ann McNamara and Suzanne Wemple, 'Marriage and Divorce in the Frankish Kingdom', in S. Stuart, ed. *Women in Medieval Society* (Philadelphia, 1976) 102–13. See also S. Wemple, *Women in Frankish Society*, especially pp. 75–96.

123. Statutes of the Synods of St. Boniface (ca. 745) no. 15; Hefele-Leclercq 3/2:

930: 'In monasteries of canons, monks and nuns, one will not admit more than the resources permit'. Council of Cloveshoe (747), 28; Hefele-Leclercq 3/2:910 'No one must accept a congregation [of clerks or monks] larger than its means permit. . . . It is the same for nuns'. Council of Arles (813), number 8; Hefele-Leclercq 3/2:1135 'One must not receive too great a number of persons in a monastery or in a house of clerks'. Council of Reims (813), number 27; Hefele-Leclercq 3/2: 1137: 'In a town and in a monastery, there must not be more clerks or monks than can be maintained'. Council of Mainz (813), number 19; Hefele—Leclercq 3/2:1140 'In monasteries of canons, monks and nuns, one must not receive more people than the monastery is able to nourish'. Capitulary of the Councils (813), number 6; Hefele-Leclercq, 3/2:1146: 'A monastery must not recieve more people than it is able to nourish'. Council of Aix-la-Chapelle (817), number 8; Hefele-Leclercq 4/1:15: 'They must not receive too large a number of nuns nor of persons who have lived in too great luxury'.

124. Baudonivia, *De vita sanctae Radegundis liber II; MGH Scriptorum rerum merovingicarum* II, 2/5: c.5, 381.

125. *Gregorii episcopi turonensis liber in gloria confessorum; MGH Scriptorum rerum merovingicarum,* I, c.104, 814.

126. A summary of canon 4 from a council of Reims in 881 states: 'The royal *missi* must, in accord with the diocesan bishops, visit the monasteries of canons, monks and of nuns, to abolish the abuse, . . . and to prepare and deliver to the king an inventory of possessions, to give the number of canons and nuns of each monastery, finally, following the circumstances, the king is able, with the help of the bishops, to augment or reduce this number;, Hefele-Leclercq 4/2:685.

127. *MGH Capitularia regum francorum,* number 19, 1:63.

128. Gregory of Tours, *History of the Franks,* X. 15:571.

129. *Capitulare de monasterio S. Crucis Pictavensi* (822–24), number 6: '*Ut omnino caveatur ne ultra centenarium numerum congregatio illa per cuiuscunque petitionem multiplicetur*', No. 7 '*Ut omnino provideatur ne clericorum numerus plus quam III augeatur*'; *MGH Capitularia regum francorum* 1:302.

130. André Duval, OP 'The Economic Organisation of Convents', trans. Lancelot C. Sheppard, *Poverty: Religious Life* IV (London, 1954) 89.

131. McCarthy, pp. 11, 15, 66–67, 70.

132. Gregory of Tours, *History of the Franks* 9.42; 535.

133. *Ibid.*; 538.

134. *Ibid.*; 536.

135. *Ibid.*

136. This is a summary of legislation found in Hefele-Leclercq, 3/1:170, 4/1:94, 4/2:784.

137. *Vita Anstrudis: MGH Scriptorum rerum merovingicarum* 6: c.16 73.

138. *Acta Sanctorum* April 3:65.

139. *Vita* 38; AA SS January, 1:523.

140. AA SS February, 1:384. See also R. Podevyn, 'Étude critique sur la Vita Gudulae', *Revue Belge de philologie et d'historie* 2 (1923) 634.

141. J. Verdon, 'Les moniales dans la France de l'ouest aux XIᵉ et XIIᵉ siècles: Étude d'histoire sociale', *Cahiers de civilisation médiévale* 19 (1976) 263. Charter six (1045) of the *Cartulaire du Ronceray* notes '*Sed quia ibi sanctimonialium congregatio degit, perpendens illius sexus invalitudinem ad res sue possessionis ab invasoribus defendendas . . .*'.

142. Catherine Boyd, *A Cistercian Nunnery in Medieval Italy* (Cambridge, Massachusetts, 1943) 109.

143. Ver. canon; Hefele-Leclercq 3/2:936.

144. Canon 33; *MGH Concilia aevi karolini* 1:256.

145. *MGH Concilia aevi karolini* 1, pars II (36) cap XII, (37) cap. XIII. 713. In light of the common problems nuns had with poverty and the maintenance of enclosure, it is interesting to read the invective of the reformer Ivo of Chartres. In writing to Gautier, Bishop of Meaux, he describes the nuns of Faremoutiers as 'female demoniacs' (*muli-*

erum daemonialium) who are 'prostituting their bodies for lewd use by every sort of male'. His observation was based on oral reports from the monks of Tours and a written complaint from Countess Adelaide. Ivo then urged the bishop to apply himself to the reform of the house. If reform proved impossible, he recommended replacing the nuns with reformed monks. *St. Fare et Faremoutiers: Treize siècles de vie monastique* (Abbaye de Faremoutiers, 1956) 40.

146. *Vita Sanctae Geretrudis* 3; *MGH Scriptorum rerum merovingicarum* 2:457. On double monasteries see Wemple, *Women in Frankish Society*, 159–62, 170.

147. Wemple, p. 171.

148. Idung, p. 186 (see above, note 82).

149. Wemple, p. 169.

150. *Ibid.*, p. 188. She also notes that 'the strict cloistering of women religious, which began under Charlemagne and continued under Louis the Pious, limited the opportunities for nuns to keep abreast of the new learning. Nuns, unlike monks, were not trained in the new schools. Abbesses were not allowed to go to the leading centers of learning to master the new skills. The restriction that convents could educate only girls undoubtedly served to justify the exclusion of nuns from the mainstream of education and intellectual life' (187–88).

151. Leclercq, 374.

152. Cain, *Review for Religious* 28/1 (1969) 109. Cain discusses this problem in relation to modern claustration for nuns and the danger of treating enclosure, which should be a means to an end, as an end in itself.

153. Idung, 169.

Benedictine Life for Women in Central France, 850–1100: A Feminist Revival

Mary Skinner

MONASTIC LIFE FOR WOMEN experienced a crisis in the late carolingian period. Many houses disappeared and others were given over to men. In the tenth and eleventh centuries, however, aided by bishops, husbands, and fathers, women sparked a revival of benedictine life in central France which led to dozens of new women's foundations. Women of means founded and endowed new houses for women; women —single, married, and widowed—entered them in large numbers. Abbesses extended their influence over dependent priories and the lands and people that surrounded them. What was the attraction of monastic, and particularly benedictine, life for so many women of this age?

Women aspiring to religious life in the tenth century had many examples of courageous christian women before them. One of their heroines may have been the sixth-century queen and nun, St Radegund, who prevailed upon a terrified bishop of Soissons to release her from her marriage vows to King Chlotar and to accept her dedication to monastic life. Freed from her bond to a man who had forced her into marriage when she was his prisoner and then killed her brother, Radegund founded Holy Cross Abbey of Poitiers and set an example to her nuns of austerity and humility, adopting for them the strict Rule of St Caesarius of Arles. Her praises were sung by her chaplain and confidant, Fortunatus, by Gregory of Tours, and by a nun of Holy Cross, Baudonivia.[1]

Early frankish women had had many possibilities for pursuing a religious life: as widows in their own homes; as recluses; as nuns in the many small monasteries clustered mostly in the towns; and as religious in houses of

87

monks and nuns usually governed by an abbess with quasi-sacerdotal authority.[2]

St Columban and St Boniface had collaborated with women in establishing monastic life. Boniface in the eighth century had encouraged the adoption of the benedictine Rule although a variety of rules persisted into the eleventh.[3] Benedict of Aniane, the carolingian reformer, became an adamant champion of the benedictine Rule. His relationships with religious women seem to have been cordial. In the early days of hardship at Aniane, women of the neighborhood saved him and the brothers from starvation with gifts of milk, and Benedict undertook to support widows and nuns living in his neighborhood.[4]

Given imperial authority, Benedict made an effort to consolidate small women's religious houses and to enforce greater enclosure, without much success. Double houses became fewer in the carolingian period as their monks were replaced by canons and, less often, the nuns by canonesses. Nuns were forbidden to teach boys and limited in their liturgical assistance at the altar. Many houses of women disappeared entirely; others were given over to men.[5] The carolingian period proved not altogether favorable to women's monastic life.[6]

There seems to have been increasing pressure for aristocratic women to marry rather than enter religious life. Fewer women were leading an eremetical life.[7] The vocation of priest's or canon's wife was becoming less esteemed by the people of the tenth century than it had been by earlier generations.[8] After 910, when women began to endow cluniac houses, they found themselves lacking in similar institutions for themselves. The last women's monastery disappeared at Tours in the mid-tenth century; after 1000, Herveus, treasurer of St Martin of Tours, had to found a new monastery to accommodate a group of women he discovered living an informal religious life at the basilica of St Martin. Many other women's houses disappeared around the time of the viking invasions.[9] Yet monastic life for women did not completely languish because religious women, like those at Tours, attempted to keep it alive and enlisted prominent clerics in their cause to reestablish old and found new religious houses. Some female foundations were given to canons (as well as to monks) in the late ninth century when men's monasteries as important as Marmoutier were also occupied by secular canons.[10] Yet women active in founding men's religious houses of the Touraine and elsewhere, were to take an even more prominent role in the establishment of benedictine houses for women.

Drawing on the excellent articles of Professor Jean Verdon,[11] my study extends from Tours, south to Bourges, Saintes and Poitiers and north to Rennes, Angers and Le Mans—analyzing charters and other sources pertaining to women's monasteries established before 1100. The monasteries considered in this article lay west of Troyes, Dijon and Macon, south of an east-west line drawn through Chartres and north of another extending from Saintes to Lyons. (See accompanying map.)[12]

At least eighteen frankish houses survived in Central France into the twelfth century but documentation on most is sparse. Three had originally been houses of men. Six women's monasteries had perished entirely by the late carolingian period and ten were given to monks or canons. Three new monasteries for women were founded in the tenth century in central France, but the revival accelerated greatly in the eleventh century with the foundation of no less than thirty-five new houses. Documentation for several of the eleventh-century foundations is abundant, thanks to the survival of cartularies from Notre Dame Ronceray, in Angers, Notre Dame Saintes, St. George Rennes, Marcigny and Molesme.[13]

Despite the carolingian reforms of Benedict of Aniane it is not certain that late tenth and early eleventh-century foundations were benedictine, but the advantages of this rule soon became apparent. All of the new monasteries surveyed here after 1020 seem to have followed the benedictine Rule.

Why did this Rule become so popular? The abbot or abbess was elected by the community, and in monasteries with privileges like those of Cluny, the founding family and the bishop were limited in the powers they might exert over the religious. The secret of the Rule was the independence it promised the religious from the clerical and lay powers that surrounded them.[14] Initial superiors were sometimes appointed by the founders, but the benedictine Rule assured independence by insisting on the free election of the abbess by the congregation, sometimes, but not always, supervised by the local bishop.[15]

Women instigated many of the new foundations, prevailing on their relatives to found new monasteries so they and their friends might enter. The entrance of a whole family into a monastery was not uncommon especially in double houses where men and women might join together. Most, but not all, the nuns were drawn from the aristocracy and quite a number were widows and married women. They brought modest, but significant gifts which their relatives sometimes sought to reclaim.

Abbesses, elected for life, served lengthy terms which contributed to the stability of their monasteries.[16] The image of the powerful abbess popularized by women scholars strongly reflects the eleventh-century charters.[17] Despite carolingian legislation (and perhaps with the exception of Marcigny) men frequently met in the chapter room of the nuns, and sisters travelled abroad when business required.[18] Canons were often associated with nunneries to provide the sacraments and assist in administration.[19] However, the abbess and her officers were fully in charge.[20] Interaction with the local aristocracy was continuous, but the newer, stronger benedictine foundations seem to have survived and prospered.

EARLY WOMEN'S MONASTERIES DESTROYED OR GIVEN TO MEN

Of thirty-eight early women's religious houses, six perished entirely before the eleventh-century.[21]

Three nuns' foundations were granted to canons although one of them was later returned to nuns. All were coincidently called St Pierre-le-Puellier; St Peter's-for-girls, as we might say, for early, urban women's houses, were often built close to cathedrals and thus particularly susceptible to occupation by canons. At Poitiers the house of this name reverted to canons in the early tenth century, but was restored to nuns in 982.[22] The nuns at Bourges[23] and Orléans[24] did not fare as well; destroyed in the ninth century, they were restored for canons in the tenth.

Seven women's monasteries were refounded for monks, and two more for male religious, who may have been monks or canons. Vézélay, the most famous, was built in 867 for benedictine nuns in honor of St Mary Magdalene by the count and countess of Vienne. In a decade the nuns had been replaced by monks and the house greatly enriched by the relics of the Magdalene.[25]

Why were so many women's religious houses turned over to men? Some scholars have assumed decadence or disorder among the nuns.[26] While such accusations occasionally appear in the documents, we may doubt their trustworthiness if we suspect the house in question was needed by men. There was a strong desire in the tenth century to restore early christian monasteries that had disappeared. Yet resources were scarce and potential nuns even scarcer; daughters of the aristocracy were wanted for marriage alliances, for, despite endemic warfare, men may have outnumbered women in the early middle ages.[27] Thus, when aristocrats founded new monasteries, usually on the sites of ancient ones, they intended them to be men's houses even if the original monastery had been for women. Only when the cluniac reform was well under way in central France, did women establish their own reformed monasteries.[28] For the twenty ancient houses that had survived the carolingian period were no longer sufficient for the number of women desiring a religious life in the eleventh century.

EARLY WOMEN'S MONASTERIES THAT SURVIVED

Although nineteen women's houses in central France failed before 1100, another eighteen early foundations survived. Three of those which continued had originally belonged to men. Six were merovingian foundations and nine were founded or completely reformed in the carolingian era. The longest-lived of all is Holy Cross of Poitiers, the foundation of St Radegund, still flourishing today in its new location south of the city.[29] Poitiers was the center of a small monastic revival for women in the tenth century.

Two early men's communities were given to women and four merovingian women's communities survived into the eleventh century.[30] Nine more monasteries for women were added or reformed in the carolingian period.[31]

Thus of two women's houses founded, only one survived. The monastic life for women not only suffered more severely, but recovered much more slowly than did that for men. Why?[32]

Professor Jean Verdon lays most of the blame on the laity.[33] The Council of Trosly in 909 had leveled the following accusations at both clergy and religious, including women's monasteries. The king and the powerful were admonished to respect the vocation of nuns. Many monasteries had been seized by them from their proper superiors. Abbots and abbesses should be elected regularly and cloister restored. Feasts and fine clothes should be suppressed, and widows and virgins consecrated to God forbidden to marry. Chastity must be better observed.[34] The Cluniac reform sought to address these problems for men, and houses for women adopted the reforms as well.

NEW FOUNDATIONS FOR WOMEN IN THE TENTH AND ELEVENTH CENTURIES

By the time of the tenth-century revival which emanated from it, Holy Cross, Poitiers, had become benedictine. It made three new foundations near Poitiers, all the work of women. In the 960s Adele of Normandy, widow of Count William, founded Trinity. Duke Hugh Capet's wife Adelaide gave to Trinity, St Pierre-le-Puellier, Poitiers, which had reverted to canons.[35] North of the city, Bonneval-les-Thouars was founded in 966 by Audearde, viscountess of Thouars.[36] St Menoux of Bourges, which had been a men's house in the seventh century, was refounded for women in the tenth.[37]

In the eleventh century, thirty-five new female foundations, mostly benedictine, followed in the wake of the many new monasteries for men inspired by the cluniac movement.[38] The century began with the foundation of Beaumont-les-Tours in 1002. Women who were already living a religious life near the basilica of St Martin requested their own monastery from the saintly treasurer, Herveus, who had rebuilt St Martin's and founded several male monasteries. But with Beaumont, he said, he restored monastic life for women, which had entirely disappeared from the Touraine.[39] Beaumont absorbed the lands of an ancient convent at Tours, Notre Dame l'Ecrignolles.[40]

Ganelon, another treasurer of St Martin, in 1045 refounded for women St Avit at Chateaudun, which had been a men's community until destroyed by the Vikings.[41] Petronilla and Haldride, daughters of Hugh de Gennes, left St Avit to found a new monastery at Pont-de-Gennes in 1092, perhaps to find a stricter life.[42] In the late eleventh century, Notre Dame de Lièze was also founded from Beaumont.[43]

Beaumont followed a rule for nuns which may not have been the benedictine rule.[44] The foundation of St Julien, by Archbishop Teotolo and Abbot Odo of Cluny, had brought benedictine reform to Tours as early as 942, however, and whether or not the nuns of Beaumont initially followed it, neighboring foundations were soon adopting the Rule of St Benedict.[45]

The diocese of Dol in Brittany was under the jurisdiction, albeit disputed, of the archbishop of Tours. The revival of women's monasticism may have spread there from Beaumont. Locmaria was founded at Dol in 1020 by a count-bishop named Benedict, his son Alan Cainart, who followed him as count of Cornaille, and Alan's wife, Judith. Their daughter, Hodierne, became the first abbess of Locmaria. The family was intermarried with those of the count of Nantes and the duke of Brittany, but they had another daughter, so Hodierne was freed for the religious life. She may even have inspired the foundation. There is no mention of Locmaria following the benedictine Rule, and Hodierne seems to have been appointed abbess by her parents and grandfather. Judith, her mother, continued to be a prime supporter of the new foundation, and it would not be exaggerating to suggest that Locmaria was primarily the project of this aristocratic mother and daughter.[46]

The most prolific of all women's monasteries in this period was Notre Dame, Ronceray, founded at Angers by Hildegarde, countess of Anjou, in 1028.[47] As patrons of St Martin's Abbey, the count and countess of Anjou were closely in touch with reformers at Tours, and Ronceray was to follow the benedictine Rule.

Ronceray was particularly the work of Hildegarde, for fully half the foundation charter is an enumeration of her personal donations of lands, mills, and vineyards. There was a special endowment for four priests who were to serve the sisters, and many serfs were given to the nuns, including one who was to do the cooking. Before undertaking a last pilgrimage to Jerusalem, Hildegarde led thirteen of her serfs to the altar of Ronceray, placing them under the nuns' protection.[48]

The initial twenty-six nuns, following the Rule of St Benedict, elected one of their number, Leoburga, abbess in 1028, but under the watchful eyes of the count, countess, and many noble men and women. No bishop seems to have supervised this election.[49] A later election in 1073 was presided over by Bishop Eusebius of Angers and confirmed by Count Fulk Rechin. In both cases the choice of the abbess seems to have been made by the nuns.[50]

The abbess of Ronceray personally supervised her extensive lands and numerous priories. For example, once she marched to the cemetery of the monks of St Nicholas to demand the disinterment of a body that should have been buried in the nuns' cemetery. She was convinced to relent, however, when advised that the body had already decomposed considerably. This was a rare instance when abbess of Ronceray gave in easily in defending her monastery's rights.[51]

From Ronceray were founded eleven priories in the later eleventh century. Two of these were endowed by women. Cohémon was given to Ronceray by Aremburgis, widow of Thevin Strobon, viscount of Thouars. She and her daughter entered as nuns.[52] They may have been advocates of reform, just as an early viscountess of Thouars had founded Bonneval-les-Thouars less than a century before.[53] The priory of St Cyr and St Julitte was given to Ronceray by Count Matthias around 1040.[54] Vernoil-le-Fourier was the gift of Geoffrey Fulrade and his wife Ameline after 1060.[55] These aristocrats seem to have founded their own monasteries, but looked to Ronceray to supervise them.

Other priories of Ronceray were St Aubin de Brigné, Plessis-aux-Nonnains, St Lambert de Lattay, St Christophe de Mareil, St Aubin de Seiches, and Notre-Dame de Prigny, which also boasted a woman founder.[56]

The priory of Avenières was given to Ronceray in 1070 by Hamon, lord of Laval, and another aristocrat. Hamon then founded the priory of St Pierre-le-Potier which he gave to Avenières.[57] The first nuns of these priories, founded and donated to Ronceray by aristocrats, may have come from the mother house, but more likely they were recruited locally among the friends and relatives of the founders. In this way benedictine life for women spread throughout the countryside. The number of nuns at Ronceray itself grew only slowly, from twenty-six in 1028 to thirty-three in 1073.[58] Any surplus sisters may well have been sent off to one priory or another. Cluny was not the only monastery in the eleventh century to develop something of an empire.

About 1028 another key monastery, St Georges, Rennes, was founded, again by a woman, Adele, the sister of Duke Alan III of Brittany. According to the charter, Adele wished to become a nun, and 'out of his great love for her Alan offered her to God and permitted her to take a vow of perpetual virginity. So that she might better embrace the monastic life and walk in the way of perfection, he gave her a suitable place to withdraw with her companions and serve God and his martyr, St George, under the Rule of St Benedict'.[59]

This charter mentions a group of women wishing to enter monastic life together and provides an excellent illustration of the way in which many of these communities may have been founded. St Georges seems to have been not only a family project but a civic endeavor as well. The first entrants represented the leading families of the city of Rennes. They included the mother and sister of Guarinus, the bishop, and the daughters of both the viscount and the vicar of the city.[60]

Alan and Adele's mother, Haduisa, and their brother, Eudes, confirmed the foundation. Haduisa later gave the nuns the town of Cavana, a gift from her son Eudes, whom it seems she and her husband had adopted. Roiantelina, Eudes' widow, had gathered another group of nuns at Cavana, but they did not have sufficient means of support. Consequently, Abbess Adele received her and her nine sisters into the monastery of St Georges.[61]

Along with lands the nuns were given a number of churches. Some of these were made into priories. At Notre Dame, Tintiniac, founded in 1032, the nuns permitted a castle to be built for which its lord pledged fidelity to them. Haduisa and Alan founded St Pierre de Marcheil in the same year; St Seglin also dated from then and St Georges d'Arz followed in 1043. When Alan died on pilgrmage to Jerusalem, his wife, Bertha of Blois, was left in a very vulnerable position with their three-month old son Conan. Bertha appealed to her sister-in-law, Abbess Adele, for prayers and protection, giving the nuns the priory of St Pierre de Plougasnow. Conan grew up safely to be a formidable duke and a constant champion of his aunt's abbey.[62]

In 1047 Agnes of Burgundy, widow of Count William of Poitou and wife of Count Geoffrey Martel of Anjou, founded Notre Dame, Saintes. Agnes wished to cement good relations between her new husband Geoffrey and her son, from whom Geoffrey held his lands at Saintes. Not satisfied with giving lands they already held, Agnes bought lands she thought the nuns would need.[63] The new house was supported primarily by ecclesiastical revenues. Lay aristocrats were increasingly willing to grant churches they had acquired to monasteries, sensing their claims on ecclesiastical properties were becoming suspect.[64]

Agnes paid six thousand *solidi* for seven manses she bought from a knight; she also gave the nuns the mint at Saintes, buying out from the bishop for one thousand *solidi* the half interest she did not already own. For an additional fifteen hundred *solidi* she bought them the island of Vis, including taxes and tolls on fishing and trade.[65]

Donations of ecclesiastical goods and revenues included: six churches and all the tithes at Maremie; fourteen manses and most of the tithes on the island of Olerone; the church of St Dionysius, and the ancient, extinct abbey of St Paladius; the church, tithes, and hunting rights at Nancras (providing meat for the table of the abbess and for the infirmary, as allowed by the benedictine Rule); and the parish and tithes of Montepolino in Anjou. The nuns were promised complete jurisdiction over all their lands and revenues, immune from king, dukes, counts, castellans, archbishops, bishops, colliberti, bailiffs, knights, and any other officers, ecclesiastical or secular.[66]

Notre Dame, Saintes, was dedicated in November of 1047. The abbess and nuns were to serve God under the Rule of St Benedict. Abbesses were to be freely elected by the sisters from their own group or another house without outside pressure or taint of simony.[67] Their foundation charter was confirmed by three archbishops, six bishops, six abbots, one bishop-elect, and many other ecclesiastical officials. It was confirmed by Pope Leo IX in 1049.[68] When Agnes' second son, Guy Geoffrey, became duke of Aquitaine, he confirmed his mother's gifts to Saintes and remained a champion of the abbey even as he fought Geoffrey Martel's nephews for his lands.[69]

Through the count and countess of Anjou, the nuns of Saintes made an exchange of priories in 1047 with the monks of Trinity, Vêndome. The women received Notre Dame de Montpollin in exchange for St Medard de Chevire-le-Rouge. When the original nuns were rejected by their founder in 1080, a monastery at Perigueux was also given to Saintes.[70]

At least five other women's houses were begun in the last part of the eleventh century. St Gènes-des-Monges was founded by St Robert, then abbot of La Chaise-Dieu.[71] Blessac also originated near 1050, founded by Ranulfe III, viscount of Aubusson, for his daughter. St Germaine des Larrey near Lyons, a men's house in the sixth century, was dedicated to benedictine nuns.[72] Not far away Notre Dame Rougemont started by the end of the century and St Urbain at Marcannay-la-Cote became a priory of St Benigne.[73] St Julien de Pré at Mans was endowed about mid-century by a pious aristocratic woman named Lezeline, who rebuilt the walls of the church and placed nuns there who would cherish the benedictine Rule.[74]

Finally, two important houses which included men and women were founded in the last half of the eleventh century, Marcigny in 1055, and Molesme in 1075. Marcigny, the first official cluniac house for women, was established by Abbot Hugh, who thought that women had no place to which they might retire to live a strict monastic life. He installed a small community of monks to assist the sisters. Abbot Hugh's family was deeply involved in the beginnings of Marcigny. His brother Geoffrey, count of Semur, co-founder with Hugh and generous donor over many years, in 1070 entered Marcigny with his daughter Lucie. In 1088 his son Geoffrey joined, along with his wife, one son, and two daughters, making extensive gifts to Cluny for use at Marcigny.[75]

Molesme was a small community of women joined to a larger group of men. Women are not prominent in the early charters that have survived, for donations were made generally to the abbot and brothers. The founding abbot, Robert, was superior of both men and women. Only the entry of women, usually with other family members, identified Molesme as a 'double' house. It was founded in 1075 by Ugo de Maligny with his sisters, nephews, nieces, and their spouses, a real family endeavor. There were nine prominent women donors, two of whom founded priories. At least twenty-two priories were founded from or given to Molesme by the end of the eleventh century. Perhaps only one of them, however, included women.[76]

As Poitiers had served as a center of women's monastic expansion in the tenth century, monastic reform in the eleventh century spread from Tours to Dol, Angers, Rennes, Saintes, and beyond. Saintly clerics and monks, like Treasurer Herveus of St Martin and Abbot Hugh of Cluny, can be credited with important foundations, like Beaumont and Marcigny. Aristocratic women who wanted to become nuns prevailed upon their fathers, brothers, and husbands to found monasteries for them, where they often became the first abbesses. In this way Locmaria was founded by Hodierne and her family, and St Georges, Rennes, came to be led by Adele of Brittany. Other wealthy laywomen, who did not themselves become nuns, nonetheless founded important houses. Two countesses of Anjou were in this group. Hildegarde founded Ronceray, and Agnes, her successor, founded Saintes. Although Beaumont and Locmaria may not have followed the benedictine Rule, Ronceray, Saintes, Rennes and their many priories firmly established benedictine life as the norm for nuns of the eleventh century in central France.

By including both nuns and monks, houses like Marcigny and Molesme solved the problem of chaplains for the nuns; the canons who served some of the earlier houses had not always been above reproach.[77] Marcigny was Hugh's attempt to create a much stricter than usual house, stressing enclosure and following the usages of Cluny. Double houses led by women had to await the founding of Fontevrault in the twelfth century.

WOMEN WHO CHOSE MONASTIC LIFE: ENTRANTS AND THEIR GIFTS

Considerable information about the nuns is provided in the charters that recorded their gifts to the monastery upon entry. These charters often reveal the marital and social status and something of the life-situation of the entrant. Professor Jean Verdon has analyzed the entry charters for Rennes, Saintes, Ronceray, and Marcigny through the twelfth century.[78] By isolating the data for the eleventh century, we can make some interesting comparisons.

Most of the nuns were drawn from the aristocracy, although this was less the case for Ronceray than for the other houses studied. Since women's monasteries were established more slowly and were fewer than men's, there seem in the eleventh century to have been fewer spaces available than women who wished to enter. The number of nuns was limited, sometimes deliberately and sometimes by the resources available to support them. Ronceray remained at around thirty nuns and Marcigny was limited to ninety-nine. Occasionally a priory failed and its nuns had to be absorbed by the mother house.[79] The few available openings were filled first by the relatives of the founders and more substantial donors. This initially left few places among the nuns for women from the poorer classes of society.[80]

Professor Verdon questions the vocations of the nuns who entered these houses suggesting that many were compelled to join, but I see little evidence for so doing.[81] Many women described as daughters entered, but they do not seem to have been children.[82] Marcigny was explicit about not accepting candidates of less than twenty years of age. Other reformed houses seem also to have preferred more mature novices. Many eleventh-century candidates were older in that they had been married women in the world before becoming nuns. The charters suggest many had had an experience of conversion to the monastic life.[83] Some younger women, like one who approached St Odo of Cluny, might defy their parents to avoid marriage and enter religious life.[84]

Women seem to have had little choice of marriage partners at this time. Did they have as little choice as to whether to become nuns? Did fathers place daughters in monasteries against their wishes and did husbands who wished to divorce their wives force them into religious houses? Professor Wemple maintains that carolingian monasteries were often refuges or even prisons for women who had no monastic vocation.[85] Professor Verdon points out that many charters quite literally say that a husband or father 'made' his wife or daughter a nun. The initiative taken by women in founding and joining the reformed benedictine houses of the eleventh century is so clear in the charters that I am not willing to concede that coercion was the rule, or even very frequent. I think rather that it was an honor to be admitted to these houses for women.

If a father 'placed' his daughter in a monastery, as one did when he went to the Holy Land with the instructions that if he had not returned in three years, she was either to enter or be married, this need not be construed as coercion. The girl may have consented to try monastic life for three years before commiting herself for life. If it did not work out she might return to her family, and her father set it in writing that in his absense an appropriate marriage would still be arranged for her. The document also specified that if his daughter returned home to be married, his niece was to have her place in the monastery. The family hoped, and sought to assure, that one of its young women have a chance to join and, if she wished, persevere in the monastic life.[86]

As the church came to insist that a bride's consent was necessary to make a marriage valid,[87] so monasteries were only successful when the religious consented to join them. I sense a tremendous enthusiasm in the charters on the part of women who founded and entered the new benedictine houses of the eleventh century. Consider, for example, the eleven entrants to St Georges, Rennes, before 1100, whose entries are recorded in the charters. Eight were described as daughters and three had been married women. Some of the charters speak of a father 'making his daughter a nun' or just 'giving' her to the monastery along with some lands, but verbs like bestowing, elevating, offering, and dedicating are also used and the impression given is one of competition to be accepted.[88] Reform sentiments were expressed by one father at his daughter's entrance to St Georges in that he sought to give the monastery some tithes that it no longer (1080) seemed appropriate for a lay person to possess.[89]

The benedictine Rule forbids private property, and strict adherence to the Rule was expected at St Georges. When nine sisters from Cavana, a small house which had failed, and their leader, Roiantelina, asked for admission to St Georges, Roiantelina wished to have some of the revenues she had brought with her used for the exclusive support of her nuns. Abbess Adele of St Georges refused saying that private property was not permitted in the Rule.[90] Where concern for the Rule was this great, I doubt very much that superiors would have accepted, or retained, women who had been forced into the monastery against their wishes. This is not to say the wishes of a parent or a husband would not be very persuasive (one is reminded of Heloise's confession in the twelfth century of having entered only for Abelard's sake) but the slow process of becoming a Benedictine was meant to weed out those who did not take to the life.

Thirty-five per cent of the nuns entering Ronceray before 1100 were widows or married women. By the end of the twelfth century the percentage would decrease to twenty-five per cent, still a significant proportion of mature women.[91] Some eleventh-century women seem to have entered monasteries in much the same way women today begin a career when the children are grown. Celibacy was lauded as the highest life, and many older women seem to have been attracted to it. Admittedly, some of their arranged marriages may not have been happy ones and they may have been just as glad to separate as were their husbands to 'place' them in the monastery.

Ronceray accepted some members of the non-aristocratic, even poorer, classes.[92] For example, one serf prospered sufficiently working for the monastery to buy his family's freedom. He and his wife entered monasteries, she becoming a nun of Ronceray.[93] The son of a draper sued the nuns for return of a gift his father had given when his sister entered the house. Perhaps recognizing his need, the nuns returned the gift.[94] His sister was a nun at the priory of St Cyr, where the nuns may have been even less aristocratic than at Ronceray itself, where the wife of a miller became a nun as late as 1100.[95]

The gifts at entry to Ronceray were not usually very large, so great wealth was not requisite in an entrant's family. Some men made gifts ahead so that their wives might later enter if they wished.[96] Sometimes litigation was undertaken to eliminate other claimants to lands, such as that by a knight who wished to make a secure gift when his two sisters entered Ronceray.[97] One father paid off other claimants in fish and eels when he made a gift celebrating his daughter's entry; he also gave her money for her veil and an annual gift of ginger.[98] Other knights whose daughters were joining gave only a few fields.[99] One father promised the nuns twenty pounds if they would accept his eldest daughter and make her a *learned* nun, or if she should not be promising then one of his younger girls.[100]

Donations of ecclesiastical lands and revenues, not uncommonly under lay control, were among the gifts families made when one of their members entered Ronceray. When his daughter entered there, for example, one father gave one-quarter of the offerings at his parish, and then increased the percentage when he and his wife also decided on religious life.[101] Commercial properties were also donated.

Walter Rage gave a port and meadows near Chateauneuf when his daughter, Lisoie, entered Ronceray. These gifts were subsequently challenged by his other daughter, Adelice, and her husband. When the case came to a judgement of God, perhaps by duel, Adelice's husband backed down, and when he died Adelice confirmed the gifts to the monastery. Nonetheless in 1075 another relative can be found challenging them. He underwent an ordeal by hot iron and won for his daughter the revenues of these lands for her lifetime only. This gift was particularly valuable as it was the site of a new burg and appreciated greatly over the years.[102]

Occasionally Ronceray had difficulties retaining lands given by entrants when family members tried to reclaim them. Nevertheless they acquired small grants of land, revenues from land and commerce, and some ecclesiastical revenues from gifts of new entrants and their families.

In the entry charters of Saintes prior to 1100, four new nuns were described as wives and eleven as daughters.[103] More than a quarter of these entrants, then, were married women, and a mixture of secular and ecclesiastical lands were included in their gifts. When Agnes of Burgundy was founding Saintes, she gave the entire island of Vis, including its church, which she bought from a man named William, whose small daughter was to be allowed to enter as part of the bargain.[104] The admittance of this child oblate is one of only three such examples I found in the charters.[105]

The first entrants to Marcigny were as likely to be widowed or married as single. Prior to 1100 there were thirteen new nuns described by name only or as daughters or sisters. Twelve were described as wives, mothers or widows.[106] The greater percentage of married entrants may be accounted for by couples entering Marcigny together. Geoffrey III of Semur entered with his wife, a son, and two daughters. They made a substantial gift including a *villa*, vineyards, fishing rights, a meadow, and a mill.[107] Could each member of a family like this possibly have had a vocation? In the enthusiasm of founding Marcigny with Uncle Hugh, abbot of Cluny, I think it possible. Marcigny was an especially strict house which stressed commitment to cluniac ideals.

In comparison to the other monasteries, Marcigny attracted more women without a father or a husband who represented them in the charters of entry. There were one independent countess, three women identified only by name, and four widows, all of whom entered and presented gifts to Marcigny independently of any male relative. One daughter and one sister seem also to have been acting on their own. Each gave a modest gift of from one-half to three manses, except the Countess Reine, who was more generous. The grants of male relatives at the entry of their daughter, sister or wife were not substantially greater than those of the entrants acting alone.[108] The charters of Marcigny were careful to express the consent of the entrant. Abbot Hugh, as we noted, expressly called for mature applicants.[109]

There were only five entry charters to Molesme before 1100 that included the entries of women. Elizabeth de Bourmont gave her allod and her small son to Molesme when she joined. This is the third example I have found of a child oblate, and this child was given to a house renowned for its strictness.[110] A brother and sister entered Molesme together, making the gift of a church.[111] A father and daughter joined, giving several manses. The daughter became a nun and the father wavered between embracing monastic life and accepting a secular prebend from the abbey; most likely therefore, he was a priest.[112] Renard of Noyers entered with his wife and one son, but left behind four sons, one of whom was still young.[113] Finally, a son confirmed a gift made by his father when his mother had entered.[114] All but one of the entry charters to Molesme which include women record the entry of family groups. Three of the entrants there were married and two were probably single, but the total number of women entering Molesme was not large.

CONCLUSIONS

Aristocratic founders, their families and friends provided the main endowment for the new women's monasteries. New members seem not to have been under obligation to provide large gifts. There may well have been unrecorded entrants who provided no gifts at all. This made it easier for several members of the same family, and people without extensive resources, to join, and may have ensured that vocations and not wealth were the criteria for entry.

The women whom I initially studied at Beaumont, those who asked Herveus, the treasurer of St Martin, for a proper monastery were the model for others all over central France, who began asking clergy and male relatives to help them establish a benedictine life for women. Monastic life for women had been through hard times. Half the ancient houses had either failed or been given to men. Undaunted, women founded new abbeys, often with priories clustered around them. Bourges and Poitiers boasted several important houses by the year 1000. The eleventh century saw new women's houses radiating from Tours, Dol, Rennes, Angers, and Saintes. 'Double' houses were begun at Marcigny and Molesme to provide a stricter monastic life for women in partnership with reformed monks.

The benedictine Rule became the key to renewal by the mid-eleventh century. Property was held entirely in common. Election of an abbess by the community protected the independence of the house. Women were very active as founders and donors, and widows and married women made up at least a quarter of all entrants. Families and community leaders entered together. Many priories were founded, but competition was keen for places available. Most, but not all, entrants came from the aristocracy, where vocations do not seem to have been lacking.

That the monastery provided much to the surrounding society explains in part the tremendous support the nuns received. Religious houses helped keep the peace, provided lodging for travellers, and protected the poor. They governed many people and administered the economy of extensive lands. Increasingly they absorbed ecclesiastical lands and revenues that the laity were uncomfortable about owning. Women's monasteries provided education for girls, offered second careers for widows and wives, and an alternative to marriage for young girls. They were centers of liturgical revival and religious renewal for entire provinces.

The popularity the renewed houses had for women cannot be explained entirely by their many benevolent effects on society; the quality of life offered within the monastery influenced them as well. In this, women's religious life was affected as much as men's by the reform ideals emanating from Cluny. These were well expressed in the life and writings of St Odo, second abbot of Cluny, who seems to have touched the reform of women's monastic life at least indirectly at several points.

According to his biographer, John of Salerno, Odo had a remarkable encounter with a woman shortly after entering monastic life at Baume under Abbot Berno. He stopped to visit a noble family on his way back to the monastery from home (both of his parents had just entered monastic life), and spent the evening with the daughter of the family and others of the household, for her parents were away. Impressed with his vocation, she came to him secretly at night begging him to help her become a nun and avoid the marriage which was being arranged for her. Odo helped her to run away with him and his companions and left her at an oratory for women near his monastery, prepared to confess all to Abbot Berno who was understandably perturbed at his returning with a woman. Convinced of Odo's sincerity, Berno permitted him to take her food and provide instruction for several days until he could find her a place in a nearby community of nuns, where soon afterwards she died.[115]

When telling this incident to John of Salerno, Odo may have been reminded of an anecdote about his own hero of an earlier generation, Gerald of Aurillac, which Odo had included in his biography of Gerald. Odo's biographer says, not that Odo was attracted sexually to the young woman whom he helped to escape from her family, but that Abbot Berno was understandably suspicious at first. Although opportunity had clearly existed, both Odo and the young woman, who wished his help to become a nun, were set on the ideal of the celibate life. At his early encounter, on the other hand, Gerald had not yet been fully converted to the monastic life-in-the-world and the incident proved a turning point for him. The lord of extensive lands, he had recently taken the title of count when his fancy was caught by a young woman who had no power to resist him, for she was one of the serfs of his estates. Gerald had gone to her parents to request her from them when he was suddenly repelled by what he was doing and by the very sight of her. He realized that he was not only giving into lust, but abusing the power over the poor that God had given him to protect. Later, when he resisted a fine marriage alliance, it became clear that he had been converted to celibacy although he was never able, because of his responsibilities as count, to enter a monastery.[116]

Men and women in the age of Odo and Gerald cherished the ideal of celibacy even when they sometimes had difficulty living up to it. St Odo, the unnamed nun, and Gerald renounced sex and marriage in favor of monastic life. As Odo explained in his *Occupatio*, they lived in imitation of the celestial life, in anticipation of the imminent end of the world, Christ's second coming, and life in paradise. Freed of sexual passion, men and women aspired to live in freedom and equality like the angels.[117] Thus Odo was freed in charity to break monastic rules and travel with a woman who had run away from home. When wrongly tempted by passion and power, Gerald, in guilt and fear, quickly arranged the marriage of the serf he had nearly seduced. As his conversion deepened, Gerald went on in love to protect the poor, administer justice, oppress the oppressors, feed the poor at his own table, and turn his castle into a veritable monastery, ruling without violence and refusing to kill in battle.[118] As with St Augustine much earlier, the key to their conversions was celibacy.

St Odo carried to extremes the christian virtues with which he endowed St Gerald. No one could surpass Odo in humility or service to his brothers. He gave even the necessities of the monks and their travelling expenses away to the poor. In imitation of the poor Christ, he rode a donkey alone among the monks of Fleury who were armed to kill him, and won them over to his reforms.[119] His monks not only shared goods in imitation of the apostles, but lived in real poverty, sacrificing to share with anyone in need. His gentleness and humility, dedication to peace, the sense of humor and holy joy for which he was known, his criticisms of the luxury of the clergy and the violence of the powerful, won his movement the whole-hearted support of devout men and women of the tenth century.[120]

At Cluny, St Odo responded to all who asked his help. This cluniac propensity to give away time, talents, and wealth may have led to an exhaustion of resources by the time of Abbot Hugh in the late eleventh century.[121]

Odo seems to have tried to simplify and limit the monastic liturgy and the grandeur of ritual that was customary in his day. He laid stress on silence and on private prayer.[122] Odo encouraged devotion to the Eucharist, to the human Christ and his mother.[123] Modeled on the family, the cluniac community was supposed to live in unity and love, reaching out to inspire others and draw them in, while maintaining a precarious independence of outside interference.

Women, frequently in danger and usually lacking power in a warrior society, were understandably drawn to these ideals. Cluniac life promised them equality, a measure of independence of their families, scope for their talents, and opportunities for leadership. Like Odo's travelling companion, a nun might avoid an unwanted marriage, the dangers of childbirth, and possibly seeing a husband or child killed. Instead, she might find security in prayer and liturgy, and a sacramentalized life in which every action had symbolic value. Ideally, she would live a holy life in a poor but loving and peaceful community awaiting a death that seemed all too imminent.

Nuns were not, however, cut off from their families at this time. Their relatives participated in the prayers and festivals of the monastery; friends and cousins entered the same community; the administration of common adjoining lands drew benefactors and religious together. Widows and married women, leaving children behind, were not completely separated from family concerns. Some had raised families, and after their husbands' deaths or with their permission had entered monastic life. By carolingian times, marriage, now more often then before monogamous, became attractive to women, but the attraction to monastic life remained stronger for some.[124] Cluniac spirituality attracted women, but few monastic houses were available at first for them. Nearly a century after St Odo, the benedictine revival for women began in full force. Credit for it must be given not only to cluniac reformers, but to the women who founded, entered, and led the new benedictine houses for women.

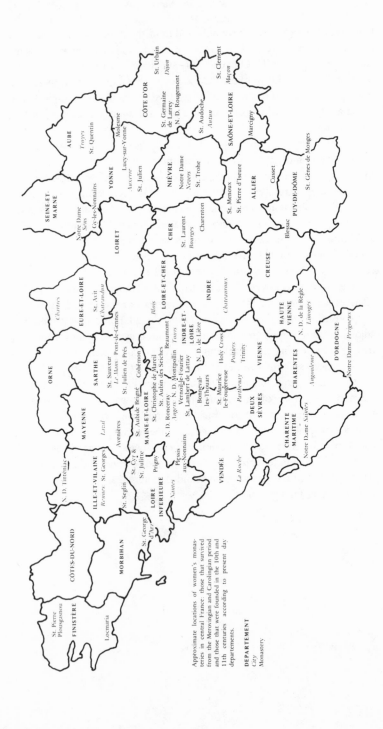

Approximate locations of women's monasteries in central France: those that survived from the Merowingian and Carolingian period and those that were founded in the 10th and 11th centuries according to present day departementes.

DEPARTEMENT
City
Monastery

ABBREVIATIONS

AM	*Annales de Midi*
BEC	*Bibliotèque de l'école de chartes*
BSAIV	*Bulletin et mémoires d'archéologique l'Illeet-Vilaine.*
CAM	*Cartulaires de l'abbaye de Molesme.* Ed. Jacques Laurent. Paris, 1911
CCM	*Cahiers de civilisation médiévale*
CM	*La cartulaire de Marcigny-sur-Loire.* Ed. J. Richard. Dijon, 1957.
CR	*Cartulaire de l'abbaye de Ronceray.* Ed. Paul Marchegay. Archives d'Anjon, 3. Angers, 1854.
CS	*Cartulaire de l'abbaye royale de Notre-Dame de Saintes.* Ed. L'abbe Th. Gragilier, Cartulaires inédits de la Saintonge. 2. Niort, 1871.
CSG	*Cartulaire de l'abbaye de Saint-Georges de Rennes.* Ed. Paul de la Bigne Villeneuve, *BSAIV* 9, 1875.
GC	*Gallia Christiana.* Paris, 1715– .
MGH SS	*Monumenta Germaniae Historic: Scriptores*
MSAT	*Mémoires de la société archéologique de Touraine*
MS BNTA	Manuscript, Bibliothèque nationale, collection Anjou-Touraine
PL	J.P. Migne, *Patrologiae cursus completus, series latina.*
RB	*Rule of St Benedict*
RHGF	*Recueil des historiens de Gaul et de France*
RM	*Revue Mabillon*
VA	Martène, *Vetera Analecta*

NOTES

1. Suzanne F. Wemple, *Women in Frankish Society: Marriage and the Cloister, 500–900* (Philadelphia, 1981) 38–39, 151–52,183–85, 220–21. Fortunatus, *De vita sanctae Radegundis* ed. B. Krusch; *MGH Scriptorum rerum Merovingicarum* 2.368. Gregory of Tours, *History of the Franks*, Vol. 2 (Oxford, 1927); Baudonivia, *De vita s. Radegundis Liber II*, ed. B. Krusch. *MGH Scriptorum rerum Merovingicarum* 2.377–95. Fortunatus *Life*, with fine tenth-century illuminations by a nun of Holy Cross, may be found in the Bibliothèque municipale de Poitiers MS 426. See René Aigran, *Sainte Radegunde* (Paris, 1918). L. Coudanne, 'Baudonivie, moniale de Sainte-Croix et biographe de sainte Radegonde', and Georges Marié, 'Sainte Radegonde et le milieu monastique contemporaine', *Études mérovingiennes: Actes de Journées de Poitiers, 1952* (Paris, 1953) 45–51, 219–25.

2. Wemple, *Women in Frankish Society* 149–65.

3. Jonas, 'Life of St. Columbanus' ed. Edward Peters, *Monks, Bishops, and Pagans: Christian Culture in Gaul and Italy 500–700* (Philadelphia, 1975) 75–113;

Wemple, *Women in Frankish Society*, 159, 165–66; Boniface, *The Letters of St Boniface*, tr. Ephraim Emerton, (New York, 1976) 34–41, 56–57, 59–61, 64–65, 77–78, 121–22, 170–73. Friedrich Prinz, *Frühes Mönchtum in Frankreich Kultur und Gesellschaf in Gallien, den Rheinlander und Bayern am Beispiel der monastischen Gntwicklung* (Munich-Vienna, 1965).

4. Ardo, 'Life of Benedict of Aniane,' tr. Allen Cabaniss, *The Emperor's Monk*, (Ilfracombe, Devon, 1979) 55–56, 64–68.

5 .See Wemple, *Women in Frankish Society*, 165–74, 187–88. See the following section of this article.

6. *Ibid.*

7. *Ibid.*, 157–74.

8. *Ibid.*, 143–48. See also J. E. Lynch, 'Marriage and Celibacy of the Clergy: The Discipline of the Western Church: An Historico-Canonical Synopsis', *Jurist* 32 (1972) 14–38, 189–212.

9. A. Salmon, 'Notice sur l'abbaye de Saint-Loup près de Tours', BEC VI (1845) 436–53. Prosper Tarbé, 'Examen critique et analytique de diverses chartes de Xᵉ, XIᵉ, XIIᵉ siècles relatives à la Touraine', *Revue retrospective* 9 (1837) 26–29. RHGE 10:589, 607. Jean Mabillon, *Annales ordinis Sancti Benedicti* (Lucca, 1745) 4:696–97, 708; MS BNTA II/1 nos. 273, 322, 376, 377; GC XIV, cols. 189, 311–17 and Instr. cols. 63, 82.

10. Émile Mabille, *Les invasions normandes dans la Loire et les pérégrinations du corps de Saint-Martin* (Paris, 1869) 26. Edmond Martène and Casimir Chevalier, *Histoire de Marmoutier* MSAT 24 [1874] 1:177.

11. Jean Verdon, 'Le monachisme en Poitou au Xᵉ siècle', *Revue Mabillon* 59:272 (1978) 235–53; 'Les moniales dans la France de l'Ouest au XIᵉ et XIIᵉ siècles: Etude d'histoire sociale', CCM 19:3 (1976) 247–64; 'Recherches sur les monastères feninins dans la France du nord aux IXᵉ–XIᵉ siècles', RM 59:266 (1976) 49–96; 'Recherches sur les monastères feminins dans la France du Sud aux IXᵉ–XIᵉ siècles', AM 88/2:127 (1976) 117–38; 'Rolé economique des monastères feminins aux IXᵉ–Xᵉ siècles', RM 58:261 (1975) 329–43.

12. See the map concluding this article; geographical references from Verdon, CCM 19:3 (1976) 247–64; Verdon, RM 59:266 (1976) 49–96 and Verdon, AM 88/2:127 (1976) 117–38. A few early houses noted by Verdon have not been included here because no evidence as to whether they survived into the eleventh century or not has yet been found. Verdon, RM 59:266 (1976) 50 (Saint-Jean-le-Grand, Autun; Meuse) 60 (Saint-Maximin, Saint-Hilaire, Sens; Notre-Dame aux Nonnains de Troyes) 61 (Saint-Pierre du Mans; Notre-Dame and Saint-Pierre de Caladon) Verdon AM 88/2:127 (1976) 123 (Clion and Notre-Dame de Sales, Bourges). The diocese of Bourges has been included while the dioceses of Agoulême, Bordeaux, and Clermont have not. This is, admittedly, arbitrary, but I have not been able to research the original sources in the archives of these dioceses yet.

13. Paul Marchegay, ed., *Cartulaire de l'abbaye de Ronceray*, Archives d'Anjou, 3 (Angers, 1854). L'abbé Th. Grasilier, *Cartulaire de l'abbaye royale de Notre-Dame de Saintes*, Cartulaires inédits de la Saintonge, 2 (Niort, 1871). Paul de la Bigne Villeneuve, 'Cartulaire de l'abbaye de Saint-Georges de Rennes', *Bulletin et mémoires de la société archéologique d'Ille-et-Vilaine* 9 (1875) 127–311. J. Richard, ed., *Le cartulaire de Marcigny-sur-Loire (1045–1144): essai de reconstitution d'un manuscript disparu* (Dijon, 1957). Jacques Laurent, ed., *Cartulaires de l'abbaye de Molesme* 2 (Paris, 1911).

14. RB 33, 50–54, 56–67. See Alexandre Bruel, *Recueil des chartes de l'abbaye de Cluny*, 1 (Paris, 1876) no. 112, pp. 124–28.

15. Marchegay, nos. 15 and 16 analyzed by Olivier Guillot, *Le comte d'Anjou et son entourage au XIᵉ siècle* (Paris, 1972) 1:181–93; Grasilier, CS, nos. 2, 3, 4, 225; de la Bigne Villeneuve, CSG, no. 1.

16. SAINTES: see CS 236–37 (Constantia, 1047–60; Lethburgis, 1060–79; Hersendis, 1079–99). RENNES: see CSG 141, 162 and the charters following (Adele,

1032–*ca*67, see nos. 7, 13, 19, 21, 23, 28, 29, 56; Hodierne, 1067–77, see nos. 30, 31, 43, 44, 58; an unnamed abbess in no. 3 and Theiphaine, (1078–84) according to 'Catalogue historique des abbesses de Saint-George', *Bulletin et mémoires de la société archéologique de département d'Ille-et-Vilaine* 10 (1876) 203–11. Adele II of Brittany (1085–1152) *Ibid.* 211 and CSG 241 and no. 32. RONCERAY: see CR (Leoburga, 1028–*ca*50: see nos. 15, 18; Bertrada, *ca*1050–73 [?], see nos. 238, 278, 280; Richilde, 1073–[followed by Tiburge elected sometime before 1122] see nos. 16, 177, 188, 225, 241.)

17. I am thinking particularly of Lina Eckenstein, *Women Under Monasticism* (New York, 1963), Eileen Power, *Medieval English Nunneries* (New York, 1964), Eleanor McLaughlin, 'Equality of Souls, Inequality of Sexes: Women in Medieval Theology', *Religion and Sexism*, ed. Rosemary Ruether (New York, 1974) 236–41, and Jo Ann McNamara and Suzanne Wemple, 'Sanctity and Power: The Dual Pursuit of Medieval Women', in R. Bridenthal and C. Koonz, edd., *Becoming Visible: Women in European History*, (Boston, 1977) 99–111. See also Wemple, *Women in Frankish Society*, 149–74.

18. *CR*, nos. 178, 180 give examples of laypeople in the chapter; no. 48 shows the abbess abroad on business. *CS* nos. 13, 57, 78, 133, 224 concern pleas held before the abbess and nuns; in no. 162 a layperson is fed in the refectory and in no. 127 the abbess is given a horse to go out on business. Verdon, CCM 19:258. See also Dom R. Gazeau 'La clôture des moniales au XIIᵉ siècle en France', RM 58 (1974) 289. J. D. Mansi, *Sacrorum conciliorum nova et amplissima collectio* (Venice, 1772) 14:266–76. G. Huyghe, 'La clôture des moniales des origines à la fin du XIIIᵉ siècle', –*Etude historique et juridique* (Rubaix, 1944) 49ff. J. Rambaud-Buhot, 'Le statut des moniales chez les Pères de l'église dans les règles monastiques et les collections canoniques jusqu' au XIIᵉ siècle' in Dom A. Galli, James O'Carroll *et. al.*, edd., *Sainte Fare et Faremoutiers: treize siècles de vie monastique* (Abbaye de Faremoutiers, 1956) 156–57. Jane Schulenberg's article in the present volume.

19. For example, *CR*, nos. 1, 4, 72 and 180. *CS*, nos. 55, 57. Ronceray no. 72 is particularly interesting because the nuns paid off a father who had bought their canonical prebend for his son, who proved unworthy and was dismissed. See also Dom P. de Monsabert, 'Documents inédits pour servir à l'histoire de l'abbaye de Sainte-Croix de Poitiers', RM 9: 58–60 (no. 2).

20. This is certainly the impression given by the charters cited in note 16 above; see Verdon, CCM 19: 255–58 on the abbess and her officers.

21. One 'double' house, at St Pierre, Rebais (founded 635), was destroyed by the Normans: GC 8:1679. Verdon, RM 59:60. At Tours, St Pierre-le-Puellier lasted until 791 and St Loup until 941. Salmon, BEC 6:436–53; Tarbé, *Revue retrospective* 9 (1837) 26–29; GC 14: 186, 189; Verdon RM 59:62. Two women's houses at Le Mans also disppeared in late carolingian times (GC 14:431–32, 438–39; Verdon RM 59:61). Notre Dame, Sens, barely escaped destruction by Count Richard in 978 and the nuns of Perigueux were driven out by their erstwhile founder in 1080 and sought refuge at Saintes (CS no. 21; Mabillon, *Annales* 3:650; Verdon RM 59:60).

22. Verdon, AM 88/2: 127 (1976) 121. R. Aigran 'Une abbesse mal connue de Sainte-Croix de Poitiers', *Bulletin philologique et historique* (1946–47) 197–202. *Cartulaire de l'abbaye de Saint-Cyprien de Poitiers*, ed. L. Redet, Archives historiques de Poitou 3 (Poitiers, 1874) nos. 52, 296. MS Bibliothèque municipale de Poitiers, collection Dom Fonteneau 27:43. See also notes 29 and 35.

23. GC 2, Instr. no. 49, col. 42. Verdon, AM 88/2: 123–24.

24. GC 8:1517. Verdon, RM 59:59.

25. M. Quantin, ed., *Cartulaire général de l'Yonne* (Auxerre, 1860) 1, nos. 43, 44, 55 and 87. Verdon, RM 59:50. V. Saxer, 'Le statut juridique de Vézelay des origines à la fin du XIIᵉ siècle', *Revue de droit canonique* 6 (1956) 230–35. St John the Evangelist, Sens, was also founded for nuns in 496, but restored for monks in 822 (GC 12:195. Verdun, RM 59:60). Notre Dame, Tuffé, and Notre Dame de Puellemontier, near Troyes, were founded for nuns in the seventh century and converted to monks in the early eleventh (GC 14:436–38. G. Busson and A. Ledru, edd. *Actus pon-*

tificum Cenomannis in urbe degentium, Archives historiques du Maine 2 [Le Mans, 1901] 179–80, 203, 284. GC 12:534. Verdon, RM 59:60–61. Eugène Vallée, *Cartulaire de Chateau-du-Loire,* Archives historique du Maine 6 [Le Mans, 1905] nos. 3, 37. Charles Menjot d'Elbenne, *Cartulaire de l'abbaye de Saint-Vincent du Mans,* 1 [Mamers, 1886–1913] nos. 178, 186). Etienne d' Entrammes, founded for women in 832, became a priory of the monks of Evron and St Martin d'Etampes was given to the monks of Morigny in 1106. (GC 14:440; Verdon RM 59:60–61; GC 12:125 and Instr. cols. 16, 17 and 20). St. Etienne of Nevers, a foundation of St. Columban for nuns, was occupied by men in 1063 as was Notre Dame de Bonne Nouvelle at Orleans at an uncertain day [GC 12:667 and Instr. cols. 326–329; Dom Beaunier and Dom J-M Besse, *Abbayes et prieurés de l'ancienne France,* Archives de la France monastique 6 (Paris, 1913) 114–15; GC 8:1514–15; Verdon 59:58–59].

26. For accusations of decadence, see GC 3:370 (Hamage). GC:1075 (Humblières ca 948). GC 8:1703 (Faremoutiers ca 1096). See Ivo of Chartres, *Correspondance,* ed., J. Leclercq, *Classiques d'histoire de France au Moyen Age* 22 (Paris, 1949) no. 70 (also Saint-Avit, no. 10). Verdon, RM 50:226 (1976) 65–67. PL 132:717–20 and PL 139:487. Maurice Prou, ed., *Recueil des actes de Philippe Ier, roi de France, 1059–1108* (Paris, 1908) no. 137, pp. 345–46, no. 161, p. 403.

27. For a scarcity of women and their importance in marriage alliances in the early middle ages, see: Emily R. Coleman, 'L'Infanticide dans le haut moyen age?' *Annales: Economies, sociétés, civilisations* 29 (1974) 315–35, and David Herlihy 'Land, Family and Women,' *Tradtio* 18 (1962) 89–120, both are included in Susan Stuard, ed. *Women in Medieval Society* (Philadelphia, 1976) 13–70 cf. Georges Duby, *Medieval Marriage,* tr. E. Forster (Baltimore, 1978); Wemple, *Women in Frankish Society* 27–123.

28. On women's monasteries, see notes 11 and 32. On monastic expansion under the influence of Cluny, see the following: Gerald Sitwell, ed., *Saint Odo of Cluny being the Life of Saint Odo by John of Salerna and the life of Saint Gerald of Aurillac by Saint Odo* (London, 1958). Mary Skinner, 'Aristocratic Families: Founders and Reformers of Monasteries in the Touraine, 930–1030', *Benedictus: Studies in Honor of St Benedict of Nursia,* Studies in Medieval Cistercian History 8 (Kalamazoo, 1981) 81–98. Noreen Hunt, *Cluny under Saint Hugh, 1049–1109* (London, 1967). Articles by Wollasch, Mager, and Diener in Gerd Tellenbach, ed., *Neue Forschungen über Cluny und die Cluniacenser* (Freiberg/Br., 1959). Jean de Valous, 'Sur quelques points d'histoire relatifs à la fondation de Cluny', *Millenaire de Cluny* (Maçon, 1910). Raffaello Morghen, 'Monastic Reform and Cluniac Spirituality', Kassius Hallinger, 'The Spiritual Life of Cluny in the Early Days', and Jean Leclercq, 'The Monastic Crisis of the Eleventh and Twelfth Centuries', in Noreen Hunt, ed., *Cluniac Monasticism in the Central Middle Ages* (Hamden Conn., 1971). Kassius Hallinger, *Görze-Kluny: Studien zu den monastischen Lebensformen und Gegensätzen im Hochmittelalter,* Studia Anselmiana 22–23 (Rome, 1950) 1:517–600 and 2:746–64. J. F. Lemarignier, 'Political and Monastic Structures in France at the End of the Tenth and the Beginning of the Eleventh Centuries', in F. Cheyette, ed., *Lordship and Community in Medieval Europe* (New York, 1968) 100–127. Ernst Säckur, *Die Cluniacenser in ihrer kirchlichen und allgemeingeschichtlichen Wirksamkeit bis zur mitte des elften Jahrhunderts* (Halle, 1892) 1:1–120, 239–56, 270–79. L. M. Smith, *The Early History of the Monastery of Cluny* (London, 1920) 1–142. Bede Lackner, *The Eleventh-Century Background of Citeaux* Washington, 1972) 1–91. Cinzio Violante, 'Il monachesimo cluniacense di fronte al mondo politico ed ecclesiastico (secoli X e XI)', *Spiritualità Cluniacense,* Convegni del centro di studi sulla spiritualità medievale, 1958 (Todi, 1960). Articles by Conant, Chagny, Laporte, Richard, Chevrier, Leclercq, and Duby in *A Cluny: Congrès scientifique. Fêtes et cérémonies liturgiques en l'honneur des saints Abbés Odon et Odilon, 1949* (Dijon, 1950). Articles by Hourlier, Talbot, and Tellenbach in Helmut Richter, ed., *Cluny: Beitrage zu Gestalt und Wirkung der cluniazensischen Reform* (Darmstadt, 1975). Guy de Valous, *Le Domaine de l'Abbaye de Cluny aux Xe et XIe siècles* (Paris, 1923) 1–54. Jean Leclercq, 'Pour une histoire de la vie à Cluny', *Revue d'histoire ecclésiastique* 57 (1962) 385–408. Barbara Rosenwein, *Rhinoceros Bound:*

Cluny in the Tenth Century (Philadelphia, 1982). Joachim Wollasch, ed. *Cluny im 10. und 11. Jahrhundert:* Eingeleitet un Zussamengestellt (Göttingen, 1967).
29. Verdon, RM 59:235–36. P. de Monsabert, RM 9 (1913) 50–88. MS Bibliothèque nationale, MS latin 12755, fols. 416–23. MS Bib. de Poitiers, coll. Fonteneau 5:523–56. Beaunier-Besse, *Abbayes et Prieurés* (Paris, 1910) 3:242–44. MS Bib. de Poitiers no. 136 (250): *Vita Radegundis* (tenth century) fols. 21–79. Louise Coudanne, 'Regards sur la vie liturgique à Sainte-Croix de Poitiers', *Bulletin de la société des antiquaires de l'Ouest* 14:1 (1978) 353–79. R. Aigran, *Bulletin philologique et historique* (1946–47) 197–202. Alfred Richard, *Histoire des comtes de Poitou,* 778–1126 (Poitier, 1904) 1: 5,8,10,32,24,35,94,104,116,169,176,214,244,252. P. de Monsabert, *Le monastère de Sainte-Croix* (Ligugé, 1952). Dom Guy Oury, *Les moniales Bénédictines* (Paris, nd) 18. E. Briand, *Histoire de sainte Radegonde, reine de France et des sanctuaires et pelerinages en son honneur ou Histoire de l'abbaye de Sainte-Croix* (Paris, 1898) 359–408. See also notes 1, 22, 35.
30. Two male merovingian monasteries were granted to women, St Audoche d'Autun in the seventh century and St Julien of Auxerre by a carolingian bishop (GC 4:483–84. G. Tessier, ed., *Recueil des actes de Charles II le Chauve, roi de France* 3 vols. [Paris, 1943–55] Vol. 1 no. 206 pp. 521–22. GC 12:414 and Instr., cols. 101–102. Quantin, *Cartulaire de l'Yonne* 1:178–80 (no. 93). Verdon RM 59:50 and 58). Charenton, a columbanian foundation, and St Eustadiole survived at Bourges. The surviving documentation does not prove, however, that these communities were occupied continuously (M. de Laugardière, *L'église de Bourges avant Charlemagne* [Paris, 1951] 169–79, 183, 202–203. L. Buttot de Kersers, 'Essai de reconstitution du cartulaire A de Saint-Sulpice de Bourges', *Memoires de la Société des Antiquaires du Centre* 35 [1912] 42. GC 2:174–78. Verdon, AM 88:123. René Crozet, *L'Art roman en Berry* [Paris, 1932] 9, 243, 245. *Archives et histoire des abbayes bénédictines et cisterciennes de Haute Berry* [Bourges, 1980]. See Charenton: Guy Devailly, *Le Berry du Xe siècle au milieu du XIIIe* [Paris, 1973] 75, 105, 153, 170. MS Archives départementales du Cher, séries H:40H2 and 40H5 (after 1154). Beaunier-Besse, *Abbayes et Prieurés* 5:42–43). St Quentin of Troyes became a priory of Molesmes in the eleventh century and Lucy-sur-Yonne was still extant in the twelfth. (GC 12:534. CAM 1:216–17. Verdon, RM 59:60. Laurent Henri Cottineau, *Repertoire topo-bibliographique des abbayes et prieurés,* 3 vols. (Macon, 1935–70) col. 1674. Verdon, RM 59:50).
31. Of the nine carolingian foundations, St Pierre d'Iseure had been started for men in the ninth century and only later was given to nuns (Cottineau, 1464. GC 4:447 and Instr., col. 46. Verdon, RM 59:50). St Maurice-la-Fougereuse began in 820, St Sauveur de Mans in 832, and Cusset was founded by the bishop of Nevers in 886 (G. Michaud, *Saint-Maurice-la-Fougereuse et son prieuré millenaire* [Parthenay, 1900] 109–11. MS Archives départementales d'Ille-et-Vilaine 24H88. Verdon, AM 88:120. Mabillon, *Annales* 2:586. Verdon, RM 59:61. M. Fazy, *Catalogue des actes concernant l'histoire du Bourbonnais jusqu'au milieu du XIIIe siècle* [Moulins, 1924] nos. 25 and 26. Beaunier-Besse, *Abbayes et Prieurés,* 5 [1912] 111–12. GC 12, Instr., col 308–12. RHGF 9:347–48, 358–59. Bibliothèque nationale MS latin 12667, fol. 309. Verdon, AM 88:125–26). St Laurent was established at Bourges, and Notre-Dame-de-la-Règle at Limoges was restored by Louis the Pious (Philippe Labbe, *Nova bibliotheca manuscriptorum* [Paris 1657] 2:62. GC 2:172–74. Verdon, AM 88:123. Guy Devailly, *Le Berry,* 107, 262. R. Mère Marie de Saint-Raphael, *Histoire d'un monastère: les Benedictines de Saint-Laurent de Bourges* [Bourges, 1891]. R. Limouzin-Lamothe, *La diocèse de Limoges des origines à la fin du moyen âge* [Strasbourg-Paris, 1951] 58. GC 2:610. MGH SS 2:616–17. Verdon, AM 88:126. Beaunier-Besse, *Abbayes et prieurés,* 5: 209–210. St Clement de Maçon was restored in 948 by Louis IV while Notre Dame and St Trohé at Nevers were renewed after the viking invasions according to a charter of Charles the Fat. (Philippe Lauer, *Recueil des Actes de Louis IV, roi de France,* 936–54 [Paris, 1914] no. 31, 74–75. Verdon RM 59:51. A. Sery, *L'abbaye des religieuses de Notre-Dame de Nevers* [Nevers, 1902]. Beaunier-Besse, *Abbayes et prieurés* 6:113–14, warns there may be two monasteries of this name. GC

12, Instr., cols. 300, 311–12. Verdon, RM 59:58, 59. Cottineau, 2066. Mabillon, *Annales* 3:259. GC 12:666). Finally, two convents were begun at Sens, Notre Dame and Gy-les-Nonnaines, which later became a priory of Faremoutiers (*Saint-Fare et Faremoutiers*, 38. Mabillon, *Annales* 3:650. Verdon, RM 59:60).

32. Work is just beginning on this important topic. See Wemple, *Women in Frankish Society*, 165–74; 187–88: the Verdon articles cited in note 11 above. Noreen Hunt, *Cluny Under St Hugh*, 186–93; Dom Philibert Schmitz, *Histoire de l'ordre de Saint-Benoit* (Maredsous, 1956) 8:*Les Moniales*, 70–76. Jean Leclercq, 'Medieval Feminine Monasticism: Reality versus Romantic Images', *Benedictus*, 57–65: the articles in the present volume. Jean Richard, 'Sur l'histoire du prieuré de Marcigny aux XIe et XIIe siècles', *Melanges d'histoire et d'archéologie offerts à professeur Kenneth John Conant* (Macon, 1977) 135–40.

33. Verdon, RM 59:64–65. P. Schmitz, *L'Ordre de Saint-Benoit*, 8:70–76.

34. Verdon, RM 59:65–66. Mansi, *Amplissima collectio* 17:263–308. G. Schnürer, *L'église et la civilisation au moyen âge*, 3 vols. (Paris, 1933–38) 2:175–76.

35. See note 22. MS Bibliothèque municipale de Poitiers, collection Dom Fonteneau 27, fols. 15–54. MS Bibliothèque nationale, MS latin 12755, fols. 105–13, 474–88. Beaunier-Besse, 3:244–45. L. Halphen and F. Lot edd., *Recueil des actes de Lothaire et de Louis V, rois de France, 954–987* (Paris, 1908) nos. 20, 47 and 59. Richard, *Poitou* 104–7, 233–37, 252. Verdon, RM 59:237.

36. MS Bibliothèque nationale, MS latin 12756, fols. 265–85, 592–612. Beaunier-Besse, 3:245–46. Verdon, RM 59:240. Verdon, AM 88:121. GC 3:1333–36. Richard, *Poitou* 1:106–7. Halphen and Lot, *Actes de Lothaire et Louis V*, no. 62. Imbert, *Histoire de Thouars* (Niort, 1871) 377–84.

37. J. J. Moret, *Histoire de Saint Menoux* (Moulins, 1907) 36–40. M. Deshourliers, 'Saint-Menoux', *Congrès archéologique de France, LXXXe session, 1913* (Paris-Caen, 1916) 24. GC 2:178–80. Verdon, AM 88:124. Beaunier-Besse, 5:43.

38. See note 28.

39. GC 14:311–17 and Instr., cols. 63 and 82. Bibliothèque municipale de Tours, MS 1329. MS BNTA II/1 nos. 273, 322, 340, 376, 377. II/2 nos. 545, 555, 569. Charles de Grandmaison, *Chronique de l'abbaye de Beaumont-lès-Tours depuis son origine jusqu'au 1657'*, MSAT 26 (1878). Fleuret, *Cartulaire des Bénédictines de Beaumont-lès-Tours* (Mesnil, 1898). Beaunier-Besse, 8:38–39. Verdon, RM 59:62. RHGF 10:589, 607. Mabillon, *Annales* 4:696–97, 708.

40. I do not agree with Verdon (RM 59:62) that there were still nuns at Notre-Dame de l'Ecrignolles since the confirmation by King Robert says explicitly *non esse in pago Turonico coenobium, ubi sanctimoniales foeminae Christo possent suae devotionis impendere officium*: RHGF 10:589. Mabillon, *Annales* 4:696. MS, BNTA II/1 no. 340. See Guy Oury, 'L'Idéal monastique dans la vie canoniale: le Bienheureux Hervé de Tours', RM 50 (1960) 21, who agrees with this position.

41. GC 8:1289 and Instr. cols. 299–300. Verdon, RM 59:58. Yvo of Chartres, *Correspondance*, letter 10, 40–49.

42. Ivo of Chartres, *Correspondance*, 40–49, complained that St Avirt was decadent by the late eleventh century. See Verdon, RM 59:61. Beaunier-Besse, 8:183.

43. Verdon, RM 59:62. Beaunier-Besse 8:45. MS BNTA II/1 no. 322.

44. RHGF 10:607: *de ecclesiâ videlicet Beata Maria Bellimontis in qua regulam sanctimonialium supradictus sanctus vir Herveus construxat*. MS, BNTA II/1 no. 376.

45. Skinner, *Benedictus*, 82–83. Guy Oury, 'La reconstruction monastique dans l'ouest: l'abbé Gauzbert de Saint-Julien de Tours', RM 54:69–124.

46. Jean Delumeau et. al., *Histoire de Bretagne* (Toulouse, 1969) 128–51. A. de la Borderie, 'Recueil d'actes inédit des ducs et princes de Bregagne', *Bulletin et mémoires d'archéologique d'Ille-et-Vilaine* 17 (1888) no. 8, 17–19. GC 14:891.

47. Dom Piolin, *Abbaye de Notre Dame de la Charité ou du Ronceray* (Angers, 1880). François Uzureau, *Les religieuses de l'abbaye dit Ronceray à Angers* (Angers, 1906). François Marie Tresvaux du Fraval, *Histoire de l'église et du diocèse d'Angers* (Paris, 1858) 1:487–95. Marchegay, CR, No. 1:1–5. Bibliothèque municipale d'Angers, MS

844–48b (760): Cartulaire de Notre Dame du Ronceray, roll 1, charter 1; roll 5, charter 52. Citations to documents in the thirteenth century cartulary preserved in Angers may be found in CR; in consulting them, however, I have not found the Marchegay edition to be entirely accurate. Olivier Guillot, *Le comte d'Anjou et son entourage au XIe siècle* (Paris, 1972) 1:25–30, 63, 309–13, 462–48.

48. CR, no. 1, 1–5.
49. Guillot, *Comte d'Anjou*, 175–76, 180. CR, no. 15.
50. Guillot, *Comte d'Anjou*, 189–90. CR, no. 16.
51. CR, no. 48.
52. CR, no. 391. Verdon, RM 59:61.
53. See note 36.
54. CR, no. 171, 172. Verdon, RM 59:62.
55. CR, no. 293. Verdon, RM 59:61.
56. Verdon, RM 59:61–62. CR, nos. 427, 428, 429, 430, 431, 432, 434 (Prigny).
57. Verdon, RM 59:61. CR, nos. 360, 361, 362, 365, 366, 372, 378.
58. Verdon, CCM 19:247
59. 'Abbesses de St Georges', BSAIV 10 (1876) 302–7. Ducrest de Villeneuve et Maillet, *Histoire de Rennes* (Rennes, 1845). Balneat, 'Le vieux Rennes', BSAIV 33:41–224 and 34:13–164. Guillotin de Corson, 'L'église de Rennes à traves les âges', *Revue de Bretagne et de Vendée*, 6e series, 7:85–99; 178–91, 255–61. Guy Devailly, 'Les documents anterieurs au XIIe siècle conservés aux archives départementales d'Ille-et-Vilaine', BSAIV 80 (1978) 9–11. CSG 152, no. 1:217–22. Verdon, RM 59:62. GC 14:782–86.
60. CSG 152, 155, no. 1:217–22.
61. CSG 154, 157, no. 1:217–22, no. 2bis:226, no. 10:234–35, no. 12:236–38.
62. CSG 156–60, nos. 2,5,6,18,27. Verdon, RM 59:266 (1976) 49, 62.
63. L. Audiat, 'Abbaye de Notre Dame de Saintes: notes et documents', *Archives d'histoire Saintonge* 11:417–48. Dom Boudet, 'Histoire de l'abbaye de Notre Dame hors les murs de la ville de Saintes', *Archives d'histoire Saintonge* 12:246–81. Verdon, AM 88:121. CS no. 1:1–5.
64. See note 89.
65. CS no. 80:72–73, no. 77:70, no. 225:143–44; no. 1:1–5
66. CS no. 1:1–5, no. 78:70–71, no. 235:154, no. 211:135.
67. CS no. 2:6–7.
68. Ibid; CS no. 3:8–9, CG 2, Instr. col. 481. CS nos. 109, 110:90–91.
69. CS no. 11. CS ii, no. 53:54, and no. 80:73. Boudet, *Archives d'histoire Saintonge* 12: 272–74.
70. CS no. 21:28, no. 235:154. Verdon, RM 59:61.
71. Verdon, AM 88:126. P.R. Gaussin, *L'abbaye de Chaise-Dieu (1043–1513): L'abbaye en Auvergne et son rayonnement dans la Chrétienté* (Paris, 1962) 335.
72. Verdon, AM 88:126: L. Lacrocq 'Le monastère de Blessac', *Memoires de la société des sciences naturelles et archélogique de la Creuse* 22, fasc. 3–4 (1922–24) 283–302. Verdon, RM 59:50.
73. Verdon, RM 59:51.
74. Verdon, RM 59:62. GC 14:501–5. Robert Latouche, *Histoire du comté du Maine pendant le Xe et le XIe siècles* (Paris, 1910) catalogue d'Actes, no 30. Ambroise Lendru, 'Englise de Pré au Mans', *La Province de Maine* 14 (1906) 159–63. *Congrès archéologique de France* 77 (1910) 288–91. Gabillot and Tournouer, 'Excavations archéologiques dans le Maine et le Pays d'Alençon', *Bulletin de la société historique d'Orne* 27 (1908) 11–140. Guillois, 'Extrait d'une notice sur l'eglse de Notre Dame du Pré, *Société française pour le conservation des monuments historiques* (Le Mans, 1853) 312. Charles Menjot d'Elbenne, *Cartulaire St. Vincent* no. 78:58
75. See note 32, and Abbot Hugh's letters to Marcigny in PL 159;947–52. CM no. 3:3–5; nos. 7–13:8–14; no 6:8; no. 15:15–17.
76. CAM no. 2:5–6; no. 4:7–8; no. 24:34; no. 26:36–38; no. 27:39–40; no. 80:86;

no. 83:88; no. 84:89–90; no. 89:95; no. 90:96; no. 91:96–97; no. 102:106; no.
119: 120–21; no. 122:122; no. 125:124; no. 138:134–36; no. 182:165; no.
183:165 –66; no. 185:167; no. 190:172–73; no. 196:176; no. 453:417–18; nos.
607–8:470–71, (priories); no. 79:85; no. 126:125–26; no. 135:131–32; no.
184:166 (entries).

77. See CR no. 72 in which the nuns pay off a father to be rid of an incompetent
son who had bought their canonical prebend *ca.* 1100.

78. Verdon, CCM 19:247–64.

79. For example, CS no. 21:28 or CS no. 10:234–35 and no. 12: 236–37. See
note 90.

80. Verdon, CCM 19:249.

81. *Ibid.* 252.

82. See notes 88, 105, 110 for possible exceptions.

83. Hunt, *St Hugh,* 190.

84. John of Salerno, *St Odo,* Book 1, part 36, 37–39.

85. Wemple, *Women in Frankish Society,* 171.

86. Verdon, CCM 19:252, citing CR no. 354.

87. Duby, *Medieval Marriage,* 17.

88. CSG no. 11:235–36; no. 35:263–64 *(fecit filiam suam monacham);* no. 41:269
(uxor ejus est sanctimonialis); no. 39:266–68 *(pro filia mea in ejus ecclesia sub monachali
jugo Deo famulatura);* no. 48:274–75 *(fecit matrem suam Maientiam monialem);* no.
49:275 *(cum Elisabeth filia sua . . . pro amore Dei dedit et concessit);* no. 54:281 *(cum
Agnete filia sua, pro amore Dei in perpetuam elomosinam possidendam dederunt et concesse-
runt, et super altare beati Georgii posuerunt)*—child oblate?

89. *Ibid.* no. 60:286 *(volens evitare illud anathema quo constringuntur et deprimuntur
omnes illi laici qui res ecclesiasticas jure possident hereditario, dono . . . faciendo filiam meam
monialem.)*

90. RB 33; CSG no. 12:236–37 *(Tradidit etiam nobis viginti boves, et duodecim vaccas
et decem et octo equas. Addidit etiam et quoque in eadem conventione ut vestitus amminiculo
eas in omni vita sua de suo sustentaret. Quod nos refugimus, ne proprietatis contagio nostra
contaminaretur religio acceptis ab ea centum solidis).*

91. Verdon, CCM 19:251.

92. *Ibid.,* 249.

93. CR no. 34.

94. CR nos. 374 and 376.

95. Verdon, CCM 19:249. CR no. 425.

96. For example, CR no. 395.

97. CR no. 349.

98. CR no. 348.

99. CR no. 233 (and a *colliberti* family), no. 234. A second wife gave a garden in
thanksgiving for her step-daughter's profession (CR no. 99). CR no. 245 shows a son
reducing his rent on lands he had already 'given' the nuns when his mother entered.
In CR no. 121 another boy, described as a child, gave up the family home when his
mother joined Ronceray. CR nos. 93, 95 and 96 desribe how a father, unhappy
about the gifts his aunt had given on her entry to Ronceray, tried to reclaim them until his two daughters also decided to become nuns there. The sisters appeased him
with a gift of ten pounds. In CR no. 237 a widow gave two allodial properties when
her daughter entered. Other widows on their own entries gave their homes and surrounding lands (CR nos. 117, 216 and 343). Meadows, vineyards, woods, and mills
were common entry gifts. (CR nos. 302, 304, 305, and 306—mills and mill tithes; no.
201, 253, 254, 283, 342, 392—lands, meadows, vines, woods). Customs (taxes) collected at markets and fairs showed the gifts of middle-class families (CR no. 404).

100. CR no. 402.

101. CR no. 273. One couple offered an eighth of the offerings at their parish
altar, including pennies, candles, and bread and an eighth of the tithes, including
lambs, pigs and calves (CR no. 271). Another father gave half of the church at Mareil

when his daughter joined; this church became a priory of Ronceray when the dean and the chapter of the cathedral of Le Mans added their interests in this church at the entrance of another daughter, who may possibly have been the daughter of one of their canons (CR nos. 413, 405).

102. CR nos. 235, 236, 237, 240, 241, and 244.

103. Verdon, CCM 19:251.

104. CS no. 225:143–45.

105. See notes 88, 105, 110. A father gave half the church of St Sulpice when his daughter entered Saintes (CS no. 95:83–84). Another father relinquished valuable disputed lands and rights for two thousand *solidi* and two daughters' entrance (CS no. 97:84). A quarrel with the monastery over a mill was settled when the litigant's daughter was permitted to enter Saintes (CS no. 54:55). Mills were popular gifts. A husband and wife who separated to enter religion gave Saintes their home and all its furnishings (CS no. 37:42–43, no. 229:149–50). A villa and variety of lands were contributed by other entrants (CS no. 81:73, no. 89:81, nos. 109, 110:90–91, no. 230:151, no. 190:106–8).

106. Verdon, CCM 19:253–54.

107. CM no. 15:15–17.

108. CM no. 17:17–18; nos. 18:18–19; 21:20–21; 22:21; no. 28:24–25; no. 33:30–31; no. 280:159–60; no. 282:161–62. When his wife joined, a husband donated their home and all wine-making equipment. A widow gave the dowry from her first marriage. A woman and the Lord of Jaligny, on behalf of his wife who was entering, each gave a church (CM no. 19:19–20, no. 24:22–23, no. 25:24, no. 32:29–30, no. 42:35–36, nos. 90, 91, 92:65–67 [winery] no. 120:89–90, no. 19:19–20, no. 21:20–21, no. 20:20, no. 280:159–60).

109. See note 83.

110. CAM no. 79:85; see notes 88, 105, 110.

111. CAM no. 135:131–32.

112. CAM no. 126:125–26.

113. CAM no. 184:166.

114. CAM no. 15:22–23.

115. John of Salerno, *St Odo*, Bk. 1, pt. 36, 37–39.

116. St Odo of Cluny, *St Gerald*, Bk. 1, pt. 9, 101–3; Bk. 1, pt. 34, 123–24; Bk. 2, pt. 16, 145–46.

117. Raffaello Morghen, 'Monastic Reform and Cluniac Spirituality', and Kassius Hallinger, 'The Spiritual Life of Cluny' in *Cluniac Monasticism*, 11–43.

118. St Odo, *St Gerald*, passim: B. Rosenwein, *Rhinoceros Bound*, 66–83, 97–100.

119. John of Salerno, *St Odo*, Bk. 2, pts. 4–8, 44–52. Bk. 3, pt. 8, 79–81.

120. Barbara Rosenwein, 'St Odo's St Martin: the uses of a model,' *Journal of Medieval History* 4 (1978) 317–31; Rosenwein, *Rhinoceros Bound*, 84–96.

121. Noreen Hunt, *St Hugh*, 200–207.

122. Kassius Hallinger, *Cluniac Monasticism*, 38–46. B. Rosenwein, 'Rules and the "Rule" at Tenth-Century Cluny,' *Studia Monastica* 19 (1977) 307–20. John of Salerno, *St Odo*, Bk. 1, pt. 32:33; Bk. 2, pt. 10–12:53–56.

123. Raffaelo Morghen, 'Monastic Reform and Cluniac Spirituality,' *Cluniac Monasticism*, 20–26; Hallinger, *Cluniac Monasticism*, 40–42; John of Salerno, *St Odo*, 64.

124. Wemple, *Medieval Frankish Women*, 122–23.

Humility and Power: Anglo-Saxon Nuns in Anglo-Norman Hagiography[1]

Susan Millinger

THE MONASTIC REVIVAL of late tenth century England—that great burgeoning of energies spiritual, intellectual, and artistic—was a revival and reformation of women's houses as well as men's.[2] We do not know much about these late anglo-saxon nuns and their communities, in large part because little was said of them in contemporary documents.[3] Indirect sources of information for the women's monasteries in the tenth century, however, and direct evidence of their life and concerns in the mid-eleventh century is provided by the *lives* of late anglo-saxon holy women composed after the Norman Conquest. Two of these works are particularly valuable, the *lives* of the tenth century nuns, Edith of Wilton and Wulfhild of Barking, written soon after the Conquest of 1066 by Goscelin of St Bertin.[4] It is the methodology of their author that make these *vitae* valuable to the student of women's monasticism.

THE HAGIOGRAPHER

From at least the 1070s Goscelin travelled around England, writing the *lives* of about eighteen male and twelve female saints.[5] Because Goscelin produced so much work, and because a substantial amount of it remains, his usual methodology can be determined. Much of the time, Goscelin was putting older *lives* into a newer, more fashionable style. When he can be detected reworking old materials, he can be seen reworking them faithfully. As one historian has said of him: 'He not only believed what he read or was told, but reported it faithfully'.[6] At one point, indeed, Goscelin criticized an author who collected *communes . . . virtues* from the *lives* of other saints.[7] This sensitivity suggests that Goscelin saw himself, in contrast, as recording specific facts about individuals, not compiling spiritual commonplaces. That Goscelin normally appears a faithful reworker of traditions makes it likely that with him we can be surer than with most hagiographers that the episodes he relates were told him by the religious he visited. Although the emphases and interpretations are probably his own, I would suggest that the anecdotes are essentially those told in late anglo-saxon communities. Thus Goscelin's *lives* seem an unusually open channel to mid-eleventh century english monasteries.

THE PURPOSES OF THIS STUDY

It is less likely that Goscelin's *lives* open a channel to late tenth-century saints. The difficulty of using hagiography as biography has been amply revealed by many scholars since Delehaye. It is true that the *lives* of Edith and Wulfhild were written within a century of their deaths on the basis of information provided by communities which had a continuing history back to the saints' lifetime. Yet over the course of that century memories may have faded, and shifts in the needs of the communities may have changed the emphases and even the outline of tales. Thus I am using these documents as evidence not for the actual deeds and personalities of the tenth-century saints— although I suspect that these *lives* are fairly reliable indicators of what their communities thought of them—but rather for the ideals and images of female sanctity held in anglo-saxon convents in the mid-eleventh century.

THE MAIN CHARACTERS

The *lives* of Edith and Wulfhild introduce us to three women saints and to several abbesses and nuns of their communities. Edith, born during the reign of her father, King Edgar (959–75), was probably born in 960, and died at the age of twenty-four in 984. Edith's *vita* contains anecdotes about her mother, Wulfthryth, who became abbess of Wilton in Edith's infancy. She outlived her daughter by a number of years; we last hear of Wulfthryth in 997. Wulfhild, their kinswoman and a woman of Wulfthryth's age, became abbess of Barking and may have lived until 1006.[8] In addition to these three, we see in some detail Leflaed of Barking, Wulfhild's successor as abbess; Aelfgifu, abbess of Wilton in the late 1060s; and a nun still alive at the time of the Conquest, Wulfrunna-Judith of Barking, who had known and loved Wulfhild.

CHOOSING THE MONASTIC LIFE

In Goscelin's descriptions of these tenth century anglo-saxon nuns, their decisions to become nuns and the consequences of these decisions loom large. The consequences are most dramatic in the life of Wulfhild of Barking. When Wulfhild was a young girl being educated in the monastery of Wilton, King Edgar began to pursue her. She resisted him, but her aunt Wenflaed, who desired a relative at the summit of power, was less resistant. Wenflaed, the abbess of Wherwell, sent for Wulfhild, pretending to be deathly ill. Inviting her niece to Wherwell, she promised to make her her heir. The dutiful niece hastened to her aunt's side. When she arrived, she found Wenflaed feasting beside the king.

Wulfhild herself was garbed in gilded robes and forced to sit between suitor and aunt. Edgar offered wealth and marriage, but Wulfhild sat in silence, internally spurning all she was being offered. She ate nothing, pretending to be ill. At last she was given permission to withdraw, but guards were placed at the doors of, and within, her chamber. When she went to the privy, she was followed even there. Once there she disrobed and left robes and jewels to two handmaidens. Then she went out through the opening. 'This was the narrow way by which she arrived at the gate of life uncontaminated', wrote Goscelin.[9] She spent the night in a humble dwelling where no one would think of looking for her, and the next day returned to Wilton. Edgar, however, did not accept his rebuff at Wherwell, but followed her back to Wilton. There one day he and his followers trapped her outside the church. She fled to the altar, like any fugitive, but her sleeve remained in the hand of her captor. Marvellously, the sleeve seemed not torn but as if neatly cut off. At this miracle, Goscelin tells us, Edgar (like David, as we are very pointedly told) became aware that he was attempting to injure a spouse holier than Uriah, for he was seeking a woman betrothed to the Lord. He then promised Wulfhild that he would not bother her again.[10]

The story of Wulfhild shows that choosing the monastic life might require an extreme strength of will. Episodes in which women had to overcome the strong opposition of family or spouse to become nuns are common in the hagiography of medieval women saints.[11] The conflict certainly became a hagiographical commonplace, but it is, I would suggest, one which often corresponded with historical reality. One interesting aspect of this commonplace is that in it two ways of overcoming opposition seem to exist. In one pattern, the woman overcomes by her own strength of will and ingenuity; in the other, the woman overcomes with miraculous assistance. These suggest at least two different contemporary understandings of the interaction of divine guidance and human will. They also may indicate different notions of the self-assurance and control over their lives that women had. In the case of Wulfhild, these two patterns are combined. In her first escape, Wulfhild won freedom by herself; in her second and final escape, she had miraculous assistance. One wonders whether these are two different versions of the same escape, and whether Goscelin in his account was knitting the two together, for he seems to have accepted both patterns with equanimity.

These two *lives* contain accounts of two other women who overcame the objections of parents or spouses using their ingenuity or strength of will. One is Leflaed, Wulfhild's successor as abbess of Barking, the child of a wealthy family who wished her to marry a powerful lord. She refused him, but told her family she would abide by the decision of Abbess Wulfhild. Wulfhild advised her to become a nun.[12] The other is Wulfthryth, who unlike her cousin Wulfhild had not disdained Edgar's advances. After the birth of their daughter, Edith, Wulfthryth decided to give up both the possession of worldly riches and the love of Edgar, and join a nunnery. Goscelin was clearly impressed by the strength she showed in making and in remaining faithful to this decision.[13]

The commitment of Edith herself to monastic life shows the pattern of directly intervening divine guidance. According to the *life*, a two-year-old Edith, living in the monastery, was given a chance to chose between spiritual and worldly goods. A cloth was spread out before the altar and on it were placed jewels suitable to royal women—crowns and bracelets. The blace veil of the nun, chalice, paten, and psalter were also placed on it. All the nuns prayed God to declare which life Edith should lead. Then the infant was set on the floor. She headed, unswerving, straight for the veil, which she placed on her head.[14] Later, according to Goscelin, Edith had another opportunity to make a choice, and this time she showed her own strength of will in her commitment to the monastic life. After the assassination of her half-brother Edward, she was, we are told, offered the kingdom by princes and people, who thought a 'lady of mature prudence' would be better than young Aethelred, 'an unlearned infant', who was entangled in the death of their half-brother.[15] Yet she rejected their pleas, as Christ rejected the temptation to rule the world. There is no reason to accept this episode as historically accurate, since no other source suggests the offer occurred, and since the Anglo-Saxons had never had a reigning queen. But it is certainly interesting that such a tale could have been told in mid-eleventh century England.[16]

Wulfhild, Leflaed, and Edith all gave up the possibility, and Wulfthryth the possession, of wealth and status, something Goscelin repeatedly expresses in terms of the rejection of golden armbands and purple robes.[17] It is surely not surprising that nun's *vitae* exhibit their strong desire for the monastic life. But it is interesting that these women's desire is shown to be unusually strong, capable of overcoming great temptations or obstacles, because this indicates that women could be perceived as very strong-willed, one might even say, assertive. It is also interesting that the alternative to monastic life is posed mainly as the allurements of a life of wealth and status. This could be Goscelin's emphasis. The women's houses of his day were still, as in the tenth and early eleventh centuries, filled with women from powerful, wealthy families, and Goscelin may have considered it important to use these episodes to point a moral.[18] Yet the anecdotes themselves, I suggest, could well reflect the communities' own priorities. Such tales of strong commitment or marvellous decision-making could have reinforced the members' belief in the correctness of their own decisions.

DEEDS OF CHARITY, ACTS OF HUMILITY

After he has recounted the nuns' resistance to the allure of alternatives to monastic life, Goscelin lets his descriptions of the activities of these women in their monasteries become general and heavily traditional.[19] Of the episodes narrated, a good proportion illustrate either the charity or the humility of the saints. For instance, Goscelin describes the abbess Wulfhild as a model of abstinence, vigils, and prayers, and a very generous giver of alms.[20] Only one of these hagiographical clichés receives the support of an illustrative episode: her charity, shown in the form of hospitality to guests. Once when she was enterataining, her liquor supply was miraculously replenished to keep her guests happy.[21]

Wulfhild is the third holy person of the late tenth century to whom this marvel is attached. A similar story is told of Bishop Aethelwold of Winchester (who, oddly enough, is the recipient of Wulfhild's hospitality), and a third version of the marvel concerns a good friend of Dunstan, Archbishop of Canterbury,—the holy woman Aethelflaed.[22] The popularity of this miracle indicates that it touches a theme important to tenth-century society. I would suggest, then, that in this episode in the life of Wulfhild we see an element in the image of sanctity which goes back to the late tenth century.

Generosity in times of celebration was also important in the life of Edith. While she was a nun under her mother Wulfthryth's guidance, although she herself preferred to fast, she encouraged servants and guests to feast.[23] Edith exhibited other kinds of charity as well. She sought to devote herself to the poor and the sick. The more deformed and diseased sufferers were, the more she served them. She tended the sick, bestowed clothing and alms on the poor, and intervened to protect criminals from their pursuers.[24] Her charity also extended to birds and animals. From the southern wall of the monastery stretched the 'suburb' of the animals, where were enclosed the foreign and native animals which she had received as gifts. She often went there alone to feed them, and they would come and eat from her hand.[25]

Although open-handedness was valued, it could also pose problems. Aelfgifu, who was abbess of Wilton sometime between 1065 and 1067, was known for her great generosity.[26] After Aelfgifu's death, Edith appeared to one of the nuns of Wilton and instructed her that the sisters should pray at once for their abbess. Edith explained that God had given to Edith all of Aelfgifu's sins but one, and Edith intended to persist until she had acquired forgiveness for that last sin. The community seems to have believed it likely that the last sins of Aelfgifu's might have been excessive charity.[27] Another hint that mid-eleventh century communities may have had ambivalent feelings about generosity lies in Goscelin's comment on Edith's care for the animals. He indicates that this was looked at askance, although he does not explain why.[28] It may have been her concern for animals itself, and not her charity to them that was considered worth criticizing. The eleventh century may not have been ready for a Saint Francis.

Humility, like charity, is the focus of a number of episodes. Leflaed, Wulfhild's appointed successor, was inseparable from Wulfhild in life and shared with her, we are told, a deep humility and sense of personal inadequacy.[29] Edith's humility, that of a king's daughter, was inspiring to all. We are specifically told that in her monastery filled with 'famous children of princes, nobles, and the great ones of the realm', one proud kinswoman, the nun Wulfwyn, stood in special need of Edith's example of loving, humble service.[30] Edith's spiritual zeal led her to wear a hairshirt, which she concealed under a delicate tunic and a purple outer garment. Goscelin was impressed with this paradox of humility concealed by display, by the hidden pearl of the hairshirt. He tells us that Bishop Aethelwold was misled by the outer finery, and rebuked Edith. Edith, not in the least abashed, politely replied that God judges the mind, not the clothing, and quoted the Bible at the bishop. Aethelwold was properly reminded that a mind can be just as pure in purple as in sackcloth.[31]

There can be little doubt that Goscelin was interested in evidences of humility because they represented so great a contrast to the status these women would have had both as members of the royal or magnate families, and as abbesses. His rhetorical elaborations make this clear.[32] Humility was always the great virtue of medieval monasticism, but it seems to have become more impressive to Goscelin when it represented great sacrifice. The virtues of humility and charity which Goscelin emphasizes were very traditional monastic virtures by the eleventh century. But the distinctness of the episodes Goscelin relates suggests that these traditional virtues were being lived out freshly in the communities he visited.

MIRACLES PERFORMED IN LIFE

The quite traditional nature of the images of sanctity of these communities is visible also in the miracle episodes. Almost all of the miracles worked by the saints in life fall into the standard categories of healing and prophecy. The spirit of prophecy, for example, was exhibited by Wulfhild when she rebuked a goldsmith of her church for riotous living. His response was a rude one, eliciting from her a prophecy that he would pay for his rudeness. Indeed he did, for he was mute for a year before his death. During that year, he came to regret his rudeness to Wulfhild more than his riotous living.[33] Wulfhild and Edith showed such foreknowledge of several events in their lives.[34]

Prophecies are not abundant in the saints' lives; healings by the living saint are even rarer. Wulfhild worked one healing in her life, curing a blind child.[35] Edith did not heal in life, but her mother Wulfthryth, with extreme reluctance, cured a blind German who insisted she could heal him.[36] According to tradition, Wulfthryth also performed major miracles of protection while still alive. In one case, two of the priests of Wilton had been imprisoned by the reeve of Wilton. Her prayers for them were answered by their return, and the death of the guilty reeve.[37] Another time, a thief took refuge at Wilton. Wulfthryth had the gates opened, and his pursuers, officials of the king, entered after him, and became blind for their daring.[38] As a more effective miracle worker in her life than either her daughter or her cousin, Wulfthryth must have made a strong impression on her community during her life.

MIRACLES WORKED AFTER DEATH

Miracles of protection of one's property and one's people, like those worked by Wulfthryth, were more commonly worked after death. These anglo-saxon abbesses exhibited such kinds of protective power after death, guarding not only their property and their people, but also their own bodies. They also continued to heal and to prophesy after death, although specific episodes of healing after death are not much more numerous than healings in life. One double cure by Wulfhild is recorded, three by Wulfthryth, and four by Edith.[39] These cures affected nuns and oblates, dependents of the monastery, or vaguely identified women and children.[40] The sphere of influence of these saints seems to have been fairly local. As we might expect, their own communities made the most demands on them.

The devotion of their communities to these saints is revealed also in the saints' appearances to their nuns to make requests or to give essential information. Wulfhild appeared before the translation of her body to ask that it be hidden from the gaze of bystanders.[41] Wulfthryth indicated to Aelfgifu that the two would lie side by side in death.[42] Edith, in particular, was a frequent visitor. She appeared to her mother thirty days after her death to reassure her that she had triumphed over Satan.[43] She appeared to King Aethelred and also to a magnate when she wished her body moved to a better site, and she appeared once to Dunstan giving him instructions about her translation and a second time reinforcing her message with St Denis's assistance.[44] Edith appeared to Cnut in response to his prayers as he was caught in a bad storm *en route* to Denmark.[45] Again she appeared far from home to a stormtossed english seafarer when Ealdred, Archbishop of York, called on her while voyaging to Jerusalem.[46] In both cases, she calmed the storm. Edith's revelation of herself to a number of great men is indicative of the greater extent of her cult, but like the others, she also appeared to her nuns: Goscelin recorded six such visits.[47]

Certain nuns seem particularly likely to have experienced visions: Aelfgifu of Wilton appears to have been such a one. Aelfgifu may also have stimulated other members of her community to be receptive of visions, because the two chapters dealing with Aelfgifu contain no less than seven manifestations (six visions and a heavenly voice).[48] At Barking, Wulfrunna, also called Judith, was deeply devoted to her community's holy abbesses. When Wulfhild appeared to one of the sisters at Barking, asking her to shield her body from the gaze of onlookers during the translation, Wulfrunna, hearing of it, asked that the sister permit her to perform the duty. Like Jacob, she received the benediction.[49] When the coffin was opened, only Wulfrunna dared touch it, to learn that the incorrupt body was indeed solid.[50] Later, Wulfrunna reminded Wulfhild that the saint now wore Wulfrunna's robe, and she asked Wulfhild to provide her with another. Miraculously, the robe was provided.[51] Wulfrunna clearly expected her saints to aid her.[52]

CARE FOR THEIR COMMUNITIES

Members of the community at Wilton sometimes complained about what they saw as Edith's lack of concern for them. At one point, the sisters murmured among themselves that Edith cared more for outsiders than for her own. In a vision to one of the nuns, Edith rebuked them for the smallness of their minds, reminding them that no one in Christ is an outsider. Moreover, she told the community, nothing was more important to her than was her daughters' salvation. Some, though, might need to be tried 'in the furnace of patience and penitence' before they would be worthy to join Edith in heaven. Edith's message strengthened the weaker sisters.[53]

The saint was less tolerant when a sister complained to the bishop (Goscelin's own patron) that Wilton was losing its property because Edith had no power with God. That night, Edith appeared to another sister stating in answer to the first sister's criticism. 'I can do anything'. On learning of this message, the original complainer asked Edith's forgiveness.[54]

In fact, Edith did take a number of measures to protect her property. The most dramatic case occurred in the lifetime of Queen Emma, wife first of Aethelred and then of Cnut. One of the king's magnates took a certain estate of Edith's and died impenitent. While his friends and kindred were sitting about the corpse, the corpse sat up and asked for help. 'The terrible majesty of Saint Edith and her intolerable indignation' were preventing his soul from finding a place of rest. He could not stay in heaven or on earth. He asked that his friends beg Emma to come to him and give the lands back to Edith . When this had been done, he died in peace, now having Edith as a protector.[55]

PROTECTION OF THEIR OWN BODIES

The saint had God's aid to protect her body as well as her lands. The body of the dead saint was protected from disrespect in a number of ways. Fraudulent craftsmen, making a shrine out of lightly gilded silver instead of the gold they were given, were struck blind for their presumption.[56] People trying to steal bits of cloth from Edith's corpse were miraculously prevented.[57] Wulfhild protected her corpse from being touched by unworthy hands on several occasions, rendering her body immobile until the unworthy ones were rejected.[58] Such miracles in which the saint's body is protected from harm or disrespect are quite common in these *lives*. The miracles, like the virtues, of the saints are fully in the mainstream of hagiographical tradition.

CONCLUSION

The concerns of Wilton and Barking (and no doubt of many another late anglo-saxon nunnery) come alive in these *lives*. In them we see the virtues that impressed the communities, and the need they had for saintly models and saintly aid. Charity and humility are the virtues the *lives* most emphasize. It seems likely to me that these interests go beyond Goscelin the hagiographer to the communities themselves. The ambivalent attitude to charity, for example, seems most easily understood as an expression of both memories of the saints' desire to respond to the needs of God's creatures and the communities' fears lest lavish giving threaten their survival. Had Goscelin himself been the source of the emphasis, it seems unlikely that he would have cast doubt on the virtue. Likewise, Goscelin may have believed that these houses needed to keep the virtue of humility in mind, but the evidence suggests that the communities did also. Otherwise, for example, Edith's community would not have remembered and passed down the name of the nun Wulfwyn, who was proud.

The nuns' dread of losing their property is revealed by the saints' miracles as well as by their caution about charity. Help in maintaining property was very important to these communities: such protection receives as much, if not more, attention than does healing the sick. The nuns perceive their patrons as women of power, protecting their own bodies from disrespect, their people from disease and mistreatment, their property from the greed of the great. For those of us who analyze the status of women in the Middle Ages, it is important to realize that these women were not second-class miracle workers in the eyes of their communities. If we were to compare these women saints to the great miracle-workers of the tenth century, especially Swithun of Winchester, Edmund of Bury, and the peripatetic Cuthbert of Durham, we would find similar powers. The male saints, too, healed ailments, freed from fetters, appeared in visions with instructions and advice, and protected their own—their bodies, their people, their property—from violence through violence.[59] Women saints were expected to provide the same services the male miracle-workers were providing in the later tenth century and, in the eyes of their communities, they obliged. The *lives* of Edith and Wulfhild provide us with a clear statement of the eleventh century's belief in the ability of women saints, like men saints, to channel God's power to those who called on them.

After death, these women remained both channels of power and enduring models of strength of will and faith. We might, for example, consider the persistent devotion of Wulfrunna-Judith; the unfazed and chilling response of Wulfhild to the insolent goldsmith; the calm self-possession with which Edith answered the criticism of her clothing made by the formidable Bishop Aethelwold. In their *lives*, the great male saints of the tenth century, like Aethelwold himself, exhibited just such strength of character. The supreme example of the strength of will and faith of these women may be their commitment to the religious life, which rendered them resistant to great temptation. In assessing the emphasis of these *lives* on the stories of overcoming royal pursuit or resisting parental pressure, we need to keep in mind the possibility that one reason why these tales loom so large for the hagiographer and for the communities which told them is because they make such excellent metaphors for, and examples of, the strength of faith that makes a saint.

NOTES

1. The original of this paper was presented at the Fifth Berkshire Conference, Vassar College, June, 1981.

2. The classic account of the revival is that of David Knowles in chapter 2 of *The Monastic Order in England*, 1st ed. (Cambridge, 1940). Knowles said little of the women's houses.

3. I discussed the evidence provided by contemporary hagiography in a paper 'Women and Monasticism in Tenth Century England' given at the 14th International Conference of Medieval Studies at Kalamazoo, May 1979. M.A. Meyer has been investigating the charter evidence for women's houses in the late anglo-saxon period. The result of his work can be seen, for example, in 'Women and the Tenth Century English Monastic Reform', *Révue Bénédictine* 87 (1977) 34–61.

4. The *life* and *translation* of Wulfhild was published by Mario Esposito, 'La Vie de Saint Wulfilda par Goscelin de Cantorbery', *Analecta Bollandiana* 32 (1913) 10–26. More recently, Marvin Colker has included it in his 'Texts of Jocelin of Canterbury which relate to the history of Barking Abbey', *Studia Monastica* 7 (1965) 418–34. Goscelin's *vita Edithae* was published by André Wilmart, 'La Légende de Sainte Édith en prose et vers par le moine Goscelin', *Analecta Bollandiana* 32 (1913) 5–101, and 56 (1938) 265–307. The *lives* are of particular significance to anyone trying to construct a picture of women's monasticism in the tenth century because they seem to be the two *lives* of tenth-century women saints written closest in time to the lives of the protagonists.

5. Goscelin has been studied more and more of late. The standard description of his life and work is that of C.H. Talbot in his introduction to The *'Liber Confortatorius* of Goscelin of Saint Bertin', *Analecta Monastica*, ser. 3, 37 (1955) 5–22. Most subsequent descriptions are based on Talbot. See, for example, Sharon Elkins, 'Female Religious in Twelfth Century England', (dissertation, Harvard University, 1976) 26–36; Colker, 'Texts', 383–92; Frank Barlow, ed. and trans., *Vita Aedwardi Regis/The Life of King Edward*, Nelson's Medieval Texts (London, 1962) 91–111. Talbot, p. 13, lists thirty-one saints of whom Goscelin is known to have written *lives* or other works of hagiography. Of the women, most were early anglo-saxon abbesses: Earcongota, Eormenilda, Ethelburga, Etheldreda, Hildelitha, Milburga, Mildred, Osyth (?), Sexburga, Werberga, and Withburga.

6. Barlow, *Vita Aedwardi* 94.

7. Quoted by Talbot, *'Liber'*, 17, note 83, from the *'Libellus Contra Inanes sanctae virginis Mildrethae usurpatores'*.

8. These dates are based on internal evidence supplied by the *lives*. David Knowles, C.N.L. Brooke, and Vera C.M. London, edd., *The Heads of Religious Houses-England and Wales 940–1216* (Cambridge, 1972) give slightly different dates. Some of their entries suggest more attention was given to twelfth-century authors than to the eleventh-century lives.

9. *Vita Wulfildae* ii: 'Haec est angusta via qua vite ianuam incontaminata attigit'. (I am using both the Exposito and the Colker editions.)

10. *Vita Wulfildae* iii.

11. Many of the fictional *acta* concern women who chose martyrdom over marriage. Goscelin himself emphasized this parallel in describing Wulfhild's spurning of Edgar (*Vita Wulfhildae* ii and iii). He compared her to Thecla, Agatha, and Lucia. Many of the frankish saints had to deal with such opposition: see Suzanne Wemple, 'Contemplative Life: The Search for Female Autonomy in the Frankish Kingdom', *Anima* 6 (1980) 131–36. Bede has given us an anglo-saxon example in the great saint Aethelthryth (in the *Historia Ecclesiastica* IV, 19–20. Another anglo-saxon example is Osyth of Essex. For Osyth's trials, see Denis Bethell, 'The Lives of St. Osyth of Essex and St. Osyth of Aylesbury', *Analecta Bollandiana* 88 (1970) 85–87.

12. *Vita Wulfildae* vii.

13. Goscelin, *Vita Edithae* 4. It was, as Wulfhild had discovered, hard to gainsay

Edgar, and according to the *vita* Bishop Aethelwold had to intervene to aid Wulfthryth.

14. *Vita Edithae* 5.

15. Ibid., 19. 'melius scilicet mature prudencie dominam quam infantilem inscitiam tanto regno imperare posse'.

16. Since Goscelin is not known as an hagiographer who added episodes to what he was told, it could well be that Edith's community was the source of this episode, which is in itself a very interesting possibility.

17. In the *vita* of Wulfhild (ii), he emphasized the rich clothing put on her in the banqueting scene at Wherwell, and later Wulfhild's divesting herself of it rather ritualistically in the privy. Leflaed lived '*inter monilia et radantia ornamenta*' while she sighed for the rewards of virginity (ch. vii). The centrality of clothing and jewelry in her choice of monastic over royal life is clear in the testing of Edith, described above. When Wulfthryth chose the convent, she went there without her royal robes: '*pro aurotexta purpura induitur nigra peregrinantis a Domino tunica, pro aureis monilibus ornatur pudore, pro regali diademate fusco velatur flammeolo, obumbrata caput in die belli divino umbraculo*' (ch. 4). Throughout these *lives*, clothing is an extremely important symbol for Goscelin. Perhaps the origin of this lies in the ceremonial clothing change of the consecration ceremony. When I read this paper at the Berkshire Conference, the chair of the session, Penelope Johnson, made the interesting suggestion that Goscelin's fascination with clothing might stem from the general emphasis of medieval moralists that women were especially prone to personal vanity, and gave excessive attention to their clothing, in particular. Thus Goscelin might have been attempting to emphasize the lack of this failing in his heroines.

18. For the presence of noble and royal women in these houses, see, for example, Barlow, *Vita Aedwardi*, 96–97, on Wilton. Goscelin himself makes such a comment on the backgrounds of the women at Wilton (*Vita Edithae* 10).

19. Sharon Elkins has pointed this out in her 'Female Religious' (note 5 above).

20. *Vita Wulfildae* iiii.

21. *Ibid.*, vi

22. Wulfstan, *Vita S. Aethelwoldi* 12; PL 137:79–104. B., *Vita S. Dunstani*, 10; ed. W. Stubbs, *Memorials of St. Dunstan*, Rolls Series 63 (1874) 3–52.

23. *Vita Edithae* 10.

24. *Ibid.*

25. *Ibid.*

26. *Translation* (Book II of the *Life of Wilmart*), 20.

27. Comments Goscelin Ch. 20: '[*Quam h*]anc *offensam estimus, nisi quod in virtute hospitalitatis* [*virtut*]*em excesserit, quem tamen excessum hospitalitas excusaveri*[*t*]'.

28. *Vita Edithae* 10. Goscelin ends the chapter: '*Si quis tamen ut nimium iustus, carpere quam laudare malit hec studia circa huiusmodi animalia, quasi ex regia natura incitata aut actu aut memoratu supervacanea, viderit ne suis virtutibus sanctior sit hec offensa, ubi ardua caritas ac vitae sanctitatis excusat, immo adornat omnia*'.

29. *Vita Wulfildae* vii.

30. *Vita Editbae* 10: '*Erat tunc illa virginialis et sponsalis Christi familia ex diversis seculi dignitatibus, ut solet, collecta: clara principium, procerum, optimatumque regni pignora*'. The kinswoman who needed the example of humility is even named (her name was Wulfwyn).

31. *Vita Edithae*, 12.

32. Examples of his thorough development of the theme of humility are *Vita Wulfildae*, vii, and *Vita Editbae*, 10 and 12. We can not be sure that the communities shared Goscelin's emphasis, inasmuch as they seem not to have provided Goscelin with many episodes illustrative of humility. Edith's hair shirt (*Vita Editbae* 12) is intended as an example of humility, and humility lies behind the rather simple episode in Wulfhild's life (vii) in which she points out that she and Leflaed are good only for carrying water, and are not very good even at that.

33. *Vita Wulfildae* viii.

34. When Wulfhild was expelled from Barking by the king's mother, she foretold when she would return (*Vita Wulfildae* viiii). She knew and foretold that Leflaed would be her successor (vii). Finally, she foretold the date of her own death (x). Edith had a dream which prefigured the death of her half-brother King Edward (*Vita Edithae* 18). She also foreknew where she would be buried (24). Edith's message to the expectant parents of a future nun and abbess, Brihtgifu, may be intended to show foreknowledge that Brihtgifu would join the community at Wilton (26).

35. *Vita Wulfildae* v.

36. *Translatio Edithae* 2.

37. Ibid., 4.

38. Ibid., 5.

39. Wulfhild, who had been abbess at Horton was well as Barking, shows her double rule by making one poor woman, blind and unable to walk, seek a cure for each affliction at a different house. Given back her sight at Horton, she had to crawl to Barking to gain the use of her legs (*Vita Wulfildae* xi). At Wulfthryth's tomb a child who had bad vision and could not walk was cured of both ailments; a paralytic woman was healed, and a sister was cured of dysentery (*Translatio Edithae* 9,10,11). Edith cured a future nun of Wilton when she was an infant living in the house, and healed the withered limbs of a kinswoman of Abbess Brihtgifu (*Vita Edithae* 17 and 18). She also healed Abbess Aelfgifu's eyes (19). The final miracle in the *vita* (23) concerns the giving of a tongue, and his speech, to a mute boy working as a laborer at Wilton.

40. The exceptions are Wulfthryth's cure of the blind German (a german priest of Wilton plays an important role in this episode) and Edith's cure of the dancer from Kolbec who was wandering through Europe looking for a cure (*Translatio Edithae*, 3 and 16).

41. *Vita Wulfildae* xiii.

42. *Translatio Edithae* 20.

43. *Vita Edithae* 25.

44. *Translatio Edithae* 1.

45. Ibid., 12.

46. Ibid.

47. She appeared to Abbess Aelfgifu when curing her eye ailment (*Translatio Edithae*, 19). Both Abbess Brihtgifu and Aelfgifu had visions in which Edith indicated that Aelfgifu would become abbess (20). Edith appeared to a sister with the message that prayer was needed that Aelfgifu be forgiven the last of her sins (20). Edith also appeared to her sisters to assure them of her protection for the community (21 and 22). The woman who appeared to the mute to instruct him what to do to be healed is, no doubt, Edith herself (23).

48. *Translatio Edithae*, 19 and 20.

49. *Vita Wulfildae* xiii.

50. Ibid.

51. Ibid., xv.

52. The *Vita Wulfildae* also contains two interesting episodes in which Wulfrunna-Judith makes demands on St Aethelburga of Barking, and gets results (xvi and xvii).

53. *Translatio Edithae* 21.

54. Ibid., 22.

55. Ibid., 14. 'Ecce sancte Edithe maiestas terribilis et indignatio intolerabilis . . .'. Another episode of Edith's persecution of someone who stole her property occurs in chaper 15.

56. Ibid., 13.

57. A woman who tried to steal part of the clothes from Edith's corpse found herself unable to leave the church until she had given back the stolen cloth (*Vita Edithae* 27); another person seeking to take a piece of Edith's garment was stopped when blood sprang from the corpse when his knife grazed the body while cutting the robe (*Translatio Edithae* 2). A sister was stopped from cutting a piece from Edith's head-band when the head of the dead saint rose in indignation (*Ibid.*, 2).

58. When the recently deceased saint was being carried from London, where she had died, back to Barking, her coffin could not be moved as long as a sinner with whom she had been angry had his hands on it (*Vita Wulfildae* xii). Years later, during her translation, her sarcophagus could not be moved as long as a sinful woman had her hands on it (*Ibid.*, xiiii).

59. I analyzed the miracles of the tenth-century saints at length in my dissertation, 'The Latin Hagiography of England, 900–1066', (dissertation, University of California, Berkeley, 1974). See especially, chapter 4: 'Miracles'.

GENEALOGICAL RELATIONSHIPS OF THE SAINTS AND IMPORTANT ROYAL CONNECTIONS

(With lists of the successors of the saints who are mentioned in the *lives*)

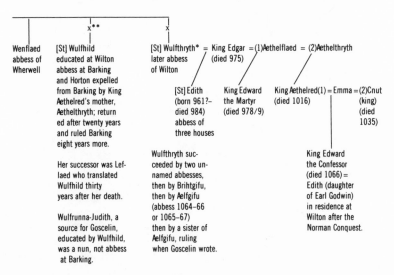

Wenflaed
abbess of
Wherwell

[St] Wulfhild
educated at Wilton
abbess at Barking
and Horton expelled
from Barking by King
Aethelred's mother,
Aethelthryth; return
ed after twenty years
and ruled Barking
eight years more.

Her successor was Lef-
laed who translated
Wulfhild thirty
years after her death.

Wulfrunna-Judith, a
source for Goscelin,
educated by Wulfhild,
was a nun, not abbess
at Barking.

[St] Wulfthryth*
later abbess
of Wilton

[St] Edith
(born 961?–
died 984)
abbess of
three houses

Wulfthryth suc-
ceeded by two un-
named abbesses,
then by Brihtgifu,
then by Aelfgifu
(abbess 1064–66
or 1065–67)
then by a sister of
Aelfgifu, ruling
when Goscelin wrote.

King Edgar = (1) Aethelflaed = (2) Aethelthryth
(died 975)

King Edward
the Martyr
(died 978/9)

King Aethelred (1) = Emma = (2) Cnut
(died 1016)   (king)
                              (died
                              1035)

King Edward
the Confessor
(died 1066) =
Edith (daughter
of Earl Godwin)
in residence at
Wilton after the
Norman Conquest.

KEY: horizontal lines represent sibling relationships
 vertical lines represent parent/child relationships
 = means married; =(1), =(2) means married first, second
 x means unnamed in *lives* and unidentifiable

NOTES: * probably not a formal alliance
 ** the *lives* seem to imply a sibling relationship

Why English Nunneries
Had No History:
A Study of the Problems
of the English Nunneries
Founded after the Conquest

Sally Thompson

THE SHORTAGE OF EVIDENCE for a study of english nunneries founded after the Conquest is remarkable and has puzzled many. Writers ranging from seventeenth-century antiquaries to twentieth-century historians working on articles for the Victoria County Histories have commented on the lack of sources for the early history of these nunneries. 'Of the early foundation of the priory of Benedictine nuns at Broomhall within the limits of Windsor Forest nothing is known', wrote Cox in the Victoria County History for Berkshire.[1] Another would-be historian of the nuns, trying to collect evidence about the foundation of a Buckinghamshire priory, solved his problem with the statement, 'The nunnery of Little or Minchin Marlow, *prioratus de fontibus de Merlawe*, may be said to have no history'.[2]

Without entering into a philosophical discussion as to whether it is possible for any institution to 'have no history', an examination of the documentary sources for the post-Conquest english nunneries provides interesting insights into the circumstances surrounding the foundation of many of these houses, and the very scarcity of documents probably highlights particular problems which faced women who wanted to enter religious life in England in the twelfth and early thirteenth centuries. By 1250 at least one hundred forty-two nunneries were in existence.[3] Only nine of these were, beyond doubt, old foundations established before the Conquest, although it is possible that others were in some sense re-foundations of earlier communities. These nine older houses in many ways formed a distinct group: they were abbeys rather than priories and they were generally considerably richer than post-Conquest foundations.[4] Leaving them aside, I propose in this study to concentrate on the houses apparently founded after the Conquest and look at the evidence for their history in the twelfth and thirteenth centuries.

Primary sources for the study of these nunneries are indeed meager. Series of original charters are extant for a handful of houses—for example, Nuneaton in Warwickshire[5] and Wix in Essex—some of them forgeries[6] —as Lacock in Wiltshire[7] and such gilbertine houses as Bullington and Sempringham.[8] Groups of charters survive for some of the Lincolnshire convents such as Greenfield, and a smaller number for Stixwould [9] and for the Cambridgeshire nunneries of St Radegund and Hinchingbrooke.[10] As for cartularies and registers, only seventeen are extant, of which two are mere fragments and one is badly burnt. There is evidence for the existence of twelve other cartularies, and short extracts from seven of these have been copied by antiquaries and so survive.[11]

But for the majority of nunneries the main sources are the documents and references transcribed in the *Monasticon Anglicanum*.[12] One Yorkshire nunnery, Thimbleby, was so obscure as to miss even the attention of Dugdale and Dodsworth and was first spotlighted in an article written in 1886.[13] There is some information about the nunneries on the royal records. The pipe rolls record occasional payments to nuns, and some charters were confirmed and enrolled on the charter rolls and other royal records. Bishops' records provide a more fertile source for the history of women's houses, and Eileen Power made great use of episcopal registers in her study of medieval english nunneries.[14] But by taking the end of the thirteenth century as her starting point, she avoided the problem of the earlier period for which there are no registers.[15] Some evidence for the nunneries in the twelfth and thirteenth centuries can be gleaned from episcopal *acta* and from papal bulls, but finding it is a hard struggle. Hugo, writing a history of the nunneries in Somerset in 1896, summed up the situation when he spoke of references which 'however at first sight or to general readers apparently small and unimportant are all that are presented by enormous masses of records, long searches among which have oftentimes to be made before the grain of information which is the object of these investigations rewards the explorer'.[16]

FIRE AND FLOOD

This brief overview of the documentary sources which survive leads to the question: why were they so few. The survival of any historical document is, of course, subject to the vagaries of historical accident. Fire was a major hazard and charters seem to have been destroyed at seven nunneries. At an early date the first buildings at Markyate were burnt down, possibly with a loss of documents.[17] The cartulary at Nun Keeling in Yorkshire, dating from the sixteenth century, was badly damaged in the fire at the Cotton library in 1731.[18] At Ickleton the priory's records were said to have been destroyed in the rebellion of 1381.[19] Floods also constituted a problem. The nuns of Stratford, Middlesex, had their lands flooded on many occasions by the river Lea[20] and the ladies at Crabhouse in Norfolk seem to have had to abandon their original site because of flooding.[21] Other evidence reveals serious floods at five other nunneries.[22] It would not be difficult to list similar accidents for houses of monks and canons, but it is not impossible that the nuns were more careless with their candles or less fortunate in their choice of sites than their brothers.[23]

IGNORANCE OF LATIN

In addition to such natural disasters there may have been particular reasons why fewer records survive for nunneries than for monasteries of men. Knowledge and understanding of Latin may have presented a special problem. Eileen Power has pointed out that in the thirteenth century there are references to nuns' ignorance of Latin and in the fourteenth nearly all the episcopal injunctions to nunneries were in French. By the fifteenth century Alnwick visitation records provide evidence for the complete ignorance of Latin in some houses, with the prioress unable to understand episcopal mandates. There is no comparable evidence for such ignorance in the men's houses visited by the bishop.[24] This lack of learning might well have had an effect on the keeping and survival of records. In 1440 the prioress of Langley informed a visiting prelate that she had the foundation charter for her house but she could not understand the writings.[25] A similar difficulty in understanding muniments is the reason given by the author of the english version of the cartulary of Godstow for his work of translating the Latin into an intelligible form—

'And, for as muche as women of relygyone in redynge bokys of latyn, byn excusyd of grete undurstondyng where it is not her modyr tonge. Therefore how be hyt that they wolde rede her bokys of remembraunce and of her munymentys wryte in latyn, for defaute of undurstondyng they toke ofte tymes grete hurt and hyndraunce.'[26]

Once charters and muniments written in Latin had become unintelligible there may have seemed little point in preserving them.

THE FAILURE OF THE NEW ORDERS TO PROVIDE FOR WOMEN

Another reason for the lack of surviving sources for the early history of nunneries may be their inevitable dependence on chaplains and the difficulties of their relationships with men. By the very nature of their religious calling a community of women depended on the services of a priest for the celebration of Mass and such other needs of their devotional life as the hearing of confession. Men would have been needed to help in other ways—managing the nuns' estates, working as labourers and acting for the women in lawsuits, particularly if the nuns were strictly enclosed. Finding men to serve the nuns seems not always to have been easy. The new Orders of the twelfth century were in many ways not able to cope with religious women. The Premonstratensians originally welcomed ladies with a religious vocation. St Norbert's dedication and the power of his personality attracted women as well as men to follow him and there is evidence of the presence of sisters as well as brothers at several of the early premonstratensian houses.[27] But problems soon seem to have arisen. In 1198 a bull of Innocent III referred to a decree passed by the Order stating that no more sisters were to be received and suggesting as the reason the discord they caused.[28] A dislike of the whole tribe of religious women was forcibly expressed by the abbot of one premonstratensian house towards the end of the thirteenth century. He and his canons decided that the wickedness of women surpassed all, and that they would in no way receive any sisters *ad augmentum nostrae perditionis*. They went on to vow that no sister would be received into their house for the next fifty years and they clearly hoped that their successors would have the sense to renew the ban.[29]

The early Cistercians firmly rejected any contact with women—religious or secular.[30] Although by the thirteenth century they had been forced to overcome their original scruples and include communities of women within their Order, they too found the *cura monialium* could be a burden. Apart from the decrees of the General Chapter in the early thirteenth century which vainly tried to stop the incorporation of nunneries, a statute of 1228 appointed special auditors to hear cases involving the nuns and so remove the tedious burden of feminine complaints from the over-worked General Chapter. In 1222 the cistercian abbots petitioned the pope with the request that they not be forced to send monks to live at women's houses to help the nuns with their temporal affairs, for this gave rise to matters to the prejudice of the Order and the danger of their souls.[31]

Robert of Arbrissel is the religious leader of the period who has the greatest claim to be a supporter of feminine vocation.[32] He attracted both men and women by the vigour and eloquence of his call to repentance and apostolic poverty, and he appears to have shown particular concern for the women. At Fontevrault he established a community for both sexes, but the men's duty was to serve the spiritual and temporal needs of the nuns, and they were placed firmly under the control of the abbess. This development has been hailed as signifying Robert's enlightened concept of the status and position of women.[33] An examination of the evidence, however, suggests that he saw this masculine subservience within the context of penitential discipline.[34] The self-sacrifice involved in serving a community of religious women was penitence indeed. On his deathbed, Robert gave his followers the choice of abandoning their charge and renouncing their obedience to the ladies of Fontevrault. His biographer, himself a brother of the order, recorded with pride that none took this easy road.[35] But papal bulls dating from the first half of the twelfth century, stating that brothers from Fontevrault were not to be received into any other Order, and urging bishops to force those who had left to return, suggest a considerable measure of discontent.[36]

THE NEW ORDERS IN ENGLAND

The new Orders of the twelfth century, therefore, did not solve the problem of providing support for nuns. In England only three houses of the Order of Fontevrault were founded for women, and three premonstratensian nunneries.[37] One house, Harrold in Bedfordshire, was founded as a member of the reformed order of augustinian canons, the Arrouaisians —another group which initially welcomed women.[38] Abbot Gervase of the mother house of Arrouaise seems to have played an important personal part in the foundation of the nunnery. According to one account some of the early members of Harrold were his blood sisters, *sorores carnales*.[39] But by the end of the twelfth century clear evidence appeared of discord between the nuns and the canons of Arrouaise. An attempt was made to subject Harrold to the abbey of Missenden, also a member of the Order. In 1177 Abbot James of Arrouaise granted the churches of Harrold and Arrouaise to the canons of Missenden.[40] No mention is made of the nuns but the intention of the grant was presumably to place them under the canons' authority. The nuns were not happy with this solution, probably because they resented the degree of control exercised by the canons. They campaigned vigorously for their independence and were eventually freed from all subjection to the houses of both Missenden and Arrouaise in return for a token payment.[41] There is no evidence that the nuns maintained further links with the canons.

There is little to suggest that in England the cistercian Order played a significant part in supporting nunneries in the twelfth and first half of the thirteenth century. Twenty-seven houses are listed as cistercian in Knowles and Hadcock, but of these, only two, and one a mid-thirteenth century foundation, were clearly officially members of the Order and had close links with cistercian monks.[42] Many of the other houses are described as cistercian only in later sources, and sixteen of them are sometimes recorded as belonging to another Order, suggesting a degree of ambivalence.[43] An entry on the close roll of 1270 reveals the abbot of Cîteaux in a letter to the king expressly rejecting the claims of six nunneries to be cistercian.[44]

An obvious solution to the problems of the intrinsic dependency of women following a religious vocation was the establishment of a double order as at Fontevrault. In England this was the achievement of the Gilbertines,[45]—the only new Order of the twelfth century which was specifically English. Gilbert of Sempringham had not wanted to found an Order and the organisation which developed under his guidance was the product of practical necessities and advice from the Cistercians,[46] themselves unwilling to undertake the care of nuns. The Order of Sempringham initially enjoyed a measure of success—it was said that by Gilbert's death it numbered about 700 canons and 1,500 nuns.[47] But there were suspicions about the moral dangers of such double establishments. In their revolt the discontented lay-brothers cited the close proximity of canons and nuns as a problem,[48] and the scandal of the nun of Watton[49] must have caused some unease and probably led to stricter rules about the segregation of the sexes. It is interesting that the later foundations of the Order were for canons only, and the gilbertine double houses never spread far beyond the borders of Lincolnshire.

PROBLEMS IN OBTAINING CHAPLAINS

St Gilbert was remarkable in that, albeit unwillingly, he founded an Order with a clear constitutional framework which provided men—canons and lay brothers—to care for the needs of nuns, and an organisation which linked the houses and provided for their mutual support. The remaining english nunneries classed as either benedictine or augustinian were largely isolated units. Some of these individual houses not belonging to the gilbertine Order seem at their foundation to have depended on a brother or canon who appears to have taken the initiative in establishing a community in the same way as St Gilbert helped the seven maidens at Sempringham. At Clerkenwell in London the earliest charter of the founder, Jordan de Briset, shows that he made his grant to a certain brother Robert who was to found the community.[50] At Swine priory in Yorkshire, another brother, Robert, seems to have gathered nuns around him for the original foundation and then acted as its director or *magister*.[51] At Nun Appleton, also in Yorkshire, the earliest extant grant of the founder was made to a brother Richard and the nuns there.[52] Such nunneries, even if originally helped by a priest or canon, were still left with the continuing problem of the need for masculine help. Difficulties in obtaining this support may well explain the apparent changes of Order of many of the nunneries. The alternate classification of numerous houses as augustinian or benedictine[53] possibly reflects the Order of the particular men whom they managed to obtain as chaplains. It is significant that the nunneries which seemed to possess the greatest sense of stability as regards their Order are the gilbertine houses and the convents of the Order of Fontevrault[54]—all double establishments where masculine support was secured by an organisational framework.

Problems in obtaining suitable chaplains and the ensuing lack of any degree of continuity may well have presented an additional hazard for the amassing of archives and the survival of documents. There is very little evidence as to who wrote the extant charters. An occasional witness list is terminated by a name—always masculine—coupled with the description 'who wrote this charter'.[55] As M. T. Clanchy has pointed out, the art of writing, frequently thought of as a laborious task equal to manual labour, was not considered an integral part of literacy as it is today, but as something in many ways distinct.[56] The translator of the Godstow cartulary gave as another reason for his labours the difficulties the nuns had in finding learned and true men to advise them.[57] The prioress of Ankerwyke returned his original mandate to Bishop Alnwick instead of the certificate he requested, saying she did not understand it herself and had she no man of skill or other lettered person to instruct her what to do.[58] Often the responsibility of drawing up charters recording grants to a monastery fell to the beneficiary. It may well be that the nuns did not have this skill themselves and found it difficult to obtain the services of those who did.

PROBLEMS OF POVERTY

Another factor that probably endangered the collection and survival of documents was poverty. The payment of scribes as well as the provision of wax and ink could be expensive, more so possibly than the parchment unless this was of very fine quality.[59] Enrollment on the royal records would have involved payment. The majority of nunneries founded after the Conquest certainly seem to have been poor.[60] Claims of poverty, particularly when made in the context of avoiding taxation, must be treated with some caution, then as now. Marham, founded in 1249, did not qualify for the Norwich taxation of 1254; probably because of this it was also omitted from the taxation of 1291, although by that date the nunnery had acquired considerably more endowments.[61] Many other nunneries are not mentioned in the returns for the taxation of Pope Nicholas. The figures that are given, incomplete as they are, vary from ten shillings *per annum* for St Margaret's Ivinghoe to nearly £200 for Godstow.[62] But a house such as Godstow, founded by a noble lady and favoured by kings, was exceptional. The majority of founders and patrons of nunneries generally came from a less wealthy and less important section of society. In Yorkshire it has been shown that William de Percy is the only representative of the baronial class to feature in the list of founders of monasteries for women.[63] Others, like William de Arches and his family, who were responsible for the foundation of three nunneries,[64] though important men locally, were not of baronial rank. The same is generally true of the southern houses. Exceptions—such as Amesbury, refounded in 1177 by Henry II, Nuneaton founded by Robert, earl of Leicester, and his wife Avicia, Elstow founded by the neice of William I, Marham, Godstow and Lacock founded by widows of noble rank,[65] were among wealthier houses that reflected the relative prosperity of their founders.

The initial endowment of many nunneries seems to have been small. At the convent of Haliwell in London an eloquent letter of Bishop Gilbert Foliot asking the Bishop of Lincoln to confirm the grant of a church to the nunnery, referred to the site and endowments of the house as so restricted as to be more suitable for burial than sustenance.[66] For the London houses, such small beginnings did not prove a permanent drawback; they were able to benefit from numerous small grants from wealthy citizens and eventually obtain a sizeable income.[67] Other nunneries were not so fortunate. The story of the foundation of Thetford even implies that impoverished surroundings were regarded as particularly suitable for nuns. Thetford was originally a small cell of Bury St Edmunds. By about 1174 only two religious survived there. Depressesd by poverty and intolerable conditions they approached Abbot Hugh and expressed a strong desire to withdraw. At their suggestion the abbot and nuns of Bury St Edmunds agreed to admit in their place some nuns who had before been living at Ling. Some additional endowments were given to the community of women there but the nuns had to make a payment to the infirmary of the abbey in return.[68] Similarly, at St Albans the *Gesta Abbatum* recorded with little suggestion of unease that the women at de Pré and Sopwell, two communities under the control of the abbey, were barely able to support the necessities of life.[69]

Apart from small initial endowments and less wealthy patrons, the poverty of the nunneries may have been compounded by pressure on them to receive more inmates than they could afford. To achieve financial stability, a balance had to be maintained between endowments and the number in the community. There are hints in the sources that patrons exerted pressure to gain admittance for their candidates. A papal bull issued at the request of the nuns of Carrow in Norfolk stated that the patrons of the house were not to force the ladies to receive more inmates than their income could maintain.[70] Another bull instructing the monks of St Albans not to lay burdens on the women at de Pré may well reflect similar pressures.[71]

In all probability it was usual for a grant to be made when a new recruit entered a nunnery. Such a gift, though necessary for practical purposes, could raise the suggestion of the sale of a spiritual benefit; and the poverty of the nunneries may have been further aggravated by anxieties about simony. According to his hagiographer, when Archbishop Edmund Rich wanted to find places for his two sisters in a nunnery, the only house which did not require a grant as a condition of entry was Catesby in Northamptonshire. This was the house the saintly archbishop chose as being the only one free of simony.[72] Numerous charters recording grants to nunneries contain the words *cum filia mea* or *cum matre mea*, showing that the donation was linked with the entry into the religious life of a member of the donor's family.[73] The size of such grants varied considerably. They could be very small indeed. In the second half of the twelfth century canonists became increasingly concerned about simoniacal entry into the religious life. It was emphasised that any gift was to be a voluntary offering and any pact about a grant made before or at entry seems to have been forbidden, while a gift made after the reception of the new entrant was more acceptable.[74] This might help to explain why charters show the Rich family making grants to Catesby in spite of the archbishop's scruples about simony.[75] But such unease and ambivalence presumably weakened the monasteries' bargaining position.

In the thirteenth century the critics of simoniacal entry suddenly shifted their concern from entry into religion in general to the malpractices of the nuns. Canon 64 of the Fourth Lateran Council (1215) was outspoken: 'Since the simoniacal stain has infected so many nuns to such a degree that they receive scarcely any sisters without a price and they wish by pretext of poverty to palliate a crime of this sort, we prohibit entirely that this be done from now on'.[76] It would seem that the nuns' financial difficulties necessitated grants on entry, but once the unease about simony had been formulated by the canonists, demanding grants which would provide realistically for a new entrant would have been made difficult. The fact that nuns are singled out for such complaints, rather than male religious, probably reflects a situation where the larger economic base of the men's houses made it easier for them either to abandon such gifts on entry, once they were regarded as tainted with simony, or to camouflage them more effectively. But as the decree of the Fourth Lateran Council suggests, it is probable that a significant proportion of grants to the nunneries were linked with the entry of a new member of the community.

PARTICULAR PROBLEMS OF THE NUNS: CONCLUSIONS

There are therefore various reasons which might explain why so few sources are extant for the history of the nunneries. Existing records may have been particularly vulnerable as the nuns' lack of understanding of Latin made them unintelligible; difficulties in finding chaplains may have caused problems both for the provision of scribes and the care of archives; poverty may have added to the problems and increased the likelihood of charters not being obtained in the first place or not being safeguarded by enrollment on the royal records. A rough analysis of the existing sources suggests that there is some correlation between the wealth of a house and the number of documents which have survived. Pre-conquest houses certainly have left more records than later, poorer foundations and, with the exception of Hinchingbrooke, none of the poorest houses has extant series of charters or cartularies.[77] It is also possible that documents belonging to nunneries were more endangered by the Dissolution in the sixteenth century than the archives of many men's houses. The sites of some of the ladies' houses seem to have changed hands frequently. Where records do exist it is sometimes possible to trace a particular reason for their survival. At Lacock it is probable that an inheritance dispute within the family of the new owners brought chestfuls of the deeds of the house into the custody of the Court of Wards, where many have survived.[78] It is also interesting that from the small houses of Broomhall and Lillechurch, whose endowments passed to St John's college Cambridge, some original charters survive in the college archives.

THE DEVELOPMENT OF NUNNERIES FROM DIVERSE ORIGINS

But apart from intrinsic vulnerability and fortuitous circumstances such as the transfer of sites, there may be more radical reasons for the lack of sources available for a study of the early years of many of the nunneries. Perhaps this lack in part reflects the diverse origins of the nunneries and the way they grew and developed, and to look for specific acts of foundation and foundation charters may be misleading. It has already been shown that foundation charters sometimes involve a telescoping of a complex and protracted process of foundation over several years.[79] It has also been pointed out that asking *when* a monastery was founded may be less significant than trying to discover *how* a house was founded.[80] This may be particularly true of nunneries, which appear frequently to have developed slowly from diverse origins which would not be contained in any foundation charter. One such process was the gradual development of a community round a particular anchoress or group of recluses.

The Life of Christina of Markyate,[81] written probably in the mid-twelfth century, tells of the struggles of a maiden to follow her religious vocation in spite of the opposition of her family and some members of the church hierarchy. In the background of her story there are hints about the gathering of a group of maidens around her and the eventual formation of a community. Initially these maidens seem to have had a considerable degree of freedom, and Christina herself seems to have made no formal profession of religious vows. Gradually over a period of some time, and partly due to Abbot Geoffrey's friendship and persuasion, Christina made formal profession at St Albans, the abbot helped with the construction of buildings and the provision of temporal necessities, and from 1145–46 charters survive referring to the nuns and the dedication of their church at Markyate.[82] The obtaining of these charters was probably due in part to the friendship of the powerful abbot. If it had not been for the survival of the Life of Christina, a unique source, and its echoes in the *Gesta Abbatum* of St Albans, the extant charters would suggest a simple foundation date of 1145–46 for the nunnery at Markyate and give little hint of its anchoretic origin. Other houses may have developed in a similar way, leaving virtually no trace on the records. At Crabhouse in Norfolk, the account—written in thirteenth and fourteenth century hands—of the origins of the house which forms part of the register,[83] tells of a certain maiden who wished to live a solitary life. Other ladies gathered around her, but eventually difficulties, culminating in a great flood, forced them to abandon the site. What happened then is not clear, but it seems as if one member remained, living as an anchoress until another group formed around her. Feeling that help was needed to overcome their difficulties, they then put themselves under the protection of a local lord. It is impossible to verify an account such as this, but a comparison with the Life of Christina and the similarities to her saga would indicate a degree of probability. One of the early charters of Crabhouse refers to a certain Leva, suggesting that she was a person of some significance, as Christina had been, and it is clear that there was a hermitage there.[84]

Other nunneries provide fragments of evidence of such an anchoretic origin—Ankerwyke in Buckinghamshire where the name gives the only hint, Sopwell where the *Gesta Abbatum* records that Abbot Geoffrey formed a community there around two recluses, at Limebrook and Kilburn where there is more evidence to suggest that anchoresses may have formed the nucleus of a subsequent community.[85] The Crabhouse account implies that patrons may sometimes have played their part in the foundation of the nunnery at a relatively late stage. It may often have been a case of several lords giving small endowments, possibly as a member of their family joined the community of women which was already established. In the absence of one clear founder who initiated a nunnery where no community had existed

before, it is not surprising to find no foundation charter extant for many of
the houses, but only references to a series of small grants apparently made
by various families.

DOUBLE FOUNDATIONS

There is another possible reason why the origins of so many nunneries are
obscure. As we have already suggested, the establishment of some form of
double organisation met a real need in providing for the spiritual and temporal support of nuns. Yet such forms of organisation increasingly came
under suspicion. At several houses where a series of early charters with witness lists are extant, there is evidence to suggest that a sizable body of men
apparently formed an integral part of the community. At Stixwould, for example, the cartulary and charters reveal at least seven men who are described
as brothers of the house, and two others who are given the title of canon.[86]
At Blackborough early charters transcribed in the cartulary suggest that the
house was originally some form of double establishment while later ones
refer only to the presence of women.[87] The same is true of Swine, Catesby,
and Legbourne.[88] Houses where a sizeable body of men formed part of the
community were in some sense a double foundation, and later unease at this
form of organisation might have discouraged the preservation of records.

Several nunneries may have been more directly the offshoots of double
foundations. This seems to have been true of two of the premonstratensian
convents. Sisters who came to be established at Orford and Broadholme
seem initially to have been regarded as an integral part of the abbey of Newhouse.[89] The nunnery of Moxby in Yorkshire developed from what had
originally been a double house of the Augustinian Order at Marton.[90] This
can be deduced from the charters, but it is not made clear. The very separation of the women in this way would imply a failure or an unease which
was not likely to be documented. Earlier evidence form the eleventh century shows that some of the old benedictine monasteries had women attached to them. In the time of Abbot Paul (1077–1093) women appear to
have been present at the abbey of St Albans,[91] and there are references to
nuns at Evesham and Bury St Edmunds.[92] The *Gesta Abbatum* goes into
some detail about Abbot Geoffrey of St Albans' foundation for nuns at Sopwell.[93] The account does not suggest that some of the nuns had originally
come from the abbey and that the cell of Sopwell was an offshoot of what
had in some sense been a double community at St Albans. Yet it is probable
that this was so,[94] and the St Albans account was content to stress the abbot's generosity to the women and his control over them without addressing the delicate question of where the ladies came from.

LINKS WITH HOSPITALS

At the end of the twelfth century, Abbot Warin of St Albans founded a community for leprous sisters at St Mary de *Pré*. A close reading of the account in the *Gesta* suggests that this was also an offshoot of a double foundation— the leper hospital at St Julians.[95] Soon after the establishment of the women at de *Pré* there are references in the records to a prioress and nuns as well as sisters.[96] It is sometimes stated that this establishment changed from a nunnery into a hospital in the fourteenth century,[97] but the distinction seems long to have been an artificial one. The line between hospital and nunnery is often by no means clear. The nuns at St Albans in the eleventh century were ordered by Abbot Paul to be housed in and around the almonry, presumably the centre from which the abbey dispensed the hospitality demanded by the benedictine rule.[98] The suggestion is that the nuns at Bury similarly were caring for poor people as well as the saint and the abbey.[99] At Carrow nunnery a reference suggests that the two sisters who played an important part in the foundations of the house had been members of a hospital in Norwich.[100] Elusive references on the pipe rolls to the nuns of Richmond may refer to sisters who served the hospital there and formed a small religious community.[101] As with a group growing up around an anchoress a development such as this might be less likely to make its mark on record sources than a new establishment. Lack of sources for the nunneries may reflect their diverse origins as well as their problems.

PROBLEM ILLUSTRATIONS

Brett in his work on the church in the reign of Henry I pointed out that studying the organisation of the church at this period involves the collecting of widely dispersed fragments of information and then asking questions which the evidence was not designed to answer.[102] This is certainly true of the nunneries. A brief examination of the evidence for the foundation of two particular houses illustrates the difficulties. Flamstead priory in Hertfordshire is reputed to have been founded by Roger II de Tosny, and a contemporary charter issued by the prioress refers to him as founder of the house.[103] But a reference in one of this same Roger's charters to grants made by his ancestors, and a papal bull to the nunnery of 1163, a date when he was probably still a minor,[104] show that the house had earlier origins. What appears to be a foundation charter of Roger II de Tosny in which he records several grants to the convent[105] does not mark the origin of the nunnery. The Life of Christina of Markyate reveals that in the early years of the twelfth century there was a venerable anchoress living at Flamstead.[106] It must remain a possibility that the priory dates back to her or her successors.[107] The origins of the nunnery at St Sepulchre, Canterbury, are equally obscure. Archbishop Anselm is given as the founder in the fourteenth-century chronicle of William Thorne, who states that the nunnery was founded in a parish church under the archbiship's patronage.[108] But the later evidence of the *Valor Ecclesiasticus* states categorically that alms were given away every Maundy Thursday by the nuns for the soul of their founder, a William Calvel.[109] There was such a man, a citizen of Canterbury, and he was known to the archbishop.[110] Perhaps he made the initial endowments with the support of Anselm who then came to be regarded as the founder. It is a possibility, however, that this community too had an anchoretic origin. There are extant letters from Anselm to a certain brother Robert, giving him guidance and theological insights to help him in his care for six ladies apparently living the life of anchoresses under his jurisdiction.[111] There is nothing specific, apart from the person of the archbishop, to link this letter with a group at Canterbury, but a connection is not impossible. Another fragment of evidence is the entry in Domesday book showing the existence of a group of nuns holding land close to Canterbury from the abbey of St Augustine.[112] As this does not conflict with what is known of the site of the nuns of St Sepulchre, it may refer to them. Yet another question is posed by the dedication of the monastery to St Sepulchre. Such a dedication was sometimes used for hospitals but is unique in England for a nunnery.[113] Lanfranc had founded hospitals at Canterbury, and Anselm may have done likewise, so another possibility is that St Sepulchre, like St Gregory's Canterbury, originated from a hospital.[114] But such hypotheses must remain tentative as the sources provide no answers.

The lack of evidence for many of the nunneries founded after the Conquest probably reflects particular problems of the nuns: difficulties in understanding Latin, difficulties in obtaining chaplains, and the general poverty of many houses. Such problems are reflected in the evidence for the existence of some ephemeral houses of nuns—communities which seem to have survived only briefly in the twelfth and thirteenth centuries.[115] But it is also possible that the scarcity of sources reflects the diverse origins of some of the houses—communities which may have developed around an anchoress or a hospital or been derived originally from a double house. Such solutions involve speculation, and speculation is a dangerous pasttime. Yet without a little of it, many of the nunneries will probably remain without any history.

Westfield College,
London.

NOTES

1. J. Cox, 'The Priory Of Bromhall' *Victoria County History* [VCH] *Berkshire* 2 (London, 1907) 80.

2. C. R. Peers, 'The Benedictine Nunnery of Little Marlow', *Archaeological Journal* 59 (1902) 307. He then proceeds to describe the archaeological evidence.

3. For the lists of nunneries in England and Wales see D. Knowles and R. Hadcock, *Medieval Religious Houses. England and Wales*, 2nd ed. (London 1971) 194, 253–55, 270, 272, 278, and 283–89.

4. The nine main pre-conquest foundations which survived after 1066 are Amesbury, Barking, Chatteris, Polesworth, Romseys, Shaftesbury, Wherwell, Wilton, and Winchester.

5. British Library [BL] Aston collection purchased 1903. The Nuneaton charters are found among Additional Charters nos 47393–53,112.

6. See C.N.L. Brooke 'Episcopal Charters For Wix Priory,' *A Medieval Miscellany For D.M. Stenton*, ed. P. Barnes, C. Slade, Pipe Roll Society (London 1962) 45–63. The charters of Wix priory are the subject of a current research project.

7. *Lacock Abbey Charters*, ed. K.H. Rogers, Wiltshire Record Society 34 (Devizes 1979).

8. *Transcripts Of Charters relating to the Gilbertine Houses of Sixle, Ormsby, Catley, Bullington and Alvingham*, ed. F.M. Stenton, Lincoln Record Society 18 (Horncastle 1922). Some of the Sempringham charters are printed in 'Charters Relating to the Priory of Sempringham', ed. E.M. Poynton, The *Genealogist*, New Series 15 (1899) 158–61, 221–27; 16 (1900) 30–35, 76–83, 153–58, 223–28; 17 (1901) 29–35, 164–68, 232–39. The sources for Alvingham and Bullington are discussed by B.J. Golding, *The Gilbertine Priories of Alvingham and Bullington: their Endowments and Benefactors*, (Oxford Diss., 1979).

9. *Documents Illustrative Of The Social And Economic History Of The Danelaw From Various Collections*, ed. F.M. Stenton British Academy (London, 1920) 279–89 (Stixwould) and 75–102 (Greenfield).

10. Some of these are listed in H.J. Ellis, ed., *Index To The Charters And Rolls In The Department Of Manuscripts British Museum* 2, *Religious Houses And Other Corporations, And Index Locorum For Acquisitions From 1882-1900* (London, 1912) 387–88 (Hinchingbrooke). Some original charters for St Radegund are in the archives of Jesus College, Cambridge; see *Priory of St Radegund, Cambridge*, ed. A. Gray, Cambridge Antiquarian Society, Octavo Series, 31 (Cambridge 1898).

11. For lists of the surviving cartularies and registers see G.R.C. Davis, *Medieval Cartularies Of Great Britain: A Short Catalogue* (London 1958).

12. W. Dugdale, *Monasticon Anglicanum*, new enlarged edition ed. J. Caley, H. Ellis and B. Bandinel, 6 vols (London, 1817–30, reprinted 1846).

13. W. Brown, 'The Nunnery Of St Stephen's Of Thimbleby' *Yorkshire Archaeological Journal* 9 (1886) 334–37.

14. E. Power, *Medieval English Nunneries c 1275-1535* (Cambridge, 1922).

15. For a list of the extant episcopal registers see D. Smith, *Guide To The Bishops' Registers Of England And Wales. A Survey from the Middle Ages to the Abolition of Episcopacy* in 1646 (London: Royal Historical Society, 1981).

16. T. Hugo, *The Medieval Nunneries Of The County Of Somerset* (London, 1867) 20–21.

17. For example, there are references to a fire at Catesby in *Calendar Of Liberate Rolls Preserved In The Public Record Office, Henry III*, vol. iii *1245-51* (H.M.S.O. London 1937) p 345; and at Malling in *The Historical Works Of Gervase of Canterbury*, ed. W. Stubbs, i *Chronicle Of The Reigns Of Stephen, Henry II and Richard I* Rolls Series [RS] (London, 1879) p 485. The reference to a fire at Markyate occurs in the *Gesta Abbatum* see *Gesta Abbatum Monasterii Sancti Albani*, ed. T.H. Riley; RS 1 (London, 1867) 103. For later evidence of fire destruction see Power, pp. 171–72.

18. Davis, no. 728 p. 82.

19. *VCH Cambridgeshire* 2, ed. L.F. Saltzman (1948) 400.

20. *Calendar Of The Patent Rolls Preserved In The Public Record Office 1358–61* (London: HMSO, 1896) 175.

21. 'The Register of Crabhouse Nunnery', ed. M. Bateson, *Norfolk Archaeology* 11 (1892) 4. For a description of the manuscript of the register, see Davis, no. 284, p. 33.

22. For later evidence of floods see Power, pp. 176–77.

23. It is possible they were more vulnerable because of their poverty.

24. Power, pp.246–51.

25. *Visitations Of Religious Houses In The Diocese Of Lincoln, Records of Visitations held by William Almwick bishop of Lincoln AD MCCCCXXXVI-MCCCCXLIX*, ed. A. Hamilton Thompson, Canterbury and York Society 24 (London, 1919) vol 2, part 1: p. 174.

26. *The English Register of Godstow Nunnery*, ed. A. Clark, Early English Text Society [EETS] (London, 1911) 25.

27. *Non solum autem virorum, sed etiam feminarum cohortes idem Norbertus ad Deum convertere studuit* . . . Herman de Miraculis B. Marie Laudunensis, *Monumenta Germaniae Historica inde ab* a.c. *500 usque ad 1500.* ed. G.H. Pertz (Berlin-Hanover, 1826–) *Scriptorum* 12 p. 657. See also H.M. Colvin, *The White Canons In England* (Oxford, 1951) p 327.

28. PL 214:173–74 (1198), listed in A. Potthast, ed., *Regesta Pontificum Romanorum Inde Ab A. Post Christum Natum 1198 AD A 1304*, 2 vols (1874–75 repr. Graz 1957) I, no. 168, pp. 17–18.

29. C.L. Hugo, *Sacri Et Canonici Ordinis Praemonstratensis Annales* . . . 2 vols (Nancy, 1734–36) 2: col. 147.

30. See S. Thompson 'The problem of the Cistercian nuns in the twelfth and early thirteenth centuries' *Medieval Women; Studies in Church History, Subsidia 1*, ed. D. Baker (Oxford, 1978) 227–52.

31. *Ibid.*, 238–39.

32. For a recent article on Robert of Arbrissel, see J. Smith, 'Robert of Arbrissel, Procurator Mulierum' *Medieval Women*, 175–84.

33. For example, see J. Michelet, *Histoire de France* 2nd ed. (1835) 2:298–300.

34. For a study of Robert's employment of synkeitism as a penitential practice, see D Iogna-Prat 'La femme dans la perspective pénitentielle des ermites du Bas-Maine (fin XIᵉ début XIIᵉ siècle)', *Revue d'histoire de la Spiritualité* 53 (1977) 47–64.

35. 'Alia Vita B. Roberti', *Acta Sanctorum Bollandiana February 3* (Antwerp, 1658) 608.

36. For example PL 163:504 (Gelasius II, 1118); and PL 179:865 (Lucius II, 1144).

37. The nunneries of the order of Fontevrault were Amesbury, Nuneaton, and Westwood; see Knowles and Hadcock, 104–5. The Premonstratensian nunneries were Broadholme, Guyzance, and Orford; *Ibid.*, 283. See also, Colvin, 327–36.

38. For a brief history of the nunnery of Harrold see Sister Elspeth, 'The Priory Of Harrold' *VCH Bedfordshire* 1, edd. A. Doubleday and W. Page. (London, 1904) 387–90. See also, *Records Of Harrold Priory*, ed. G.H. Fowler, Bedforshire Historical Record Society 17 (1935). For the order of Arrouaise see L. Milis, *L'Ordre Des Chanoines Réguliers D'Arrouaise. Son histoire et son organisation, de la fondation de l'abbaye-mère (vers 1090) à la fin des chapitres annuels (1471)*, 2 vols (Bruges, 1969).

39. *The Cartulary of Missenden Abbey*, ed. J.G. Jenkins, *Buckinghamshire Record Society* [3 vols II, X and XII (1938–62)] 3: no. 809, p. 182.

40. Milis, Appendix ii, p. 599. For a later abbot's account of Abbot Gervase's welcome to women see *MGH Scriptorum* 15 (2) p. 1121.

41. *Cartulary Missenden*; 3:183 and 189.

42. Thompson 'Cistercian nuns', 242–44.

43. Knowles and Hadcock, 272. Note the houses where another Order is recorded.

44. *Calendar Of The Close Rolls Of The Reign Of Henry III Preserved In The Public Record Office* [14 vols] (London: HMSO 1903–27), 14 [*1268–72*] (1938) 301.

45. For the Gilbertines, see R. Graham, *S. Gilbert Of Sempringham And The Gilbertines* (London, 1901).

46. For links between the Gilbertines and the Cistercians, see B. Golding, 'St. Bernard And St Gilbert' in *The Influence Of St Bernard. Anglican Essays with an Introduction by Jean Leclercq*, ed. B. Ward (Oxford: Fairacres, 1976) 42–52.

47. *Monasticon* 6 (2) p. xxix. The numbers to which the houses were limited c 1185 –90 are given in Knowles and Hadcock, p. 194.

48. D. Knowles, 'The Revolt of the Lay Brothers of Sempringham', *English Historical Review* 50 (1935) 469–70. Knowles suggests this charge was entirely false.

49. For a recent article on the story of the nun of Watton, see G. Constable 'Ailred of Rievalux and the nun of Watton, an episode in the early history of the Gilbertine order' *Medieval Women*, 205–26.

50. *Cartulary Of St Mary Clerkenwell*, ed. W.O. Hassall, Camden Society, 3rd series, 71 (London, 1949) no. 40, pp. 30–31.

51. Thompson 'Cistercian nuns', p. 251 and note 168.

52. *Early Yorkshire Charters*, edd. W. Farrer and C.T. Clay [12 vols] (Edinburgh/ Wakefield, 1914–65) (1914) no. 541, pp. 419–21.

53. Knowles and Hadcock, 253–55, and 278.

54. Their charters often make reference to the order of the house, whereas those of benedictine or augustinian communities rarely do so.

55. For example, BL Additional charter 48093 (Nuneaton c 1240–50.)

56. M.T. Clanchy, *From Memory to Written Record, England 1066–1307* (London, 1979) 88 and 90.

57. *Register Godstow*, p. 25.

58. *Visitations Lincoln* 2, part 1, p. 174.

59. Clanchy, pp. 93–94.

60. For a further discussion of the nuns' financial problems, see Power, 161–236.

61. J.A. Nichols, *The History and Cartulary of the Cistercian Nuns of Marham Abbey 1249–1536* (Diss. Kent State University, Ohio, 1974) 33–36.

62. Knowles and Hadcock, 264 (Ivinghoe) and 259 (Godstow).

63. J. Burton, *The Yorkshire Nunneries in the Twelfth and Thirteenth Centuries*; Borthwick Papers 56 (York, 1979) p. 24.

64. *Ibid.* p. 18.

65. Knowles and Hadcock, 104–5 (Amesbury and Nuneaton), 275 (Marham), 259 (Godstow), and 281 (Lacock).

66. *The Letters And Charters Of Gilbert Foliot*, edd. A. Morey and C.N.L. Brooke (Cambridge, 1967) p. 245, no. 172.

67. C.N.L. Brooke and G. Keir, *London 800–1216. The Shaping of a City* (London, 1975) 329–30.

68. BL Harleian, MS 743, f. 271ᵛ–72ᵛ; a text of this charter is printed in *Monasticon* 4; 477–78.

69. *Gesta Abbatum* 1:368.

70. BL Harl., Charter 43 A 34, printed *Monasticon* 4:71.

71. *Calendar of Entries In The Papal Registers Relating To Great Britain and Ireland*, ed. W.H. Bliss. 1: *Papal Letters 1198–1304* (London, 1893) p. 90.

72. C. Lawrence. *St Edmund of Abingdon. A Study in Hagiography and History* (Oxford, 1960) 107 and 222.

73. For a discussion of the question of dowries and entry fees in relation to the Yorkshire nunneries, see Burton, 21–23.

74. J.H. Lynch, *Simoniacal entry into religious life from 1000–1260; a social economic and legal study* (Columbus, Ohio, 1976) *passim* and particularly pp. 98 and 116.

75. Lawrence, 316–17, and Lynch, 215–16.

76. Lynch, 193–94 and note 57.

77. For Hinchingbrooke there are references to a register no longer extant (Davis no. 490, p. 55) and a number of charters for the house are preserved in the British Library. See note 10.

78. *Lacock Charters*, pp. 2–4.
79. V.H. Galbraith, 'Monastic Foundation Charters Of The Eleventh And Twelfth centuries' *Cambridge Historical Journal* 4 (1934) 205–22.
80. J.C. Dickinson, 'The Origins of St Augustine's Bristol' *Essays In Bristol And Gloucestershire History* edd. P. McGrath and J. Cannon, Bristol and Gloucestershire Archaeology Society centenary volume (1976) pp. 112–13.
81. *The Life Of Christina Of Markyate, A Twelfth Century Recluse*, ed. C.H. Talbot (Oxford, 1959).
82. BL Cotton charter xi 6, printed in *Early Charters Of The Cathedral Church Of St Paul, London*, ed. M. Gibbs; Camden Society 3rd series, 58 (London, 1939) no. 154, pp. 119–20; BL Cotton charter xi 8 printed in *English Episcopal Acta Lincoln 1067–1185*, ed. D.M. Smith (London, 1980) no. 49, pp. 30–31.
83. *Register of Crabhouse*, pp. 2–5 and pp. 12–13. See also, Davis, no. 284, p. 33.
84. BL Harl MS 2110 f. 82ᵛ (Register of Castle Acre). See also *Monasticon* 5:69, no. 4.
85. *Gesta Abbatum* 1:80 (Sopwell), for the possible anchoretic origins of Lime-brooke and its connection with the Ancrene Wisse, see E.J. Dobson, *The Origins Of Ancrene Wisse* (Oxford, 1975); there is considerably less evidence to link the Ancrene Wisse with Kilburn priory (see R.W. Chambers, 'Recent Research upon the Ancren Riwle', *Review of English Studies* 1 (1925) 4–23, but early charter evidence shows that this community also originated around a group of anchoresses, see BL Cotton MS Faustina A iii f 325ᵛ, printed *Monasticon* 3:426, no. 1.
86. Thompson, 'Cistercian nuns', 247.
87. BL Egerton MS 3137. Some of the charters from this are printed in *Monasticon* 4:206–7. One charter, no. 3, refers to brothers and sisters.
88. Thompson, 'Cistercian nuns', 247–48.
89. For example, a charter of Henry II grants protection to the sisters as well as the canons of Newhouse, (*Documents Of Danelaw* no. 243, p. 178.) Cf. the view of Colvin that although the houses of nuns were closely associated with the canons they did not begin as double establishments (Colvin, 328.)
90. Knowles and Hadcock, 262.
91. *Gesta Abbatum* 1:59.
92. Knowles and Hadcock, 65 (Evesham); for the reference to the nuns at Bury see D. Knowles, *The Monastic Order in England . . . 940–1216*, 2nd ed. (Cambridge, 1963) 136–37 and note 2.
93. *Gesta Abbatum* 1:80–82.
94. L.F. Rushbrooke Williams, *History Of The Abbey Of St Alban* (London, 1917) 59, suggests this as a possibility. See also Knowles and Hadcock, 265.
95. *Gesta Abbatum* 1:199–202.
96. For example BL Additional charters 19279 and 19962. See also the bull of Alexander IV printed *Monasticon* 3:356, no. 4.
97. See W. Page, 'The History of the Monastery of St Mary de Pré' *Transactions St Albans and Hertfordshire Architectural and Archaeological Society*, NS 1, *1895–1902* (St Albans, 1898) 12–13.
98. *Gesta Abbatum* 1:59.
99. Knowles, *Monastic Orders*, 136–37.
100. W. Rye, *Carrow Abbey, Otherwise Carrow Priory, Near Norwich In The County Of Norfolk, Its Foundation, Buildings, Officers And Inmates, With Appendices* (privately printed Norwich 1889). Appendix 1 prints this extract from Tanner MS 342, f. 149.
101. For example see *The Great Roll Of The Pipe For The Eighteenth Year Of King Henry II, A.D. 1171–2*, Pipe Roll Society 18 (London, 1894) 5.
102. M Brett, *The English Church Under Henry I* (Oxford, 1975) 3.
103. *The Beauchamp Cartulary Charters 1100–1268*, ed. E. Mason, Pipe Roll Society, NS 43 (London, 1980) p. 210, no. 370.
104. Flamstead cartulary, Hertfordshire Record Office MS no. 17465, f. 3. The papal bull is printed in Holtzmann, *Papsturkunden in England*, Abhandlungen der

Gesellschaft de Wissenchaft in Göttingen, phil-hist Klasse, Berlin-Göttingen, 3:586 no. 494. Roger was a minor when his father died in 1162 and may not have come of age till several years later. (*The Complete Peerage* by G.E.C., revised edn. V. Gibbs, H.A. Doubleday, Lord Howard de Walden, G.H. White and R.S. Lea [London, 1910–59] 12 (1) p. 765.)

105. Flamstead cartulary printed *Monasticon* 4:300, no. 1. This must date from before 1209 (the date of Roger's death) and a similar charter in the cartulary (Hertfordshire Record Office MS no. 17465) is dated 1204.

106. *Life Of Christina*, 92.

107. Compare the view of Talbot, who rules out tthis possibility: *Ibid.*, note 1.

108. See R. Twysden, *Historiae Anglicanae Scriptores 10* (London, 1652) col. 1893.

109. For a discussion of the claims of William Calvel see W. Urry, *Canterbury Under The Angevin Kings* (London, 1967) 62–63, and note 7.

110. *Ibid.*, p. 386, no.2.

111. PL 159:167–68 and 257–58.

112. Urry, 62 and note 7. He uses this as evidence for William being the founder rather than Anselm, but this entry in Domesday could also indicate the existence of an earlier community..

113. Examples of hospitals with this dedication are Warwick, St Sepulchre, which later developed into a priory (Knowles and Hadcock, 178–79); Hedon Yorkshire, and Hereford (322).

114. *Ibid.*, 152.

115. For example, there is an isolated reference to a community of nuns at Spinney which does not seem to have survived. (*Acta Lincoln* p. 160, no. 256.)

Male/Female Cooperation:
The Example of Fontevrault*

Penny Schine Gold

AMIDST THE PROFUSION of new Orders founded between the late eleventh and the thirteenth centuries, the Order of Fontevrault presents an especially interesting case in the history of women in monasticism. All communities of women had needs for spiritual and material assistance (the *cura monialium*), and until the end of the twelfth century, most monastic Orders were willing to participate in a more or less close relationship with female communities in order to provide such assistance. But while many Orders in the early thirteenth century moved to exclude women or severely to restrict cooperation with women religious, Fontevrault continued to exist and thrive.[1] This essay will explore the roots of Fontevrault's success in its foundation and organization, looking especially at its institutionalization of cooperation between male and female religious.

ROBERT OF ARBRISSEL AND THE FOUNDING OF FONTEVRAULT

Fontevrault was founded in 1100 or 1101 by Robert of Arbrissel, a native of Brittany who had been born around 1060 into a poor peasant family.[2] Robert's early career was shaped by the spirit of gregorian reform so prevalent in the late eleventh-century church. After studying in Paris, Robert returned to Brittany, entering the service of Sylvester, Bishop of Rennes. He spent four years there as archpriest, 'making peace between quarrelers, liberating churches from slavery to the laity, separating the incestuous unions of priest and laity, opposing simony, and manfully opposing all sins'.[3] But these reforming activities were not uniformly popular, and when Bishop Sylvester died, Robert was forced to leave. He taught in Angers for a

151

short time, but then became caught up in the contemporary enthusiasm for eremeticism.[4] Accompanied by another priest, Robert went into a deserted area in the forest of Craon to devote himself to contemplation. As so often happened with hermits, however, his isolation did not last long—he soon had visitors, may of whom wanted to remain with him. In order to provide for them, he founded a congregation of canons who were to live by the rules of the primitive church. Robert developed a reputation for his skillful preaching, and when Urban II was in Anjou in 1095, it was arranged that Robert preach at the dedication of a church in Angers. The Pope, impressed with his zeal, enjoined him to preach. Robert then began his career as an itinerant preacher, a way of life he continued until his death. He was so successful in this role that he gave up the community of canons at Craon in order to have more time for preaching. As he travelled, he was joined by many persons of both sexes.[5] Again Robert founded a community for the people who had gathered around him, this time at a deserted place called Fontevrault, at the intersection of the boundaries of Anjou, Poitou, and Touraine. Robert's biographer, Baldric, attributes the foundation to Robert's fear that some persons within the enlarging crowds might act indiscreetly. Noting, however, that 'women should live with men', Baldric describes Robert's decision to look for a deserted place where they could live 'scrupulously, without scandal'.[6]

Thus Robert of Arbrissel established a community that included both women and men. Contact between the men and the women was, however, strictly limited, and labors were divided according to sex. The women were assigned a silent life in the cloister; the men were subjected to labor, spiritual for the clerics and physical for the laymen. In this way, Robert 'commended the more tender and weaker sex to psalm-singing and contemplation, while he applied the stronger sex to the labors of the active life'.[7] These people were not only of both sexes but of all conditions: 'Many men, of every condition came; women, poor and noble, widows and virgins, young and old, whores and man-haters assembled'.[8]

The numbers of men and women at Fontvrault are not known. It seems clear, however, that women outnumbered men. Baldric notes in his *Vita* that after building the oratory, they built cloisters, yet 'three or four did not suffice for such a great gathering of women'.[9] The special importance of women in the community is also indicated by Robert's choice of a woman, Hersende, to govern the community as prioress when he recommended life as a wandering preacher. Petronilla of Chemillé, who was later chosen abbess, was at this same time assigned the office of procurator.

During the next fifteen years, Robert travelled through most of western and southwestern France, preaching, setting up priories of Fontevrault, and receiving donations for the growing order.[10] The events of the last year of

Robert's life, as described by his second biographer, Andrea, are particularly interesting, as they reveal quite clearly the purpose Robert had in founding Fontevrault.[11] The first section of Andrea's biography focuses on two events: first, Robert's request that the brothers of Fontevrault pledge to remain in the community under the rule of women and, second, Robert's choice of an abbess to govern the community.[12] Andrea tells the following story, using long 'quotations' from Robert himself.

Robert, gravely ill at Fontevrault, calls the brothers to his bedside. He tells them that he is about to die, and that he would like to ascertain whether the brothers want to continue in their purpose at Fontevrault, that is, for the sake of their souls to obey the command of the handmaidens (*ancillae*) of Christ. He reminds them that whatever he has established, he has subjected to the rule of these women. If the men do not want to stay at Fontevrault, he gives them permission to join another Order. With an almost unanimous voice, the brothers declare that there is no better life possible, and they pledge to remain.[13]

Not many days later, Robert sends for several bishops and abbots. When they have assembled, he tells them that he is near death, and that he has called them to Fontevrault to help him in the choice of an abbess. Robert instructs them that all he has built has been for the nuns, that he has given them full authority over his goods, and that he has committed himself and his disciples, for the salvation of their souls, to the service of the nuns. On this account, with their advice, he would like to appoint an abbess while he is still alive, lest after his death someone might presume to oppose his goal. Robert then discusses the choice of the abbess. He considers the question of whether he should appoint a 'lay convert' (*laica conversa*) or a virgin.[14] The dignity of the Order would seem to demand governance by a virgin, but Robert expresses concern that someone who had been brought up within the life of the cloister would not have the worldly knowledge needed to run a monastic Order, and he is concerned that the community he has built not deteriorate. A Martha-type woman is needed for an abbess; let Mary gaze longingly at heaven.[15] The assembled men agree wholeheartedly.

Seven months later Robert chose as abbess Petronilla of Chemillé, who had been one of his early followers.[16] In announcing his choice, Robert mentions that she had been married once, and that to him nothing seems more in accordance with the authority of abbess.[17] This is apparently not meant simply as a loop-hole for Petronilla—Andrea tells us that Robert had it written into the rules of Fontevrault that the abbess should never be someone who had been brought up in the cloister; many churches, he notes, had been ruined by such inexperienced abbesses. Robert did not choose to perpetuate his own role by appointing a male master of the Order, either instead of or in addition to an abbess. In contrast, Gilbert of Sempringham, whose gilbertine houses in England for men and women are frequently compared to Fontevrault, personally selected a male successor, and the position of master was included in the Institutes of the Order, institutionalizing male control.[18]

The two saint's lives of Robert give us a picture of a self-consciously ordered community of men and women. The sexually mixed composition of the crowds that followed Robert in his first years as a wandering preacher may have been due to the general attraction of such figures; but whatever the reason for the initial mixture, his biographers show Robert very purposefully organizing a continuing association. The principles are clear: Robert's works have been done for the sake of women; the men should, for the sake of their souls, carry on their service of the women; the governance of both the men and the women of the community should be carried out by the abbess. Baldric also mentions a concern for the physical separation of the women from the men. The Rule of the community reinforces this picture.

Three versions of the Rule for Fontevrault have survived.[19] None of these appears to be the original Rule drawn up by Robert, as described by Andrea. Andrea reported that, beside a regulation concerning the election of the abbess, Robert also dictated regulations directing both the men and the women with respect to speech, acts, food, and clothing. Yet none of the existing Rules contain consideration of all four things. Rule I (if we follow the order in Migne) consists of forty-four rules for women and twenty-seven rules for men. Rule II contains seven rules for women and seven for men. Rule III is composed of eight rules for women. Von Walter judges that Rule II is a fragment of the original rule, and dates from 1116 or 1117. He considers Rule I to be a reworking of the original rule, completed sometime before 1155, and probably before Petronilla's death in 1149. Rule III seems to him to be a later form of Rule I, and may date from around 1150.[20] This chronology is only an estimation, but it is worth exploring the differences between Rule II, judged to be closest to the original, and Rule I, the most detailed elaboration of the rules, judged to date sometime after Rule II.

Rule II contains a strong statement of the spiritual and secular jurisdiction of the abbess over Fontevrault and all its dependents:

> Petronilla, chosen by master Robert and constituted abbess by the common will and by the devoted request of the nuns as well as of the brothers religious, is to have and maintain the power of ruling the church of Fontevrault and all the places belonging to that church, and they are to obey her. They are to revere her as their spiritual mother, and all the affairs of the church, spiritual as well as secular, are to remain in her hands, or be given to whomever she assigns, just as she decides.[21]

This Rule also states that the male members of the community (*presbyteri, clerici, laici*) have promised to serve under the bond of obedience to the nuns, and that this subjection should be followed not just at Fontevrault, but at the other communities in the Order as well. The governance of the nuns in everyday matters can be seen in three of the seven statutes for the men: the men are to be content with what is given them by the nuns; they are to bring their leftover food to the door of the nuns' quarters where it will be distributed to the poor; the men are to receive nothing from the outside without the permission of the abbess.[22] The nuns were not strictly confined to the cloister; one provision, for example, ordains that the cloistered nuns should always maintain silence, except for those who attend to business on the outside.[23] Another statute assumes the prioress travelled outside, ordering that she be received and obeyed in all the communities of the Order.[24] Only one statute relates to the separation of men and women. This is an injunction that sick nuns are never to be anointed or receive communion, except in the church, a rule presumably intended to prevent the possibility of a priest entering the nuns' quarters.

All but two of the statutes of Rule II are included in Rule I, either unchanged, or with slight changes. The rule that described the authority of Abbess Petronilla is omitted, as is a prohibition of meat-eating. Of the numerous statutes included in Rule I, but not found in Rule II, many concern dress, a topic not touched upon in Rule II. More important to us here are the rules directed at restricting contact between men and women in the community. Eleven of the forty-four rules for women (nos. 4, 28, 29, 30, 32, 33, 34, 35, 38, 40, 41) and one of the twenty-seven rules for men (no. 14) deal with such restrictions.[25] Most of these women's statutes are concerned with preventing contact between the sexes during the various religious offices. For example: 'When the priest comes to celebrate mass, the door to the choir will not be open to the nuns, unless for communion, and when they do receive communion, the abbess, or deaconess, *(decana)*, or cellarer should always watch over them'.[26] The one men's statute is concerned with the possibility of women entering the male quarters: 'The brothers are not to receive women [*mulieres*] into their houses to do their work'.[27]

Other added rules spell out a stricter discipline for women than was apparent in Rule II. For example, the statute is repeated that enjoins the cloistered nuns to silence, while excepting those who need to do business outside, but a rule is added specifying that, within and without, they are to maintain the honesty and seriousness of the cloister as much as they can. No nun is to go outside the cloister to do anything unless it has been ordered by the abbess; no nun can go outside without the company of at least two men, one religious and one secular, and there is to be no speaking *en route* except by the abbess or prioress.[28]

These surviving fragments of the Rule confirm the picture formed by the saint's lives of Robert of a religious community based upon a well-thought-out relationship between men and women. Even though reliant on men for the conducting of religious services, the women, in their lives of contemplation, were the focus of the community. The men were there to serve the nuns, both spiritually and materially. Robert's choice of a woman to be the superior of the community, and the complete charge of both men and women given to the abbess by the Rule, confirm the dominant importance of the female element at Fontevrault.

THE RELATIVE ROLES OF MEN AND WOMEN AT FONTEVRAULT

Fontevrault is often referred to by scholars (though not by its contemporaries) as a 'double monastery' because its male and female communities lived in such close proximity and because a woman held administrative authority over both communities. Although double communities of men and women, governed by an abbess, had been common in the earlier Middle Ages, they had died out in the tenth and eleventh centuries, and Fontevrault has been seen as representing a twelfth-century revival of this form. The term 'double monastery' is misleading, however, and a detailed investigation of the foundation and development of Fontevrault can help clarify the term, often used with the implication that the two communities, joined for convenience under the authority of one person, were of equal importance. But the term 'double' disguises the fact that most of these communities were originally founded for the benefit of either men or women rather than both. The anglosaxon double monasteries seem to have been primarily communities for women. A. H. Thompson remarked that 'it is difficult to regard these religious houses . . . as anything but nunneries in connection with which there were communities of brethren to do such work and perform such services as the nuns could not do or perform themselves'.[29] In these early foundations, as at Fontevrault, where the nuns were also the predominant element, it was the norm to have an abbess rule over both men and women. Yet there were other communities referred to as 'double monasteries' that were in origin male communities to which a group of women became attached. Such an association might begin gradually, by the offering of protection to a female recluse, or large numbers of women might be associated from an early date, as happened in the Premonstratensian Order.[30] Not surprisingly, this type of double monastery had an abbot as head. The use of the term 'double monastery' thus disguises a variety of organizational structures, a variety influenced by the original purpose and mode of foundation of the communities. The importance and role of women in these communities could be very different, as in some cases the community was at its foundation organized around the needs of women and women were in charge of governance, while in others women were taken into predominantly male communities, perhaps because they sought a religious life and could not find suitable nunneries. In the former, men were attached to a female community for the convenience and support of the women; in the latter, women were attached to a male community as a favor to the women and for their protection. Between these two extremes were a variety of establishments responding to local needs and pressures. Rather than speaking of these communities as 'double monastries', we would be more exact to recognize the diversity of arrangements and purposes by referring to the general phenomenon of religious men and women living in close proximity to each other, and by specifying the particular purpose and arrangements at the communities in question.[31] Fontevrault, as we have seen above, was a community intended by its founder to be centered on women. The men were an important part of the community, but their importance rested upon their subservient role: they were there to serve the women.

A wide range of documents—chronicles and letters, as well as charters from the monastery itself—confirm this picture of the relative roles of men and women at Fontevrault. In fact, sources from outside the monastery rarely even mention the men at Fontevrault. All letters addressed to Fontevrault were addressed to the abbess, the abbess and the nuns, or the nuns; the salutations never include the men.[32] The content of these letters, and of letters written about, as well as to, Fontevrault, only infrequently mention the men of the community.[33]

Occasional mentions of Fontevrault in chronicles give us another view of how outsiders perceived the institution. Here again, Fontevrault is most frequently described as a community of nuns. William of Malmesbury, writing not very long after Robert's death, identified Fontevrault very clearly as an establishment for women:

> [Robert of Arbrissel] was the most celebrated and eloquent preacher of these times: so much did he excel, not in frothy, but in honeyed diction, that from the gifts of persons vying with each other in making presents, he founded that distinguished monastery of nuns at Font-Evraud, in which every secular pleasure being extirpated, no other place possesses such multitudes of devout women, fervent in their obedience to God. For in addition to the rejection of other allurements, how great is this! that they never speak but in the chapter: the rule of constant silence being enjoined by the superior, because, when this is broken, women are prone to vain talk.[34]

William of Newburgh's account, written in the 1190s, similarly mentions only women,[35] and another english chronicle records that Henry II and Richard I were buried with 'the nuns of Fontevrault'.[36] A treatise on the various monastic orders, written in 1154, mentions only nuns at Fontevrault.[37]

Another chronicle notes that Robert of Arbrissel drew to him many persons of both sexes,[38] and one chronicle, oddly, mentions only male followers.[39]

Internal documents—most voluminously, charters of donation and disputes over property—make it clear that the large population of monks at Fontevrault was there to serve the nuns, just as Robert had ordained. The following analysis of the relative roles of the monks and nuns as seen from within Fontevrault is based on a study of the hundreds of charters that survive.[40] Of them, only a handful mention men as the recipients of a gift. The donations are usually made to 'God, blessed Mary, and the nuns of Fontevrault' or to 'God, blessed Mary, and the church of Fontevrault'.[41] The huge proportion of donations addressed to the nuns of Fontevrault rather than to the monks, or to the nuns and monks together, demonstates that outsiders (here the people donating property) viewed Fontevrault as a community of women rather than as a special community of both men and women.[42] But the salutations might also be considered an insider's point of view, since the language with which a charter was worded must frequently have been the work of the scribe, or perhaps a representative of the church who dictated to the scribe. The salutations of the donations might, then, present a good image of the self-definition of the community.

Whether the salutations present an inside or an outside perspecive, the circumstances of the drawing up of the charters makes even more significant the predominance of the nuns in the salutations, as the monks were more involved in these business transactions than were the nuns. It is likely that the charters were drawn up by monks, rather than nuns, as the few charters we have that indicate the scribe name a man.[43] Futhermore, the donors were more likely to have had direct dealings with the monks of the community than with the nuns, other than the abbess or prioress. The witness lists of many of the charters from the first half of the twelfth century show the abbess and prioress of Fontevrault with some regularity as witnesses (in thirty-three charters out of 305 from the first half of the century). Even if not witnessing, one of them is often mentioned as having arranged the donation, having paid a *quid pro quo* to the donor, or as having received the donation (or consented to the donation) *in manu*. But other nuns appear rarely—only three of the 305 charters were witnessed by nuns other than the abbess or prioress. In contrast, monks of the community appear as witnesses even more frequently than do the abbess and prioress, in sixty-three charters.[44] The monks also did other business involved in seeing a donation through to completion; they might measure the land to be given,[45] or go to a donor's home to secure consent from a wife and children who had not come to the ceremony at the monastery.[46] In fact, it was not uncommon for the donation itself to be made at the donor's home, rather than at the monastery.[47]

The handling of business affairs, as these charters show concerned most of the nuns very little. Many tasks were taken care of by the monks, who often travelled outside the community on business. But the dominant figure on these journeys was clearly the abbess or the prioress, who often coordinated the whole transaction. In one case in which a dismissal of a claim was made 'in the hand' of a monk Gaufridus, we are told that it was done this way 'because the abbess was not there'—that is, the expectation was that the abbess would have received the dismissal, but in her absence the monk subsituted for her.[48] But while the abbess and prioress were busy with the economic concerns of the abbey, the other women in the community were left free for their spiritual duties, the life of contemplation, while the monks took care of the necessary work involved in keeping up with the stream of donations. The ready availability of the monks made it unnecessary, for example, for the nuns to travel outside the community on business matters. Such travel had been allowed for in the Rule of the community, so it was not that a strict cloistering of the nuns required that business be carried out by the monks. Rather, at Fontevrault, despite the fact that the nuns were not strictly cloistered by their Rule, it was considered preferable to have the monks do this necessary but spiritually unrewarding work.[49]

Two examples illustrate the utility of having monks available to carry on business outside the abbey. In 1114 Geoffrey of Vendôme, the abbot of an important monastery in a neighboring province, came to Fontevrault to give a salt revenue from the domain of his abbey. In return, the anniversary of Geoffrey's death was to be observed at Fontervrault. The charter records that this transaction was made 'in the chapter of Fontevrault, in the presence of lord Geoffrey abbot and of lord Robert our master, with the assent of all the sisters'.[50] We see, then, some business involving Geoffrey, one of the monastic celebrities of the area, taking place at Fontevrault in the chapter of nuns; no monks are mentioned. Yet when the concession of this revenue was later confirmed at the chapter of the monastery of Vendôme, two monks from Fontevrault were present.[51] The important business, including the reception of the abbot, was done in the presence of the nuns, and then the necessary, but time-consuming task of seeing the transaction through to its confirmation (a task that also entailed travel away from Fontevrault) was taken care of by the monks.

In another example, the monks took care of the groundwork for a transaction that was later confirmed at Fontevrault by the chapter of nuns. Sometime during the second quarter of the twelfth century Abbess Petronilla gave a house to a couple and their heirs, who were to pay a certain amount in dues for it to Fontevrault. The transaction was witnessed by nine men, including the prior, two monks, and two priests of Fontevrault. This transaction apparently took place away from the abbey, for we are told that a short time later the abbess confirmed the gift in the chapter, with the nuns consenting .[52] The chapter of nuns clearly acted as the formal governing body before which business matters were brought for conclusion. A donation confirmed in the chapter might have involved much preparation by the monks, as well as by the abbess or prioress, but it was in the chapter of nuns that the act would be finally formalized.[53]

What of the internal governance of the community? Did that work out as Robert had hoped, with the monks 'content with what is given to them by the nuns'? Unfortunately, documents recording internal affairs are virtually non-existent; many directions were likely given verbally rather than in writing, or the documents that were generated were not deemed worthy of preservation. Two documents survive from the first half of the thirteenth century that illustrate the relative roles of the abbess, nuns, and monks in decisions affecting the whole community. A charter from 1210 records a transfer of revenue from the nuns to the monks: 'I, Abbess Adele, and the convent of Fontevrault announce that on the petition of our brother Harduinus, we give to God and blessed John the Evangelist and the convent of our clerics and brothers of the Habit of Fontevrault, ten *solidi* to be rendered annually to the prior.'[54] Ten *sous* is a very small sum. Were there circumstances that made this particular revenue especially important to the monks, or was this the type of transaction that went on all the time at Fontevrault without being recorded or preserved? The second document records a decision made in 1241 by a later Abbess Adele with the assent and counsel of the prioress, prior, and the whole chapter (of nuns, presumably), regulating the mixture of grains with which bread was to be made for the whole community—nuns and brothers, both cleric and lay.[55] Scanty as these documents are, it is reassuring to find at least this much confirmation of Robert's intentions that the abbess govern both the men and the women, even with respect to the details of material life.[56]

THE SUCCESS OF FONTEVRAULT

What factors protected Fontevrault from the difficulties experienced by many other female communities? Perhaps contributing to its success was the relatively large number of men at Fontevrault, at least during its first two centuries of existence. We do not have extensive information on the numbers of monks and nuns at Fontevrault and other communities, but it seems that Fontevrault had an unusually large community of men. Seventy-nine different monks appear among the witnesses to charters from Fontevrault between 1100 and 1149. An account of pensions to be paid to the monks and chaplains of Fontevrault, dating from 1228, lists some one hundred twenty names.[57] The large number of co-resident men provided a large 'staff' available to carry out the various tasks necessary to the continued financial success of the institution—and Fontevrault was highly successful in drawing in donations. The large pool of help also meant that the burden of service could be spread widely (few monks appear as witnesses more than once or twice); perhaps this eased a resentment that might otherwise have been felt. And when we think of the variety and number of business tasks and trips undertaken by the many monks of Fontevrault, the resentment that was expressed by some monks and canons at the 'burden' of women becomes understandable.[58] But more information is needed before we conclude that the simple fact of numbers was particularly important to the success of Fontevrault. Scholars may have underestimated the number of men usually resident at a nunnery.[59] On the other hand, the many priories of Fontevrault may not have had nearly as high a proportion of monks as did the motherhouse.[60]

The major difference between Fontevrault and other Orders must have been that in the very early stages of its development, the founder and early members of Fontevrault formally institutionalized, through detailed written regulations, the relationship that was to exist between the men and the women of the community: that the women were the focus of the community; the men were there to serve the women. In commenting on the exclusion of women from Arrouaise and other Orders at the turn of the century, Ludo Milis refers to the importance of the organizational inclusion of women:

> Around 1200, many Orders began a movement to abolish or diminish the female presence. It is likely that the origin of part of the discontent could be found in an inadequate organization: statutes appropriate to the sisters of Arrouaise were never drawn up; for the Norbertine sisters, there were only a few, added on to the Customary of the men.[61]

In the earlier Middle Ages—the sixth to ninth centuries—women were very active in the monasticism of the frontier, but were excluded from the later, more thoroughly organized, period of monastic development in the tenth and eleventh centuries. A similar pattern seems to have occurred in the twelfth and thirteenth centuries. The new frontier was both territorial and spiritual: territorial in the desire to set up communities in a wilderness area, spiritual in the desire to push the boundaries of monastic spirituality beyond those of the current institutions of the church. These frontiers dissipated more quickly than the frontier of initial conversion, and we see a similar degeneration of women's situation with regard to these twelfth-century movements.

The women of Fontevrault were apparently spared this decline because the inclusion of women was written into the legislation of the Order, whereas elsewhere women, having attached themselves as they could to a predominantly male structure, were easily viewed as peripheral and were likely to be forced out as the organization of the Order was tightened. In other words, the early formalization, or institutionalization, of women's participation at Fontevrault prevented the attacks suffered in other Orders. The participation of women at Fontevrault was not unusual for the first half of the twelfth century, but the formal structuring of an arrangement dominated by women was.

The structured inclusion of men was also very important to Fontevrault's success. In most other cases, arrangements were made with men on a more casual basis, using whatever resources were available locally. There were several variables in the arrangements: would the fulfillment of the material and spiritual needs of the nuns be cast as service or supervision, would they be fulfilled by an individual man or a community of men, and would that individual or community reside with the nuns or at a distance? The particular arrangement could make a great difference in the reliability of services for the nuns. Those nuns dependent on priests from a neighboring community, for example, had a less convenient and secure arrangement than nuns who could call on a resident chaplain or group of chaplains.[62] Whether this male participation was structured as service or supervision also made a difference. The business trips undertaken by the monks of Fontevrault were a different phenomenon from the cistercian use of a male supervisor (*custos*) for temporal affairs.[63]

The system at Fontevrault tended to avoid the antagonisms that could occur in more casual arrangements. The men at Fontevrault were part of the community and they identified with it. What was unique about Fontevrault was not that it had some men associated with the community, but that it had a particularly large group of men actually integrated into the community, by the original design of the founder. Robert of Arbrissel also firmly established the role of the men in the community as one of service, not supervision.[64] Although this may have been the intent at many other female communities, it was rare in twelfth- and thirteenth-century institutions to have the power of the abbess so little curtailed by male authority of one kind or another. This undoubltedly enhanced the prestige of Fontevrault, and contributed to its reputation as one of the foremost communities for women in France.

These institutional arrangements enabled Fontevrault to survive the period of monastic retrenchment that occurred at the end of the twelfth and the beginning of the thirteenth century, and to escape the knife of necessity or convenience that severed women from many monastic communities. The woman-centeredness of Fontevrault was not unique, but its firm institutional expression was, and this made it impossible to view the nuns at Fontevrault as burdensome, unimportant, or peripheral.

Knox College
Galesburg, Illinois

NOTES

*I have given a fuller treatment of the relationship of Fontevrault to other contemporary monastic movements in [Penny S. Gold,] *The Lady and the Virgin: Image, Attitude, and Experience in Twelfth-Century France* (University of Chicago Press, forthcoming).

1. For the development of reluctance on the part of many Orders to accommodate women desiring the monastic life, see Micheline de Fontette, *Les religieuses à l'âge classique du droit canon: Recherches sur les structures juridiques des branches féminines des ordres* (Paris: J. Vrin, 1967); R.W. Southern, *Western Society and the Church in the Middle Ages* (Baltimore: Penguin, 1970) 309–31; Herbert Grundmann, *Religiöse Bewegungen im Mittelalter: Untersuchungen über die geschichtlichen Zusammenhänge zwischen der Ketzerei, den Bettelorden und der religiösen Frauenbewegung im 12. und 13. Jahrhundert und über die geschichtlichen Grundlagen der deutschen Mystik* (Hildesheim: Georg Olms, 1961); Brenda Bolton, 'Mulieres Sanctae', in *Women in Medieval Society*, ed. Susan Mosher Stuard (Philadelphia: University of Pennsylvania Press, 1976) 141–58; Eleanor C. McLaughlin, 'Equality of Souls, Inequality of Sexes: Women in Medieval Theology', in *Religion and Sexism: Images of Woman in the Jewish and Christian Traditions*, ed. Rosemary Radford Ruether (New York: Simon & Schuster, 1974) 233–51. Another order that, to a certain extent, followed the pattern of Fontevrault was the Gilbertine Order in England, founded by Gilbert of Sempringham; see Rose Graham, *S. Gilbert of Sempringham and the Gilbertines: A History of the Only English Monastic Order* (London: E. Stock, 1901) and Sharon Elkins, article above and 'Female Religious in Twelfth Century England',(Dissertation, Harvard 1977).

2. René Niderst, *Robert d'Arbrissel et les origines de l'ordre de Fontevrault* (Rodez: G. Subervie, 1952) 38. The following details of Robert's life are taken from the two saint's lives devoted to Robert (PL 162:1043–78). The first was written by Baldric, Bishop of Dol, shortly after Robert's death in 1117. The second, concerned only with the events leading up to Robert's death, was written by a Fontevrist monk after Baldric's biography had been written, but sometime before 1120. A thorough discussion of the dating, authorship, reliability, and usefulness of the various sources of Robert's life, including the two saint's lives, can be found in Johannes von Walter, *Die ersten Wanderprediger Frankreichs: Studien zur Geschichte des Mönchtums*, vol. 1: *Robert von Arbrissel* (Studien zur Geschichte der Theologie und der Kirche, vol. 9, no. 3) (Leipzig: Dieterich, 1903) 9–94.

3. Baldric, *Vita*, ¶ 3; PL 162:1048–49.

4. This aspect of Robert's life, and the lives of others like him, are described by L. Raison and R. Niderst, 'Le mouvement érémitique dans l'Ouest de la France à la fin du XIe siècle et au début du XIIe siècle', *Annales de Bretagne* 55 (1948) 1–46.

5. Baldric, *Vita* 16; PL 162:1051: '. . . *sexus utriusque plures adjuncti sunt ei*'. This instance of both men and women following a wandering preacher is not an isolated phenomenon. The preachers of the First Crusade also drew mixed crowds. See, for example, the description of the career of Peter the Hermit in Steven Runciman, *A History of the Crusades* (New York: Harper & Row, 1964) 1:113–33.

6. Baldric, *Vita* 16; PL 162:1051: '*Videns autem subsequentium multitudinem dilatari, ne aliquid ageretur inconsulto, quoniam mulieres cum hominibus oportebat habitare, ubi possent sine scandalorum scrupulositate conversari et vivere, deliveravit perquirere, et si quod desertum contigisset reperire*'.

7. Baldric, *Vita* 17; 1052: '*Mulieres tamen ab hominibus segregavit, et inter claustrum eas velut damnavit, quas orationi deputavit; homines vere laboribus mancipavit. Non sine discretione id agere videbatur, quia sexum teniorem et imbecilliorem commendabat psalmodiae, et theoriae; fortiorum autem applicabat exercitiis vitae actualis. Laici et clerici mi [x] tim ambulabant; excepto quod clerici psallbant, et missas celebrabant, laici laborem spontanei subibant*'.

8. Baldric, *Vita* 19; 1053: '*Multi confluebant homines cujuslibet conditionis; conveniebant mulieres, pauperes et nobiles, viduae et virgines, senes et adolescentes, meretrices et mas-*

culorum aspernatrices' (see also *Vita* 22; 1055). Robert was drawing married women as well as widows and virgins: Niderst, p. 25, n. 22; Andrea, *Vita* 36 (PL 162:1075); J. de Petigny, 'Lettre inédite de Robert d'Arbrissel à la comtesse Ermengarde', *Bibliothèque de l'École des Chartes*, ser. 3, 5 (1854) 209–35.

9. Baldric *Vita* 20; PL 162:1054.

10. Niderst, 41–50. There is general agreement on the number of priories founded by mid-century (about twenty by the time of Robert's death in 1117 and another twenty by the time of the death of Petronilla, the first abbess of Fontevrault, in 1149). But estimates on the number founded after 1149 vary considerably, ranging from eighteen to one hundred additional priories. The reason for the discrepancy probably lies in the difficulty of distinguishing a priory from a simple domain, that is, a parcel of land worked or supervised by one or more members of the order (Françoise Grelier, 'Le temporel de l'abbaye de Fontevrault dans le haut-Poitou, des origines à la réforme du XVe siècle' [thèse Ecole des Chartes 1960,] 121–39).

11. Andrea; PL 162:1057–78. The identity of the author is not certain. For a discussion of the question of the authorship, see von Walter, 17–25. Andrea's story appears to be addressed to the men at Fontevrault, rather than to the men and women or women alone. There is no opening saluatation, but towards the middle of the *vita*, the author exclaims: *'Licet mibi, fratres, dicere virum bunc . . .' (Vita* 21; 1068). In contrast, Baldric's *vita* is addressed explicitly to the abbess and nuns of Fontevrault. His *vita* begins: *'Baldricus, Dei gratia Dolensium sacerdos, licet indignus, ancillae Christi Petronillae, venerabili monasterii Fontevraldensis abbatissae, omnibusque ejusdem coenobii sanctimonialibus sub ejus regimine, salutem'* (col. 1043). The different topics emphasized by the two authors may perhaps, then, be related to the different audiences intended. It is also a commentary on the separateness of the male and female communities that one *vita* would be addressed to the women, and one to the men, although Andrea refers to the life written by Baldric, and indicates that his purpose is to fill out the description of the events surrounding Robert's death (¶ 1; col. 1057).

12. These events comprise roughly the first quarter of the *vita*; the rest of the *vita* describes Robert's journeys during the seven months between the choice of the abbess and his death at the priory of Orsan.

13. Andrea, *Vita* 3; PL 162:1058–59. The pledge is described first as being almost unanimous, but later as unanimous. This is a matter of some interest, as a non-unanimous pledge could be taken as a sign of some dissatisfaction among the men. Such dissatisfaction was a distinct problem at various times from the fifteenth century onwards (F. Deshouillières, 'Le prieuré d'Orsan en Berry', *Mémoires de la Société des Antiquaires du Centre* 25 [1901] 51–137).

14. Andrea, *Vita* 5; PL 162:1060. The exact meaning of *conversa* and *virgo* are not clear. In this context, the distinction emphasized is someone who has joined the community somewhat later in life, as opposed to someone brought up from childhood in a monastery. For a discussion of the difficulty of establishing a precise meaning for the word *conversa* see Ursmer Berlière, 'Les monastères doubles aux XIIe et XIIIe siècles', Académie Royale de Belgique, Classe des lettres et des sciences morales et politiques, *Mémoires*, sér. 2, vol. 18, fasc. 3 (1923), pp. 27–31.

15. Andrea, *Vita* 5; PL 162:1060.

16. It is not clear why the choice was delayed seven months. Andrea also does not indicate whose counsel was sought in the selection of Petronilla. He only says that Robert made the choice 'not without the counsel of religious men' (*non sine religiosorum virorum complevit consilio*) (7; 1061).

17. Andrea, *Vita* 7; 1061: *'Licet enim monogama fuerit, cogente tamen necessitate, nulla mibi convenientior videtur buic praelationi'*. A seventeenth-century 'translation' of this passage adds an apologetic note not present in the original: Qu'il est vray qu'elle a esté une fois mariée: mais que cét empeschement a esté levé, comme quelques-uns d'eux qui y ont assisté, sçavent tres-bien, dans l'assemblée de Messeigneurs les Prelats, qui tous unanimement ont conclu, qu'on peut élire une Abbesse qui ait passé par cét Estat. Qu'elle estant instruite & despuis plus long-temps, mieux que toutes les autres Dames,

de ses Maximes, de son Esprit, & de ses desseins, elle les pourra facilement perpetuer dans l'Ordre' (Sébastien Ganot, *La vie du bien-heureux Robert d'Arbrissel, fondateur de l'Ordre de Fonteurauld* [La Fleche, 1648]). Robert was being considered for canonization in the seventeenth century, and his association with women caused much defensive writing. See Reto R. Bezzola, *Les origines et la formation de la littérature courtoise en Occident (500-1200)*, Bibliothèque de l'École des Hautes Etudes, vol. 313², (1960), p. 283, n. 1.

18. Elkins, 'Female Religious', 241, 271.

19. PL 162:1079-86.

20. von Walter, pp. 65-82.

21. ¶ 5; PL 162:1083-84.

22. ¶ 14; PL 162:1085.

23. Enclosure at Fontevrault was less strict than at cluniac and cistercian nunneries (Roger Gazeau, 'La clôture des moniales au XIIe siècle en France', *Revue Mabillon* 58 [1974] 295).

24. We also know from Andrea's *vita* that the abbess and prioress of Fontevrault travelled extensively (PL 162:1068ff). Petronilla's travels can also be gauged by the many scattered charters bearing her signature (Niderst, pp. 67-74).

25. The statutes are numbered differently in von Walter's edition of the Rule. He combines some statutes, and ends up with only thirty-nine rules for women; he retains twenty-seven for the men. In the following list, the first number is that in PL, the second (in parentheses), von Walter's: Women's 4(4), 28(28), 29(28), 30(29), 32(31), 33(32), 34(32). 35(33), 38(34), 40(35), 41(36); Men's 14(15). Von Walter's edition of Rule I is better than Migne's, and is cited in the notes that follow.

26. von Walter, p. 192 (Statute 32). Compare canon 27 of the Second Lateran Council (1139), which forbids canons or monks to sing in the same choir with nuns (J. D. Mansi, *Sacrorum Conciliorum Nova et Amplissima Collectio* [Venice, 1776] 21:533).

27. von Walter, 194 (Statute 15). This probably refers to servants rather than nuns.

28. von Walter, 190-91 (Statutes, 3, 26, 18, and 19).

29. Alexander Hamilton Thompson, 'Double Monasteries and the Male Element in Nunneries', in *The Ministry of Women: A Report by a Committee Appointed by His Grace the Lord Archbishop of Canterbury* (London: SPCK, 1919) 148.

30. Stephanus Hilpisch, *History of Benedictine Nuns*, trans. Sister M. Joanne Muggli, ed. Leonard J. Doyle (Collegeville, Minnesota: St John's Abbey Press, 1958) 23-24. Benedictine monasteries commonly had such an attached group of nuns (Dom Philibert Schmitz, *Histoire de l'ordre de Saint-Benoît*, [Maredsous, 1956] 7:45-50). For examples from twelfth-century Cologne, see Frederick Mark Stein, 'The Religious Women of Cologne: 1120-1320' (Dissertation, Yale 1977) 37-38.

31. On this point, see Sharon Elkins, 'Double Monasteries of Twelfth-Century England' (Paper delivered at The Seventeenth International Congress on Medieval Studies, Kalamazoo, 1982). I am grateful to the author for sharing with me this and other unpublished material.

32. For example, letters from Honorius II (PL 166:1268); from Lucius II (PL 179:864, 924); from Paschal II (PL 163:296, 419); from Calixtus II (PL 163:1121); from Innocent II (PL 179:72, 304, 320, 634, 635); from Eugenius III (PL 180:1037, 1396, 1413).

33. Some letters do mention *fratres* at Fontevrault: from Calixtus II (PL 163:1122); Lucius II (PL 179:865); Gelasius II (PL 163:504); Honorius II (PL 166:1268); Eugenius III (PL 180:1037).

34. *Chronicle of the Kings of England*, trans. J. A. Giles (London, 1904) 471. The Latin can be found in the Rolls Series, no. 90, 2:512 (Book 5, §440). Giles translates the word *egregium* as 'noble'; I have changed this to 'distinguished'.

35. *Historia Rerum Anglicarum*, Rolls Series, no. 82, 1:51-52.

36. *Ex Radulphi Coggeshalae Abbatis Chronico Anglicano; Recueil des historiens des Gaules et de la France* 18:62, 85.

37. Robert of Torigny, *Tractatus de immutatione ordinis monachorum*; PL 202:1312.

38. The *Annals* of Saint-Sergius of Angers, entry for the year 1116, in *Chroniques des Églises d'Anjou*, edd. Paul Marchegay and Emile Mabille (Paris, 1869) 143.

39. The *Chronicle* of Saint-Maxentius of Poitiers records that in the year 1100 Robert began to build the monastery of Fontevrault and to support churchmen (*patres*) and monks in many places (in *Chroniques des Églises d'Anjou*, 420).

40. The cartulary of Fontevrault, of which less than half (about 400 charters) still exists, is in two pieces; the bulk of it is in the Bibliothèque Nationale in Paris (nouv. acq. lat. 2414) and nine folios are in the Archives départementales of Maine-et-Loire, bound with a nineteenth-century copy of the part of the cartulary that is in the BN (Maine-et-Loire, 101H225). (For an account of the history of the cartulary, see R. I. Moore, 'The Reconstruction of the Cartulary of Fontevrault', *Bulletin of the Institute of Historical Research*, London University 41 [1968] 86–95.) The bulk of the charters in the cartulary date from the first half of the twelfth century. I have supplemented these with other charters dating through 1249, both original charters deposited in the archives of Maine-et-Loire (hereafter abbreviated M&L), and a large collection of charters made at the end of the seventeenth century and now preserved in Paris (BN ms. lat. 5480; hereafter abbreviated as BN5480; this manuscript is paginated rather than foliated). When referring to charters from the cartulary of Fontevrault, my reference will be F, for Fontevrault, followed by the number of the charter in the nineteenth-century copy (M&L 101H225), followed by a folio number, if it is from BN nouv. ms. lat. 2414, or a page number if it is from the nine manuscript leaves in M&L 101H225 (these leaves are paginated, 1–18); thus, for example, F781, fol. 75ʳ. This system should facilitate reference to either the original in Paris or the copy in Angers. Folio references are to the folio on which the given charter begins, although the quotation itself might come from the next folio.

41. Donations that mention both men and women (all from the first half of the twelfth century): F720, fol. 52ʳ; F743, fol. 62ʳ; F746, fol. 63ᵛ; F754, fol. 66ᵛ; F787, fol. 77ʳ. Donations that mention monks, or the monk of the church of St Jean de l'habit, with no mention of nuns: BN5480, p. 77 (1199); BN5480, p. 49 (1232); BN5480, p. 83 (1237); F809, fol. 84ʳ (first half twelfth century). In 1199, Eleanor of Aquitaine founded the chapel of St Laurence at Fontevrault (BN5480, p. 465), and some later gifts provide for a chaplain for that chapel: M&L 101H55; BN5480, p. 226; BN5480, p. 286.

42. In contrast, donations to gilbertine houses in England, houses frequently compared to Fontevrault, are commonly addressed to 'the nuns and their brethren, cleric and lay', or to 'the canons and nuns': F. M. Stenton, *Transcripts of Charters Relating to the Gilbertine Houses of Sixle, Ormsby, Catley, Bullington, and Alvingham* (Horncastle: W. K. Morton and Sons for the Lincoln Record Society, 1922) 77 and *passim*.

43. For example, F574, fol. 2ʳ; F760, fol. 68ᵛ.

44. One ironic result of this practice is that we can draw up a list of monks at Fontevrault, but not a list of nuns. Most of the monks who witnessed charters appear only once or twice in the documents.

45. F830, fol. 89ᵛ; F910, fol. 133ʳ.

46. F580, fol. 6ᵛ.

47. F719, fol. 51ᵛ; F780, fol. 74ᵛ; F772, fol. 72ʳ: a monk of Fontevrault was present on all three occasions, and the abbess in F780.

48. F719, fol. 51ᵛ. The action took place away from Fontevrault.

49. Cf. Abelard's recommendations to Heloise regarding the role of monks in taking care of the external needs of nuns (*The Letters of Abelard and Heloise*, trans. Betty Radice [Baltimore: Penguin, 1974] 209–10).

50. F698, fol. 43ᵛ.

51. Ibid.; an abbreviated version (lacking mention of Fontevrist monks at Vendôme) is found in PL 162:1095–96.

52. F575, fol. 3ʳ.

53. The chapter at which such ceremonies took place was apparently only for nuns, not nuns and monks: '*capitul* [*um*] *piae et justae congregationis sanctimonialium*'

(F692, fol. 41ᵛ). On at least one occasion, however, the nuns and monks met together in chapter. In 1119 Calixtus II visited Fontevrault and confirmed the possessions and privileges of the abbey. The charter of confirmation mentions his attendance at the chapter 'of brothers as well as sisters': '*Sequenti sane die in capitulum venientes, in pleniorii* [sic] *tam fratrum, quam sororum conventu . . .*' (PL 163:1122). But it seems likely that the men joined the assembly just for the special occasion of hearing Calixtus, which perhaps explains the use of the comparative form of *plenus*.

   54. BN5480, p. 340.

   55. BN5480, p. 439.

   56. The fifteenth-century reformed Rule of Fontevrault detailed a decision-making process for the community. When an important decision had to be made, the prioress was to call together all the nuns. After getting their advice, she could, if she so desired, ask for advice from secular experts or from some of the brothers. But if she did ask for advice from the brothers, they were to give it in humility and subjection, and not push their advice in an impudent manner (*Regula ordinis Fontis-Ebraldi. La reigle de l'ordre de Font-Evrauld* [Paris, 1642] 198). As the tone of the Rule indicates, the fifteenth-century monks did not seem as willing to devote themselves to the nuns as were the twelfth-century members of the Order. Certainly by the seventeenth century, the whole arrangement must have seemed quite odd. At least two treatises were written that were largely apologies for the organizational subjection of men to women at Fontevrault: *Noviciat des Enfans de la Vierge dicts religieux de l'ordre de Fontevrauld*, faict par le Solitaire de la Sacrée Vierge mère de Dieu (Poitiers, 1634); *D la Puissance et jurisdiction des religieux pères confesseurs de l'ordre de Fontevrauld au sainct sacrement de poenitence* (Poitiers, 1634). No such apologies seem to have been needed in the twelfth century.

   57. M&L 101H225.

   58. For a good description of the 'burden' from the male cistercian point of view, see Sally Thompson, 'The Problem of the Cistercian Nuns in the Twelfth and Early Thirteenth Centuries', in *Medieval Women*, ed. Derek Baker (Oxford: Basil Blackwell, 1978) 239.

   59. For information on numbers of men and women at some benedictine houses, see Schmitz 7:52.

   60. Alfred Jubien gives some statistics on the population of ten priories of Fontevrault in 1209:

   Saint-Aignan: 60 nuns, 2 monks, 2 clercs
   Le Breuil: 52 nuns, 9 monks
   Saint-Croix: 75 nuns, 2 clercs, 2 laymen   *lais*
   L'Espinasse: 100 nuns, 2 clercs, 3 laymen
   Le Paravis: 59 nuns, 3 priests, 1 clerc, 10 laymen
   Vaupillon: 56 nuns, 1 priest, 11 laymen
   Saint-Laurent: 76 nuns, 2 monks, 22 laymen
   Boulac: 70 nuns, a prior, 2 priests, 1 clerc, 31 laybrothers   *frères lais*
   Langages: 79 nuns, 4 monks, 4 laybrothers
   Mommère: 60 nuns, 1 chaplain, 20 laybrothers

Jubien, *L'abbesse Marie de Bretagne et la réforme de l'ordre de Fontevrault d'après des documents inédits* (Angers, 1872) p. 11, n. 2. Grelier also comments on the small numbers of men (often just two, three, or four) at many of the priories (p. 150).

   61. *L'ordre des chanoines reguliers d'Arrouaise: Son histoire et son organisation, de la fondation de l'abbaye-mère (vers 1090) à la fin des chapitres annuels (1471)* (Bruges: De Tempel, 1969) 1:516–17.

   62. A. Thompson, pp. 157–58.

   63. John A. Nichols, 'The Internal Organization of English Cistercian Nunneries', *Cîteaux. Commentarii Cistercienses* 30 (1979) 30. For details on various arrangements, see also Louis J. Lekai, *The Cistercians: Ideals and Reality* (Kent, Ohio: Kent State University Press, 1977) 350–52; Elkins, 'Female Religious', p. 6; Nicolas Huyghebaert, 'Les femmes laïques dans la vie religieuse des XIe et XIIe siècles dans la province

ecclésiastique de Reims', *I Laici nella 'societas christiana' dei secoli XI e XII* (Atti della terza settimana internazionale di studio, Mendola, 21–27 agosto 1965) (Milan, 1968) 371.

64. For an interpretation that minimizes Robert's role in the structuring of the institutions of Fontevrault, see Jacqueline Smith, 'Robert of Arbrissel: *Procurator Mulierum*', in *Medieval Women*, 175–84. Smith is a good antidote to Bezzola and others who elaborate, with little evidence, on Robert's intentions in founding and structuring Fontevrault, but I think she goes too far in the opposite direction, ignoring Robert's continuing involvement in the community after its foundation, as evidenced in Anrea's *Vita* and in many charters of donation.

The Emergence of a Gilbertine Identity

Sharon K. Elkins

WHENEVER A NEW RELIGIOUS ORDER is created, questions arise about its necessity. Are the purposes it serves and the needs it meets ignored elsewhere in the Church, or could the same functions be performed by groups already established? Has a charismatic figure, so often the impetus for the new Order, given rise to a personality cult or has a neglected form of genuine christian ministry been articulated? Often such issues are addressed by members of the new Order, eager to authenticate their legitimate place in the christian tradition.

By the end of the twelfth century, the Gilbertines had recognized the need to justify their existence.[1] Originating in mid-twelfth century England, they had become by the century's close a prominent, successful Order of nuns, canons, lay sisters, and lay brothers numbering twelve hundred religious in nine houses for both sexes and in four canonries, all located in England.[2] Since many men's Orders were reluctant even to supervise religious women,[3] since monasteries for both sexes had often been tried and often mistrusted,[4] the Gilbertines needed to enunciate reasons why their celibate men and women shared the same abbeys. Why had they devised a whole network of such monasteries for men and women, incorporated in a complex institution with a host of regulations and customs? How could they best vindicate their organization?

In addition to justifying their unusual organization, the Gilbertines were confronting an identity problem which had lingered from their inception. In 1147 their founder, Gilbert of Sempringham, had attempted to convince the Cistercians to assume supervision of Sempringham and Haverholme, the first two communities he had established, composed at that time of nuns, lay sisters, and lay brothers.[5] The Cistercians had refused Gilbert's request;

169

what explanation could then be offered for his development of an institutional arrangement so unlike that of the Cistercians? If he had been attracted to the Cistercian model, why had he deviated from it so markedly and why had he created instead an order of double monasteries?

The ideology which the Gilbertines developed to answer these questions emerged gradually. One version was provided before his death in 1189 by Gilbert of Sempringham himself, who wrote a succinct history of his formation of the Order; his account was preserved as the prologue to the Institutes of the Gilbertine Order.[6] A much longer, somewhat different rendition of the Order's early development was produced by an anonymous canon of the Order in 1201 for his *Vita* of Gilbert, part of a campaign to convince Pope Innocent III to canonize the founder.[7] Aware of the numerous objections which could be raised about the form, wisdom, and necessity of the new Order, the anonymous canon offered a self-conscious rationale for the Gilbertines. A comparison of Gilbert's history with the canon's *Vita* shows a gilbertine identity evolving.

GILBERT OF SEMPRINGHAM'S NARRATIVE

Gilbert's own account is a sparse chronological reconstruction of events in the 1130s and 1140s. As a young man, Gilbert had inherited two churches in Lincolnshire and rights in others. Rather than profit personally from their income, he wanted to give the revenue 'to the divine cult and for the sustenance of those choosing poverty for God'.

> But when I could not find men (*viros*) who wanted to submit their necks for the love of God to a strict life according to my wish, I found young women (*virgines*) who, often instructed by us, wanted to aim without any impediment for divine slavery, disregarding the cares of this world.[8]

Gilbert's bald assertion that he had originally intended to give his inherited wealth to men sets the motif of his whole story; repeatedly his preferences were altered by events.

'Since virginity is pleasing to God', Gilbert enclosed seven women 'whom I had stirred up with divine love' in a cloister he had built with the aid of Bishop Alexander of Lincoln, probably in 1131. 'I was not thinking of adding any more to those living there', but it seemed dangerous to have the enclosed women served by secular girls 'running here and there', able to do 'more harm than good'. So circumstances again altered his inital intention. After a visit from 'the first abbot of Rievaulx who had come by for me and had praised my plan' (*propositum*), Gilbert decided 'to permit my serving women themselves to be regulated in dress (*habitus*), in poor food and clothing, and to minister to those enclosed for Christ'.[9]

In elaborating the instructions he had given these serving women when he formed them into the lay sisters of his Order, Gilbert stressed their own desire for poverty, chastity, obedience, and humility. He was persuaded to form the lay sisterhood only after he had been 'entreated with great devotion' by the women themselves. The creation of the lay brothers he presented almost as an after-thought:

> Likewise, when I had only secular men who were in charge of the possessions of my house and the agriculture, [I gave them] a similar mode and order . . . as I had commanded for the lay sisters. I took for myself male servants, giving them the habit of religious, just as the lay brothers (*fratres*) of the Cistercians have.[10]

This organization with nuns, lay sisters, and brothers, would have satisfied Gilbert if circumstances had not, once again, intervened. With the growing appeal of Sempringham and the addition of another house at Haverholme, on property provided by Bishop Alexander of Lincoln, Gilbert became uneasy. 'There were not yet literate religious necessary for the care of them (*illas*) and the guidance of the laity'.[11] As Gilbert remembered events, he began to doubt his own ability to provide sufficient supervision and priestly service after the expansion. He sought outside help.

'I went to the chapter of the Cistercians, Pope Eugene being present, a man of great counsel and holiness, so that I might deliver up to their regulation our houses and the handmaids of Christ and our brothers'. The background had been set: Gilbert sought a strict religious life, the Cistercian abbot of Rievaulx had praised his plan, and he had adopted the cistercian *conversi* system; when he wanted regulation of his foundations, Gilbert turned to the Cistercians. Again, his wishes were foiled. 'I suffered a refusal altogether. Forced by necessity, I gathered to me clerics for the regulation and care of the women and men who had given themselves to external labor'. The clerics were to lead a life of vigils and fasts, following the Augustinian Rule.[12]

The remainder of Gilbert's account emphasizes how carefully the men and women were separated in the communities. The canons were to have access to the women only when they were dying and in need of unction and *viaticum*; even then witnesses were to be present. Mass was celebrated in a church with a partition which prevented the canons from seeing or being seen by the women; the canons' own chapel and buildings were separate from the nuns' area and were closed to the women.[13] Gilbert had been led by events repeatedly to change his plans, but he was not lax or remiss. His terse account was a history, not an apology; yet he was sure that each innovation, introduced to meet real needs, was fitting and proper.

Gilbert's version has the ring of veracity in its simplicity and straightforward narration. No master plan dominated his actions; no vision directed his steps. Women he had inspired by his preaching were willing to undertake the strict religious life he wanted to support, and everything else followed logically. Such a chain of events supports one of the theories which has been proposed to explain in general the appearance of double monasteries. In the words of Thompson, 'the male element is intended merely to fulfil the necessary duties from which the inmates of the cloister are disqualified by canonical and physical disabilities, and to supply assistance upon occasion in the management of temporal affairs'.[14]

Yet presuppositions abound in Gilbert's (and in Thompson's) explanation. The complicated double arrangement need not have been chosen to provide the services of sacraments and labor. Most nunneries over the centuries, and in twelfth-century England, were single-sex houses served by chaplains and hired hands. Gilbert devised a system in which resident male clerics directed and supervised an Order composed primarily of women. Basic assumptions about the necessity of enclosing nuns, separating them from the world, and providing ordained men to regulate them and the lay brothers and sisters underlay Gilbert's decisions.

Gilbert was not unique among his contemporaries in choosing a double arrangement, even though certain of his Order's features were unparalleled. Yet his account makes no mention of other examples which might have inspired him, neither the double monasteries formed by his peers, as at Fontevrault, nor those known from tradition, as the Anglo-Saxon monasteries described by Bede. Nor does his version of the early history contain any hint of an explanation some scholars have proposed for the proliferation of double monasteries in certain historical epochs and their virtual nonexistence in others: that they were a continuation of the practice of *mulierum consortia*— celibate men and women dwelling together to prove their ascetic virtues.[15] Mary Bateson has suggested that 'double monasteries arose . . . as the natural sequel to an outburst of religious enthusiasm' which led to 'a recrudescence of the conception of a purer form of chastity in the shape of a fresh development' of double monasteries.[16] However accurate this assessment may be for other monasteries and other epochs, it had no place in Gilbert's understanding of his Order. Even though there was a revival of enthusiasm for religious life, Gilbert never claimed to imitate other foundations nor to practice a purer than usual form of chastity. Rather, Gilbert held the conviction that female religious and lay orders needed close and extensive supervision and guidance by literate, ordained men, the type of regulation which inclusion in a men's Order or a double Order would provide.

THE IDEOLOGY OF THE VITA

By the beginning of the thirteenth century, Gilbert's explanation for his creation of the double arrangement was no longer sufficient. After the revolt of the lay brothers[17] and the less widely known affair of the nun of Watton,[18] questions had been raised about the wisdom of Gilbert's plan. In the *Vita* prepared by an anonymous gilbertine canon to convince Pope Innocent III of Gilbert's sanctity,[19] a more elaborate ideological justification for the Order was provided.

To show that Gilbert was not an idealistic enthusiast, naively unaware of sexual temptations, the *Vita* traced the slow germination of Gilbert's idea. The son of a norman knight of Lincolnshire and a saxon lady, Gilbert was prevented from becoming a knight himself by physical deformity, and acquired respect in his own right only after he was educated on the continent. When, on his return, he established a school for local children in his inherited church at Sempringham, Gilbert was already promoting literacy and discipline.

During the period he served as master of this school, Gilbert himself experienced sexual temptation. While lodging with a local family, Gilbert dreamed one night that he saw the daughter of his host, placed his hand on her breast and could not take it away. Fearing that the dream 'portended a future crime of fornication', Gilbert moved to a dwelling he constructed in the cemetery of the church. In the canon's view, this dream prefigured 'glorious merit', for this girl was later one of the first seven whom Gilbert enclosed at Sempringham; her bosom was 'the secrecy and peace of the church', 'a place of good conscience and perpetual peace' from which Gilbert's hand, his unshakable care, could not be removed.[20]

To explain Gilbert's gradual victory over his fear of close association with women, the canon elaborated the history of the Order's formation. Instead of simply describing how Gilbert had inspired the girls of Sempringham, the canon connected Gilbert's acts with the text in John 4:34–38 in which Jesus declared that he and his disciples had a mission to reap the harvest prepared for them, to bring in the grain for eternal life. Thus, the women whom Gilbert had 'stirred up with divine love' became in the canon's version 'certain secular girls (*puellae*) in the village of Sempringham whose minds had received the seed of the word of God which [Gilbert] had often ministered to them and now, having been cultivated with dew and heat, were white for the harvest'.[21] In imitating Christ and the disciples, Gilbert had launched into a mission of apostolic significance; moreover, he extended the disciples' task, for Gilbert both sowed and reaped while the disciples had only reaped what had been prepared by others.

In conferring his wealth on women instead of men, Gilbert was, the canon claimed, following an injunction of Jesus. With a reference to Luke 16:9, in which Jesus was quoted as saying, 'Use money, tainted as it is, to win you friends, and thus make sure that when it fails you, they will welcome you into the tents of eternity', the canon reasoned:

> When he did not find men who wanted to live so strictly for God, he considered it worthy to confer all his wealth for the use of such who were truly poor in spirit and who might purchase for himself and others the kingdom of heaven. Therefore he made himself friends (*amicos*) by means of unrighteous mammon, who might receive him into the eternal tabernacle. But he did not make men his friends (*amicos*) first, but women; for he called together for rejoicing female friends (*amicas*) found by the coins who later produced many male friends (*amicos*) by their chastity.[22]

The theme of Gilbert's support of the 'truly poor in spirit' was developed even further. '[Gilbert] repeatedly said, and divine counsel admonished, that more freely should be benefitted those who are naturally weaker and more compassionate, and thus more fully could reward be hoped for'.[23]

By the time the anonymous canon was writing for Innocent III, Gilbert's actions on behalf of women could not simply be recounted; they needed to be justified. In his complex chain of arguments—the reinterpretation of Gilbert's sexual dream, Gilbert's response to an undeniable readiness on the part of women, his use of funds to support female followers who would then attract men to his plan, his aid of women as an expression of true charity to the poor—the canon hoped to vindicate Gilbert's decision to become involved in the religious life of women. Attention to women needed explanation; in the canon's view, it was unusual and in itself showed Gilbert's admirable sanctity and apostolic lifestyle.

In recounting the addition of the lay orders, the anonymous canon followed Gilbert's explanation. Gilbert organized the serving girls with their own rule and habit because he had been advised 'by religious and prudent men that it was not safe for secular young women, wandering all around, to minister to religious'. 'Seeing that without male solace the female care was of little use', Gilbert added lay brothers. 'Since tender virgins are accustomed easily to be tempted by the wiley serpent', Gilbert provided dependable servants who would enable the women to be secluded 'away from the tumult of the world and the sight of men', 'so that entering the room of the king alone in solitude, the brides might be free for the embraces'.[24] According to the canon, nuns should be isolated from secular society in order to devote themselves to prayer.

The only mention the canon made of the Cistercians was in his short account of Gilbert's decision to 'deliver up the care of his houses to the guardianship of the cistercian monks' after the growing community made him want 'to put off the honor and burden' and lay it upon others whom he judged 'stronger and more able'. Since this was the first reference to cistercian influence, the canon explained why Gilbert chose the Cistercians:

> he had more familiarity of these than of others, having received frequent hospitality, and he judged them more religious than others because they were more recent and stricter of rule. Therefore he believed it safer to give them command of his work, because the rigor of the Order and newness of their conversion made them guard that *conversatio* which he considered the stricter.[25]

The canon portrayed the Cistercian's rejection of Gilbert's application as an advantage: 'The Lord did not want the congregation of Sempringham to be deprived of its own pastor, who was better for its future than ten others.' The mission to Cîteaux was a success, for Gilbert impressed Pope Eugene who asked him to assemble regulations for his community. 'Moreover blessed Malachy, archbishop of Ireland, and Bernard, abbot of Clairvaux, having become Gilbert's friend (*familiaris*) on that trip', gave him a staff as a sign of their love. The cistercian rejection enabled Gilbert to add the canons, the wisest possible choice; as the *Vita* explained, Gilbert chose men so that they would be able to rule others and protect the women; literate men so that they would know how to rule others and could show the way of salvation to men and women; ordained men so that by Church law they could preside and perform the office of pastor for all.[26]

In this summary of the addition of the canons and lay orders to the original gathering of women, the anonymous canon accepted Gilbert's own assumptions that women profited from seclusion and that they and the lay orders should be supervised by priests, preferably priests also bound to community life. The most significant difference between Gilbert and the canon's explanation was in the treatment of the cistercian connection; to this I will return shortly. But the canon was not content with this chronological recounting of the formation of the four groups. If circumstances and presuppositions dictated the creation of the Order, the final result was of apocalyptic significance. In a lengthy section of the *Vita*, the canon piled image on image in his enthusiasm for Gilbert's creation.

Most of the symbols stress the number four: 'Father Gilbert gathered the sons of God from the four winds and put them together in one construction —a house of God with four walls, having arranged four stones upon a humble foundation with Christ Jesus as the corner stone'. Or, the order was 'a new chariot of Aminadab', with four wheels—the clerical and lay men on one side and the literate and illiterate women on the other. This four-wheeled

chariot was pulled by two yoked teams, 'the clerical and monastic disciplines', led by Gilbert.[27] Although a wealth of symbols utilizing the number
four would have suggested themselves to a medieval writer—the four cor-
ners of the earth, four evangelists, four rivers of Paradise, to name just a few
—the canon passed over more obvious choices for esoteric images which
emphasized how unusual Gilbert's creation was.

In incorporating these four groups, Gilbert continued his imitation of the
apostles, already noted in the canon's account of the original 'harvesting' of
the souls of the women. For in combining groups which represented the
basic divisions of the Church—lay and religious, cleric and monk, male and
female—Gilbert had fulfilled the injunction given to Peter in his vision in
Acts: 'This [Order] is the dish of Peter, a four-sided piece of linen lowered
from heaven, filled with every kind of animal,' those honored according to
the world and those rejected. Since he had included in one Order groups
which the world normally kept apart, Gilbert had become 'the vicar and imitator of Peter'.[28]

Through a paraphrase of Isaiah 11, the canon presented the harmony of
these four diverse groups as a prefiguration of paradisiac harmony. The new
concord between usually discordant groups was likened to the wolf living
with the lamb, the panther with the kid, the calf and lion led by the small
boy; 'there the fox is not cunning, and the raven scorns the offered cadaver'.
Love having overcome hatred, all lived as one, united without murmurings.
The women who were part of this arrangement were able, miraculously, to
follow the institutes of men with only a few alterations. 'There,' as psalm
148:12 proclaimed, 'young men and virgin girls, the old with the young,
will praise the name of the Lord, because', the canon went on to say of the
Gilbertines, 'all ages, every condition, and both sexes exalt there not their
own but the name of the Lord alone'.[29]

How had such marvelous unity come about? In the canon's view, God
alone could be the author of a plan which combined such unlikely types in
one Order, under one master. Such an assortment of members under one
head had never before existed: Gilbert could not have discovered the arrangement or learned it from others. Like the apostle Paul, Gilbert had received his institutional organization from God, through the teaching of
Christ and the unction of the Holy Spirit.[30]

A new chariot bearing the ark of the Lord, formed by an 'imitator of
Peter' instructed by Christ and the Holy Spirit, prefiguring the millennial
kingdom, the Gilbertine Order was presented by the canon as a miraculous
new creation. Despite the precedent of anglo-saxon monasteries with abbesses ruling a community of monks and nuns, or the presence of Fontevrault with its abbess and a mixed community, the canon insisted on the
novelty of Gilbert's form. Strictly speaking, given the dominance of the

canons in the Order, he was right. Yet his assertion was not simply that the organization of the communities was unprecedented. 'Double orders' had been previously created for a plethora of reasons and understood by their participants in myriad ways. Yet the Gilbertines were impressed with their own uniqueness and with the wisdom and apocalyptic significance of their four-fold arrangement.

GILBERT AND BERNARD: THE ORIGIN OF THE DOUBLE ORDER

If this explanation for the origin and existence of the Gilbertines has survived in the two primary documents extant, why has cistercian influence on Gilbert's Order been so greatly emphasized in literature on the Gilbertines? [31] In part the assessment stems from a papal bull, printed by Dugdale and credited by him to Pope Innocent III, which has been interpreted to mean that Bernard of Clairvaux was one of the founders of the gilbertine Order.[32] Near the end of a long discursive section of this bull occurs the clause cited as evidence of Bernard's role: '*sancto Gilberto, primo priore ordinis de Sempringham, institutus, et à beato Bernardo quondam Clarevallis abbate.*'[33]

A comparison of the manuscript with Dugdale's printed edition shows that Dugdale's punctuation has misled scholars. Instead of being linked with Gilbert, Bernard was singled out by name among 'others' who approved, not the entire Institutes of the Gilbertine Order, but a particular decision of Gilbert's to recite the office in plain chant. Punctuated as in the manuscript, the passage reads:

> Moniales quoque in omnibus illum modum officii sui in ecclesia servent qui et supradicto Sancto Gilberto primo priore ordinis de sempringham institutus, et a Beato Bernardo quondam clarevallis abbate necnon et allis plerisque religiosis personis primo fuerat approbatus, scilicet non musice cantando seu honeste moderate ac distincte psallendo atque legendo.[34]

> Moreover the nuns always observe in church that style of [reciting the Divine] Office which was instituted by the aforementioned Saint Gilbert, first prior of the Order of Sempringham, and which was first favored by Blessed Bernard, Abbot of Clairvaux, as well as by many other persons in religion; namely [the nuns perform] the Office not by singing musically but by chanting or reading distinctly, with dignity and at a moderate pace.

Instead of identifying Bernard as the co-founder, the bull specified that he was one of the first to favor the simple plainchant used by the Gilbertines. The bull's importance as proof of Bernard's role is further undermined by its date. It came not from the reign of Innocent III, as Dugdale thought, but from that of Innocent IV,[35] a pontiff unlikely to have any special information about the early history of the Gilbertines.

Except for this papal bull and the mention of Bernard in the *Vita*, the only other source connecting Gilbert with Bernard is William Parvus of Newburgh's *History of England*, written at the end of the twelfth century just a few years before the *Vita*. According to William Parvus, after Gilbert had begun to attract numbers of women to a religious life, he wanted more specific direction, 'lest by chance he would be running, or had run, in vain', a reference to Galatians 2:2 in which Paul explained his decision to go to Jerusalem to verify his mission with the apostles after fourteen years of independent work. Comparing Gilbert to Paul, William Parvus recounted that Gilbert went to 'a wise and holy man with a clear title, namely the venerable abbot of Clairvaux, Bernard', who gave him venerable counsel and strengthened him in his plan (*proposito*).[36]

Proponents of Gilbert like Willaim Parvus and the anonymous canon who wrote the *Vita* could not have helped but be aware that Bernard's support for Gilbert's plan would have great apologetic value. Even though they saw Gilbert as another Paul, independently formulating his understanding of the christian life, they emphasized that Gilbert, like Paul, later verified his plan with a respected authority. If a suggestion of Foreville, the editor of much gilbertine material, is accepted, the anonymous canon may have decided to add the reference to Bernard in a second edition of the *Vita*, written between 1202 and 1205.[37] Was he inserting a tradition then in vogue, reported by William Parvus, perhaps unknown to him earlier? Were he and William, a half-century after Gilbert's visit to Cîteaux, finally publicizing the full range of events that had actually happened there, the support from Bernard as well as the rejection by the General Chapter? Or were they elaborating a link between Bernard and Gilbert to give additional justification to the Gilbertines?

The third alternative has much to recommend it, especially when a long-noted chronological detail is taken into account: for Gilbert to have met both Bernard and Malachy during his stay at Cîteaux, he would have had to remain there for more than a year.[38] So extended a visit seems most unlikely after the Cistercians had rejected his plan, especially when Gilbert himself made no mention of Bernard or any lengthy stay, and when the sole sympathetic figure Gilbert mentioned at Cîteaux was Pope Eugene.

Is the issue of cistercian influence then an unresolvable conundrum that does not warrant reinvestigation? In my view, the problems are solved if three stages are distinguished in the formation of the gilbertine identity: Gilbert's ideas before he went to Cîteaux; his view between his return to England and his death; and the concept advanced by his proponents at the turn of the century. When the early stage is considered, the cistercian influence is apparent. Gilbert himself said that the Abbot of Rievaulx praised his plan; that he had gathered the lay orders in imitation of and on the advice of the Cistercians; that he admired the strictness of the cistercian Order and wanted it to take over the regulation of his houses. An independent source, the foundation charter of Haverholme, verifies this early cistercian influence. When Bishop Alexander of Lincoln granted Haverholme in 1139 to the nuns 'under the custody and teaching of the priest Gilbert', he said, 'these women, seizing on the narrow life, the holy life, namely the life of the monks of the cistercian observance, as much as the weakness of their sex permits, strive to keep it, and they do keep it'.[39]

After the Cistercians refused his request, Gilbert initiated his most experimental and original phase. Studying the ideas of his contemporaries and predecessors but accepting none of their models intact, he devised a system in which ordained, literate men were bound by the Augustinian Rule and joined to the community. Apart from his fundamental assumption that male leadership and supervision were crucial for nuns and lay brothers, Gilbert was willing to make adjustments. When the Order was shaken by the revolt of the lay brothers, and when the dangers inherent in close association of chaste men and women were made apparent in the episode with the nun of Watton,[40] Gilbert accepted the advice that women and men should be secluded from each other. But he never lessened his conviction that the canons were essential for the welfare of the other groups.

During the later years of Gilbert's life, he continued certain cistercian-inspired practices. A gilbertine missal, probably prepared for the priory of St Catherine's Lincoln sometime after 1148, is 'generally speaking, Cistercian'. The editor concluded, 'there can, I think, be no doubt that it was copied from a Cistercian Missal . . . '.[41] Nonetheless, at this stage, Gilbert, following his own inclinations, selected practices from a wide range of monastic customaries which he combined in a unique way with his own ideas.

After Gilbert's death deprived them of his presence and charism, the Gilbertines sought a clearer sense of their identity to justify the continuation of Gilbert's plan, to explain why his creation should not die with him. They emphasized Bernard's approval of the developed organization, not just cistercian inspiration for the early formation. Instead of recounting the cistercian basis for the lay orders, the canon who wrote the *Vita* claimed support from both Bernard and Malachy for the fully developed order, especially for the addition of his own group, the canons. But even the reputed advocacy of a person of Bernard's stature was not sufficient to insure the Order's legitimation. Furthermore, the Gilbertines were unlikely to be protected by a cistercian canopy. Whatever their inspiration and whoever their supporters, the Gilbertines could not claim, like the Cistercians, to be a stricter observance of the benedictine Rule when Augustinian canons formed an essential part of their Order. The *Vita* therefore elaborated a justification for the four-fold order, a developed gilbertine ideology which did not depend on links with the Cistercians.

Viewing the Gilbertines' emerging identity in three stages not only accounts for their changing attitudes toward the Cistercians. It also shows the process by which an Order which had been created to meet specific circumstances gradually developed an understanding of its place in the christian tradition. Some Orders put into practice the ideals of their founder. Even though the history of the Franciscans illustrates how visions can resist institutionalization, Francis' ideals shaped the order. Gilbert gave his Order no such compelling vision; he was only one of many mid-twelfth century figures attracted to a strict benedictine life and willing to support it with his finances. Concrete situation had encouraged him repeatedly to modify his plans until finally his unique institution was devised. The Gilbertines had to develop gradually their own rationale. With the millennial vision of four-fold harmony, not with a pretense at cistercian imitation, the Order finally found its justification. The Gilbertines decided to be judged on the wisdom of that ideal—of men and women, clerics and monastics, ordained and lay persons living together and jointly striving for a christian society.

Wellesley College

NOTES

*I am grateful to Professor Giles Constable for his comments and suggestions, and to Drs Penny Gold and Mary Skinner for advice on earlier drafts. Any errors are, of course, my own.

1. The standard history of the Gilbertines is still Rose Graham, *S. Gilbert of Sempringham and the Gilbertines* (London, 1901). For biographical information on Gilbert, see note 19 below.
2. The most reliable estimate is that given by David Knowles and R. Neville Haddock, *Medieval Religious Houses, England and Wales*, 2nd ed. (London, 1971) 491–93: between 310 and 457 nuns; a smaller number of lay sisters; 214 to 264 canons, and around 300 laybrothers. For the difficulty in estimating membership, see David Knowles, *The Monastic Order in England* (Cambridge, 1966) 207.
3. A growing literature on this theme began with Herbert Grundmann, *Religiöse Bewegungen in Mittelalter* (1935, rpt. Hildesheim, 1961), and continues in R. W. Southern, *Western Society and the Church in the Middle Ages* (Harmondsworth, 1970) 312–18; even popular histories have developed the idea: Frances and Joseph Gies, *Women in the Middle Ages* (New York, 1978) 87–96. For a treatment of situations particularly relevant to the Gilbertines, see Jacqueline Smith, 'Robert of Arbrissel: *Procurator Mulierum*', and Sally Thompson, 'The Problem of the Cistercian Nuns in the Twelfth and early Thirteenth Centuries', *Medieval Women*, ed. Derek Baker (Oxford, 1978) 175–84, 227–52.
4. On double monasteries, see Alexander Thompson, 'Double Monasteries and the Male Element in Nunneries', *The Ministry of Women* (London, 1919) 145–64; Ursmer Berlière, *Les Monastères doubles aux XIIe et XIIIe siècles* (Brussels, 1923) and

Mary Bateson, 'Origin and Early History of Double Monasteries', *Transactions of the Royal Historical Society* N.S. 13, (1899) 137–98.

5. On the relation between the Gilbertines and the Cistercians, see Graham, pp. 10–14; Knowles, *Monastic Order*, pp. 205–7; Francis Giraudot and Jean de la Croix Bouton, 'Bernard et les Gilbertins', *Bernard de Clairvaux*, Commission d'histoire de l'order de Cîteaux (Paris, 1953) 327–38; and Brian Golding, 'St Bernard and St Gilbert', *The Influence of Saint Bernard*, ed. Sister Benedicta Ward (Oxford, 1976) 42–54.

6. Preserved in an early thirteenth century manuscript in excellent condition, the Institutes of the Gilbertine Order are introduced by a first-person narrative claiming authorship by Gilbert: Bodleian Douce 136, folios xii^v–1^v, printed with no significant variations in William Dugdale, *Monasticon anglicanum*, edd. John Caley, Henry Ellis, and Bulkeley Bandinel, 6/ii (London, 1846) insert after p. 954, pp. xix–xx. Since Gilbert could have written his account for the original version of the Institute adopted in the early 1150s or as much as forty years later, shortly before his death in 1189, the narrative is difficult to date; the assertion that the nuns' chapel was partitioned in a way which prevented the nuns from seeing or being seen by the canons would suggest a date after 1167, when modifications were introduced in response to the revolt of the lay brothers. For this revolt, see Raymonde Foreville, *Un Procès de Canonisation à l'aube de XIIIe Siècle (1201–1202)* (Paris, 1943) 83–89, and David Knowles, 'The Revolt of the Lay Brothers of Sempringham', *English Historical Review* 50 (1935) pp. 465–87. Although Gilbert's recollections could have been shaped by challenges to his organization, this is the only account purporting to be by him.

7. For a discussion of the manuscript tradition of the *Vita*, see Foreville, *Un Procès*, xiv *ff*, and for a suggestion of the author's identity, pp. xx–xxii. The version preserved as Bodleian Cotton Cleop. B. I. was printed by Dugdale, pp. v *ff*.

8. Douce, fol. xii^v; Dugdale, p. xix. The translations are mine.

9. Douce, fol. xii^v–1^r; Dugdale, p. xix.

10. *Ibid.* In the text of the Institutes, an account of uncertain date provides more details about this cistercian influence on the lay brothers. The Abbot of Rievaulx who advised Gilbert is identified as William, and the serving men themselves are said to have longed to follow the austerities of the cistercian laybrothers whom they saw on William's visit to Sempringham. See Douce fol. 38^r, and Dugdale p. xxxvi. Since this section could be considerably later than Gilbert's and the canon's accounts, and since the greater specificity elaborates, without changing, Gilbert's version in the introductory section of the Institutes, I have not set this expansion on a par with the other two account. Compare Golding, p. 47, and Giraudot-Bouton, 328–30.

11. Douce fol. 1^r; Dugdale p. xix.

12. *Ibid.* The standard date for this visit to the cistercian General Chapter is 1147.

13. Douce fol. 1^{r-v}; Dugdale, pp. xix–xx.

14. Thompson, 'Double Monasteries', 164.

15. Literally referring to the men who consorted with women, the phrase *mulierum consortia* should include as well the women who proved their conquest of temptation by living with men. See Roger Reynolds, '*Virgines subintroductae* in Celtic Christianity', *Harvard Theological Review* 61 (1968) 547–66, and Louis Gougaud, '*Mulierum Consortia*: Étude sur le Syneisaktisme chez les ascètes Celtiques', *Ériu* 9 (1921) 147–56.

16. Bateson, p. 197.

17. See above, note 6.

18. Giles Constable, 'Aelred of Rievaulx and the Nun of Watton: An Episode in the Early History of the Gilbertine Order', in Baker, *Medieval Women*, 205–26.

19. The biography of Gilbert is based primarily on this *Vita*. Born in Lincolnshire in the 1080s, Gilbert fled to the continent for his education in order to escape ridicule at home for his deformity and slow learning under his father's tutor. After teaching at the school he founded at Sempringham, Gilbert was called to the court of

the bishop of Lincoln in 1122. He remained there until around 1130, primarily serving with Bishop Alexander, who ordained him to the priesthood. From 1131, when he gathered the women at Sempringham, until his death in 1189, Gilbert was chiefly concerned with the affairs of his new Order. The *Vita* served its purpose, for Innocent III canonized Gilbert in 1202. We possess the expanded *Vita* from 1205.

20. Cotton Cleop. fol. 41; Dugdale, pp. v–vi. The translations are mine.

21. Cott. Cleop. fol. 46; Dugdale p. vii.

22. *Ibid.*

23. Cott. Cleop. fol. 47; Dugdale p. vii.

24. Cott. Cleop. fol. 47–51; Dugdale pp. vii–viii.

25. Cott. Cleop. fol. 50–51; Dugdale p. viii.

26. Cott. Cleop. fol. 51–53; Dugdale pp. viii–ix.

27. Cott. Cleop. fol. 55; Dugdale p. ix. The chariot of Abinadab bore the ark in 2 Samuel 6:3ff; the reference to it in Song of Songs 6:11 would help explain its familiarity to the canon. The division of the women into literate and illiterate women instead of nuns and lay sisters is unusual in the *Vita.*

28. *Ibid.* The image of a dish in Peter's vision is not preserved in most modern translations, but it would be one interpretation of the Vulgate, Acts 11:4ff.

29. Cott. Cleop. fol. 55–56; Dugdale p. x.

30. Cott. Cleop. fol. 56–57; Dugdale p. x Galatians 1:11–13 was paraphrased by the canon, the text in which Paul claimed he received his gospel through a revelation, not from men.

31. See most recently, Giraudot-Bouton, 327–38, and Golding, 42, 50.

32. Graham, p. 13, ftn. 56; her claim has been followed by later scholars.

33. Dugdale vi, 2, p. 961.

34. The bull, printed by Dugdale, vi, 2, pp. 960–61, is from a general cartulary of the gilbertine house of Alvingham, written mainly in a thirteenth-century hand, Bodleian Laud. mis. 642, fol. 2.

35. C. R. Cheney and Mary G. Cheney, edd., *The Letters of Pope Innocent III (1198 –1216) concerning England and Wales* (Oxford, 1967) 61; Élie Berger, *Les Registres D'Innocent IV,*[1] (Paris, 1884) 161.

36. William Parvi de Newburgh, *Historia Rerum Anglicarum,*[1] ed. Hans Claude Hamilton (London, 1856) 45–46.

37. Raymonde Foreville argues that the few references to Gilbert as blessed (*beatus*) instead of master, his usual title in the *Vita*, occur in sections added in the expanded version of the *Vita* after his canonization; hence, 'Le paragraphe intitulé *Quod commissum est ei a domino papa regimen ordinis sui* [the passage which mentions Bernard] . . . où l'épithète *beatus* précède le nom de Gilbert à l'instar de ceux de Thomas de Canterbury, Bernard de Clairvaux, et Malachie d'Armagh, respectivement canonisés en 1173, 1174, et 1190, semblent postérieurs au décret d'Innocent III concernant la canonisation de Gilbert (30 janvier 1202)' *Un procès,* pp. xvii–xviii.

38. Golding, 42–47, following the reconstruction by Giraudot-Bouton, 331–32.

39. Dugdale, 948, an accurate transcription of Bodleian MS Dodsworth 144, a cartulary of Haverholme copied in the seventeenth century.

40. See above, notes 17 and 18.

41. Reginald Maxwell Woolley, ed., *The Gilbertine Rite,* 1, Henry Bradshaw Society, *59* (London, 1921) xv and xxv.

Feminine Lay Piety in the High Middle Ages: The Beguines

Dennis Devlin

A PIOUS WOMAN who desired to devote her life to God and religion during most of the Middle Ages had two choices: she could become a nun in the traditional monastic sense, or she could become a recluse in a cell attached to a church or chapel. Even these were not viable choices for most women: a sizable dowry was often required to obtain one of the few available places in an abbey; the life of a recluse was closely regulated by the clergy, and was a life unsuited to many persons. Women from backgrounds of little wealth usually had no choice at all; religious life was seldom a possibility for them.[1]

This was not the case, however, everywhere in Christendom during the late twelfth and the thirteenth centuries. There grew up in the urban centers of the Low Countries, the Rhineland, and northern France a new form of religious life for devout women from all walks of life. Contemporary sources refer to these women in a variety of ways: *mulieres religiosae, mulieres santae,* and, especially in sources from unsympathetic ecclesiastical authorities, *mulieres quae beguinae dicuntur.* Though some ecclesiastical officials used the term to apply generically to heretics, the women involved in this new 'movement' apparently used 'beguine' sometimes to describe themselves. The origins of the term as well as the origins of the movement seem obscured by time, though modern scholars have offered various theories regarding both issues.[2] Regardless of its origins, the evolution of the beguine life can be traced from near its inception to its institutionalization over the course of nearly two centuries, and the lifestyle of these pious women can easily be differentiated from that of most nuns and lay women.

ORIGINATION AND DEVELOPMENT

Scholars have generally agreed that the development of the beguine movement has four stages, one flowing into the next.[3] The first, spontaneous
development resulting from the waves of religious excitement which had
swept over european Christendom during the twelfth century, saw individual
women searching for a more intense spiritual life. Church reform, currents
of mysticism, new popular religious ideals and practices, crusading fervor,
and numerous socio-economic changes had all combined by the late twelfth
century to produce a new phenomenon in western Europe's urban centers:
women—usually from the wealthier classes—began living a life dedicated to
God and religion, but outside of the traditional forms of monasticism or
reclusion. These early beguines were regulated neither by vows nor rule,
nor did they necessarily renounce the possibility of marriage. Moreover,
they did not withdraw from the world as did nuns or recluses, but lived in
their own houses or those of friends and relatives, in most cases earning
their own living through some sort of manual labor in the cloth industry.[4]

By the early thirteenth century many of these women had become associated in informal groups under the unofficial guidance of friendly and
sympathetic monks and clerics. At this stage, the beguines were essentially
unregulated; they took no perpetual or even long-term vows, and worked in
the world; each household developed its own form of spiritual life complete
with devotional activities and exercises.[5] The lack of ecclesiastical discipline
and official hierarchical approval proved threatening in this public phase of
the beguine movement. The beguines were fortunate to find support from
the Cistercians (as we shall see shortly) and a protector and ardent patron in a
rapidly rising young cleric, Jacques de Vitry, who advanced from a parish
ministry in the Low Countries to become bishop of Acre and eventually
friend, spiritual advisor, and cardinal-legate to Pope Gregory IX.[6]

A third phase began when beguine houses and associations were granted
an indirect quasi-legal recognition by Gregory IX's papal bull of 1233, *Glo-
riam virginalem*. From this point onward, the beguines came increasingly
under clerical control and organization. Many houses were forced to accept
a sort of modified conventual rule—a variation on the cistercian customary
seemed preferred—and to submit to clerical supervision of their spiritual and
devotional life. The freedom earlier beguines had enjoyed became increasingly curtailed, though at the same time the 'cloistered beguines' of this
third stage of development were less threatened with being disbanded or
painted as heretics by detractors. Indeed, beguine houses and the beguine
lifestyle still differed substantially from the traditional monastic pattern, and
the beguines remained officially laywomen living in an established parish
under the spiritual guidance of the local curates.[7]

The last stage of their development was the official episcopal organization of beguine houses into parishes. This move made beguinages legal religious and civil entities, granted them certain privileges and protections, but also brought them directly under clerical authority—most often Dominican— and substantially reduced their autonomy. The beguines never, however, became officially recognized as a religious order nor were the women ever legally 'religious.'[8]

Throughout its two centuries of development, the beguine movement seems to have been at its liveliest and most dynamic in its first stages, particularly in the early thirteenth century during the lifetime of Jacques de Vitry (D. 1240). It was at this point in its growth that these associations of pious women first gained widespread notice—notoriety, according to some sources —and made their greatest impact on medieval spirituality. The beguines had by this time attracted the attention not only of Jacques de Vitry, who supplies considerable information concerning the lifestyle and spirituality of some of them,[9] but also that of the cistercian Order. Caesarius of Heisterbach includes numberous stories of *mulieres religiosae* and *mulieres sanctae* in his collections of miracle tales,[10] while the relationship between some cistercian abbeys of men and women and various beguine houses was extraordinarily close until the mid-thirteenth century.[11] Cistercian foundations at Cologne, Villers-en-Brabant, Aulne, St Bernard on the Scheldt, Herkenrode, and Parc-les-Dames, among others, provided the beguines with protection, spiritual guidance, and material sustenance through land grants and pensions.[12] The beguines benefited from this relationship. But so too did the Cistercians; by their contact with the beguines they remained in touch with fresh currents of spirituality. According to E.W. McDonnell: 'On Cistercian nuns themselves it appears that beguine mentality left a deeper imprint than that of the order which had adopted them'.[13] Yet through these exciting first two phases of their development, the beguines remained lay women, unregulated and uncloistered; very few of them ever became nuns or *conversae*.

Clearly, there was something about the lives of these holy women which touched a responsive chord in the heart of the most vital and dynamic monastic Order of the time, and which seemed admirable to an ardent reformer of the stature of Jacques de Vitry. The beguines did not fit the ordinary pattern: they were women who were in the world, but not really part of it; pious women whose devotional ardor often surpassed that of cloistered nuns. Like them they dedicated their lives to God in a disciplined lifestyle, but unlike them they were not professed religious. In sum, it was the lifestyle of the early beguines, a lifestyle founded on an intense spirituality, which differentiated them on the one hand from other laywomen and on the other from nuns.

Rooted in the fertile soil of the religious ferment following the gregorian reforms, beguine spirituality during its early phases exhibited most of the charasteristics associated with the popular religious movements of the period. Chief among these was the concept of the *vita apostolica* which, in its various forms and interpretations, contributed heavily to the creation both of new religious orders and of new heterodox groups.[14] While there were different interpretations as to what constituted the true apostolic life, most agreed that a few basic principles were always involved. These included a return to the primitive Church and its scriptural foundation, a concern for the conversion and salvation of souls throughout the world, and evangelical poverty which included the common life and honest manual labor. The lack of consensus occurred in defining precisely what was meant by the 'primitive Church', 'concern for souls', and 'evangelical poverty'; indeed, different groups within society applied different interpretations to these concepts, usually including only their own constituency within their particular definition of spiritual perfection.[15] A product of the times, beguine spirituality was also based on an interpretation of apostolic life.

The popular fascination with the primitive Church in the twelfth and thirteenth centuries derived in a large measure from a rejection of the socioeconomic conditions of the time. Social dislocation caused by the revival of commerce and the growth of towns, together with a distaste for an increasingly wealthy institutional Church whose leaders were numbered among the political powers of the age, led many lay persons and some clerics to yearn for a simpler life and a salvation easier to attain. Scripture provided guidelines; the lifestyle imitated that of the apostles; the Rule was the gospels. Thus could a Jacques de Vitry not be disturbed by groups such as the beguines who had no rule: 'It is, in my judgment, not only those people who renounce the world and go into religion who can be called "regulars", but all the faithful of Christ who serve the Lord under the rule of the gospel and live under the orders of the one highest Abbot of all'.[16] The return to the primitive Church was, in fact, the essence of the apostolic life for, people believed, the primitive Christians showed great zeal for the cure of souls, lived in common, worked with their hands, and practiced voluntary poverty.

MARY OF OIGNIES

All these features were hallmarks of the spirituality of the early beguines. Again and again in reference to the beguines, expecially in their *vitae*, the ideals associated with the concept of the primitive Church are mentioned.

Jacques de Vitry's biography of Mary of Oignies (d. 1213), the woman who became the prototypical beguine, constantly reiterates these aspects of beguine spirituality.

He states that though she was enlightened directly by the Holy Spirit, nonetheless Mary still revered the scriptures and was guided by them.[17] She followed 'the most fundamental of all evangelical teachings: "Whosoever will come after me, let him deny himself and take up his cross and follow me"; and she made it her life to follow Christ'.[18] As a girl, yet unable to follow Christ, Mary seemed to recognize the great virtues of the Cistercians and when coming upon them 'was fond of stepping after them in their footprints'.[19] Later, as an adult, Mary modeled her life on the life of Christ and followed in his footsteps, using the scriptures for guidance.

She also 'burned with zeal for the salvation of souls' to such an extent that, being a woman and thus forbidden by church law to preach, she prayed God to send her a preacher through whom she could save souls.[20] She loved and supported preachers and their work, supported and prayed for the crusading movement, and endeavored through example and counsel to help others seek spiritual perfection. In comparing Mary's charitable work to her concern for souls, Jacques de Vitry echoes the general attitude of his contemporaries who felt dedicated to the apostolic life: 'For though it is a pious and charitable work to relieve physical ills, it is much greater to exhaust time and work on the cure of souls; nor is there any sacrifice more pleasing to God than zeal for saving souls'.[21] As her biographer he relates numerous incidents of Mary's concern for saving souls, in addition to mentioning several cases where her intercessions helped free souls from purgatory.[22]

Jacques de Vitry also provides ample testimony to Mary's conformity to the most visible aspects of apostolic life: poverty and manual work. 'As she grew in years, her love of poverty and religion increased', he wrote, referring to her childhood.[23] Later 'she not only renounced what was her neighbor's by not wanting it but what was her own by leaving it',[24] even though 'she was born of parents in the middle rank of society, and in such a well-to-do situation that she was surrounded with comforts and luxury'.[25] Of her insistence on poverty, he added: 'She developed a great love of poverty, so great that she hardly retained the necessities of life . . . yet Christ always supplied her the necessities.'[26] Her love of poverty was, in fact, so intense that 'often she meditated on the poverty of Christ . . . and had a strong desire to leave and follow Christ, begging her bread as he did . . . being dependent on the hospitality of strangers'.[27]

She supported herself through alms and work, the latter not because she needed to work but because of work's penitential value. 'She labored with her hands as much as possible so as to afflict her body with penance and to relieve the needs of her poor neighbors, and also having left all to follow

Christ, to have the means of providing herself food and clothing. . . . Nor did she find manual labor anything but most sweet . . . she labored with her hands and ate her bread in quiet and silence in conformity to the apostolic command.'[28] It was, in fact, Mary's dedication to poverty and manual work which, according to Jacques de Vitry, so strongly instilled in her the humility and obedience requisite to spiritual perfection. Hence his frequent examples and many references to Mary's practice of these important elements of the apostolic life.

Voluntary poverty and the manual work associated with it were perhaps the key ingredients of the apostolic program of devout lay people who, forbidden by canon law to preach, were necessarily limited in their ability to save souls and imitate the lifestyle they associated with the primitive Church. Apostolic poverty was, however, difficult to achieve in a manner acceptable to church officials, partly because of its idealism and impracticability and partly because of its tendency to point an accusing finger at the institutional Church. The temptation was always great among laymen and radical clerical reformers who espoused apostolic poverty to attack the wealth of the Church and its many vested interests in the social and economic structures of the time.[29] It was in this point that Mary of Oignies and the beguines distinguished themselves from other layfolk who desired to practice the apostolic life, for the beguines rarely ran afoul of church authorities by turning the virtue of poverty into a vice by attacking the ecclesiastical power structure. Like St Francis and his early followers, the beguines succeeded in living a virtuous apostolic life essentially by minding their own business, by providing example rather than criticism, and by remaining humble and obedient to church authority.[30] Consequently, de Vitry frequently emphasizes Mary's obedience and humility; 'she denied herself by submitting to another by obedience', and 'after her usual manner, trying humbly and with dove-like simplicity to obey everyone'.[31] Because of this, she was able to live the apostolic life without falling victim to pride. Other lay apostolic groups, such as the Waldensians and the Spiritual Franciscans, fell away on this very point. Instead of becoming saintly examples of lay spiritual perfection as did many beguines and early followers of St Francis, they ran aground on the shoals of heterodoxy.

There was yet another value to the practice of voluntary poverty and labor of the hands. Since the earliest days of the Church, these practices had been associated with asceticism and penance. They were considered necessary to the achievement of spiritual perfection, since they presupposed the attainment of humility and obedience through mortification and corporal discipline.[32] They were also one of the cornerstones of institutional monasticism; the gentle erosion of them had been both a factor in the founding of new Orders in the twelfth century and in the simultaneous criticism of monastic groups. De Vitry placed beguine life therefore within the traditional, acceptable standards of christian spirituality by his emphasis on poverty and humility when he described them as 'large bands of holy women who . . . clinging to the heavenly Spouse in poverty and humility, earning a poor subsistence by the work of their hands.'[33]

Through their practice of the apostolic life and espousal of evangelical principles the beguines accomplished two things. First, they were able to devote their lives to the pursuit of spiritual perfection in the mainstream of christian tradition, within the limits allowed by church officials. As they posed no threat to the institutional Church, but in fact accepted its authority and traditional spiritual values, they were able to enjoy the protection and patronage of a Jacques de Vitry and of the Cistercian Order, whose basic values they reflected. Second, since by the thirteenth century most experts on the matter had conceded that laypersons could live a certain kind of apostolic life and might achieve spiritual perfection, it was not yet necessary for the beguines to accept a rule or enclosure, or to become nuns.[34] Herein lay their strength. Living an acceptable form of the apostolic life, they could remain within the boundaries of traditional spirituality; but being laywomen and free of the restrictions imposed upon cloistered nuns, they had the liberty to experiment and break new ground.

CISTERCIAN NUNS: SIMILARITIES AND DIFFERENCES

Though they were laywomen, the beguines did nonetheless have much in common with their cloistered benedictine and cistercian sisters. Virginity or continence, one of the great virtues of the cloister, was also important to the beguines. Jacques de Vitry makes much of the chastity of Mary of Oignies who, though she was married, refrained from sexual activity. At first her husband yielded 'merely from the gentleness and kindness of an indulgent husband' but later as a result of a vision from God he even 'imitated her religious works and saintly life, leaving all to the poor to follow Christ'.[35] Beguines drew women drom all socio-economic ranks. Some, like Mary of Oignies, were married, some unmarried, some widowed. Regardless of their social rank or marital status, however they considered the virtue of chastity as essential to the beguine lifestyle as to that of professed nuns. Jacques de Vitry describes them as 'bands of holy virgins, despising carnal pleasures and riches . . . holy matrons serving God, zealously guarding the chastity of maidens and instructing them in wholesome lessons to desire only the heavenly Spouse . . . widows, too, fasting, praying, watching, working . . . to serve the Lord in the spirit as earlier they had tried to please their husbands in the flesh'.[36] So important to the beguine lifestyle was the virtue of chastity that McDonnell, echoing other scholars, calls it one of 'the two cardinal objectives of beguine life' the other being poverty in an apostolic context.[37]

The beguines were also similar to nuns, especially cistercian nuns, in developing a mysticism which went beyond that of most contemplatives. Jacques de Vitry tells of many beguines who 'were so taken out of themselves by plentiful drinks from the Holy Spirit that they passed the whole day in ecstatic silence'.[38] Nearly every page of his *life* of Mary of Oignies provides examples of her mysticism. This is the case with the *vitae* of other thirteenth-century beguines, as it is with the *vitae* of contemporary cistercian nuns.[39] Among mystical experiences common to beguines and cistercian nuns were communication with saints and angels, visions of Christ and the Virgin, appearances of the infant Jesus, numerous eucharistic phenomena, and a variety of ecstatic trances, out-of-the-body experiences, and revelations of the future.[40] In addition, holy women of both groups could cure the ill, speak in tongues, and see into others' consciences, and they often had gifts of clairvoyance, tears, and prophecy.[41] This great similarity between the spirituality and mystical experiences of both beguines and cistercian nuns undoubtedly accounts for much of the cistercian monks' interest in these lay *mulieres sanctae*, and indicates the monks' possible influence on both groups of women.

Some of the devotional interests and spirituality of beguines and cistercian nuns were so markedly similar that contemporaries often made little distinction between them. McDonnell even claims that the nuns were so closely intertwined with 'the beguine movement that they passed under the eyes of the public as beguines'.[42] Moreover, Greven's basic thesis was that the beguine movement was not only quite similar to that of the Cistercians but was, for all practical purposes, derived from it.[43] Part of such confusion of the two groups undoubtedly stemmed from the Cistercian Order's late recognition of a feminine branch as well as the legislation of the General Chapters, which vacillated between encouraging the acceptance of women into the order (until 1226) and limiting the activities of monks engaged in the *cura monialium*.[44] A further point of confusion was the clearly obvious fact that not only were there similarities between beguines and cistercian nuns, but that the relationship between them—before the appearance of the friars—was remarkably close. Nonetheless, a beguine-cistercian affinity and parallelism did not necessarily make the beguine lifestyle and spirituality merely a derivative form of cistercianism.

Despite the similarities between the two groups and their mutual influence on one another, there were differences even beyond the beguines' official lay status and lack of rule. The beguines' version of the apostolic life was more in the lay mold which had developed during the twelfth century than it was in the traditional monastic framework. While the beguines exhibited certain apostolic virtues found among nuns, such as humility and obedience, they had a different interpretation of poverty. Cloistered nuns were hardly able to support themselves by manual work in the cloth industry, by mendicancy, or by the extremes of physical poverty favored by the beguines.[45] Nuns, like monks, took vows of poverty and practiced spiritual poverty, an acceptable and traditional form of apostolic poverty but not the type of apostolic poverty found among beguines.[46] Roisin, in fact, claims that the beguines heavily influenced the cistercian nuns' practice of poverty.[47] The early beguines, living in towns and unrestricted by vows of stability, were able to work in cottage industry occupations and to beg—practices favored by the secular but not the monastic interpretation of apostolic poverty. Moreover, most beguine houses lacked the endowments of nunneries, and in many cases the beguines' practice of apostolic poverty must have been dictated not only by a desire for spiritual perfection but by simple economic necessity.

In yet another area of spirituality the beguines differed from cloistered nuns. Beguine ascetic practices were often far more extreme than those found, or even allowed, in abbeys. Jacques de Vitry tells of a beguine who rolled herself in the fire, and stood in freezing water in the dead of winter.[48] He relates numerous ascetic practices of Mary of Oignies, including her 'great loathing for her own flesh so that she cut off pieces of it with a knife'.[49] She would also go for long periods neither eating nor drinking and, as her biographer says, 'wonderfully enough, did not suffer headaches from it'.[50] Her *vita*, and those of other beguines, are replete with examples of extreme asceticism of a type rarely found among their monastic contemporaries. There were some examples from cistercian circles, however, but, as Roisin remarks, 'this sort of extreme mortification is found among nuns in close contact with the beguine movement'.[51]

EUCHARISTIC DEVOTIONS

While beguines and cistercian nuns had in common certain devotional interests and shared the same mystical inclinations, there was one devotional theme much more strongly associated with the beguines. This was devotion to the Eucharist, especially to the real presence of the human Christ. Indeed, if there was a 'beguine devotion', this was it. The bishop of Toulouse, Foulques, driven from his city by the Albigensians, 'could not sufficiently admire the faith and devotion he found in Liège, especially among the holy women, who were most zealous in their devotion to the Church of Christ and its sacraments'.[52] Jacques de Vitry tells of beguines who experienced physical and mental changes and sensations when receiving communion or in the presence of the host, a reference to the beguines' eucharistic devotion, which de Vitry thought should 'make unbelievers and heretics blush with shame'.[53]

The *life* of Mary of Oignies contains countless examples of her devotion to the sacrament and eucharistic miracles associated with her life. 'She could find no rest except in the presence of Christ in the Church', claimed Jacques de Vitry.[54] 'The holy bread strengthened her heart, the wine intoxicated and gladdened her heart. . . .' To receive Christ's body was the same thing with her as life itself.'[55] The *vita* of Odila, the widow of Liège (d. 1220), provides another very early example of beguine eucharistic devotion.[56] There are many others, notably the beguine credited with the institution of the feast of Corpus Christi, Juliana of Mt Cornillion (1193–1258).

Though a beguine, Juliana at times sought refuge from persecutors in cistercian convents, and her *vita* is illustrative of an individual serving as intermediary between lay beguines and cistercian nuns, and having close contacts with both groups.[57] Not surprisingly, then, while the earliest examples of intense devotion to the eucharist are primarily to be found among beguines, this devotion—and the mysticism emanating from it—soon found its way into cistercian nunneries and, occasionally, monasteries.[58] The *vitae* of many cistercian nuns begin by the second quarter of the thirteenth century to reflect an intense devotion to the eucharist, though the experiences of even the most devout, such as Ida of Louvain (d. 1302), do not surpass those of the earlier beguines. Undeniably, however, devotion to the eucharistic real presence was one of the strongest elements of cistercian spirituality from at least the early thirteenth century.[59] Especially among cistercian nuns was this the case; and if their intensity many not quite have matched that of the beguines, it was because the nuns surpassed the devotional intensity of their spiritual cousins in other areas and were at the same time more subject to the traditional disciplines of the monastery.

There was, finally, one other significant difference between the beguines and the cistercian nuns. The nuns were never accused of heresy, and their name was not occasionally used synonymously for 'heretic'. This problem plagued the beguines from the very beginning well into the fourteenth century, in large measure because of their ill-defined status and origins, in the lay apostolic movement.[60] Indeed, given this background, any woman could call herself a beguine until the days of strict regulation in the fourteenth century. The beguines were often viewed with suspicion and seem always to have had detractors whom Jacques de Vitry attacked as 'the enemies of religion who, maliciously criticizing the pious practices of these religious women, ripping and tearing them apart like mad dogs, attack customs so unlike their own; and finally, unable to do more, they use against them new names they invented'.[61] These are the same men who 'being wise in their own conceit, lacking the Spirit of God, believe nothing their reason cannot comprehend and hate and mock things they do not understand'.[62] At one time or another, the beguines were accused by their enemies of being associates of the Albigensians, the Waldensians, The Fraticelli, the Brethren of the Free Spirit, and a host of lesser groups. In all likelihood some women calling themselves beguines probably did associate with such groups. Such women were probably, assuming their good intentions, closer to the lay extreme of the beguine spectrum, and thus lacked those aspects of traditional spirituality found in a Mary of Oignies who, though 'in the world', nonetheless practised the virtues of humility and obedience as did any nun. Despite the similarities in their spirituality, beguines like Mary had a problem their cistercian counterparts avoided: beguines were not cloistered and did not take permanent vows. Until the reorganization of the movement by Pope John XXII, the beguines were laywomen seeking spiritual perfection with no universal regulation, no ecclesiastical superior, and no legal offical to check any excesses or deviations in action or thought that might develop. The freedom afforded by this lack of ecclesiatical regulation made the beguines suspect in the eyes of church officials, who took vows and enclosure as guarantees of good behavior. Churchmen knew the lifestyle and spirituality of cistercian nuns; they could never be certain of these things among the beguines.[63]

Beguine lifestyle and spirituality represent what McDonnell calls 'the via media', a state halfway between that of a professed religious and that of a laywoman leading an ordinary but devout life in the world.[64] In a sense, they combined elements from both worlds, drawing together aspects of both the practical and contemplative lives. Such a lifestyle and spirituality were, in and of themselves, neither good nor bad; they had their strengths, but also their weaknesses. In the earlier phases of the movement, its adherents became some of the more independent women of the medieval period. Under the strict control of neither church officials nor fathers nor husbands, the early beguines were able to live a life they chose, preferred, and more or less controlled. The life that most of them apparently wanted was one of devotion to God in a search for spiritual perfection within the lay world.

Grand Valley State Colleges
Allendale, Michigan

NOTES

1. On the dowry system, see Eileen Power, *Medieval English Nunneries c. 1275–1535* (Cambridge University Press, 1922–rpt New York: Biblo and Tanner, 1964) 16–25.

2. For a brief discussion of the origins of the term 'beguine', see E. W. Mc Donnell, *The Beguines and Beghards in Medieval Culture* (New Brunswick, N.J., 1954) 430–38. McDonnell's book is the most thorough treatment of the beguines available in English. For another scholar's view of it, see Alcantara Mens, 'Les béguines et les beghards dans le cadre de la culture médiévale. A propos d'un livre récent E. W. McDonnell, *Beguines and Beghards in Medieval Culture*' in *Le Moyen Age* 54(1958) 305–15. See also, among others, H. Logeman, 'The Etymology of the Name Beguine', in *Leuvensche Bijdragen* (1928) 110–37; F. Callaye, 'Lambert le Beges et les Béguines' in *Revue d'histoire ecclésiastique* 33(1927) 245–59; G. Kurth, 'De l'origine liégeoise des béguines' in *Bulletin de l'académie royale de Belgique* (1912) 437–62.

3. The classic work on the subject is by L. J. M. Philippen, *De Begijnhoven, Oorsprong, geschiedenis, inrichting* (Antwerp, 1918). The first stage of beguine develop ment is discussed in pp. 40–57. For a local study in depth, see Dayton Phillips, *Beguines in Medieval Strasbourg. A Study of the Social Aspect of Beguine Life* (Stanford, 1941); and E. G. Neumann, *Rheinisches Beginenund Begardenwesen. Ein Mainzer Beitrag zur religiösen Bewegung am Rhein* (Meisenheim-am-Glan, 1960). Regarding the beguines in general, see J. Greven, *Die Anfänge der Beginen, Ein Beitrag zur Geschichte der Volksfrömmigkeit und der Ordenswesens in Hochmittelalter* (Münster/W., 1912).

4. See Philippen, 58–68.

5. *Ibid.* For devotional interests of the beguines in the Low Countries, see Alcantara Mens, *Oorsprong en Betekenis van de Nederlandse Begijnenen Begardenbeweging* (Louvain, 1947); Simone Roisin, *L'hagiographie cistercienne dans le diocèse de Liége au XIIIᵉ siècle* (Louvain, 1947), pt. 2; 'Thèmes en faveur dans le milieu Cistercien-béguinal'; *idem*. 'L'efflorescence cistercienne et le courant féminin de piété an XIIIᵉ siècle', *Revue d'histoire ecclésiastique* 39(1943) 342–78; McDonnell, *passim*, especially 281–405.

6. For a biography of Jacques de Vitry, see Philipp Funk, *Jacob von Vitry, Leben Und Werke* (Berlin, 1909). Among the works of Jacques de Vitry which have been edited and published are: *The Historia Occidentalis of Jacques de Vitry*, edited by J. F. Hinnebusch (Fribourg, Switz., 1972), hereafter cited as HO; *Vita Maria Oigniacensis* in *Acta Sanctorum* June, 5: 547–72 (Paris, 1867), hereafter cited as VMO; *Lettres de Jacques de Vitry (1160/70–1240) évêque de Jean -d Acre*, edited by R. Huygens (Leiden, 1960); T. Crane, *The 'Exempla' or Illustrative Stories from the 'Sermones vulgares' of Jacques de Vitry*, Publications of the Folk-Lore Society, no. 26 (London, 1890); J. Pitra, ed., *Analecta Novissima spicilegii Solesmensis. Altera continuatio*, 2(Paris, 1888), 344–442 (a partial edition of *Sermones vulgares*). For a complete bibliography of works and secondary literature, see Hinnebusch, ix–xix.

7. Philippen, 69–88. For the beguines in this period, see also H. Grundmann, 'Zur Geschichte der Beginen im 13. Jahrhundert' in *Archiv für Kulturgeschichte* 21 (1931) 296–320.

8. Philippen, 89–126. A good recent study of the beguines' problems from the late thirteenth century is by Jean'Claude Schmitt, *Mort d'une hérésie: l'église et les clercs face aux béguines et aux béghards du Rhin supérieur du XIVᵉ an XVᵉ siècle* (Paris, 1978).

9. See especially *VMO*, but also occasional reference in letters and *Sermones vulgaribus*, particularly his *Secundus sermo ad virgines*.

10. Caesarius of Heisterbach, *The Dialogue on Miracles*, edited and translated by H. Scott and C.C.S. Bland (London, 1929); *Die Fragmente der Libri VIII Miraculorum des Caesarius von Heisterbach*, in *Römische Quartalschrift für christliche Alterbunskunde und für Kirchengeschichte*, 13(1901). For some examples, see *Dialogue*, book 3, ch. 6; 3:47; 4:84; 5:46; 5:47; 5:50; 6:34.

11. Cf. J. Greven, *Die Anfänge*, who claims the beguines were a derivation of Cîteaux; also McDonnell, 320–40, 365–87; and Roisin, *L'hagiographie*. Specific studies of most of the cistercian foundations in the Low Countries can be found in J. Canivez, *L'ordre de Cîteaux en Belgique des origines (1132) an XXᵉ siècle* (Forges-lez-Chimay, 1926).

12. Numerous examples in McDonnell, 170–86. See also *Cronica Villariensis Mo-*

nasterii, edited by G. Waitz in *Monumenta Germaniae Historica, Scriptores* 25:192–219.

13. McDonnell, 321. Roisin says much the same thing, frequently and more emphatically; cf. *L'hagiographie*, pp. 94, 96, 103, 111ff., among others.

14. Concerning the *vita apostolica* and its ideals, see P. Mandonnet and M. H. Vicaire, *St. Dominic and His Work*, translated by M. B. Larkin (St Louis, 1944) 272–81; J. Dickenson, *The Origins of the Austin Canons and Their Introduction into England* (London, 1950) 7–90; and Herbert Grundmann, *Religiöse Bewegungen im Mittelalter*, second edition (Hildesheim, 1961).

15. See M. D. Chenu, 'Monks, Canons, and Laymen in Search of the Apostolic Life', *Nature, Man, and Society in the Twelfth Century*, translated by Jerome Taylor and Lester K. Little (Chicago, 1968) 202–38. See also Mandonnet, *St. Dominic*, 258–90; Grundmann, *Religiöse Bewegungen, passim.*

16. de Vitry, *H.O*, p. 165.

17. *VMO*, p. 563B.

18. *VMO*, 51, F, citing Lk. 9:23.

19. *VMO*, 550B.

20. *VMO*, 562F.

21. *VMO*, 560A.

22. See *VMO, liber* II *passim.*, esp. capitula 3 and 6 (pp. 557ff.).

23. *VMO*, 550B.

24. *VMO*, 551F.

25. *VMO*, 550A.

26. *VMO*, 557E and 558A.

27. *VMO*, 557F.

28. *VMO*, 555F. For pauline injunctions to physical labor, see for example: 1 Th 2:7–11; 1 Co. 4:12; Ac 18:1–4; Eph 4:28.

29. For a discussion of some of these problems, see M.D. Chenu, 'Monks, Canons, and Laymen in Search of the Apostolic Life', and 'The Evangelical Awakening' in *Nature, Man and Society*. Also see Grundmann, *Religiöse Bewegungen*, 13–38; M.D. Lambert, *Franciscan Poverty, The Doctrine of the Absolute Poverty of Christ and the Apostles in the Franciscan Order, 1210–1323*, (London, 1961); M. Mollat, ed., *Études sur l'histoire de la pauvreté* (*Moyan Age–XVI siècle*) 2 vols (Paris, 1974); T. Manteuffel, *Naissance d'une hérésie. Les adeptes de la pauvreté voluntaire au Moyen Age*, translated by A. Posner (Paris, 1969); Decima Douie, *The Nature and the Effect of the Heresy of the Fraticelli* (University of Manchester Press, 1932).

30. Jacques de Vitry usually associates the Franciscans with the primitive Church, citing both them and the beguines as examples of the proper form of the apostolic life. See *HO*, p. 349f.; *Epistola 1, ed.*, R. Robricht, 'Briefe des Jacobus de Vitriaco', *Zeitschrift für Kirchengeschichte* 14(1894) 104, and *ep.* 6, *idem.* 16(1896) 83; See also Pitra, p. 414f., *Sermo XXXVIII, Ad fratres ordiniis militaris.*

31. *VMO*, 552A, and 551B.

32. Cf. E. Dublanchy, 'Ascétisme', *Dictionnaire de Théologie Catholique*, 1:2055–77; M. Viller, J. de Guibert, *et.al.*, 'Ascèse, Ascétisme', *Dictionnaire de Spiritualité*, 1:964–81; and Paul Pourrat, *La Spiritualité chrétienne* 4 vols. (Paris, 1919–28) The last has an especially abundant bibliography, as does Louis Bouyer, Jean Leclercq, François Vandenbroeck, *Histoire de la spiritualité chrétienne*, 3 vols. (Paris, 1969), English trans. *A History of Christian Spirituality* (New York: Desclee, 1968).

33. Jacques de Vitry, *VMO*, 547f., Prologue – to Foulques, Bishop of Tolouse.

34. For examples of lay persons living the apostolic life, see Chenu, *Nature*, 219–30; Mandonnet, *St. Dominic*, 272–81; J. B. Russell, *Dissent and Reform in the Early Middle Ages* (Berkeley, 1965).

35. *VMO*, 550D.

36. *VMO* Prologue, 547F.

37. McDonnell, p. 145.

38. *VMO* Prologue, 548D.

39. Beguine examples include Odila the Widow, Juliana of Mt. Cornillion, Eve of St Martin's, Gertrude van Oosten, Christine of Stommeln; Cistercian examples include Beatrice of Nazareth, Ida of Louvain, Ida of Leau, Ida of Nivelles, Lutgard of St Trond, Alyce of Schaerbeek. For editions of their *vitae* (most in *Acta Sanctorum*) see McDonnell, or Roisin, *L'hagiographic cistercienne.*

40. For many examples, see McDonnell, *passim.*, esp. pp. 320–40; and Roisin, *L'efflorescence, passim,* and *L'hagiographie* pp. 106–23, and 165–84.

41. See Roisin, *L'hagiographie cistercienne,* 185–92.

42. McDonnell, 438.

43. Cf. J. Greven, *Anfänge,* and 'Der Ursprung des Beginenwesens. Eine Auseinandersetzung mit Godefroid Kurth' in *Historisches Jahrbuch* 35(1914) 26–58, 291–318.

44. Roisin, 'L'efflorerence', suggests that perhaps the cistercian nuns were not so much an Order of Cistercian nuns but rather a feminine cistercian branch.

45. There are a few examples of some of this activity among cistercian nuns. An example is Ida of Louvain, a nun at Val-des-Roses, who worked at night to earn alms for the poor; see *anon., Vita Ida Lovaniensis; Acta Sanctorum,* April 2:161 (Paris, 1866). Some other examples are given by Roisin, *L'hagiographie,* 93–98, and *passim.*

46. For a brief discussion of the differences between the monastic, canonical, and lay interpretations of apostolic poverty, see Chenu, *Nature,* pp. 203–46; Mandonnet, *St. Dominic,* 272–81; and Grundmann, *Religiöse Bewegungen, passim.*

47. Roisin, *L'hagiographie cistercienne,* p. 94.

48. *VMO* Prologue, 549A.

49. *VMO,* 551D.

50. *VMO,* 552C.

51. Roisin, *L'hagiographie,* 96; see 95ff. for examples.

52. *VMO* Prologue, 547D.

53. *VMO* Prlogue, 548D.

54. *VMO,* 355E.

55. *VMO,* 568A.

56. *Anon., Vita Julianae Corneliensis, Acta Sanctorum,* April, 1:435–75(Paris, 1865).

58. For examples and the place of the beguines in eucharistic devotion, see Roisin, *L'hagiographie,* 111ff., 178–84, and *passim.* For eucharistic devotion in general in the Middle Ages, including the roles of the beguines and Cistercians, see Peter Browe, *Die Verehrung der Eucharistie im Mittelalter* (Munich, 1932); see also *idem.,* 'Die Ausbreitung der Fronleichnamfestes' in *Jahrbuch für Liturgiewissenschaft* 8(1928) 107–43.

59. Cf. Roisin, *L'hagiographie,* n. 58, and Browe, *Die Verehrung,* 107ff. and *passim.* On p. 115 Roisin claims that 'C'est à la Vièrge que va l'affection sensible des moines comme l'amour ardent des moiniales tend vers la Christ eucharistique, l'Espouse céleste.'

60. Cf. McDonnell, 430–55, 488–538, and *passim;* J. C. Schmitt, *Mort d'une hérésie;* and Grundmann, *Religiöse, passim.*

61. *VMO* Prologue, 548A.

62. *VMO* Prologue, 449F.

63. For Jacques de Vitry's opinion of cistercian nuns, for whom he has great admiration, see *HO,* 116–18.

64. Cf. McDonnell, 120–40.

The Nun as Anchoress: England 1100–1500

Ann K. Warren

ANCHORITISM FLOURISHED in medieval England.[1] From the Conquest to the Dissolution a steady stream of persons asked to be enclosed in solitary cells for the remainder of their lives. Women more commonly than men, lay as well as religious, they chose a life that harked back to the days when St Anthony withdrew to the desert.

The English anchoress of the Middle Ages was a woman vowed to chastity and stability of abode. Her usual home was a small house attached to a village church or chapel, though it might be found within a hospital or as part of a monastic compound. She might be a woman for whom the *reclusorium* represented the first stage in her religious conversion, or she could be a former nun embarking on a more advanced and difficult kind of life in a way Benedict had long before described:

> The second [kind of monks] are the anchorites, that is, the hermits; those, namely, who not in the first fervor of their conversion, but after long probation in the monastery, have long since learned by the help of many others, to fight against the devil, and being well armed, are able to go forth from the ranks of their brethren to the singlehanded combat of the desert, safe now, even without the consolation of another, to fight with their own strength against the weaknesses of the flesh and their own evil thoughts, God alone aiding them.[2]

Anchoritism included thus two professions. On the one hand, it was an alternative religious vocation: the laywoman chose it in lieu of the monastery. On the other hand, it was an advanced form of monastic life: the nun took, beyond her original vow, a new and irrevocable step to greater austerity and an intensified spiritual life. Once in the cell and ritually enclosed, however, the former laywoman was difficult to differentiate from the former nun. Both were expected to lead ascetic lives and to earn the respect and awe accorded their new condition. Both were subsumed under the titles *inclusa* and *anachoreta*. In chronicles and *lives* the anchoress is called *venerabilis, domina, mulier Deo amabilis . . . professioni anachoreticae*, without reference to her previous status. As an anchoress she had attained a new status.[3]

The earliest clear picture of anchoritism in medieval England emerges from documents of the twelfth century. One comes upon it *in medias res*. It was already a flourishing institution with established patterns of organization and control. There existed ecclesiastical guidelines for the enclosure of recluses, private letters giving advice on how to conduct one's life, and a society willing to support anchorites financially. Twelfth-century anchorites, moreover, are discovered in these documents to have been part of a broader phenomenon. Their choice of this specific form of solitary life was but one of several options possible during a period of religious revival experienced by all of western european society in the eleventh and twelfth centuries.[4] In an age characterized by asceticism, innovation, and the creation of new and varied forms of religious life, many vocations were reckoned as eremitic. In order to place the english anchoress in the context of diverse contemporary movements, we must first distinguish between the hermit and the anchorite.

The words 'anchorite' and 'hermit' were synonymous in primitive usage. To be an anchorite or a hermit was to be a solitary, to withdraw (*anachōrein*) to the desert (*eremus*). Such a life could imply total seclusion and stability or allow considerable freedom of movement and social intercourse. One could live quite alone or with a group of like-minded solitaries. One was *anachoreta* or *eremita* interchangeably: the greek roots turned into first declension latin nouns which, moreover, include both genders.

During the Middle Ages, the word 'hermit' continued to express the general meaning initially sustained by both words while the word 'anchorite' became more restricted in use. To be a hermit was still to be able to encompass a wide variety of behavioral patterns, while to be an anchorite meant to take on a narrowly defined vocation: the anchorite was *inclusus* or *reclusus*, enclosed and stable, with limited access to the outside world. Thus, to be an anchorite meant to limit oneself to only one of the range of possibilities available to hermits; to be a hermit meant to exclude a rigid anchoretism in favor of more varied, if still ascetic, lifestyles.

Twelfth-century english documents consistently make these distinctions. Early in the century William of Malmesbury wrote of two anchorites in his latin translation of the anglo-saxon *Life of Wulfstan* by Coleman, a monk of Worcester. He speaks of one, a woman, *reclusa*, of Brumeton, 'inferior to no man in holiness', and of a man, *inclusus*, 'a servant of God' (also termed *reclusus* in another sentence).[6] Dominic of Evesham, also in the first quarter of the century, wrote of three *anachoretae*, two of whom were *reclusi* for periods of seventy-two and seventy-five years.[7] John of Ford, telling the story of Wulfric of Haselbury later in the century, termed both Wulfric and a fellow male recluse, John of Winterbourne, '*anachoretae*'. Each of five anchoresses he called '*inclusa*'. All seven were 'of the profession of anchorite', that is, confined to their cells and dependent upon others for sustenance.[8] On the other hand, in the same period, St Robert of Knaresborough, a 'hermit', ran an establishment with several co-hermits; he farmed, he collected alms.[9] So too did Hugh Garth, a founder of Cockersand Abbey, a 'hermit of great perfection', who collected alms for the hospital that preceded the monastery.[10] Alternately, Godric of Finchale was a stationary hermit living in seclusion, yet he too could grow his own food, have a cow, and fish.[11]

The Pipe Rolls record gifts to '*heremitis et reclusis*', two classes of persons.[12] In *The Life of Christina of Markyate*, both Edwin, who 'leads a religious life in solitude' yet moves about freely, and Roger, who does not leave the general confines of his household but is not formally enclosed, are called hermits. Alfwen, on the other hand, the woman with whom Christina first took refuge, was clearly an anchoress, being identified in the *Life* both as *anachoreta* and *inclusa*, words never used for Roger or Edwin or any of the other hermits who play a role in the story. Christina herself is called *inclusa* only once in the text, at that point when she is physically enclosed in her hidden cell. At other stages of her saga, when living alone or with her 'maidens' as an unregularized group of women, she is referred to only as *virgo* and *ancilla domini*.[13]

Men and women lived both as anchorites and hermits in the twelfth century. The two ways of life were well defined and distinct from each other.[14] The twelfth-century Englishwoman who desired a religious life had three choices: she could become a nun, an anchoress, or a hermitess. To choose to be a nun or an anchoress was to have a fairly sure notion of what that experience might entail. To become a hermitess was to enter into a much less charted land, one so unclearly drawn for women that no name for them quite existed. Both men and women are *anachoretae*; they are *inclusi, inclusae, reclusi, reclusae*. But women are not styled *heremitae* in biographies and chronicles. We call them 'hermitesses' because they are women living the equivalent of a hermit's life, but they are not so named in the texts.

Even so, many kinds of eremitic life for women are described in or implied by twelfth-century sources. Each kind was unique, bound only by the nature of the individual involved, or of the group, or of the site; each unfolded under the dynamics of its own inner propulsion and determined by its own sense of rightness. The sister of Godric of Finchale was one such pioneer of the eremitic life. She, *virgo Deo devota*, settled down some distance from where her brother dwelt, in a hut which he had prepared for her. She came to his oratory from time to time to attend mass, but otherwise seems to have stayed apart from him, living alone during the years she remained there. She sustained her solitary life rigorously until a mortal illness overwhelmed her and she went to a hospital in Durham where she died.[15]

Many who lived as hermitesses in twelfth-century England did not endure to death or near death. We can mention two, '*duae sanctae mulieres*', who settled in a wood near St Albans sometime around 1135. There, in rough shelters made of tree branches, ' . . . *vitam ducere coeperunt vigiliis et orationibus, sub mirabili abstinentia*', a life that included not only vigils and prayers but perfect chastity and a diet of bread and water. The dangers inherent in their self-imposed isolation, however, soon brought Abbot Geoffrey of St Albans to involve himself in their situation. He built a cell for them, and in time their primitive retreat became the nucleus of Sopwell Priory, a nunnery dependent upon St Albans.[16] In similar fashion, women who gathered round Christina of Markyate ultimately (in 1145) found themselves shifted from being hermitesses to members of a community when their household, after many independent years, was reconstituted as Markyate Priory, again dependent upon St Albans.[17] Kilburn Priory also emerged from eremetical beginnings. Charters indicate that three young maidens, Emma, Gunilda, and Christine—former maids of honor to Maud, wife of Henry I—were settled in a former hermitage then in the possession of the abbey of Westminster. In 1130, they were placed there under the protection of a warden named Godwin, himself the former hermit of the place. By 1139, Kilburn had been refounded as a priory.[18] In every case the hermitess became a nun.

The foundation story of Crabhouse Abbey is more fanciful yet not otherwise too different:

> Once upon a time there was a maiden whose heart the Holy Spirit moved to seek a desert place where she might serve God without disturbance by any earthly thing; so she found this place, which is now called Crabhouse, all wild, and far around on every side there was no human habitation.[19]

Lena, the hermitess, had come to a remote area of Norfolk to live a truly solitary life. After a time she supplicated her friends and her supporters to enable her to found a community. Crabhouse charters indicate that Lena was granted a hermitage by the prior and the canons of Ranham, with the permission of their founder, William de Lesewis. The deed calls her a 'nun' and reports that she was soon joined by 'other maidens'. They did come, and the priory was founded around 1180.[20]

These experiences create a certain rhythm. Women who were caught up in a desire to be alone found that there was nothing to preclude their eventual absorption into full-fledged communal life.[21] Though community was a choice they had, presumably, once rejected, it was one they subsequently made. The pressures against their sustaining the life of the hermitess, a life without even a name, proved too great. After the twelfth century one hears no more of the hermitess—by any name. Widespread female eremitism had proved to be only an interlude in english religious life. Susceptible to change and vulnerable to extinction, as a life style it was too fraught with danger, both physical and spiritual, long to survive, especially in the climate of the growing ecclesiastical control of all religious in the twelfth and thirteenth centuries.

The english anchoress of this paper was not one of these women. Her experience was parallel to theirs and was fed by the same spiritual climate, but her expression of it came within the context of a *conversatio* already well-defined at the outset of the twelfth century. Unlike the hermitess, the twelfth-century anchoress was not experimenting. It was she who would be able to become a recluse and stay a recluse for the remainder of her life. Her vocation would persist as a permanent feature of the english religious landscape, and, it alone, after the twelfth century, remained to accomodate the woman of solitary need and desire.

The anchorite life, then, was the most successful form of reclusive life for women in the twelfth century in England (if success is measured by endurance), and the only form available thereafter. It sustained its vitality and validity throughout the Middle Ages until the Dissolution in 1539. Throughout the period it absorbed both laywomen and nuns. While both were formally of equal status once in the cell, the nun-anchoress was, in fact, considered to be a more ideal candidate. Even as the anchorite life proved more successful than less-structured eremitic models, and was in this sense 'ideal', so the nun-anchoress was thought more likely to be an appropriate anchoress than was her lay sister. Nothing makes this so clear as the literature that was composed for her.

THE LITERATURE OF ANCHORITISM

Alone in her cell the recluse lived without formal written guidance. Unlike the cloistered nun she was not bound by monastic routine. Her day, her life, were of her own devising. Whatever her expression of her commitment to God, whatever her pattern of prayer, work and meditation, whatever the clothes she wore, the silence she endured, the food she ate, all this was to be her own decision. But freedom brought both responsibility and anxiety:

responsibility for achieving her goals; anxiety over the possibility of failure. As Benedict had warned, the anchoress depended on her own inner strength to sustain her fidelity to her commitment. Concern about the capacity to endure when freed of the primary monastic demand of obedience lay behind the request of anchoresses for private works of guidance, works to protect them, alone in their cells, from the dangers of anarchy, hypocrisy, even heresy. To meet this need a whole class of literature developed in medieval England. With the lone exception of the thirteenth-century *Ancrene Riwle*, all of the significant works of the genre were addresssed to women who formerly had been nuns.[22]

The nobility of her calling brought Eve, first a nun of Wilton and later an anchoress at Angers, a torrent of prose framed in knightly simile. From the pen of Goscelin, c. 1082, the *Liber confortatorius* consoled the author as much as the recluse for whom it was penned as it described the loneliness, the harshness, and the martyrdom of Eve's newly-chosen life, as well as its sublime nature and its eventual rewards.[23] More famous yet is the letter composed by Aelred, Abbot of Rievaulx, for his sister, a nun turned anchoress. This *De institutis inclusarum*, written c. 1160, lauds Aelred's sister, the mature and thoughtful nun who has accepted this new discipline with grace and dignity, and it contrasts her to other anchoresses (laywomen) who, having taken no vows of poverty, remain concerned with their holdings.[24] In one passage Aelred remarks how little his sister needs to read his opening comments—his outer rule—because she is perfection, but he writes them for young girls, *adolescentiores*, who will ask her for advice.[25] As Aelred moves beyond his outer rule and into the second and third parts of his work, the inner rule and a three-part meditation, he ceases to insist that his words are not for his sister. The meditation is indeed for her. She is worthy of it.

By the fourteenth century the language of these treatises, even when directed to nuns, had become English. Richard Rolle and Walter Hilton created major works for anchoresses who had been nuns. Their works are more overtly mystical than those composed for earlier anchoresses. With Julian of Norwich (herself an anchoress) and the anonymous author of the *Cloud of Unknowing*, they form a group now known as the Fourteenth-century English Mystics. All the members of this group were themselves solitaries at some point in their lives, and most of their writing was directed to other solitaries, persons who had been or perhaps still were regulars. Rolle's *Form of Living* was written for Margaret, a former nun of Hampole and a disciple of Rolle, who had earlier composed for her his *English Psalter*.[26] Hilton's *Scale of Perfection* was created for a nun still bound to read the daily office of her Order while living as an anchoress within the compound of some monastery.[27] In the next century, Richard Misyn, a Lincoln Carmelite, translated into English one of Rolle's latin works, *The Fire of Love*, at the request of a later Margaret, also a former nun and now an anchoress.[28] The *Form*, the *Scale*, the *Fire of Love*, are primers of contemplative technique and were written to teach their recipients the way to reach God. That such literature was directed to english anchoresses who had been nuns tells us several things about english spirituality in general and the central place of the anchoress within that tradition.

The strong eremitic tradition in England had ancient origins and was very orthodox. In securing a place for women within that tradition, the anchoress, as we have seen, first prevailed over the hermitess. Next the nun-anchoress rose over the lay-anchoress as the ideal female recluse, the woman most likely to guard the orthodoxy that lay at the heart of english spirituality. The nun-anchoress was a woman who understood religious life and had already progressed within it. Her growth now permitted her to become a recluse. She was a woman who could be expected to climb further, who had been disciplined by her monastic training and was less likely than the untutored to fall into error. For her, caring men could describe a perfect life of religion.

These letters of instruction were written for anchoresses already in their cells, for women who had made that transition from community to the *reclusorium* that forms the substructure of this inquiry. To understand how they moved from the cloister to the anchorhold is to leave the world of the ideal and to enter the world of the real. It is to touch the person behind the myth, the practical behind the theoretical. It is time to follow our nun in her migration.

ENTERING THE ANCHORHOLD

The nun who wished to become an anchoress first informed her abbess of her desire. The superior, in her turn, would counsel against such a choice, and only after repeated, insistent, and convincing pleading by the petitioning nun would she allow the case to move forward.[29] Application would then be made to the bishop within whose diocese the anchoress would dwell after enclosure and into whose jurisdiction she would pass after leaving her monastery. The bishop's legal responsibility to her was sixfold. He, usually through a commission set up for the purpose, first passed upon the personal credentials of the candidate and on her fitness for such a life; second, he determined if there were financial provisions adequate to sustain her for her life-time, for in leaving abbatial discipline she left abbatial support as well; third, he aided in finding or building a suitable *reclusorium* if a site had not already been secured; fourth, he released her from her vows of obedience to her abbess; next he performed (or ordered performed) rites of enclosure; and finally, he entered into an extended oversight of the now enclosed nun.[30]

It is the bishop's role in this migration of nuns that allows us to trace the process, for records of these procedures were enrolled by the various episcopal secretariats and have thus come down to us. Though these records offer only incomplete data, we can, by piecing together information from several sources, assemble a reliable overview. The most common notice to appear in the registers is the licence to enclose. It must have been the final document in a series of letters or commissions, but perhaps the only one deemed important enough to be permanently transcribed. A typical licence concerns an atypical woman, atypical because she was the anchoress for whom Richard Rolle wrote *The Form of Living*. The notice to enclose her, found in the register of the Archbishop of York, William Zouche, is dated 12 December 1348. It is in the form of a commission to the Abbot of Eggleston to enclose 'Margaret le Boteler, a sister of the [benedictine] house of nuns of Hampole, . . . who, having conducted herself as an anchoress, desires greatly to be confirmed in that healthful way of life and to lead a solitary life, so that in it she may be in a condition to act as a servant of God, giving herself more freely and more quietly to pious prayers and vigils'. She was to be enclosed in 'a certain house, attached to the chapel at East Layton, in the archdeanery of Richmond in our diocese, in which house she will stay perpetually until her death'.[31]

How long the process had taken to reach this point we do not know. The petition of another Margaret, a nun of Arden, took more than six months to proceed through the ecclesiastical bureaucracy. On 13 November 1320, Archbishop William Melton, Zouche's predecessor at York, issued a proclamation stating that Margaret of Punchardon had asked that she '. . . might be enclosed in a proper and worthy place so that she might serve God more strictly by leading the solitary life'. The archbishop further declared that he already had made inquiry as to her past life and found her deserving of enclosure. The notice implies that Margaret had no specific anchorhold in mind when she made her request and, in effect, was asking the archbishop to find her one. The register records her licence for enclosure six months later. She was to be interred in the '. . . house of St Nicholas, Beverly [a hospital], to obtain the fruits of a better life in company with Agnes Migregose, already a recluse there'.[32]

The six-month interval between the first and second notices may represent the time needed to find a suitable *reclusorium*. Generally, *reclusoria* became available only upon the deaths of their incumbents. Otherwise a new establishment would have to be built or an existing one enlarged to accommodate an additional person. As a final resort, two persons could double up. The notice does not make clear which of these courses had been taken by the archbishop to meet Margaret's needs. Quite possibly no *reclusoria* were available and none seemed likely to come on the market in the near future, and so, after a six-month wait, she was placed in one that already had an occupant.

An exchange of letters between a bishop and the abbot whom he had charged to act for him in a similar case gives a more complete picture of procedure, although it too is not without limitations. On 3 January 1435, Bishop William Gray of Lincoln requested that the abbot of Thornton, an augustinian house, examine a benedictine nun who desired to become an anchoress. The abbot was to proceed in four stages. First, he was to satisfy himself that the nun's resolve in this matter was in no way capricious; next, he was to examine the premises of the suggested *reclusorium*, a small house attached to the parish church at Winterton; third, he was to survey the attitudes of the general community; and finally, if continually reassured that all was in order, he was to perform rites of enclosure in the name of the bishop and report back to him the full details of the investigation and its outcome.[33]

The abbot's subsequent communication to the bishop set out his manner of conducting his commission and announced that he had arrived at Winterton on the twenty-first of January. The nun, Beatrice Franke of Stainfield Priory, was waiting for him on his arrival. He examined her with regard to the length of time during which she had persisted in desiring such a move and of the peril in which she placed herself should she fail. Satisfied that she neither wavered nor faltered in any way and that she had desired to become an anchoress almost from her childhood, he released her from her bond of obedience to the prioress of Stainfield and enclosed her the next day in a ceremony in which, during mass, she publicly made her new profession, reading it 'openly and clearly', and promised obedience and chastity to John, representing the bishop.[34]

The letter from Hoton to Gray, signed and dated the twenty-third of January, when the abbot was again back home at Thornton, is followed in the register with the prioress's licence to Beatrice. Noting, as had Hoton, the extended duration of time during which Beatrice had persevered in her resolve to become a recluse, the prioress, Margaret Hulle, cited the episcopal decision to allow Beatrice to become an anchoress and gave her own permission. The monastic licence of release, then, was necessary but secondary. This tallies nicely with proper procedure as expressed in the *Provinciale* of William of Lyndwood, a fifteenth-century compendium of correct episcopal practices. No one lesser than a bishop might licence an anchorite and, specifically, no abbot might give licence to his own monk to be enclosed. (*nec Abbas potest licentiare Monachum suum ut includatur*). On the other hand, the abbot was to (even had to: *nec obstat*) give license for his monk's transference to the solitary life,[35] as Prioress Margaret Hulle had done.

In Beatrice's case, the dates suggest that the whole process was perfunctory. The abbot received Gray's letter some time after 3 January. On the twenty-first, he arrived at Winterton, where the nun awaited him. It is unclear whether she was already living in the cell without formal approval and liturgical enclosure, or had been brought by prearrangement to the site on that day from her monastery. Whatever the sequence, her presence at the site, already beyond the confines of her cloister, indicates that the process was expected to go forward. In fact, the busy abbot examined her on that day, enclosed her on the next (the twenty-second), and was sufficiently reestablished at home to take up his correspondence on the twenty-third.

Clearly much had been arranged in advance. The site was accounted for and all seem to have been of one mind that Beatrice Franke's commitment to be a recluse was neither lightly taken nor likely to be transitory. Enough time elapsed between the third of January and the twenty-first for some correspondence between John at Thornton and Margaret at Stainfield, a correspondence which established that this was to be an uncomplicated procedure. As there is no mention of what financial arrangements had been made (unless the bishop's reference to the 'consent' of the community implies their acceptance of financial obligation[36]), this too may have been previously reviewed.

Money issues are dealt with openly in many anchoress notices. The absence of any discussion of financial matters in the cases cited above suggests that the subject already had been addressed satisfactorily. An endowed cell might have been found or private funding secured. In 1493, for example, the Bishop of Lichfield enjoined the Abbot of Cockersand to enclose a woman named Agnes, a nun of Norton Priory, at Pilling in Garstang, a chapelry of Cockersand. He made no mention of money. But a 1501 entry in the account books of the abbey notes that this same Agnes 'hasse payn to James ye Abbot of Cockersand for her lyving – ii^s ii^d to [the collector] and vi^s viii^d to ye Convent'.[37] She was responsible for her own expenses and paid them like any other tenant of the abbey. Someone or some institution had to be providing her with funds, for no one was allowed to be enclosed without adequate and permanent support.

One fifteenth-century nun, Matilda Newton, gained that support from Henry V. Her story takes us out of the pure and un-substantial world of spiritual and ascetic desire and into a more earthly realm, for Matilda sought in the anchorhold both a holy life and the solution to a practical problem. A nun of Barking, Matilda was invited to become abbess of Syon when Henry V founded a bridgettine house there in 1415. She went, but her administration was not a success (Margaret Deanesly suggests that she lacked sufficient tact). Her position became untenable. She did not choose to stay on as nun where she had been abbess; she could not return to benedictine life after adopting the more rigorous obedience of the order of St Saviour. She resolved the situation by her entrance into a *reclusorium*. She became an anchoress and her endowment was subscribed by the king at twenty marks per annum,[38] (reclusion may have seemed like heaven after the politics of the monastery!)

Need as well as desire played its part in the placing of a woman named Joanna in a Norfolk *reclusorium*, c. 1200. Joanna had lived at Crabhouse, the nunnery founded through the exertions of the hermitess, Lena. Crabhouse dispersed within twenty years of its establishment when extensive flooding wasted the area. All the nuns drifted from view save Joanna:

> Many years after there came a flood of water, which overwhelmed their habitation, wherefore they went away and did not again return, and how and where they lived is not known, except only of the one who made herself a recluse in the cemetery of Mary Magdalene of Wiggenhall.[39]

A typical English anchoress, Joanna lived in an anchorhold attached to a parish church. The records impart a sense of her commitment to her stability as a nun, a notion that precluded her leaving the region and made the anchorhold a suitable alternative.

The story of Beatrice de Hodesack, just a hundred years later, provides another example of a nun finding a *reclusorium* in time of need, and elaborates the continuing relationship of bishop and recluse over the years of her confinement. One first learns of Beatrice from a series of episcopal letters of the early fourteenth century. In the year 1300 an entry appears in the *sede vacante* register of the see of York. The notice, in a fashion now familiar, records a request that the Abbot of Roche enclose Beatrice, the daughter of Thomas de Hodesack, in the dwelling for anchoresses in the chapel of St Edmund, near Doncaster Bridge in Sprotburgh. Her credentials had been validated and the consent of all with an interest in the matter received.[40]

Beatrice was next heard of ten years later when she became the subject of a letter from Archbishop William Greenfield to the Bishop of St Andrews. Here she is identified as a former nun of Coldstream, in the scottish diocese of St Andrews. After having lived in community for many years, she had run away from the monastery when war seemed imminent in that part of Scotland and had no wish to return there. Yet she remained without any license for withdrawal, either from her prelate or from her prioress. She lived now in the anchoresses's house at Doncaster. Greenfield's tone turned philosophical as he mused on how all good shepherds have wandering sheep who escape their flocks and how zeal must be tempered with just compassion to help the erring quiet their fear and return to the sheepfold. The bishop, William de Lamberton, was asked to look into the matter, Archbishop Greenfield pledging to be guided by his decisions.[41]

Five years later, in 1315, Beatrice was again the subject of a Greenfield letter, this one addressed to William of Creasacre, who held (perhaps as agent) the lands and tenements which his ancestor, Lord William Fitz-william, had specifically set aside for the support of the anchoress establishment at Doncaster, an endowed *reclusorium* for two women. Thomas was in arrears with his payments, which were of the order of ten quarters of wheat annually, five due to Beatrice and five to the other anchoress. The letter chided Thomas for his recalcitrance in paying his debt and then moved on to describe Beatrice's history and current status. Greenfield wrote that she left Coldstream with the license of her prelate, the diocesan bishop (the aforementioned William de Lamberton) as well as with that of her prioress; that there was just and reasonable cause for her decision to leave her house; that she entered the Doncaster *reclusorium* with the license of Thomas Corbridge, formerly Archbishop of York, and continued there with his [Green-field's] permission; and that the convent at Coldstream had been devastated and despoiled during the scottish wars and was now dispersed so that Beatrice could no longer return, even if she so desired.[42]

In this complicated story we see the bishop playing many roles, all of which bear witness to his sense of the seriousness of Beatrice's enclosure, his desire that it be made ecclesiastically proper, if indeed it was not; his concern for her physical and spiritual welfare. The letters cover a span of fifteen years. Other data affirm that Beatrice lived in the cell until 1328.[43] Whatever the initial forces which moved her to seek the *reclusorium*, once within it she remained for over a quarter of a century, to her death.

A final vignette plays upon all of the themes touched upon here: a concerned bishop, a homeless nun, a need for endowment, a profound commitment to the *reclusorium*. It shifts back and forth between the practical and the spiritual, for in their wisdom medieval bishops understood that man, not God, must provide.

Christine Holby was a canoness of Kildare when raiding irish foresters 'destroyed and devastated' her convent. She went to Edmund Lacy, Bishop of Exeter, seeking a *reclusorium*, bringing letters of consent from her prioress. The letters recommended that she be accepted by the bishop as an anchoress, but her enclosure was not to be effected so easily.

The bishop handled her petition as he would have any other; the fact of her convent's dispersal served only to explain her presence and not to excuse any special treatment. On 14 September 1447, Lacy commissioned the precentor of the cathedral, Walter Collys, to examine her on her desire to enclose herself as an anchoress in the churchyard of St Leonard's, Exeter. Collys was to look into her heart to make sure that Satan had not transformed himself into an angel of light to lead Christine to her downfall, and that Christine was indeed ready to take this new vow. All persons connected to St Leonard's were to exercise their right to discuss her acceptability as a candidate. Finally, Collys was to 'make sure that she had secure and certain sustenance, and who will bestow it and sustain it to the end of her life, and of how much, where and of what things this manner of dowry ought to consist, so that we and our successors in this place shall never be burdened by this reclusion'. Lacy thought highly of Christine and saw the life of an anchoress as a work of great holiness. Yet he demanded a fixed endowment *before* reclusion, lest 'in opprobrium of this work, she is forced fearfully to violate her solemn vow because of the failure of her fixed endowment'.[44] If man does not provide, the devil will have his play.

The real and the ideal interact constantly throughout this story. Nuns ought not to be threatened by wars and raiding, yet they are. Anchoresses ought not to have to concern themselves with money, but they must. In order to live the ideal life one had to make a bargain with real life.

Nuns became anchoresses in medieval England for many reasons. Most of them chose reclusion out of deeply felt desire, fully understanding that the new life was to be the supreme test of their dedication to God. Others— Beatrice, Matilda, Christine, Joanna—used the anchorhold as a physical and psychological refuge as well as a spiritual retreat. Their motives were complex and subject to forces beyond their control. Satan is said to have sent the rains that flooded Crabhouse. External devils in the shape of scottish soldiers and irish foresters created havoc for Christine and Beatrice. Who can speak for Matilda? If the anchorhold was for most nuns a transition of the heart, for some it was a transition of necessity. Yet the realities of life did not diminish in medieval english eyes the fundamental perception of the nun as quintessential anchoress in a religious culture that valued the solitary vocation above all others. Throughout the period the nun-anchoress embodied an ideal harking back to the same desert that had sheltered Mary the Egyptian as well as St Anthony.

Case Western Reserve University
Cleveland, Ohio

NOTES

1. The study of anchorites has been a neglected field. See Giles Constable, *Medieval Monasticism, A Select Bibliography* (Toronto, 1976), for the few relevant works exist.
2. RB 1:3–5, trans. *The Holy Rule of St. Benedict* (St Meinrad, Indiana, 1975) 6.
3. See, for example, *The Life of Christina of Markyate*, ed. and trans. C. H. Talbot (Oxford, 1959) 92, 96 [*Christina*]; and John of Ford, *Wulfric of Haselbury*, ed. Maurice Bell (Somerset Record Society 47, 1933) 81, 84, 90, 111 [*Wulfric*].

4. See the articles in *L'eremitismo in occidente nei secoli XI e XII* [*L'eremitismo*] Miscellanea del Centro di Studi Medioevali 4 (Milan, 1965).Hubert Dauphin describes the English scene in the volume in his 'L'érémitisme en Angleterre aux XIᵉ et XIIᵉ siècles', 271–310.

5. Jean Leclercq, in '"Eremus" et "Eremita"'. Pour l'histoire du vocabulaire de la vie solitaire,' in *Collectanea o.c.r.* 25 (1963) 8–30, deals with the development of the word 'hermit' in linguistic and historical context. Leclercq finds that distinctions between the anchorite and the hermit are 'rare and artificial' (p. 25). This is not generally true in the documents I have examined. For similar remarks, see Bell's introduction to *Wulfric*, pp. xlviii–li.

6. William of Malmesbury, *Vita Wulfstani*, ed. Reginald R. Darlington (Royal Historical Society, Camden Third Series 40, 1928) 65, 67. For a brief discussion of the authorship of this work, see Antonia Gransden, *Historical Writing in England, c.550–c.1307* (Ithaca, New York, 1974) 87–88. The anglo-saxon text is now lost.

7. *Chronicon abbatiae de Evesham, ad annum 1418*, ed. William Dunn Macray (RS 29, 1863), 322.

8. *Wulfric*, pp. 81, 82, 90, 111. Henry of Huntingdon, a contemporary of Wulfric and an independent chronicler of his life, also wrote of him as an anchorite: '*In provincia quae vocatur Dorsete, apud villam quae vocatur Heselberge, degit quidam Dei servus Wlfricus nomine, officio sacerdos, conversatione anachorita.*' *Historia Anglorum*, ed. Thomas Arnold (RS 74, 1879) p. xxix.

9. *The Victoria County History*, [= VCH] *Yorkshire 3:296#97, summarizes data on St Robert's life well. See also Memorials of the Abbey of St. Mary of Fountains*, ed. John R. Walbran Surtees Society 42, 67 (1863, 1878) 1:166–71n.

10. *VCH Lancashire* 2: 103, 154.

11. Reginald, *Libellus de vita et miraculus S. Godrici, heremitae de Finchale, auctore Reginaldo monacho Dunelmensi* [*Godric*] ed. Joseph Stevenson; Surtees Society 20 (1847).

12. *The Chancellor's Roll for the Eighth Year of King Richard the First, Michaelmas 1196*, ed. Doris M. Stenton; Pipe Roll Society, N.S. 7 (1930) 209.

13. *Christina*, pp. 80, 84, 86, 92, 102, 109, *et passim*.

14. One twelfth-century source that fails to make the distinction is the *Vita Bartholomaei Farnensis*, which calls Bartholomew an anchorite as he lives austerely on his island retreat. For the text, see *Symeonis monachi opera omnia* I, ed. Thomas Arnold, (RS 75 (1882–85 295–325.

15. *Godric*, pp. 140, 143

16. *Gesta abbatum monasterii sancti Albani* I, ed. Henry T. Riley, RS 28, pt. 4 (1867) 80–82.

17. *Christina*, p. 29; David Knowles and R. Neville Hadcock, *Medieval Religious Houses: England and Wales* (New York, 1972) 261. See also C. J. Holdsworth, 'Christina of Markyate', *Medieval Women*, ed. Derek Baker, Studies in Church History, Subsidia 1 (Oxford, 1978) 185– 204, esp. pp. 185–89.

18. W. Dugdale, *Monasticon Anglicanum*, ed. J. Caley, H. Ellis and B. Bandinel (London, 1817–30) 3: 426; see also Knowles and Hadcock, 259, which corrects the date in the *Monasticon*, as does Roy Midmer, *English Mediaeval Monasteries 1066–1540* (Athens, Georgia, 1979), 180.

19. Mary Bateson, 'The Register of Crabhouse Nunnery' [= Bateson, 'Register'] in *Norfolk and Norwich Archaeological Society* 11 (1892) 2.

20. Bateson, 'Register', 1–6.

21. See Leopold Genicot, 'L'érémitisme du XI siècle dans son contexte economique et social' in *L'eremitismo*, 45–69, esp. p. 66, where he talks of this phenomenon as 'anchoritism frequently slipping into cenobitism'.

22. For the *Ancrene Riwle*, see the list of publications of the Early English Text Society. Since 1944 EETS has printed no fewer than six editions of the *Riwle* in English, two in French, and one in Latin. M. B. Salu has published a modern english version of the text (Indiana, 1955). For a discussion of english anchoritism in thirteenth-century England, see Ann K. Warren, 'The English Anchorite in the Reign of Henry

III, 1216–72' in *Ball State University Forum* 19, No. 3 (Summer, 1978) 21–28. Aside from the *Ancrene Riwle*, not only were the letters written for women anchorites addressed to religious, but also the letters written for male anchorites. P. Livarius Oliger has edited three such rules for men: *Regula reclusorum Dubliensis* in 'Regulae tres reclusorum et eremitarum Angliae saec. XIII-XIV', *Antonianum* 3 (1928) 170–83; *Regula reclusorum Walteri reclusi* in 'Regula reclusorum Angliae et quaestiones tres de vita solitaria, saec. XIII-XIV', *Antonianum* 9 (1934) 53–84; *Speculum inclusorum* in *Lateranum*, New Series 4, No. 1 (Rome, 1938). There is also a short letter, edited by Antonia Gransden, 'The Reply of a Fourteenth-Century Abbot of Bury St. Edmunds to a Man's Petition to become a Recluse', *English Historical Review* 75 (1960) 464–67. The letters written for men had nowhere near the power, the beauty, or the popularity of the literature written for women. They do, however, speak of the monk-recluse as 'ideal' in the same manner as the nun was considered a worthier candidate for the reclusorium than was her sister in the world.

23. *Liber confortatorius*, ed. C. H. Talbot, in *Analecta Monastica* 3; *Studia Anselmiana* 38 (1955) 1–117.

24. *De institutis inclusarum*, ed. C. H. Talbot, in *Analecta S.O.C.* 7 (Rome, 1951) 167 –217, and specifically, 178–79. An english translation may be found in *Aelred of Rievaulx*: Treatises and the Pastoral Prayer (Cistercian Publications, 1971) CF2:41–102.

25. Ibid., p. 182.

26. *Form of Living*, in Hope Emily Allen, *English Writings of Richard Rolle, Hermit of Hampole* (Oxford, 1931: repr. St. Clair Shores, Michigan: Scholarly Press, 1971) 85–119. For the disciple Margaret, see *idem*, *Writings Ascribed to Richard Rolle Hermit of Hampole and Materials for his Biography* [Allen, *Writings*] (Modern Language Association of America, 1927; repr. New York, 1966), pp. 187–88, 256–68, 502–11.

27. *The Scale of Perfection*, ed. Evelyn Underhill (London, 1923); see also David Knowles, *The English Mystical Tradition* (New York, 1961), p. 102.

28. Allen, *Writings*, p. 223.

29. There exists a letter written by St Bernard to a nun at such a stage in this process: 'I have been told that you are thinking of leaving your convent under the pretext of seeking a harder way of life, and that although you will not listen to your Reverend Mother and sisters trying every argument to dissuade you and every means to prevent you from doing this, you are yet prepared to take my advice in the belief that whatever I suggest would be for the best.' St Bernard suggested 'no' to this nun of the monastery of St Mary of Troyes, but other would-be recluses found more support for their project than Bernard was wont to give. Bernard's letter 115 is translated by Bruno Scott James (as number 118) in *The Letters of St. Bernard of Clairvaux* (London, 1953) 179–80: cf. *PL* 182: 261–62, and J. Leclercq - H. Rochais, edd., *S. Bernardi Opera*, 7: 294–95.

30. For an extended discussion of this process see Ann K. Warren, *The Anchorite in Medieval England 1100–1539* (Dissertation, Case Western Reserve University, 1980) 53–95.

31. Allen, *Writings*, p. 502.

32. *VCH Yorkshire* 3:15: *ob frugem melioris vitae.* . . .

33. *Visitations of Religious Houses in the Diocese of Lincoln* I, ed. A. Hamilton Thompson; Canterbury and York Society 17 (1915) 113–14.

34. *Ibid.*, 114–15.

35. William Lyndwood, *Provinciale . . . cum adjiciuntur Constitutiones legatinae d. Othonis et d. Othoboni . . . cum . . . annotationibus Johannis de Anthona* (Oxford, 1679) 214–15.

36. For example, Lyndwood, ibid., suggested that the best places for anchorites to live were in the city as compared to the country because city folk were more numerous and thus more able to succor anchorites.

37. *VCH Lancashire* 2: 103; Rotha Mary Clay, *The Hermits and Anchorites of England* (London, 1914), 104–5.

38. *Calendar of the Patent Rolls* (London, Public Record Office, 1891–), *1416–22*,

p. 102; *1422–29*, p. 43; Margaret Deanesly ed., *The Incendium Amoris of Richard Rolle of Hampole* (Manchester, 1915) 115–16.

39. Bateson, 'Register,' p. 4.

40. *Registers of John le Romeyn, Lord Archbishop of York, 1286–1296, pt. ii, and of Henry of Newark, Lord Archbishop of York, 1296–1299*, ed. William Brown (Surtees Society 128, 1917) 322–23.

41. *Historical Papers and Letters from Northern Registers*, ed. James Raine (RS 61, 1873), 196–98.

42. Ibid., pp. 196–97n.; see also *Register of William Greenfield, Lord Archbishop of York 1306–1315*, ed. A. Hamilton Thompson (Surtees Society 145, 149, [1931, 1934]) 2: 221.

43. Clay, *Hermits and Anchorites*, p. 94, citing Reg. Melton, f. 175.

44. *Register of Edmund Lacy, Bishop of Exeter 1420–1455*, ed. G. R. Dunstan (Canterbury and York Society 60–63, 1963–71) 2: 394–96.

Stixwould in the
Market-Place

Coburn V. Graves

ANY ATTEMPT TO DESCRIBE the economy of a medieval english cistercian nunnery must begin with a statement of just what is being studied and under what limitations. In the first place, the singular nature of the institution that is described as english cistercian needs to be established, for up to recent times there has been some confusion among historians of medieval women religious. By the end of the thirteenth century only two abbeys of women in England were recognized as full-fledged members of the Order of Cîteaux, and both were founded after the first quarter of the century. Yet a full hundred years earlier had been founded the first of some twenty-five houses of nuns which claimed for themselves a cistercian quality and which had by 1270 gained recognition of that character in all quarters except Cîteaux. To distinguish these houses from the two fully cistercian abbeys, they may most conveniently be styled english cistercian nunneries.[1]

The availability, quantity, and nature of the sources useful for the study of these nunneries have had the effect of rendering their early histories little or ill known. While a significant amount of source material is available for the period from the fourteenth century down to the Dissolution, sources for the twelfth and thirteenth centuries are scanty. For that era some isolated documents from a house such as Kirklees in Yorkshire have survived and have been published, but only two Lincolnshire houses have left whole collections of records. These are in the form of cartularies,* both of which are at present unedited and unpublished.[2] Other information about the early medieval period must be gleaned from a variety of scattered ecclesiastical—

*A glossary of terms is found on page 231.

chiefly episcopal—and royal records. As a result, no comprehensive study embracing all or even a large number of the english cistercian nunneries is possible. The economy of one house can, however, be described and analyzed with a high degree of reliability, and such a study will allow for some understanding of the activities of the sister-houses of the group. This last consideration is especially important, for up to now students of the economy of the english cistercian nunneries have had to rely chiefly on the material found in Eileen Power's classic study of medieval english nunneries.[3]

Indispensable as Miss Power's work is for all students of the history of women religious in medieval England, those who want to know about the life of nuns in the twelfth and thirteenth centuries discover in it limitations that cannot be overlooked. Not exclusively, but certainly for the most part, Miss Power relied on sources that date from the years after 1300, and in the area of economic activities she has placed great reliance on data drawn from Dissolution documents. Further, she has assimilated material from all kinds of nunneries from diverse regions and varying periods of time to produce a composite that offers many problems for the study of a particular nunnery's history. With reference to financial difficulties Miss Power indicated that the nunneries were, like the monasteries, beset with poverty which she attributed to causes beyond the control of the nuns (such as natural disasters and intrusions of external lay and ecclesiastical authorities). In addition she adduced substantial evidence to support her interpretation that nuns were guilty of bad management and incompetence, concluding that because of these deficiencies the nuns contributed largely to their own misfortunes.[4] She was dealing with a period of decline, and the student is left to wonder how it was in the early centuries of dynamic growth.

To answer that question this present study looks at the economy of one Lincolnshire house, Stixwould, in the years from its foundation, *ante* 1135, to the end of the thirteenth century, the period covered by its cartulary. Because the cartulary remains the chief source of information, the analysis of the economy of the house is severely limited.[5] Day-by-day activities cannot be described because there is no narrative history for the house; account-books of income and expenditure are likewise lacking. On the other side of the ledger, the cartulary does provide information about the mode of acquisition and the status of property rights; it also provides an index to complex economic assests.

FOUNDATION

Stixwould was founded as a priory for nuns by the thrice widowed Lucy, countess of Chester, between 1129 and 1135.[6] Although it was not for another century and more that its cistercian quality gained public recognition or confirmation, one may reasonably consider that it was intended from its origins to be of that kind which has been identified as english cistercian and which committed itself to a cistercian observance. There is no evidence that Stixwould or her sister-houses in the diocese of Lincoln ever sought incorporation into the Order of Cîteaux, but that would not have been exceptional; from its inception the Order had no vision that included women. When the Order did agree to the formal incorporation of houses of women religious, it did so passively and reluctantly, that is, the Order reacted to requests or (papal) commands. On its own initiative it not establish nunneries.[7]

On the other hand, from early times individual leaders in the Order did offer support and encouragement to groups of women who sought to organize a communal life.[8] Everywhere in the twelfth century the vigorous cistercian vision of monastic life inspired imitation. For the most part scholars have recognized the attractive force of the cistercian ideal in matters of organization, liturgy, and spirituality. They have not always been as quick to see an integral relation between those factors and the economic prescriptions of the founders of Cîteaux involving such institutional consequences as the lay brotherhood. The commitment to withdraw from the world of feudal involvement and to live by their own labor may not have lasted as long as earlier historians thought, but it was an ideal that inspired the early generations of the white monks and their female imitators.[9]

Certain adjustments to that pristine cistercian austerity had to be made where women were concerned; they could not be expected to engage in the heavy manual labor that the monks found necessary in their physically isolated foundations. In fact, the work was so demanding that from the beginning the monks associated with themselves lay brothers to help with their activities outside the choir. It was, accordingly, entirely consistent with the monastic structure elaborated in early cistercian *Institutes* that the nuns at Stixwould maintained a company of *conversi* to help at home and afield.[10] The presence of *conversae* in the community itself proves simply an appropriate translation of gender, not of function.[11] Since the laybrothers were charged with external affairs in the fields and in the marketplace, the laysisters were probably restricted to domestic duties at Stixwould itself.

ADMINISTRATION

The administrative structure of the economy was set forth in detail early in the thirteenth century by Hugh of Wells, Bishop of Lincoln, 1213 to 1235.[12] To be sure, his provisions were addressed to the ladies at Nun Coton, another english cistercian nunnery in Lincolnshire, but it may readily be assumed that he was prescribing a structure for similar houses in his diocese.[13] Like

Nun Coton, Stixwould operated under the administrative leadership of a prioress and a master. The master, who normally served as both chaplain and business manager, could have been a religious or a secular cleric.[14] The other males in the community were apparently religious professed to Stixwould; it is not clear whether from the beginning there were canons in addition to lay-brothers, but both were present at the end of the thirteenth century.[15]

The master's part in the administration of the economy of the house was well defined. He shared custody of the seal of the house with the prioress and an elected committee of nuns; he presented to them a monthly account of current expenses, and once a year he was required to render a major account of revenues and expenditures. At the least he had a supervisory role in the conduct of business affairs outside the wall, the execution of which could be carried out by deputies such as the cellarer or a brother assigned to the role of purchasing agent *(frater emptor).*[16] After the middle of the thirteenth century, secular bailiffs managed outlying agricultural properties.[17]

ECONOMIC HEALTH

In the absence of account-books for the period under study, we have no evidence for the year-by-year statements of financial condition, but there are occasional indices to the health of the nunnery. Stixwould appears to have have been more prosperous than her sister houses of the diocese for, when in 1269 Bishop Gravesend spoke of the dire poverty suffered by the english cistercian nunneries of his see, he did not include Stixwould in his list.[18]

Another approach to the question of economic status is the investigation of the size of the population of the house. No figures are available for the period before 1300 but for the period after that date (whenever numbers are available) Stixwould consistently had a larger number of nuns than did her sister houses.[19] It is reasonable to assume that in the earlier years, which were more prosperous in all respects, she enjoyed the same preponderance. The larger the number of nuns, it should be noted, the larger the number of supporting personnel, such as laybrothers and laysisters. For purposes of comparison it is useful to see that, when Hugh of Wells was trying to bring into balance the number of inhabitants and the material resources of Nun Coton, he fixed the numbers there at thirty nuns, ten laysisters, three chaplains, and twelve laybrothers.[20] And, we may add, Nun Coton was included in the list of poverty-stricken houses that Gravesend compiled.

Other random data reveal that in the thriving wool trade of the late thirteenth century, Stixwould was exporting fifteen sacks a year while Nun Coton, her closest rival among the english cistercian nunneries of the diocese, exported ten.[21] A similar indication of the relatively greater prosperity of Stixwould is established in the taxation of Pope Nicholas in 1291, which evaluated the temporalities of Stixwould at about £ 117 while rating those of Nun Coton, again second to Stixwould, somewhere between thirty-five and sixty pounds.[22]

From whatever angle we approach the question, Stixwould appears to be the largest and most prosperous of the english cistercian nunneries in Lincolnshire. To the degree that this is so, she cannot be seen as wholly typical. How well or how poorly the nuns managed their resources cannot be set forth in any detail, but if some nunneries fell into debt and hard times, at least one, Stixwould, was able to survive her first two centuries in sound economic condition. This could not have been achieved without a respectable degree of managerial competence.

SOURCES OF SUPPORT

Before presenting an analysis of the specific resources of Stixwould, we should examine the sources of those holdings. For the most part the patrons of the nunnery made their grants in the twelfth century, usually within two generations of its foundation. Most of them came from what has been called the 'county society', [23] that is, those who were vassals of vassals of the crown, although the nunnery itself was founded by a noblewoman of the first rank who was a tenant-in-chief, a vassal of the crown without any intermediary.

The motives behind many grants seem multiple, but they fall into two main types: some were clearly in aid of the foundation; others were an enrichment of a going concern. In both cases there was often expressed a desire for participation in the spiritual benefits associated with the religious character of the house either by way of the right of burial for the donor himself or one of his relatives, or for the kind of association in life that might be characterized as fraternity.[24] In cases too numerous to cite such phrases as 'with my body [for burial]' (*cum corpore meo*) or 'so that we might share' (*ut simus participes*) occur. One especially elaborate expression included both concepts in a single charter of the twelfth century:

> And I will be faithful and loyal to them [the nuns] in all things so that I and my wife, my father and my mother, and all my relatives may share in all the [spiritual] benefits which are conferred in their church, both now and in the future. And the nuns will receive my body after my death along with whatever property I shall be able to give them at that time.

In another arrangement, made in 1183, Swayn, a cleric of Panton, and his wife gave all their lands and buildings in Great Panton on the condition that as long as they lived in secular garb they would give the monastery a certain amount of money (*quoddam talentum*) each year on the feast of All Saints as a token of their fraternity with the nuns. If they died as seculars, the nuns were to celebrate a full service for them just as for one of the brothers or sisters of the community.[26]

Among gifts of this type were bits of land as small as two *selions* or as large as half a knight's fee. Other grants included salt works, lands to support the work of the infirmary, money for the purchase of wine to be used in the celebration of Mass or for candles for the altar, or in one case an unspecified gift of thirty shillings a year.[27]

One special source of support derived from dowries given when women were received into the community. Twenty-three such dowered entries can be indentified with precision, and in all instances the payments were in the form of temporal holdings or rights which produced income into perpetuity, or at least until the Dissolution.[28]

In addition to being expressions of personal piety and charity, requests for fraternity, or dowries for entrants, grants also took the form of diverse amounts of money to sustain pittances for the nuns. These revenues would have to have been entered into the ledgers as specified funds and should not have been available for general purposes. In the seven notices of endowments for pittances that have been recorded, the amounts varied between four shillings and one mark.[29] By the end of the thirteenth century the pittance fund allowed an annual expenditure of just under three pounds.

The spiritual motives of patrons have long been considered not only as the primary but as the exclusive source of donations, but some historians have felt that other and, in some cases, more economically pragmatic reasons lay behind the gifts. Marginal lands yet uncultivated or too worn out for cultivation were gifts cheap for the patron. While there may be a measure of truth in this view so far as the white monks are concerned, it cannot be accepted whole, at least not for Stixwould; many of its acquisitions came in settled areas, as the host of references to grants of arable lands makes clear. In fact, in one instance the nuns were given an entire *assart*.[30]

In like manner the records of Stixwould will not support the theory that pasture rights were given only when patrons sought to improve the quality of their own flocks.[31] There are, for instance, three clear-cut instances in which the nuns were permitted to enclose their flocks, and they do not include additions to the demesne. According to the terms of one of these grants the nuns received the right to pasture two hundred sheep and to maintain a movable sheepfold. The sheep were to be enclosed by hurdles supplied by the donor, who, for his part, retained rights to fold and manure (*faudicium et sterquilinium*).[32] This suggests self-interest on the part of the donor, who probably wanted fertilizer for his fields, but the fact of enclosure does argue against the idea that the improvement of his flock by cross-breeding was the grantor's prime consideration.

SPIRITUALITIES AND TEMPORALITIES

Modern historians have usually divided the economic assents of medieval religious houses into the two classes that were established for purposes of taxation in the Middle Ages: spiritualities and temporalities. There is a certain artificiality in the scheme, for, except in the case of specified gifts, the revenues went into the same pot. The moneys were spent indiscriminately on various needs or obligations. It may be observed, in addition, that income from both classes of sources was in reality greater than might appear to be the case at first glance, for nunneries recognized as cistercian enjoyed an exemption from tithes and other levies which popes allowed to the Order and bishops and kings certified to the english cistercians nuns.[33]

Despite these reservations, the traditional division does provide a measure of convenience in analyzing the economy of a nunnery, and so it will be followed here. After an examination, then, of those assets usually categorized as spiritualities, we shall consider those resources usually arranged under the heading, temporalities.

SPIRITUALITIES

Spiritualities included revenues obtained from the possession of the advowson of parish churches, including the alms and oblations that were appropriate to those churches and their dependent chapels. To be sure, the administration of those churches was provided by vicars whose stipends had to be subtracted from total income, but that expenditure was slight. At Stixwould, for instance, revenues were over four pounds; the vicar ate at the master's table and received twenty shillings a year for clothing. The nuns were responsible for the costs of hospitality for the archdeacon, *sinodalia*, and other incidental levies. Profits were higher elsewhere. At Hundelby income was over five pounds; the vicarate was rated at five marks. The ratio at Honington was thirteen pounds to five marks. At Lavington twenty-one pounds was received; the value of the vicarate was ten marks. At Thorp spiritualities were estimated at over thirteen pounds, and the vicarate was valued at five marks.[34] In some cases altar-gifts and lesser tithes were assigned to the vicars, but not always. Greater tithes, on the other hand, were always reserved to the community, and they obviously formed a significant part of the income of the nunnery. Since access to that income was assured only when the nuns had clear title to the patronage of churches, they proved willing to resist challenges whenever they arose.

The nunnery at Stixwould had a solid economic base in her possession of seven churches. At the very beginning of her history Stixwould received the rights of her founder, Countess Lucy, in the churches of Stixwould, Honington, and Bassingthorpe.[35] Shortly thereafter Alan Crosby, who was a vassal of William de Roumare, Lucy's son and Earl of Lincoln, granted his rights in the church at Bucknall.[36] According to the terms of a subsequent formal concession recorded before the chapter of Lincoln Cathedral in 1160, the nuns were obligated to give Emma, Alan's widow, one mark of silver for as long as she lived in secular garb in exchange for her forswearing her rights of dowry in the church. In consultation with the master and nuns of Stixwould, Ralph, the son of Alan and Emma, retained the right to institute an honest and suitable vicar in that church.[37]

Ralph Fitz-Gilbert, another feudal tenant of William de Roumare, donated two churches: one at Lavington, including its chapels, and another at Wainfleet. The nuns' possession of the church of Lavington was confirmed by both Bishop Hugh of Avalon (1186–1200) and the crown. The nuns were also clearly in possession of the church of Wainfleet St Mary and its chapel at Sailholme as early as 1183, for in that year the nuns' rights were recognized in an agreement they made with the abbot of Bury St Edmund's. According to this agreement the nuns were to hold the church and its chapel for an annual payment of forty sesters of salt to the abbey. The monks of the abbey who were resident at the chapel were to exercise no parish rights, by land or by sea, beyond the walls of the chapel, nor was any secular priest to serve in the chapel without the consent of the mother church. It was further agreed that no one except a monk or a person mortally ill should be received there for the *viaticum* or penance unless there was a scarcity of priests of the mother church (*pro penuria sacerdotis*).[39]

The initial compact between Stixwould and Bury St Edmund's (restated in 1219 by Hugh of Wells) underwent a revision in 1256 when Henry of Lexington, then Bishop of Lincoln, allowed the nuns to substitute an annual payment of twenty pounds in lieu of the salt. With reference to the chapel Henry decreed that, however many monks should go to that chapel, they should have free ingress only to celebrate Mass. All offerings (*obvenciones*) were to belong to the mother church. When divine services were completed, the chapel was to be closed under lock and key, and the key was to be in the care of the chaplain (*capellanus*) or his designate.[40]

While this controversy between the nuns and the monks was being resolved, another issue had arisen, this time over the advowson of the mother church. In 1252, the nuns came to a settlement with Simon of Wainfleet: for a consideration of ten marks of silver Simon renounced his claim and the nuns gained clear title to the church.[41]

The church at Hundelby, given by Ralph de Roumare, probably should be regarded as a part of the foundation-endowment of Stixwould.[42] An equally substantial part of the early endowment of Stixwould came from the addition of further rights in the church of St Andrew the Apostle at Bassingthorpe and its chapel of St Leonard, gifts of the Baswin family.[43]

The church of Muston, southwest of the city of Lincoln, was granted before 1176 to the nuns by William Albini III, son of Matilda de Seynliz.[44] Despite a confirmation of the original grant by William's son, William IV (d. 1221), the husband of William IV's daughter Isabelle tried for some time to obstruct the right of Stixwould to present a vicar to that church. In the end, a review of earlier charters convinced him that the right of patronage properly belonged to the nuns and he withdrew his objection. To make amends for the difficulties he had caused, he gave the nuns three selions in the field of the manor.[45]

With the exception of the churches at Wainfleet and Muston, the rights of Stixwould were peacefully and quickly established. In the case of Wainfleet St Mary the nuns were alert to the economic advantages of an unchallenged possession of the church and were willing to pay for a clear title. Equally worthy of observation is the nuns' ability to pay, and in cash. The commutation of the payment of salt to Bury St Edmund's to a cash equivalent may be seen as a sophisticated adjustment on the part of the nuns to the changes in the economy of the thirteenth century when money payments were displacing traditional payments in kind. In that era of rising prices, fixed obligations measured in money clearly represented a gain for the nuns.

Contradictory and incomplete records make it impossible for us to clear up the confusion that surrounds the nuns' claim to the church at Willoughby (Scotwilloughby). The cartulary of Stixwould contains the simple record of a grant of the patronage of the church of St Andrew at Willoughby, made by Alexandria, daughter of Ralph Bernard, and her sisters, Matilda, Havis, Beatrix, and Anneis.[46] Among a set of charters independent of the cartulary we find further evidence of the gift. According to their terms Alexandria, after the death of her husband, Robert of Herierbi, gave the nuns twelve bovates of land; for their part the nuns were to pay her *in fraterna caritate* three shillings, eight pence *per annun* for the rest of her life and to have quitclaim after her decease. Should she die in the world, the nuns were to take her body and do for her the same full service as for one of their own. Were she to enter the nunnery, she was to surrender to the nuns her patrimony at Willoughby both in land and rent, and renounce the payment of the three shillings, eight pence. That her patrimony included rights in the church becomes evident when, we learn that, after her death, Hugh Scotun made a grant to the nuns of the church of St Andrew in pure alms. Yet, according to royal records, there was dispute between the nuns and Hugh over the right of advowson to the church. The parties were given the right to settle the dispute before the date set for a formal adjudication of the matter. Apparently they were able to come to an agreement out of court, for there is no record of any official court proceedings. Whatever the settlement, the nuns did not obtain the patronage of the church, the spiritualies of which were rated at over fifteen pounds.[47]

This survey of the church holdings of Stixwould reveals how churches came to the nuns, how vigorously they pressed their claims when there was need, what were associated problems with gaining title. That economic considerations were of primary importance cannot be doubted; the question that remains is that of measuring the value of these assets. Imperfect as it might be, the taxation schedule of Pope Nicholas IV, drawn up in 1291, allows some estimate of that value. When a pension of one pound from the church at Alford is included,[48] the sum of the values associated with the churches of Stixwould was rated at just over ninety-four pounds. Broken down by individual units,[49] the taxation reveals the following:

	£	s.	d.
Hundelby	5	6	8
Thorp	13	6	8
Bucknall	10	6	8
Stixwould	4	13	4
Honington	13	6	8
Lavington	21	6	8
Wainfleet	13	4	8

Just as it is true that the chief income from the possession of churches came in the form of the tithes payable from the people of the parish, so is it also true that tithes could be subject to controversy and litigation. No more than any other body was Stixwould able entirely to avoid disputes over tithes, but except for a very few cases the house was able to gain her own in peace.

At Rigsby in the parish of Alford, Jollan Neville granted two parts of the tithes of grain of his demesne to the nuns when he made provision for the admission of his two daughters into the community. He included in his grant the right to a toft where the grain might be stored.[50] Innocent as the donation appeared, it proved to be the seed of controversy between the nuns and the gilbertine canons of Lincoln St Katherine. The squabble began as early as 1183 and persisted until 1256, when the initial grant gained formal and final confirmation from Honorius III. According to the pope's settlement, the canons were to agree to make an annual payment of twenty shillings in place of all tithes customarily due the nuns. If the canons failed to make payment at the appointed times, they were to pay ten shillings in penalty.[51]

A decade earlier (1247) the nuns had to come to terms with the dean and chapter of the cathedral church in Lincoln over the tithes of the produce of their grange at North Stoke. The lands at the grange had probably been absorbed into the nuns' demesne from fields which had previously owed tithes to the dean and chapter, and the issue was more one of the establishment of ultimate rights than of money. The terms of settlement at the same time favored the nuns economically and protected the rights of the chapter; the nuns were obliged to make an annual payment of two pounds of wax, and they were freed from making any payment of tithes.

As early as the mid-twelfth century the nuns found themselves embroiled in trouble over tithes and parish rights with the church of Barkston as a result of having been possessed of the neighboring church at Honington. The resolution of the conflict allocated the tithes of grain produced on five and a half bovates on the nuns' demesne to their church at Honington. From another four and a half bovates which were cultivated by their serfs (*rustici*) and not by the nuns themselves, one moiety of the tithes of grain was to go to Honington, the other to Barkston. All the lesser tithes and profits of these four and a half bovates, viz. on wool, sheep, and orchards (*de lano, de agno, de ortis*) were to go to the church of Barkston. The children of the parishoners were to be baptized at Honington, and the wives were to be churched there. Whenever wills were made, the first bequest was to go to Honington and the second to Barkston. There were similar divisions of rights to confession, Easter offerings, and the like.[52]

Apart from the gifts that came to Stixwould to sustain the well-being of the corporation, certain offerings were intended solely for the support of uniquely religious activities. In 1261 Osbert of London, rector of the church at Silkeston, paid eighty marks of silver to acquire the right to the quitrent of 100 shillings *per annum* which the nuns had been paying for their holdings at the manor of Horsington. Then he remitted the 100 shillings to the nuns with the provision that each year four marks were to be spent on wax and oil for the lights necessary to the use of the nunnery both inside the church and without, including one lamp which was to be kept burning perpetually before the principal altar of the Virgin.[53] A small parcel of land was given earlier by Hugh of Westby for the maintenance of a lamp at the altar of St Michael.[54] In another instance, thirty-two pence *per annum*, the rent from thirty-two acres, was given for the support of a lamp in the church.[55] To aid the nuns in the choir duties, Hugh Russell of Frieston provided them with a humble but laudable one-half pound of cumin, or, in its stead, *unum obolum* (halfpenny) so that they might be free to attend to their prayers (*ut quiete possint laudibus vacare divinis*).[56]

TEMPORALITIES

Clearly a variety of lands or holdings came to the nuns out of religious considerations, but they were not content to rest their fortunes on haphazard expressions of their patrons' and benefactors' piety. On their own the nuns became vigorously involved in the development of their resources, chiefly by purchasing desirable properties or exchanging others in order to gain maximum returns from the lands they held.

To sustain conventual life the nuns had themselves to be, or to employ in their service, business managers in the world. Activities in this sphere were concerned with holdings which are customarily identified as temporalities, and in the management of them the nuns collectively differed not at all from other 'economic persons'. If the taxation of Pope Nicholas is given any credence, temporalities played a large part in the total economy of the house. In that rate schedule the nuns were credited with holdings valued at £117. This figure must be considered only a rough statement of minimal value, for there is no certainty that the *Taxatio* is accurate.[57] It probably understates values, and we must remember that the temporalities were capital assets, that is, they were sources of the production of revenues each year, and it was the revenues which were rated in the *Taxatio*. There is no reliable indicator to what proportion of capital value was represented by the yearly income, and so if measurement of total value is attempted, annual returns must be considered in conjunction with capital assets, assets which in many cases retained or even increased their value over time.

Two characteristics stand out in the matter of temporalities: the variety of possessions and their geographic distribution. The variety of the nuns' holdings quickly makes it evident that the economy was diversified and, to the degree that this was true, balanced. There is sufficient evidence to show that the nuns were involved in the production of grain crops, the rearing of livestock and sheep, and water-related activities such as the production of salt and the exploitation of fisheries. In addition there were isolated, special actiivities such as the management of a tannery and the operation of mills. The records do not allow for a precise statement of the depth of involvement in these activities; they simply attest to the fact of variety.

The single most important type of temporal holding of the nuns was the grange. Just what kind of estate is embodied in the term 'grange' is difficult to assess, for according to medieval usage the term was applied to all sorts of outlying estates or even to a single building.[58] It is worth noting in this context that the term was not used to describe the tithe-barn at Rigsby. At the least it may be assumed that ordinarily a small complex of buildings surrounding lands were involved as at Ferriby where, of three perches of arable that were given to the nuns, one and one-half were said to lie on the west side of the nuns' grange.[59] The language of the charters make clear that this grange was a center of grain production. Such was the case at Horsington, where three selions immediately adjacent to the grange were acquired in an apparent expansion of the grange.[60] Elsewhere, at Hundelby, the grange was said to possess a *curia*, some sort of farmyard or space enclosed by farm buildings.[61] There was at least one building at Bassingthorpe, for it is men-

tioned as the site of the delivery and recording of a formal grant or donation.[62]

Altogether the nuns directed activities at eight granges: Horsington, Ferriby, Honington, Bassingthorpe, Wymondham, Lavington, North Stoke,
and Hundelby.[63] North Stoke may well have been the largest; a terrier of
this grange reveals that a very sizeable total of arable was held in many small
parcels intermixed with the parcels of others,[64] as was also the case at Horsington.[65] Since assessments of the values of granges are almost nonexistent,
a valuation of the grange at Honington made in 1247 has special importance. According to the inventory, the assets of the grange amounted to
twelve pounds, distributed thus:[66]

2 cart horses	20s.
20 sheep	40s.
10 quarters of barley	100s.
3 quarters of draget	34s.
hay and forage	10s.
1 cart	6s.

At all the granges, as well as at other places, the nuns were engaged in
sheep-rearing and the production of wool. According to one set of records
from the last half of the thirteenth century, amongst the english cistercian
nunneries in Lincolnshire Stixwould was the greatest seller of wool to one
group of italian merchants. She delivered fifteen sacks; Nun Coton, the second leading seller of the group, sold only ten.[67] This index, however, cannot
be used to estimate the size of the flocks belonging to Stixwould, for it is
likely that the enumerated sacks contained not only the wool gathered by
the house from its own sheep but also *collecta*, i.e., wool produced by others
in the vicinity of the house or its granges and delivered to the merchants at
Stixwould by the nuns who acted as intermediary in the business.[68] That
this was the case is suggested by the fact that, according to a tally made
within thirty years of the italian schedule, Nun Coton had eleven score
sheep. If each sack was made up of two hundred fleeces, Nun Coton's own
flocks would have produced only about one sack; yet the schedule called for
ten sacks, or the equivalent of flocks numbering at least 2,000 sheep.[69] For
Stixwould we may with certainty assume a minimum of 1,390 sheep on the
basis of the grants to pasture rights.[70] It should be noted, however, that
these data are derived exclusively from grants of pasture rights; there is no
way of knowing just how many sheep the nuns kept on their own lands.
Grants of this type would not reveal, for instance, the presence of the
twenty sheep on the grange at Honington noted above. Nor is there any
reason to think that Stixwould sold all her wool to only one company of
Italians.[71] In the end, if reasonable minimal calculations are made, we may

assume that Stixwould had flocks of approximately 1,500 sheep, or enough to produce seven or eight sacks a year. If this is so, then Stixwould was producing approximately half of the wool she was delivering; the other half came from non-conventual producers.

To arrive at the value of wool produced, all we need is a knowledge of the market price per woolsack at the end of the thirteenth century. Prices varied according to the type of wool, but we may estimate the price available to the nuns at fourteen marks per sack.[72] At that rate Stixwould earned five pounds *per annum* from her own wool—less, of course, the costs of production. There is no index to those costs or to the sums earned for the handling the wool of others.

The sheep were frequently raised on the granges, but not always. Sheepfolds (*bercariae*) were maintained outside grange limits at Horsington, Winelle, Hungerton, Stoke, and Edmesthorpe.[73] Pasture rights for flocks ranging from fifty to two hundred sheep were distributed even more widely over the countryside at Ferriby, Hundelby, Barkston, Panton, Winelle, Hungerton, Stoke, Wymondham, and Edmesthorpe. Where rights of common pasture were granted, the kind of land used is evident; but in some instances the lands attached to sheepfolds were taken from arable, and on occasion the reduction of arable to pastoral use seems to indicate an economic sensitivity to where the greater profit lay. The production of manure was an important part of arable farming, and so the removal of small parcels represents not a major redirection of effort, but rather an increment to the arable. By maintaining some sort of balance between commitments to crops and sheep, the nuns avoided the potential disasters attendant on a commitment to a one-crop economy. In this sector of their economy the nuns gave clear proof of managerial prudence and competence.

Evidence of their involvement in grain production is so abundant that it would be tedious to enumerate the data. Worth noting in the records are the signs of a sense of economic rationalism in the land management policy of the nuns. Time and again the nuns tried to consolidate their scattered lands. Exchanges, such as that at Horsington where seven selions adjacent to the nuns' lands were gained by the surrender of nine scattered selions, were not unusual.[75] In other cases, the nuns made major commitments to acquire lands: they gave thirty shillings for one bovate in Honington, to Gilbert of Sempringham and his chapter; for lands in Horsington and Bucknall they paid an entry fee of one hundred marks and assumed the responsibility of an annual payment of ten pounds.[76] On the other hand, when opportunity allowed, the nuns were willing to lease their lands to gain cash revenues.[77]

A miscellany of lesser assets, most of which are barely described in the records, includes livestock at several sites,[78] a tannery at Horsington,[79] a quarry at Great Panton,[80] and salt works at Wainfleet.[81] Rights to fish ponds or pools were an important part of the total economy of the convent, since these could provide fish for the domestic consumption of the nuns as well as produce a commodity for sale at the market. Those rights were nearby on the River Witham and on the Humber, some thirty-five miles distant from Stixwould.[82] In most cases the nuns were passive recipients of grants to these rights, but once on their own initiative they sought a fishery by exchanging landed property for it.[83]

Exclusive or partial rights to the management of mills caught the nuns up in the economy of society as well as of their own community. They had a total of eleven water mills, two each at Ferriby, Hundelby, Caythorpe, and Panton, and one mill on each manor at Methringham, Honington, and Dunnington.[84] The mills were gained in various ways: (1)as a part of the endowment (Hundelby and Honington),[85] (2) by gift, as when Ralph Fitzgilbert granted his mill at Ferriby with full rights of multure of all his lands on that manor,[83] (3) by dowry, as when the nuns received John of Hesel's mill at Ferriby when his three daughters joined the community;[87] or when Walter of Methringham, preparing to go to Jerusalem, provided for the entry of his sister into the nunnery,[88] (4) by lease, as when the nuns agreed to pay annually four marks, eight pence for the two mills and multure rights at Caythorpe;[89] or when they committed two marks, six pence *per annum* for rights to a mill between Great and Little Panton.[90]

The value of mill rights can only be approximated. If we assume, on the basis of admittedly very scanty data, that a mill had an annual minimal yield of twenty-seven shillings—the amount committed at Panton and Caythorpe—then the annual income from mills was something in excess of fifteen pounds, or about ten percent of the temporalities estimated in the taxation of Pope Nicholas. In actuality, the yield may easily have been twice that amount.

Urban holdings allowed the nuns to have depots for the storage of their own produce, to serve as stations for their own purchasing agents, or as revenue producing rental units. In Boston, the nuns had three parcels of land, one of which carried the privilege of free entrance and egress with their servants and horses and wagons and carts (*cum hominibus et equis et carris et carrectis*)[91] both at the time of the fair and at other times. Not only did the nuns sell there, they also bought. In one grant of money, for instance, if was provided that the cellarer or a *frater emptor* should use the money at the fair for the purchase of oil for a lamp at the altar of St Michael.[92]

In the city of Lincoln, the nuns held eight pieces of land distributed among six different parishes.[93] In five instances, they were small landlords receiving rents ranging from as little as two shillings to seven shillings, three chickens and a rooster at Christmas. From another piece of property the nuns received an annual income of twenty-three shillings, four pence. This property had come in free gift from Geoffrey of Leicester, but since he in fact held it from William, son of Fulco, the nuns had to settle with William. For a payment of ten shillings *per annum* to William, or to his assigns, the nuns were able to retain a net annual return of thirteen shillings, four pence. So attractive was the prospect of regular income in cash that the nuns invested thirteen marks to acquire one other piece of real estate in the city.[94]

The nuns were not only landlords in Lincoln, they also did business of their own in the city. To get a depot useful for this activity, they negotiated in the thirteenth century with John, Count of Richmond, to gain a landing place on the River Witham at Washingborough, three miles outside the city. According to the terms of the arrangement the nuns held in the town (*villa*) of Washingborough a parcel with its buildings, access to the common road, and docking rights whenever they wished, by day or by night. They were free to tie up their boats there and to remain for however long they wished. In addition to this particular transaction, John gave the nuns the annual revenue of thirteen shillings, four pence from a piece of property in the city of Boston in exchange for a certain property in that commercial center.[75]

CONCLUSION

The picture of Stixwould that emerges from this study is one of a house which developed a dynamic economy in the period between her foundation and the Black Death. If the house did not amass sufficient wealth to become a significant factor in the economy of England, within more modest limits it consistently knew prosperity. Put simply, the characterization of english nunneries drawn by Eileen Power as houses beset with hardship, managerial incompetence, and indebtedness does not apply to Stixwould, at least not in the first two centuries of her history. The nuns of the house took advantage of opportunities to enhance their material base and, when opportunity allowed or occasion required, they built a rational economy, enlarging or exchanging to consolidate whatever came to them in casual ways. At other times they made deliberate decisions to purchase whatever was needed to strengthen or round out their economy. We may suspect that they were not beyond using the spiritual character of the house to attract assets of one kind or another in exchange for such benefits as admission to the community, burial rights, or confraternity.

One result of this activity was the creation of an economic world that extended over a large territory. Practically all the holdings of Stixwould were included in a triangular zone that ran from Edmesthorpe in the south to Ferriby in the north, sixty-eight miles away; thence to Skegness on the coast, fifty-two miles from Ferriby on one side and another fifty-two miles from Edmesthorpe on the other. It may be true that Stixwould was a local nunnery insofar as its holdings were all contained within the limits of a single diocese but, as these distances suggest, it was more than a neighborhood convent.

Beyond the matter of geographical extent, the economy of the house was marked by a diversity of engagement. The nuns themselves may well have stayed at the priory giving primary attention to their religious duties, but their officers and officials were responsible for the management and administration of a number of parish churches, the cultivation of crops, the production of wool, leather, salt, and fish, the exercise of manorial rights, especially those related to the possession of mills, and the use of some, the renting of other, urban holdings.

The successful supervision of all these activities, spread as they were over such distances, allowed the nuns of Stixwould to escape the poverty and distress that troubled other nunneries within the diocese. The nuns charged with administration, or their male helpers, exhibited a degree of managerial competence that has not been sufficiently recognized. The economic health of the house provided the material conditions for the maintenance of a decent standard of religious life, and that, after all, was the justification for any economic program. While there is no direct evidence that the nuns used their prosperity to further their religious lives, it is worthy of note that contemporary episcopal registers reveal no instances of problems of religious discipline among them.

Kent State University
Kent, Ohio

NOTE ON MONEY AND VALUE

Money was reckoned and used in two ways in medieval England. A silver currency of coins circulated, and there was one common unit of reference, known as a money of account, the mark, worth two-thirds of a pound sterling or 13 s. 4 d. The pound (*libra*) was made up of twenty shillings; each shilling (*solidus*) was worth twelve pennies, and the penny (*denarius*) was composed of two half-pennies (the *obolum*). The talent referred to in the text was neither a common nor a precise unit of money; it seems simply to have meant 'some money'.

Attempts to correlate values expressed in medieval units of currency with modern values are bound to be disappointing because of a number of variables. Differences in standards of living, the constant changes in price levels that follow long periods of inflation, and the share of the value of the economic product obtained by wage-earners in the twentieth century are some of the factors that need to be taken into account before facile formulations of equivalents are set forth. One attractive estimate of modern equivalents has been offered by Doris Stenton who suggested a ratio of fifteen or twenty to one to arrive at sums of approximate equal value for England on the eve of World War II.[1] Needless to emphasize, those figures would be totally inadequate in 1981.

Even if it is impossible to develop any reliable set of equivalent values over the centuries, certain medieval economic characterictics may still be worth consideration. Normally prices remained firm in the twelfth and thirteenth centuries when they were related to customary payments whether rendered in kind or commuted to cash. Thus, the knight's fee, reckoned at forty days' armed service each year, was commuted to an annual payment of twenty shillings early in the twelfth century and remained at that figure throughout the entire period under study here.[2] On the other hand, when prices were attuned to market conditions, the period was characterized by a rise in those prices. The wage of a hired knight around 1175 was eight pence a day; by 1200 the daily wage had increased by three or four times, that is to two or three shillings (24 *d.*–36 *d.*).[3] The consequences of these conditions are all too familiar: where the nuns owed fixed obligations, they prospered; where their income was made up of fixed revenues they suffered a loss, for that fixed income steadily lost purchasing power in the face of rising prices.

1. *English Society in the Early Middle Ages*, 2nd. ed. (repr. Harmondsworth, 1955) 27–28.
2. Stenton, *English Society*, 71.
3. Stenton, *English Society*, 88–89.

GLOSSARY

ADVOWSON. The right of presenting a nominee to a vacant ecclesiastical benefice, such as the rectorship of a parish.

ALMS, PURE. The tenure of lands, etc., bestowed upon God, that is, given a religious corporation for pure and perpetual alms, free from any temporal service.

ASSART. A piece of land converted from forest-land into arable.

BAILIFF. An agent who collected rents or who managed an estate for a landlord.

BOVATE. As much land as one ox could plow in a year; varying from ten to eighteen acres.

CARTULARY. A book where the records of a monastery are kept.

COMMON PASTURE. The use of pasture by the cattle of a number of owners.

DEMESNE. The land possessed and held by the owner himself, and not held of him by any subordinate tenant.

KNIGHT'S FEE. A feudal tenure held from a superior on condition of serving in the field as a mounted and well-armed man. The service was valued at twenty shillings *per annum*.

MOIETY. A half part.

MULTURE. A toll or fee assessed for grinding grain at a mill.

PATRONAGE. See advowson.

PERCH. A measure of length of land; about five-and-a-half yards, but varying locally.

PITTANCE. A pious donation or bequest to a religious house or order to provide extra food on particular occasions; the allowance or dole itself.

QUITCLAIM. A formal discharge or release.

QUITRENT. A rent, usually of small amount, paid in lieu of services.

SELION. A portion of land of indeterminate area comprising a ridge or narrow strip lying between two furrows formed in dividing an open field.

SESTER (SEXTER). A dry measure containing the sixth part of a *modius* which, in turn, was a measure of capacity of varying size. In antiquity the *modius* was equal to about a peck.

SINODALIA (SYNODALS). A payment made by the inferior clergy on the occasion of an episcopal or archidiaconal visitation.

TERRIER. A register of landed property, including lists of tenants, with particulars of their holdings, services, and rents.

TITHES, GREATER. The chief agricultural tithes, as corn (grain), hay, wood, and fruit.

TITHES, LESSER. Tithes of agricultural products other than those subject to greater tithes.

TOFT. The site of a house and its outbuildings.

NOTES

ABBREVIATIONS

EHR .... English Historical Review

HMC................... Historical Manuscripts Commission Reports

LRS .... Lincoln Record Society

Mon. Angl.............. W. Dugdale, *Monasticon Anglicanum*. New edition by J. Caley, H. Ellis, and B. Bandinel. London, 1846.

OED .... Oxford English Dictionary

Placitorum . . . Abbrevatio . . . . Placitorum in domo capitulo Westmonasterii asservatorum abbrevatio. Richard II-Edward II. Record Commission; London, 1811.

VCH, Lincs............... The Victoria History of the County of Lincoln. Ed. W. Page. London, 1906.

1. Sally Thompson, 'Cistercian Nuns in the Twelfth and Early Thirteenth Centuries', in Derek Baker, ed., *Medieval Women* (Oxford, 1978) 227–52; C.V. Graves, 'English Cistercian Nuns in Lincolnshire', *Speculum* 54 (1979) 492–99.

2. The Kirklees documents were published by S. Chadwick, 'Kirklees Priory', *Yorkshire Archaeological Journal* 16 (1902) 319–68, 464–66. The two english cistercian nunneries whose cartularies have survived are Nun Coton (Bodl. Top. Linc. d. I) and Stixwould (BL Add. 46701, hereafter, *Cart. Stix.*).

3. Eileen Power, *Medieval English Nunneries* (Cambridge, 1922; repr. New York, 1964).

4. Power, chapter 5.

5. In addition to *Cart. Stix.* there are a number of charters related to holdings at Honington, calendared in *Historical Manuscripts Commission*, Report 11, Appendix 7 (1888) 58–81.

6. *Cart. Stix.*, fol. 1ⁱ; VCH, *Lincs.*, 2:146. Documents numbered 1–3 in HMC, 11:7, p. 59, indicate that the nunnery was in existence in the time of Henry I, i.e. before 1135. For the early date, see Frank Stenton, *The First Century of English Feudalism*, 2nd ed. (Oxford, 1961) 93. According to Bennett Hill, *English Cistercian Monasteries and Their Patrons in the Twelfth Century* (Urbana, 1968) 35, Lucy's son, Ranulf Earl of Chester, was the greatest single benefactor of the cistercian monks in England. Her other son, William de Roumare, was the founder of Revesby and a patron of Gokewell, an english cistercian nunnery like Stixwould; David Knowles and R. Neville Hadcock, *Medieval Religious Houses*, 2nd. ed. (London, 1971) 271.

7. Thompson, 'Cistercian Nuns', 227–42; Graves, 'English Cistercian Nuns', 493–94.

8. Thompson, 'Cistercian Nuns', 229–35; Graves, 'English Cistercian Nuns', 493.

9. Louis J. Lakai, *The Cistercians: Ideals and Reality* (Kent, Ohio, 1977). See especially his comments on p. 283 and the translation of chapter 15 of 'The Institutes of the Cistercian Monks Who Departed from Molesme', pp. 458–60.

10. Their presence is attested by the contitution issued by Hugh of Wells for Nun Coton; *Monasticon Anglicanum*, 5:677.

11. The presence of laysisters at Stixwould is noted only in a letter of Henry III (1270): '*Cum per inspeccionem privilegiorum priorisse et monialibus de Stikeswald et eiusdem domus sororibus concessorum intellexerimus quod eedem moniales sunt de ordine et regula Cistercien . . .*'. Bodl. Top. Linc. d. I, fol. 48ʳ.

12. *Monasticon*, 5:677.

13. VCH, *Lincs.*, 2:151.

14. Rosalind Hill ed., *The Rolls and Register of Bishop Oliver Sutton, 1280–1299*, LRS 60 (1965) 5:155, 200.

15. I have dealt with questions of organization and personnel in 'The Organization of an English Cistercian Nunnery in Lincolnshire', *Cîteaux* (1982) 333–50. For the presence of both types of male religious, see *Cal. Pat. Rolls*, 2 Edward II (1308) 166. The earliest reference to the presence of canons is in 1194, *Rotuli Curiae Regis*, 1:87. In 1199 the master was referred to as a *confrater, ibid.*, 1:308.

16. *Cart. Stix.*, fol. 105ʳ: '*ad feriam sancti Botulfi ad oleum emendum per manum celerarii vel fratris emptoris.*'

17. Ibid., fols. 101ᵛ–102ʳ.

18. Graves, 'English Cistercians Nuns', 497.

19. Ibid., n. 33.

20. *Monasticon*, 5:677.

21. Dorothy Owen, *Church and Society in Medieval Lincolnshire*, History of Lincolnshire 5 (Lincoln, 1971) 66.

22. The value of the temporalities of Stixwould is derived from *Taxatio Ecclesiastica Anglie et Wallie* (London, 1802), pp. 59–73. The value of twelve pounds supplied in VCH, *Lincs.*, 2:149, represents only the value of the home manor of Stixwould. The figures for Nun Coton are found in VCH, *Lincs.*, 2:150.

23. Owen, *Church and Society*, 49.

24. Owen, 50.

25. HMC, 11:7, no. 4, 59: '*Et ego eis fidelis et legalis in omnibus ut ego et sponsa mea, ut pater meus et mater mea, et omnis parentes mei, simus participes omnium beneficiorum quae fiunt, vel fient in ecclesia sua. Et ipsae suscipient corpus meum post obitum meum cum qualicumque catello ego potero eis dare ad illam horam.*'

26. *Cart. Stix.*, fol. 67ᵛ.

27. Ibid., fols. 9ʳ⁻ᵛ, 29ʳ⁻ᵛ, 30ʳ, 105ᵛ, 108ʳ, 113ᵛ.

28. See note 15 above.

29. *Cart. Stix.*, fols. 12ʳ, 39ᵛ, 40ʳ, 78ʳ, 101ʳ⁻ᵛ, 109ᵛ, 115ᵛ.

30. Owen, *Church and Society*, 48–51; Susan Wood, *English Monasteries and Their Patrons in the Thirteenth Century* (Oxford, 1960) 4; Hill, *English Cistercian Monasteries*, 46, 54–55; *Cart. Stix.*, fols. 89ʳ, 92ʳ.

31. Hill, *English Cistercian Monasteries*, 75–76.

32. *Cart. Stix.*, fol. 89ᵛ.

33. Graves, 'English Cistercian Nuns', 499.

34. Power, *Nunneries*, 113–17; Owen, *Church and Society*, 16. For the vicarates, see W. Phillimore, ed., *Rotuli Hugonis de Welles*, LRS 3 (1914) 3:62–63. Income from spiritualities are based on references cited in note 49.

35. *Cart. Stix.*, fol. 1ʳ.

36. *Cart. Stix.*, fols. 1ʳ, 10ʳ⁻ᵛ, 11ʳ.

37. *Cart. Stix.*, fols. 11ʳ⁻ᵛ.

38. *Cart. Stix.*, fols. 38ᵛ–39ʳ, 47ʳ, 98ᵛ, 99ʳ⁻ᵛ, 107ᵛ, 112ᵛ; VCH, *Lincs.*, 2:146.

39. *Cart. Stix.*, fols. 47ʳ⁻ᵛ. Owen, *Church and Society*, 19, 65, 74, appears to have misread the text; the salt was paid by the nuns to the abbey, not the other way around, as she has it; *Cart. Stix.*, fol. 47ᵛ: *moniales de Styk' dictam ecclesiam tenebunt redendo ecclesie sancte Eadm' de eadem ecclesiam nomine transaccionis annua quadraginta sext' sal' in festo sancti Petri ad vincula apud Waynfleth.* The crown's confirmation of the church at Lavington came early in the reign of John, *Placitorum . . . Abrevatio*, 58.

40. *Cart. Stix.*, fols. 47ᵛ–48ʳ: *quod monasterium beati Edmundi de ecclesia predicta de Wainflet in perpetuum singulis annis per manum ipsius qui eiusdem ecclesie pro tempore rector extiterit, vigil' vel die sancti Botulfi apud Wainfleth xxᵗⁱ sol' annuos nomine salis predicti percipiet.* For Hugh's restatement, see *Rotuli Hugonis de Welles*, LRS 3 (1912) 1:114–15.

41. *Cart. Stix.*, fol. 112ʳ.

42. *Cart. Stix.*, fols. 54ᵛ, 107ᵛ.

43. *Cart. Stix.*, fols. 69ᵛ, 70ʳ, 70ᵛ, 82ʳ.

44. *Cart. Stix.*, fols. 89^v, 111^r.
45. Cart. Stix., fol. 111^v.
46. *Cart. Stix.*, fol. 58^v.
47. HMC, 11:7, nos. 5, 7, 59–60; VCH, *Lincs.*, 2:146; *Rotuli Curiae Regis*, 1:308, 311; *Taxatio*, 61.
48. *Taxatio*, 59. This pension was related to the holding of the nuns of a chapel at Rigsby which was in the parish of Alford. This was a gift of Ralph Fitzgilbert, donor of the churches of Lavington and Wainfleet, *Placitorum . . . Abbrevatio*, 46.
49. The ratings of the churches are found in *Taxatio*: Hundelby, Bassingthorp, Bucknall, Stixwould, 59b; Honington, 62; Lavington, 61; Wainfleet, 58b; Muston, 65.
50. *Cart. Stix.*, fol. 57^r. Owen, *Church and Society*, 14, 50, says that the grant was of two-thirds of the tithes; the text of the charter reads *duas partes*.
51. *Cart. Stix.*, fols. 46^r, 47^v, 48^r.
52. *Cart. Stix.*, fols. 102^{r-v}; Owen, *Church and Society*, 17.
53. *Cart. Stix.*, fols. 11^r–12^r; Owen, *Church and Society*, 53.
54. *Cart. Stix.*, fol. 83^r.
55. *Cart. Stix.*, fol. 2^v.
56. *Cart. Stix.*, fol. 69^{r-v}.
57. Rose Graham, 'The Taxation of Pope Nicholas IV', EHR 23 (1908) 450, warns that the assessments used in the taxation do not accurately represent the income of a house. Anne Chapman, *Granges and Other Land Holdings of Robertsbridge Abbey* (unpublished dissertation, Kent State University, 1977) 173, n. 21, found that the figures were 'in reasonably good agreement with information derived from other sources' so far as Robertsbridge was concerned.
58. Recent studies of granges appear in Colin Platt, *The Monastic Grange in Medieval England* (New York, 1969) and R.A. Donkin, *The Cistercians: Studies in the Geography of Medieval England and Wales* (Toronto, 1978) 51–67. A keen, critical assessment of the nature of granges and other estates is in Chapman, *Granges of Robertsbridge Abbey*, 36–164.
59. *Cart. Stix.*, fol. 41^r.
60. *Cart. Stix.*, fol. 15^r.
61. *Cart. Stix.*, fol. 49^r.
62. *Cart. Stix.*, fol. 68^r.
63. *Cart. Stix.*, fols. 15^r, 41^r, 60^r, 68^r, 96^v, 99^r, 123^r, 124^r.
64. *Cart. Stix.*, fols. 123^r–24^v.
65. *Cart. Stix.*, fol. 21^r.
66. HMC, 11:7, no. 25, 62. 'Draget:' a mixture of various kinds of grain, esp. of oats and barley sown together; OED, s. v. *dredge*.
67. Owen, *Church and Society*, 66.
68. There is a discussion of wool-handling by cistercian monks in C.V. Graves, 'The Economic Activities of the Cistercians in Medieval England', *Analecta S.O. Cist.* 13 (1957) 25–28.
69. Power, *Nunneries*, 111, n. 2.
70. *Cart. Stix.*, fols. 42^r, 44^r, 48^v, 62^v, 68^v, 89^v, 90^r, 91^v, 94^r, 96^r, 96^v, 97^v.
71. W. Cunningham, *Growth of English Industry and Commerce*, 5th ed. (London, 1910) 1:545–47.
72. *Ibid.*, 548; Power, *Nunneries*, 111, n. 2.
73. *Cart. Stix.*, fols. 13^r, 14^r, 16^r, 17^{r-v}, 18^r, 20^v, 22^r, 89^v, 91^v, 96^r.
74. See note 70 above.
75. *Cart. Stix.*, fols. 16^v, 17^r.
76. *Cart. Stix.*, fols. 8^v, 9^r, 16^v, 17^r.
77. *Cart. Stix.*, fol. 101^r.
78. *Cart. Stix.*, fols. 3^r, 8^r, 69^v, 80^r; HMC, 11:7, no. 25, 62.
79. *Cart. Stix.*, fols. 13^v, 15^v, 17^v, 18^v, 19^r.
80. *Cart. Stix.*, fol. 68^r.

81. *Cart. Stix.*, fols. 54^r, 54^v, 99^v, 108^r.
82. *Cart. Stix.*, fols. 6^v, 38^r, 38^v, 99^v, 104^v, 105^r, 107^r.
83. *Cart. Stix.*, fol. 6^v
84. *Cart. Stix.*, fols. 5^r, 38^r, 44^r, 45^r, 49^r–53^v, 63^r, 65^v, 66^v, 68^v, 100^v, 104^r.
85. *Cart. Stix.*, fol. 100^v.
86. *Cart. Stix.*, fol. 38^r.
87. *Cart. Stix.*, fol. 49^r.
88. *Cart. Stix.*, fol. 44^r.
89. *Cart. Stix.*, fol. 63^r.
90. *Cart. Stix.*, fol. 65^r.
91. *Cart. Stix.*, fol. 37^r.
92. *Cart. Stix.*, fol. 105^r.
93. *Cart. Stix.*, fols. 55^r–58^r.
94. *Cart. Stix.*, fol. 54^v.
95. *Cart. Stix.*, fol. 114^v.

Medieval Cistercian Nunneries and English Bishops

John A. Nichols

On the seventeenth of July in 1442, William Alnwick, Bishop of Lincoln, visited Catesby Priory, a house of cistercian nuns in medieval England.[1] As bishop, Alnwick was charged with the visitation of monasteries in his diocese to review the quality of their religious life.[2] The investigation of Catesby was one of many conducted by bishops of Lincoln over the years with the intent of making whatever reforms might be needed. At this nunnery in 1442, there was much in need of reform.

During the visitation the bishop detected or discovered, according to the episcopal register, the following facts about Catesby: the prioress, Margaret Wavere, reported that young girls were sleeping in the nuns' dormitory; secular folk were walking about the cloister and disrupting the religious offices of the nuns; the religious services were not sung when they were supposed to be observed; the nuns were sending letters out of the priory without her approval, revealing wrongfully the internal affairs of the house, and being disobedient to her. Isabel Benet, in particular, did not obey the prioress and had ruined the priory's reputation by having an affair with William Smythe, sometime chaplain of the place, and had in fact conceived by him a child.[3]

The bishop next heard Sister Juliane Wolfe complain that the prioress did not share the financial accounts of her administration with the other sisters, that she pawned the jewels of the community, and that she threatened that if any of the nuns told of these matters during his visit, then that person would be placed under lock and key. A further complaint charged the prioress with not keeping the monastery in good repair so the buildings were becoming dilapidated.[4]

When it was Dame Isabel Benet's turn to have a private audience with Alnwick, she said that the mother superior could not keep her temper and

237

called the nuns whores and even pulled their hair while they were in choir. She said that the prioress' mother was privy to the internal affairs of the community and published them at Catesby; that the income of the priory, which had been worth sixty pounds yearly, under her management was scarcely fifty pounds; and that she had defamed herself with Sir William Taylour of Brampton. The other nuns reported similar things against their prioress, Margaret Wavere.[5]

In response to these individual charges, Wavere swore to Bishop William that she never called the nuns whores or pulled their hair. She had pawned the sacramental chalice only with the knowledge and consent of the community. She denied threatening the nuns if they made disclosures. As to the dilapidation of the buildings, she said that some were partly in repair and some were not. As for not showing an account of the priory's financial state, she confessed that she had not, and gave as her reason that she did not have a clerk who could write. As to Sir William Taylour, she flatly denied the crime at any time.[6]

The bishop gave the prioress until the next day to clear herself by having four of her sisters come forward and testify to her innocence of the articles. When she was unable to produce any compurgators, Alnwick found her guilty as charged. The bishop ordered the prioress and any of the nuns who confessed or were found guilty of wrong-doing to receive penance. Dame Isabel Benet, for example, confessed committing her crime, but not, she said, with Sir William Smythe, but with another man. Nevertheless, she was to avoid all possible contact with Smythe in the future as was the prioress with Sir William Taylour. Because of the prioress' apparent mismanagement, Isabel Benet and Agnes Halesley were appointed receivers of the priory's money and were charged with keeping an account of all income and expenses.

The report of Alnwick's visitation included the following injunctions sent to Catesby soon after his visit: he ordered that the nuns follow the rules of their Order and live in common with each other; that all secular persons be removed from the cloister and dormitory; and that the nuns, under pain of excommunication, not reproach one another by reason of the visitation disclosures. Moreover, Margaret Wavere was to set a proper example for the nuns under her care by avoiding those misdeeds for which she had been found guilty. With the publishing of his injunctions, Bishop William's visitation to Catesby Priory was officially ended, with his hope, it seems certain, that all was set in order.[7]

A slip of parchment in Alnwick's register, untitled but with information obviously meant to supplement the 1442 Catesby visit, suggests that his efforts at reform were not fully successful. The note read that Isabel Benet and Agnes Halesley, nuns of Catesby, did not obey the injunctions of the lord bishop but refused to give up their private chambers, asserting that they were not subject to the same regulations as the other nuns, since the bishop had intrusted them with financial management of the house. 'Also the said Dame Isabel on Monday past did pass the night with the Austin friars at Northhampton and did dance and play the lute with them in the same place until midnight, and on the night following she passed the night with the friars preacher at Northhampton, luting and dancing in like manner.'[8]

BISHOPS AND THE CISTERCIAN ORDER

The purpose of recounting this visit is not to reveal the sordid state of religious life practised at Catesby in the middle of the fifteenth century, but rather to make the point that no such visit by a bishop or the recording of it in his register would have occurred if this monastery had been a cistercian house of men. Traditionally bishops had considerable authority over monasteries, exercising such privileges as canonical visitations, direction over abbatial elections, punitive powers, and the right to receive oaths of obedience from newly-elected superiors. During the early years of cistercian development in the twelfth century, the bishop enjoyed such privileges over the Order's houses but eventually diocesan jurisdiction was eliminated by a steady stream of papal exemptions from episcopal control. As a consequence, except in the rare case of a papal legate, supervision of a cistercian abbey was performed only by a visiting father-abbot who was obliged to visit his daughter houses and demand that they conform to the benedictine rule as interpreted by cistercian customs and usages.[9]

While this unique system of visitation was applicable to all the monks it did not apply to all nunneries because the General Chapter at Cîteaux had refused for almost one hundred years to recognize the nuns as associated with the Order.[10] By the time affiliation was extended to the nuns in 1213, the bishops' right of supervision had become so commonplace that only two of the twenty-seven cistercian convents founded in England during the Middle Ages were exempt from diocesan jurisdiction.[11] While Tarrant Kaines and Marham Abbey's filiation was recognized by the General Chapter of the Order and entitled to its privileges and immunities, the other twenty-five houses, while claiming to belong to the cistercain community, were not free of episcopal jurisdiction.[12] The relationship between these nunneries and the english bishops, as a consequence, is the focus of this study.

SOURCES FOR AND LOCATIONS OF NUNNERIES

The dealings between nuns and bishops can be gleaned from the legal documents of the nunneries, charters in public archives, and records—such as the visitation of Catesby—in episcopal registers of the dioceses in which the cistercian nunneries were located. Of the twenty-seven houses, only two were located south of London, Tarrant Kaines and Whitney, in Salisbury and Winchester dioceses respectively. Three nunneries were founded in the Midlands of Worcester diocese, while only Marham Abbey lay in the Norwich diocese of East Anglia. The remaining nunneries were in the north of England: nine in the diocese of Lincoln, and no less than twelve in the archdiocese of York. Students of this subject then would be advised to start with the episcopal records of Lincoln and York where the majority of the cistercian convents were located.[13]

From these documents, we can conclude that the most numerous interactions between nuns and bishops concerned the issue of confirmation. In order for an action to be official, the nuns needed the bishops to confirm such things as the election of conventual officers, the appointment of monastic chaplains, or the presentment of parish clergy.

THE CONFIRMATION OF PRIORESSES

The process of selecting a superior began with the death of an abbess or prioress. The bishop of the diocese was notified and his permission asked for the election of a successor.[14] At Catesby, for example, the cellaress of the house, Joan of Northhampton, was elected by the nuns, but since episcopal permission for the election had not been obtained, the Bishop of Lincoln declared the election invalid. When the ordinary's permission had been obtained, Joan's election was confirmed.[15] In another situation, in 1308, the Archbishop of York was informed that the post of prioress at Keldholme was vacant and he appointed a commission to ascertain when the vacancy occurred, how long the house had been without a prioress, and whether the vacancy extended for six months. This episcopal interest in the temporal sequence of these affairs was noteworthy, for if the nuns did not elect a prioress within six months, their privilege of selection would go to the archbishop who would then appoint a nun to that office.[16]

The next step in the creation of a mother superior was her election by the nuns of the house, Although a unanimous vote was desirable, the abbess could be elected by a simple majority. If a consensus could not be achieved, a committee of three or four nuns (*pars sanior*) might, according to the benedictine Rule, settle on a single sister who would be acceptable to the rest as the new reverend mother of the community.[17] The details of a unanimous election were recorded by a nun of Whistones Priory who gave the following account to the bishop of Worcester.

> On the vigil of the Apostles Peter and Paul she and the whole convent had
> assembled in their chapter house and had appointed the Monday following

to . . . [hold] the election. On that day, mass being over, [and] being instructed in the form of the election by two sisters of the priory, Alice de Seculer and Isabel de Aston, all who were present, unanimously, 'as if inspired by the Holy Ghost', chose Alice de la Flagge, 'a woman of discreet life and morals, of lawful age, professed in the nunnery, born of lawful matrimony, [and] prudent in spiritual and temporal matters'. But as yet, Alice, with a modesty befitting her virtues, could not be persuaded to agree to the election. But, 'weeping, resisting as much as she could, and expostulating in a loud voice as is the custom', she was carried to the church and her election proclaimed. At length, on the following Wednesday, 'being unwilling to resist the divine will', she consented, and after reference to the bishop's commissary and the prior of Worcester, the election was confirmed.[18]

From this episode, we know that the bishop or his representative was present during the election process in priories subject to episcopal jurisdiction. After the newly-elected prioress gave an oath of obedience to the bishop, she was installed by him as the superior of the house.[19] In the two nunneries exempt from diocesan control, the election ceremony was presided over by a father-abbot from a nearby cistercian monastery who was appointed by and represented the Cistercian General Chapter. The father-abbot or the bishop had the responsibility of ratifying the election and blessing the nun selected to lead the convent.[20]

THE CONFIRMATION OF CHAPLAINS

Episcopal confirmation was also needed by the nuns when they wanted to appoint their resident mass-priest and ordinary confessor. Because the women were canonically prevented from administering their own sacramental needs, it was necessary for them to select chaplains who could enjoy permanent employment so long as they had the nuns' approval. Once confirmed by the bishop, the chaplains were subservient to the mother superior, and in a solemn ceremony before the whole community made professions of obedience to her *usque ad mortem*.[21] These chaplains usually resided on the premises in chambers outside the nuns' cloister, and their number varied according to the spiritual needs of the individual community. In houses with large religious populations, such as Stixwould, Nun Appleton, and Nun Coton, two and sometimes three chaplains would be required with one man assigned primacy.[22] But for most of the cistercian nunneries in England, the size of the community dictated but one resident chaplain.

THE CONFIRMATION OF PRIESTS

The nuns also needed to appoint priests to serve in churches owned by the convent. It was not uncommon during the Middle Ages for a benefactor to give to a monastery the advowson of a parish church, that is, the right to nominate a person to the vacant pastorate. When this occurred the bishop of the diocese in which the church was located had to confirm the advowson gift and at the same time grant to the nuns and convent the right to convert the church 'to their own uses' (*ad proprios usus*). In essence, the nunneries had the right of appropriation, i.e., the right to the income due the parish church. As rector appropriate, a nunnery was entitled to the revenues of the rectory, and the vicar whom they presented was either paid an annual stipend by the nuns or was given a *congrua portio* of the revenues that were perpetually relinquished from the income which went to the church from tithes, offerings, and altar dues.[23]

The appropriation of churches by most of the twenty-seven english cistercian nunneries created a constant relationship between the nuns and the bishops who defined regulations on the operation of these churches. When a vacancy occurred, the nuns presented a vicar-nominate to the bishop who, in turn, confirmed the man's institution and had the event recorded in the episcopal register. At the time of the appropriation, it was the bishop who established the amount of incomes for the vicar and the nuns, and assessed taxes for the vicarage and the rectory. The bishop's role was that of overseer, and as long as the nuns performed their administrative responsibilities, his role was limited.[24]

It was the nuns themselves, then, who had to execute the major administrative functions. They had 1) to find a competent candidate to serve as vicar when a vacancy occurred, 2) to insure that he received his allotted income, 3) to collect what was due the nunnery from the proceeds of the rectory, 4) to maintain the physical and spiritual needs of the vicarage, and 5) to pay the taxes assessed on the rectory's value. On the whole, an examination of the extant records proves that the nuns fulfilled these major responsibilities for the churches appropriated by them.[25]

Yet while the nuns were successful administrators with regard to churches in their charge, they also found that such responsibilities sometimes led to litigation. Stixwould Priory, for example, had a number of lawsuits during the thirteenth century concerning the advowsons of their churches in Willoughby and Wainfleet.[26] Swine Priory, Yorkshire, in 1337 got itself involved in a dispute with the parishioners of Skirlaw which was not concluded until Archbishop William Melton provided a settlement.[27] Cook Hill in Worcestershire became entangled in a suit in 1367 with the Prior of Studeley over rights of burial in the churchyard of Spernall,[28] and Marham Abbey had to settle with the Prior of West Acre in 1294 over the tithes for the churches of St Andrews and Holy Trinity in the village of Marham, Norfolk. On the other hand, the presentaton of vicars was normally accomplished with little difficulty except in a few instances, as when Robert de Gayton was prevented by the prioress and nuns of Legbourne from receiving a vicarage he wanted. With the support of the dean and confirmation by the bishop of Lincoln, however, Robert sought and secured a papal mandate which won him a benefice from the nuns in 1326.[30] Such litigation is but one example of the nuns' active role in affairs external to their cloistered life.

EPISCOPAL SUPERVISION

As has been demonstrated, then, there was frequent interaction between the cistercian nuns and english bishops in the realm of confirmation. Bishops were also charged, however, with the care of the nuns, *cura mulierum*, in their diocese, and this is the next and last category of investigation. It seems profitable to divide the bishops' responsibilities into the areas of temporal concerns on the one hand and spiritual concerns on the other. The areas are not mutually exclusive, for a community's poor fiscal state might be the cause for a moral breakdown requiring reform; but the division is a matter of convenience in the analysis of the relationships between the nuns and bishops and so it will be followed here.

Temporal Reforms

The bishop on visitation to nunneries sometimes detected that prioresses were not always administering their convents properly. Bishops' registers relate not only instances of spiritual lapse by the nuns, but also include their financial dilemmas. To solve the latter, the bishops appointed male officials to remedy economic problems. Such officials, called masters or wardens (*custos*), are mentioned at fifteen of the twenty-seven nunneries in England.[31]

The appointment of these custodians by the bishop was in most cases temporary. At Cook Hill, for example, an entry in the episcopal register for the year 1285 shows that the priory was not managing its affairs properly. The bishop let the prioress and nuns know 'as a result of the visitation of John de Farley, his official, that for the better conduct of their temporal business Thomas the chaplain should have full charge of their temporal affairs.'[32] At Nun Appleton in Yorkshire, 'Archbishop Greenfield appointed Roger de Saxton to the care of the goods of the nunnery'. And it appears that Roger remained at the house until his duties were fulfilled, because the archbishop directed ' . . . that the *custos* of the house was to have his meals daily in the chamber assigned to him, unless it happened that the prioress was having her meals in her own chamber, on account of entertaining strangers, in which case, for the sake of company, the *custos* might join them'.[33]

In a few houses, however, perhaps owing to the uniqueness of the foundation or the small size of the convent, a full-time master was appointed who had, at least at Catesby, administrative authority over income from spiritualities and temporalities. 'Robert of Wadington, canon of Canons Ashby, was appointed master of the priory by Bishop Sutton in 1293, and in the following year was succeeded by William de Grutterworth. . . . Richard of Staverdon, canon of Catesby, was appointed master in 1316, in succession to Roger of Daventry, [who was appointed in] 1297.' There is no record of a master or warden at Catesby after the fourteenth century, '. . . but so long as it lasted the master appears to have been recognized as [the] official head of the priory in pecuniary matters.'[34]

The development of a permanent master may have had its origin in the foundation of Catesby, for this house and seven others appear to have been founded as double monasteries like those of the Gilbertine Order, which allowed monks and nuns to live in the same monastery.[35] When Archbishop Giffard visited Swine in Yorkshire in 1267, he reported that the house had nuns and lay sisters as well as canons and *conversi*. There were two windows through which the nuns and sisters passed food and drink to the canons and brothers, and the archbishop became distressed when he found that more than just nourishment was being exchanged at these windows.[36] In earlier years the monks or canons held temporalities jointly with the nuns, but after the first decade of the fourteenth century double monasteries for cistercians ceased to exist and the nunneries were obliged to carry on alone.[37]

The appointment of male guardians to manage the nuns' financial affairs was apparently well intended and in some cases caused improvement, but more often than not such supervision did not help the situation and in fact caused it to deteriorate. In 1289, for example, Robert Bustard was appointed master at Swine but he did not administer affairs properly and in the next year he was dismissed.[38] Moreover, there is evidence that men deliberately used their supervisory authority at the expense of the nuns. At Swine, 'canons and *conversi*, under pretense of taking care of the external property of the house, wasted it, which, if it were carefully looked after, would suffice for the maintenance of all. The nuns were only receiving bread, cheese, and ale, and on two days in the week they only had water. The canons, however, and their accomplices were having plenty, and were daintily provided for. . . . Moreover, the house was in debt to the amount of 140 marks at least. . .'.[39] The archbishop ordered corrections of these matters.

Does the appointment of masters and wardens mean that the nuns were unable to manage their financial affairs? A review of the evidence shows other-

wise. Episcopal registers make us aware of nuns' houses with economic difficulties to which custodians were assigned, but about financially sound convents, the documents are mute. In almost half the cistercian nunneries in
England, no notice is made of a warden or master, and from the last half of
the fourteenth century to the dissolution of the houses in the sixteenth century, there is no mention of the presence of such an official. The silence of the
records indicates that the mother superiors were administrators of their own
temporal affairs.

Spiritual Reforms

In addition to setting a convent's fiscal house in order, the bishops also tried
to establish guidelines for the nuns' spiritual state. And this brings us back to
the account of the visit to Catesby which introduced this study. When the
bishops' injunctions are examined, one must remember that these documents
were never intended to be read by anyone other than the nuns for whom
they were written. As a consequence, students of this subject must exercise
caution in the use of visitation records; they present the nuns in a very negative light, spelling out only their problems and never documenting their
achievements.

The surviving visitation records reveal that the bishops frequently received
the reply 'that all things are well' to their queries about the conditions of
religious life in a specific community.[40] On occasion serious problems existed,
as at Catesby, and efforts were made by the ordinary to correct these matters. As one reads the list of irregularities found by the bishop and see his
attempts at reform, one is reminded of the english nun made immortal by
the caricature of the worldly prioress of Geoffrey Chaucer in the *Canterbury
Tales*. When Eileen E. Power wrote her now classic *Medieval English Nunneries* in 1922, she gave historical validity to the prioress of Chaucer because
the major source of Power's information was data obtained from episcopal
visitation records. Until recently the prevailing view in the scholarly world
has been that the medieval nun in general and the english nun in particular
contributed little to the religious tradition of which they were a part. Power
said sixty years ago of the moral state of english convents:

> to pass a final judgement on the moral state of English nunneries, as revealed
> by the bishops' registers during the later middle ages, is, as has already been
> suggested, a difficult task. From the monastic standard it cannot be said to
> have been high, . . . and the evidence of the bishops' registers for the second
> half of the [thirteenth] century does not give an impression of much greater
> strictness of life than is found in the nunneries of the fourteenth and fifteenth
> centuries, when monasticism had, by the admission of its apologists, passed
> its prime.[41]

It is ironic that the persons who tried most to help the nuns, the bishops, are the same persons who would provide the information which historians have used to undermine the good that the nuns did do. It was a cistercian nun at Hampole Priory named Margaret Kirkby, for example, who inspired the devout and popular hermit Richard Rolle to write his *Form of Perfect Living*.[42] In the later years of his life, Rolle lived in a cell not far from the nunnery and it is a known fact that he acted as the spiritual guide and director for the nuns at Hampole. History has shown the correctness of the nuns' judgement in selecting him as their religious advisor. When Richard died in 1349, the community at Hampole honored him and themselves by having his body buried in the conventual courtyard.[43] Ten months before his death, his disciple, Margaret Kirkby, followed his saintly example and had herself enclosed in a cell in East Layton. We know she was still alive on January 16, 1356–57, for Bishop Thoresby granted her permission to transfer to another cell near the parish church in Ainderby because her former anchorhold did not allow her to see the sacrament on the altar or hear the mass.[44] Even as long as seven years afer the death of her mentor, Margaret obviously maintained or even refined the spiritual life she was living.

If it were not for the preservation of Rolle's writings, we would not know of the influence this cistercian nun had on him or that which Rolle in turn had on the nuns at Hampole. If the only information on Hampole in the fourteenth century came from the archbishop's visitation records we would be informed that: in 1311, the nuns were condemned for not eating in common but in private chambers in the priory; in 1320, the nuns were forbidden to permit male children over the age of five to live in the nunnery as the archbishop had found being practised; in 1324, the nun Isabella Folifayt was found guilty of incontinency with Thomas de Raynevill; in 1353, a commission was appointed to inquire into the condition of the nunnery because 'according to public report, through unwise rule and other causes' Hampole had suffered serious financial losses and there was fear that the dispersion of the nuns was imminent.[45] If we were to use only the archiepiscopal visitation findings, the impression would be one of a sordid religious life at Hampole. When one adds, however, the story of Margaret Kirkby and her relationship with one of the most influential english mystical authors to the visitation records of condemnations, a more positive picture of the religious life practised by these nuns begins to emerge.

A SUMMARY OF THE RELATIONSHIP

There is no denying that some of the cistercian nunneries had spiritual breakdowns, and this study, by investigating the relationship between nuns and english bishops, has uncovered efforts made to solve the problems. Since the women could not leave the cloister, their care was in the hands of the bishops. If a convent was poorly endowed or in a dire financial state, claustration made it difficult for the nuns to become self-sufficient. With improper funding, the women could not live the type of monastic life many of them so ardently desired. Bishops and their male appointees tried to work within the ecclesiastical system to aid the nuns in fulfilling the requirements of their Rule. For their part, the nuns needed the bishop to confirm their elections or appointments, while the bishop was obliged to visit the nunnery and order temporal or spiritual reforms. Up to this time, the fullest information we have about the cistercian convents in medieval England is from episcopal visitation records which, as this study has shown, is unfortunate because the records present the nuns in such a very negative light. What is needed is further research into the lives and actions of these female religious so that a more accurate assessment can be made on the role and contribution these women made to the Middle Ages.

Slippery Rock University

NOTES

1. A. Hamilton Thompson (ed.), *Visitations of Religious Houses in the Diocese of Lincoln, 1436–49*, vol. 2 (for the Canterbury and York Societies, 1919) 46–53.

2. An excellent description of the procedures for visitations by bishops can be found in David Knowles, *The Religious Orders in England*, vol. 1 (Cambridge: University Press, 1962) 78–84.

3. These facts or *detecta* were gathered by Alnwick by talking in private with each professed member of the monastery beginning first with the head of the convent. The Latin text of the visitation is found in Thompson, *Visitations*, pp. 46–47.

4. As with above and below, these were not the only facts gathered by the visitor, but certain ones were selected by the author to illustrate the abuses at Catesby. *Visitations*, 47.

5. *Visitations*, 47–48.

6. *Ibid.*, 49.

7. *Ibid.*, 51–52.

8. *Ibid.*, 50.

9. Louis Lekai, *The Cistercian: Ideals and Reality* (Kent: Kent State University Press, 1977), 28–29.

10. John A. Nichols, 'The Manner of Monastic Filiation for English Cistercian Nunneries', *Hidden Springs: The Cistercian Monastic Woman* (forthcoming).

11. David Knowles and R. Neville Hadcock (eds.), *Medieval Religious Houses: England and Wales*, 2nd edition (New York: St. Martin's Press, 1971) 271–77. See Coburn V. Graves, 'Stixwould in the Marketplace', above.

12. See Sally Thompson, 'The problem of the Cistercian nuns in the twelfth and early thirteenth centuries,' *Medieval Women*, edited by Derek Baker (Oxford: Blackwell's, 1978) and Coburn V. Graves, 'English Cistercian Nuns in Lincolnshire', *Speculum* 54 (July, 1979) 492–99, for difficulties the nunneries caused the Order by their effort to gain recognition as cistercian monasteries.

13. Knowles and Hadcock, *Medieval Religious Houses*, 272.

14. Lina Eckenstein, *Women Under Monasticism* (New York: Russell and Russell, 1896) 367 and Eileen Power, *Medieval English Nunneries* (New York: Biblio and Tannen, 1922) 43.

15. J.C. Cox, *Victoria County Histories: Northbamptonshire*, 2 (London: James Street, 1906) 123.

16. T.M. Fallow, *VCH: York*, 3 (London: Constable and Co., 1913) 167.

17. Justin McCann, ed., *The Rule of St. Benedict*, 3rd edition (Westminster, MD: Newman Press, 1963), ch. 64, 144.

18. A.A. Locke, *VCH: Worcestershire*, vol. 2 (London: James Street, 1906) 156. Quoted matter is Locke's translation of Lucy de Soler's account, found in The Register of the Bishop of Worcester, 114.

19. Examples of an oath of obedience are printed in 'Archbishop Lee's Visitations, 1534–35', *Yorkshire Archaeological Journal* 16 (1900–1901), 431 and 439 for the prioresses of Baysdale and Sinningthwaite.

20. Lekai, *Cistercians*, 351, and Power, *English Nunneries*, 43–44.

21. J.T. Fowler, 'Cistercian Statutes', *Yorkshire Archaeological Journal* 10 (1887–89) 514: *Fratres Capellani, Clerici, et Conversi Monialium, expleto noviciatus anno, in Capitulo ipsarum ante analogium venientes, prostrati veniam petant. Deinde eisdem breviter exposita Ordinis asperitate, perseverentiam promittentes, proprietati ibidem renunciem more Ordinis consueto. Postea libro Regulae super genua Abbatissae sedentis apposito, flexis genibus, et manibus super dictum librum positis, dicant, 'Promitto vobis obedientiam de bono usque ad mortem.' Abbatissa vero respondeat, 'Det tibi Deus vitam aeternam.' Conventus vero respondeat, 'Amen.'*

22. Sister Elspeth, *VCH: Lincoln*, 2 (London: James Street, 1906) 147, 151.

23. R.A.R. Hartridge, *A History of Vicarages in the Middle Ages* (New York: Barnes and Noble, Inc., 1930) 8, and George C. Homans, *English Villages of the Thirteenth Century*, rev. ed., (New York: Harper and Row, 1970) 384–87.

24. *Ibid.*

25. An excellent example of the success can be seen in John A. Nichols, 'The History and Cartulary of the Cistercian Nuns of Marham Abbey, 1249–1536,' (Dissertation: Kent State University, 1974) 117–22.

26. Elspeth, *VCH: Lincoln*, 146; the conflict arose over who had true ownership of the advowsons, the nuns or secular lords.

27. Thomas Thompson, *The History of the Church and Priory of Swine in Holderness* (Hull: Thomas Topping, 1824) 39–40, records the dispute was settled so that the parishioners would find a vicar whom the nuns would present to the archbishop for confirmation.

28. Locke, *VCH: Worcestershire*, 157 (ended in favor of the prior of Studeley).

29. Nichols, 'Marham Abbey', p. 222, cited the cartulary of the house, which details the nuns' need to purchase the right of tithes from West Acre Priory.

30. W.H. Bliss, ed., *Calendar of Entries in the Papal Registers Relating to Great Britain and Ireland*, vol. 2 (London: H.M.S.O., 1895) 249.

31. For the houses were Baysdale, Hampole, Handale, Keldholme, Kirklees, Nun Appleton, Swine and Wykeham of York diocese, see Fallow, *VCH: York*, 159, 163, 166, 168, 170–71, 180, 182; for Cook Hill in Worcester diocese, see Locke, *VCH: Worcestershire*, 158; for Catesby, Gokewell, Greenfield, Legbourne, Nun Coton, and Stixwould of Lincoln diocese, see Cox, *VCH: Northbamptonshire*, 123; Elspeth, *VCH: Lincoln*, 151, 156; and Knowles, Christopher Brooke and Vera London, edd., *The Heads of Religious Houses England and Wales 940–1216* (Cambridge: University Press, 1972) 212, 214, 220.

32. Locke, *VCH: Worcestershire*, 158.

33. Fallow, *VCH: York*, 171.

34. Cox, *VCH: Northbamptonshire*, 123.

35. Knowles and Hadcock, *Medieval Religious Houses*, 200, and Rose Graham, *S. Gilbert of Sempringham and the Gilbertines: A History of the Only English Monastic Order* (London: Elliot Stock, 1901) 11–14, and Knowles, *Heads*, 212, 214, 220.

36. Fallow, *VCH: York*, 179.

37. Evidence for joint ownership comes from the early charters of these communities, in which the property was conferred to the *priori et santi monialibus* or *fratribus et sororibus*, but mention of male religious attached to the houses does not occur in the later centuries.

38. Fallow, *VCH: York*, 180.

39. *Ibid.*

40. Some visitations records have been printed: A. Hamilton Thompson, *Visitation of Lincoln*, for Catesby, pp. 46–53; for Heynings, pp. 132–35; for Legbourne, pp. 183–87; for Nun Coton, pp. 248–52. A. Hamilton Thompson, *Visitation in the Diocese of Lincoln 1517–31*, vol. 3 (Lincoln Record Society, 1947), Nun Coton, pp. 36–38; Stixwould, pp. 101–5. 'The Register of Walter Giffard, Lord Archbishop of York, 1266–79', *Surtees Society*, 109 (1904), Hampole, pp. 20–21; Handale and Baysdale, p. 54; Swine, pp. 146–48, 248–49. 'The Fallow Papers', *Yorkshire Archaeological Journal*, 21 (1910–11), Nun Appleton, pp. 225–53. The *VCH* also provide excellent insight to the sources.

41. Power, *Medieval Nunneries*, 471–72.

42. Hope Emily Allen, *Writings Ascribed to Richard Rolle, Hermit of Hampole* (New York: Modern Language Association, 1927) 256–68.

43. Herbert Thurston and Donald Attwater, edd., *Butler's Lives of the Saints*, 4 vols. (New York: P.J. Kenedy and Sons, 1956), vol. 3: 682–85, and Hope Emily Allen, ed., *English Writings of Richard Rolle, Hermit of Hampole* (Oxford: Clarendon Press, 1931) 1–4.

44. Allen, *Writings*, 502.

45. Fallow, *VCH: York*, 163–64.

Ten Centuries of Growth: The Cistercian Abbey of Soleilmont

Elizabeth Connor

Of all the houses of nuns in the Cistercian Order of the Strict Observance, Soleilmont goes back further in history than any other. The monastery itself was founded before Cîteaux. There is unfortunately no evidence as to the exact date of its origin, but tradition has it that in 1088 Albert III the Peaceful, Count of Namur, built a monastery for nuns following the benedictine Rule at a place known as the 'hill of the sun',[1] where according to legend there had been an ancient shrine to the sun god.[2] The earliest documentary of Soleilmont dates from 1185 and concerns a donation by Enguerrand d'Orbais of his *alodium* at Soleilmont to the Abbey of Floreffe.[3]

This latter part of the twelfth century saw an expansion of the order of Cîteaux. Many convents of nuns in the Low Countries were requesting affiliation to the Order. Among them were Solières in the district of Liège, Aywières in Brabant, and Soleilmont. A tradition based on early writings affirms that because the community of Soleilmont had diminished in numbers, the Count of Namur arranged for cistercian nuns from the monastery of Flines, near Douai, to come both to strengthen their ranks and to aid them to make the transition to cistercian observances. The General Chapter of Cîteaux delegated the Abbots of Villers, Val St Lambert, and Grandpré to visit Soleilmont and examine conditions there. Once this visitation was completed, affiliation was approved and paternity of the monastery was accorded to the Abbey of Aulne in May 1237.[4]

Two months later, by an official act dated 11 July 1237, Beaudouin de Courtenay, Count of Namur and Emperor of Constantinople, made known

251

that he fully ratified a donation 'consisting of a fish-pond, a *bonnier* of meadow, and a mill', made by Jeanne, Countess of Flanders and Hainaut, to the Ladies of Soleilmont of the Order of Cîteaux.[5] In 1239 Pope Gregory IX took the abbey under his protection and ordered that 'in this place the Rule of St Benedict and the Observance of Cîteaux shall be observed inviolably and in perpetuity'.[6] This was to be the case in reality, for the community of Soleilmont has continued without interruption until our own times.

Today anyone visiting the places bearing the names which recur in the history of Soleilmont—Gilly, Charleroi, Châtelet, Fleurus, Farciennes—will find them strongly marked by industrialization. But in the Middle Ages the monastery had horizons of fields, meadows, woodlands, and ponds; contrary to the name it had been given, it was nestled in a small green valley.

Most events of the early history of Soleilmont, that is, before the fifteenth century, have become hidden under the veil of time. Notations can be found, however, about several of the abbesses. Aleyde in 1251, fourteen years after the incorporation of the abbey into the Order of Cîteaux, signed a contract with the church of Floreffe for five *bonniers* of land. Names of other abbesses appear in obituaries or registers: Oda of Virsel, Marguerite, Hedwide of Louverval who was buried in the cloister, and Catherine d'Avesnes who was ordered by the General Chapter of 1412 to leave Soleilmont and return to the monastery where she had made profession, Montreuil-sur-Laon.[7]

Soleilmont's domain in the early period was just about sufficient to keep the nuns alive. By a document dated 24 June 1284, we know that Squire Godefroid de Wangenies authorized the nuns to pasture their animals on land belonging to the township. These animals were one hundred twenty sheep, four horses, and four cows, probably the sum total of the nuns' domestic animals. The sisters made their habits from the sheep's wool and used the fleece for keeping warm during the damp, cold winters.

The Bull of Gregory IX, mentioned above, stated that the farm of Benoîte-Fontaine at Heppignies, in the County of Namur, was also the property of Soleilmont. Add to this some meadow land (three *bonniers*) and arable land (eighteen *bonniers*) in the district of Vieuville, and seventeen *bonniers* near Châtelineau, and we have an idea of the full extent of the abbey's property during the thirteenth and fourteenth centuries. This land was the nuns' only source of livelihood.[8]

Soleilmont did not escape the general eclipse of fervor that darkened the monastic world during the fourteenth century. Dom Bruno Maréchal, a monk of Aulnes who in the eighteenth century was confessor at Soleilmont for nine years, left an *Histoire de la Fondation de l'Ancienne Abbaye de Soleilmont* which gives interesting information about the community during its early centuries, even though his work is not always exact and is strongly colored by his personal interpretation of events. About the decline he wrote:

The forementioned abbey was quite renowned and well-known for the holiness of its religious during the first century after it was admitted into the Order of Cîteaux. At that time the holy women lived a life of unequaled austerity with great fervor, following all the strictness of the Rule of St Benedict, which is the Rule of the Order of Cîteaux. . . . But unfortunately there was a relaxation of the original fervor. Little by little this slipped into the whole Order of Cîteaux . . . and the demon preyed on the minds of these holy women, who let themselves slide toward remissness without even noticing it.[9]

Other factors besides zeal on the demon's part contributed to monastic decline. In the late fourteenth century the plague struck the community and sharply reduced its numbers. The buildings fell into a state of ruin, either because of general neglect or some unrecorded calamity, or perhaps both. Many of the nuns' monasteries in the Low Countries had begun as communities of beguines,[10] and in times of hardship some tended to revert to their original form of life. Thus it was that communities often took in small children to educate, with the intention of forming them to become novices one day. Elderly persons were accepted as boarders for the rest of their days, and other persons received lodging in return for domestic services. Enclosure was not observed, therefore, and solitude was obviously impossible. Although it cannot be affirmed that Soleilmont had begun as a community of beguines, the community seems to have followed this type of orientation as an attempt at survival. According to Dom Bruno: 'It was no longer an Order, but open dis-order'.[11]

Having received complaints from the Count of Namur about the situation at Soleilmont, and seeing no way of remedying it, the General Chapter of 1413 ordered the nuns, as well as those of Moulins, Argenton, and Jardinet, who were passing through a similar period of relaxation of discipline, to vacate their monasteries and cede them to monks who would live a regular cistercian life. The Abbots of Clairvaux, Charlieu, Villers, and Aulne were asked to implement this order. The community of Moulins, composed of only a few sisters, was replaced by six monks of Aulne. Eventually, monks were also sent to Jardinet. Argenton was maintained as a nuns' monastery, but was permitted to receive novices only if a complete reform was effectuated. Soleilmont was temporarily suppressed by the Abbot of Aulne, but in six months it was repopulated and on its way to a remarkable reform.[12]

REFORM

Even before the decision of the 1413 General Chapter a reform had already been undertaken among nuns themselves in the Provinces of Namur and Liège.

Influenced by a monk of Aulnes, Dom Jean de Gesves, several nuns joined Dame Marie de Bervier with the intention of returning to a stricter observance of the Rule. Hindered in their good resolution by the Abbess of Robermont (where Dame Marie was a nun) and the Abbot of Aulne, the Visitor, by the intermediary of Dom Jean de Gesves they obtained the abbey of Marche-les-Dames, where they took up residence on 15 December 1406. The new community had at that time four religious from Robermont, two from Vivegnis, three postulants from Huy, one laysister, the confessor and chaplain [Dom de Gesves], and a family-brother.[13]

The spark of reform quickly became a flame and radiated to neighboring monasteries, among them Jardinet and Soleilmont. Dame Marie de Senzeilles came down from Marche-les-Dames to introduce reform at Soleilmont and become one of its greatest abbesses. Idleness, contacts with seculars, and vanity were banished. Humility, poverty, solitude, silence, and work were restored. To sum up briefly the work of Dame Marie, we may say that she succeeded in bringing about a fervent renewal of monastic life and observance. The reform went deep spiritually, and was lasting. In only a few years the little abbey's influence began to spread, and Soleilmont itself became a seedbed of reform. Argenton was the first house to request religious from Soleilmont to effect renewal. First Marie de Gentines was sent, to be followed by Nicaise de Harby. In the middle of the sixteenth century another nun of Soleilmont, Anne de Bievre de Rubemprez, was to continue this work at Argenton. Jeanne de Warluseille undertook a similar task of reform at the monastery of Olive, where she became the eighteenth abbess. Jeanne de Senzeilles, niece of Dame Marie, was sent to Salzinnes, where she too became abbess. Marie de Potte, still another nun of Soleilmont, reformed Boneffe. Marguerite of Austria headed the abbey of Orienten.

During this fifteenth-century reflowering, Dame Isabeau de Lannoy undertook restoration of the monastery buildings. The church, with its sharply sloping roof, was a gem of gothic architecture which somewhat resembled the church of the cistercian nuns of La Cambre. Consecrated most probably in the latter part of the fourteenth century, it had deteriorated during the period of decline and was in urgent need of repairs. It and other parts of the monastery were renewed. An inscription attests that the foundation stone of the dormitory was laid on Christmas Day 1476, and that the first two wings of the cloisters were begun at the same time. The original high, massive, rampart-like walls with towers at each corner remained intact. They would be useful time and time again, as armies passed through the region during the centuries to come.

THE DOMAIN

The extent of the nuns' land doubled during the fifteenth century, chiefly by the addition of property at Farciennes in the territory of Liège. There was first of all the farm of Fontenelle, given to Soleilmont by the abbey of Floreffe and comprising buildings, stables, sheepfold, garden, ponds, and prairies totaling one-hundred-thirty *bonniers*. A second farm at Farciennes, received as an inheritance by one of the sisters, and the farm of Escaille at Gilly also became property of the monastery. In addition, the abbey of Floreffe offered the nuns its share of the tithes from Lambusart, Fleurus, and Farciennes. Official records of Gilly dating from 1745 indicate that in 1470 Soleilmont possessed forty horned beasts, twelve horses (counting colts and fillies), twenty hogs, and one-hundred-fifty sheep.[14]

Last, but certainly not least, we should mention the woods belonging to Soleilmont. In the Middle Ages, and up until the eighteenth century, forests and woods meant something quite different than they do to men in our time. Whereas we consider woodland paths ideal for hiking and contemplation on the glories of creation, medieval man saw the forest as an unfriendly, labyrinthine, shadowy place which was nevertheless essential to his survival. Forests bordered every village and town and, aside from the parts set aside by the lords for their personal use, were considered public property. All villagers were free to gather wood in the forests to build their houses and then to furnish, heat, and light them. Everyone had the right to hunt in the forests. The only way in which the lords could hope to find workers for their land was, in fact, to grant the right to use the forests. Frequently rights for portions of the forests were rented to particular persons, but this gave rise to innumerable squabbles.

Soleilmont became involved in conflicts with both the Chapter of St Barthélemy at Liège and the inhabitants of Châtelineau about the use of the Flichée Wood.[15] After much vying, an accord was reached in the aldermen's court at Fleurus on 28 December 1473: in return for a fixed sum, two-thirds of the Flichée Wood (called also St Lambert's Wood) became the outright property of the abbey, and the other third remained the possession of the town of Fleurus.

By a similar agreement the abbey in 1479 obtained Thiéri Wood, later called Soleilmont Wood, the location of the present-day monastery. This wood covered approximately one hundred-thirty-four acres. A condition for the acquisition of these two woods is worth mentioning.[16] In July 1463, Soleilmont had found itself with a 'Court of Justice'. At the time the Chapter of St Barthélemy had exchanged its rents and arable land, meadows, and woods which it had as *allodium* at Châtelineau, for the rents it owed to the abbey of Soleilmont. By this transaction the monastery was given the power known as 'The Court of St Barthélemy'. Unlike the Assize Court which dealt with more important transgressions, the Court of St Barthélemy was a minor one. The abbess did, however, have the right to name such officials as the mayor and the aldermen, to receive rents, and to register contracts and inheritances. She even had judiciary power in matters of lesser importance. These 'honors' held by Soleilmont also imposed a great burden, and when an opportunity came in 1479 to cede the court to Lambert, Lord of Maubertingue and Châtelineau, in exchange for the Flichée and Thiéri Woods, it was with relief that Abbess Isabeau de Lannoy signed the transaction.

From the time of the fifteenth-century reform until the Revolution the abbey domain remained more or less the same, permitting the nuns a frugal existence.

POLITICAL INTERFERENCE

In the early sixteenth century Archduke Charles, later the Emperor Charles V, was trying methodically to stamp out the ancient flemish liberties. Since the abbeys were often important landowners, a key political move was to limit the freedom of election in monasteries. Pope Leo X finally gave in to Charles' insistence and agreed to name as superiors of monasteries only persons whom the sovereign found acceptable. The jurists who favored Charles promptly interpreted this to mean that Leo X had ceded his legitimate right to designate abbots and that free elections in the abbeys were henceforth suppressed.[17]

From that time on, as soon as a vacancy occurred in an abbey, the prince governing the Low Countries designated commissaries to preside over the coming election. An abbot—in the case of the Cistercians, the Father Immediate—usually assisted them. Among the persons who received the most votes, the commissary who represented the prince had the right to choose who would be elected. Political considerations obviously influenced the choice. One abbess who was designated in this way was Dame Anne Robert. Before he retired to the monastery of Yuste in 1555, one of Charles V's last official acts was the signing of nominations of superiors for a certain number of abbeys. Among them, Anne Robert was listed as superior of Soleilmont.[18]

By the same method Anne Etienne, a local lady from Châtelet, became abbess of Soleilmont in 1639, even though Adrienne de Henry, a 'foreigner' from the territory of Liège, received the most votes.[19] When Dame Anne died ten years later, Adrienne again received the greatest number of votes in the election, but the commissaries gave preference this time to Marie de Burlen, once again because of Adrienne's birthplace.

DISPERSION OF THE COMMUNITY

In 1578, during the conflict between Philip II and the Calvinists, the nuns of Soleilmont were obliged to flee their monastery. The community was dispersed and the building burned. Dame Anne Robert, abbess at the time, took refuge at Mons, where she died the same year. A group of the sisters went to Thuin, where they set up house in a dwelling belonging to the abbey of Aulnes. There it was that the government commissaries came to hold the election after Dame Anne's death. Practical considerations entered into the choice of the new abbess. Louise Heller, who was a virtuous woman, came from a very wealthy family, and the community needed funds to repair the damage done in the war. But the choice for pecuniary motives was an unwise one; within a few years there began to be complaints about Dame Louise's conduct, and she was dismissed from her charge in 1583.[20]

The commissaries did not want to be inconvenienced for the next election, and so they ordered all the nun voters to assemble at Mons in the abbey of Epinlieu. There, by unanimous vote, they elected Madeleine Bulteau as their abbess. Shortly after, it became possible for the nuns to return to Soleilmont, and Dame Madeleine governed the community with wisdom and great virtue until 1603, when she was obliged to resign because of blindness.

ECONOMIC CONDITIONS

Soleilmont, like numerous other monasteries of nuns, was frequently obliged to cope with poverty, even though the nuns lived frugally and the domain was well-managed. In additon to repeated and expensive lawsuits over the woods and the lake (as we shall see a bit later), there were taxes to be paid both to the Church and to civil officials. In time of war—and numerous were the times when armies filed past the abbey—taxes were especially high. And they were all the more burdensome because crops were sometimes destroyed by passing troops, and sometimes gathered by the soldiers for their own use. The advance of every new army brought theft and pillaging.

Another scourge was the 'abbey's bread' (*pain d'abbaye*). This was defined as a favor by which the prince, in virtue of his royal right, gave an abbey charge of providing sustenance for a person for life. It was a type of pension, and candidates were not lacking. A monastery taxed in this way could be asked either to support a person living outside its walls or to take a person into the monastery and provide for all her needs. Some of the people involved were unobtrusive; others were extremely demanding and caused a great deal of trouble. Catherine Amand, the widow of the porter at the royal stable,[21] had been granted 'abbey's bread' at Soleilmont, but she was never satisfied. In 1609 she took her complaints to court. The abbess, Dame Jacqueline Colnet, received a reprimand and was quite simply ordered to comply with Catherine's demands.

On the other side of the ledger were the dowries offered by the parents of girls who entered the monastery. The following document is not necessarily typical, but it does nevertheless give an idea of the kind of dowries the monastery sometimes received:

> By an act of 7 December 1621, in return for acceptance of his daughter, Jeanne-Catherine de Henry, into the convent of Soleilment, Master Nicolas de Henry promises to give a dowry of seventy florins of rents in perpetuity; a rent of thirty florins for the support of his daughter; at her death another rent of twenty florins; one hundred fifty florins to cover all the costs of the banquets at the time of her clothing; and to assist with the expenses on the day of her profession he promises to give the house a fatted calf worth fifty florins, to pay with honesty for the convent recreation and a suitable reception for the prelate who will receive his daughter at profession; and lastly, to provide his daughter with clothes and habits, utensils, furniture, and all other necessities, and to give her also dishes worth fifty florins, which will remain in the house.[22]

NOTRE DAME DE ROME

Dame Jacqueline Colnet, who succeeded Dame Madeleine Bulteau in 1603, came from a noble family of Venetian origin. She was abbess during the Thirty Years' War, and consequently was at the head of the community when the first, very fierce, battle of Fleurus occurred in 1622. In speaking of Dame Jacqueline, we must also add a few words about the painting of Notre Dame de Rome, without which no paper on Soleilmont would be complete. This miraculous painting, venerated by the nuns for centuries, bears the following inscription engraved on a silver plaque: 'This image of Our Lady was made following the painting by St. Luke. It is the one which Pope Gregory carried in procession against the pestilence, which thereupon ceased.' No one knows exactly when this painting became the property of Soleilment, but it seems to date from the fifteenth century. According to a continuous tradition recorded in the annals of the abbey, and confirmed by the veneration of the faithful, the painting of Notre Dame de Rome was given to Soleilmont by a cardinal of the Church at a time when an epidemic was taking a high toll in the community. In 1635, when there was an outbreak of the plague, the painting was loaned by Dame Jacqueline to the town of

Châtelet. The wave of sickness ceased, and in gratitude the burgomaster, Monsieur de Trooz, offered Soleilmont an organ of great worth which was used in the Abbey church until 1963.[23] Today Notre Dame de Rome continues, as in the past, to draw pilgrims and visitors who come with confidence to pay homage and ask for favors.

MORE WARS AND DESTRUCTION, AND RESTORATION

Dame Eugénie de la Halle became abbess in 1661 and governed the abbey for more than thirty years, through more troubled times. Five years after she took office Charles II of Spain succeeded Philip IV, and Louis XIV lost no time in claiming the Spanish Netherlands in favor of his wife, Marie-Thérèse of Austria. In this 'War of Devolution' the French General Turenne invaded the Low Countries and took possession of Charleroi. Peace came for a time with the Treaty of Aix-la-Chapelle in 1668, but hostilities began again in 1672 with Holland. More fighting took place in Charleroi. Then came the Peace of Nijmwegen in 1678, followed by still another outbreak of war in 1684. That year Gilly was burned. During the siege of Namur troops were going and coming continually, and the whole region around Charleroi was prey to pillaging and destruction. For the nuns, the climax was the violent battle of Fleurus, which took place almost in their backyard in 1692.

In addition to these man-made calamities, nature contributed still others. While Dame Humbeline de Bavay governed the abbey (1730–1739), a devastating hurricane ruined the crops of the abbey and its farms. If that were not enough, lightning struck the farm of Fontenelle and destroyed it. Such times were obviously not favorable for vocations: only six entries are recorded for the years 1694–1712.

Dame Humbeline faced these disasters valiantly. She also set about decorating the cloisters, chapter room, church, and refectory of the monastery. This 'renovation' unfortunately masked the original architectural beauty behind monumental altars and doric columns in the Renaissance style popular at the time. But it was also Dame Humbeline who, with the aid of the Abbot of Aulne, built the abbatial quarters of the monastery, with its splendid staircase and reception hall. Yet more than for any of her material achievements, she was remembered for her deep charity and humility.[24]

Dame Humbeline was followed by an abbess with exquisite taste: Dame Joseph Berger. She had placed in the choir the Louis XV stalls and a magnificent wrought-iron grille which graced the abbey church until 1963. As the inscription on Dame Joseph's tombstone affirms, she led her flock with wisdom and knew how to maintain peace, charity, and unity within the community. Her business talents also permitted her to pay all the debts of the abbey, to put a new roof on the house, and to have the pond cleaned up.

THE POND

This pond was as important to the abbey as the woods. It had come into the nuns' possession by an outright donation by Beaudouin, Count of Namur, in 1237, as we have seen above. By the pond there was a small mill whose wheel turned willingly—except in the height of summer when the water was low—to grind grain not only for the nuns but for local people who paid a small fee to the abbey in return for this service.

The pond was also plentifully stocked with fish, and the villagers from Gilly persisted in coming there to fish, claiming that at the end of the thirteenth century Wauthier I had accorded them a concession which had been confirmed by the Abbot of Lobbes. Disputes about fishing rights were taken to court many times, from the thirteenth until the eighteenth century. These costly lawsuits, just as those about forest rights, kept the community of Soleilment in a state of penury and settled nothing definitively. The villagers promptly returned with their rods and lines.

The situation came to a head in 1776, with what has been called the fishermen's 'mutiny'. This was the third year that the same scene had taken place: villagers came with food, tackle, and baggage, and camped at the edge of the pond. They lit bonfires at night and sang rowdy songs in hearing of the nuns who, in spite of all this, had to rise for Vigils at the regular hour. A letter of Dame Scholastica Daivier, abbess at the time, gives an account of these events. The letter was addressed to the Procurator General of Namur, and states in part:

> . . . People of Gilly—more than three hundred—come each year for several days and spend the funds of their families in taverns. They build fires around the pond day and night, cutting hedges and wood without sparing even His Majesty's Wood. They forsake their work in the coal mines, to the great jeopardy of both the public and the proprietors of the mines. . . .[25]

The third time this spectacle took place the nuns' patience was taxed to the limit. They agreed to pay six hundred florins if the villagers would give up their fishing 'rights'. More bickering followed, and the community was finally obliged to pay the enormous sum of eight hundred florins. Peace returned at last, but Soleilmont would enjoy its rights to the pond only for some twenty years. Then the Revolution changed the nuns' life radically.

Dame Scholastica Daivier was the last abbess of the *ancien régime*. Her coat of arms meaningfully portrayed a cross raised on a hillock, for it was under the sign of the cross that she governed Soleilmont from 1776 until 1805. From French refugees she learned of anti-religious laws being enforced by the Directory. Fearing that the monastery would soon be engulfed in the swelling current of terror, Dame Scholastica felt there was no solution but to flee. In the hope of finding refuge across the german border, the nuns headed for the Rhine, taking with them the treasured painting of Notre Dame of Rome. After traveling for three weeks they finally reached the river, but so great was the number of refugees who had already sought safety in Germany that they were refused permission to cross. The community set out on the road back to Soleilmont, hoping against hope that there was some way to escape the suppression of their monastery. This return trip was broken by a six weeks sojourn at the abbey of Boneffe.

Then the second battle of Fleurus, in 1794, crucial in the war France had declared on Austria, subjected the Low Countries to the tyranny of the Directory. About two years later, commissaries of the Republic came to Soleilmont with offers of secularization and compensations. The renunciation they proposed to the community was as follows:

> We, the undersigned, ex-ladies and ex-sisters of the ex-abbey of Soleilmont, willingly consent to abandon our former property and consent to the suppression of our former Order of Bernardines; and we receive in exchange for this voluntary and spontaneous declaration the sum of 12,000 *livres* for each lady and 8,000 *livres* for each sister.[26]

When the commissaries had finished speaking, the answer of the community was unanimous: they would never consent to such proposals. A final warning was given: 'Sign, or you will have nothing . . .'. The nuns held firm.

Several weeks later, on 26 January 1797, the property of Soleilmont was sold at public auction to a Monsieur Paulu. The community took refuge in the old château of Farciennes, a part of which had been placed at their disposal by Philippe Drion, a loyal friend. There the sisters earned their living by spinning wool and by various types of handiwork, while the uninhabited monastery four kilometers away remained ever present in their thoughts. Soleilmont was resold in 1801 to a Monsieur Devraux. The following year the new owner consented to rent a part of the abbey and its garden to the nuns; even though they could not return as proprietors they were home again.

Dame Scholastica Daivier died in 1805. Shortly afterwards, at the request of Napoleon's Minister of Justice, the abbey was placed under interdict by the Bishop of Tournai. The imperial police believed Soleilmont to be a nest of 'Stevenites'.[27] Stevenism was a movement of resistance to the oppressive measures of the napoleonic government concerning the practice of religion. It took its name from Corneille Stevens, Vicar General of Namur, and had many members in the Provice of Namur, principally clergymen and religious who had been despoiled of their property. Prejudicial documents were found in some of the out-buildings of the abbey, where known members of the resistance had been hiding. For six weeks celebration of Mass was prohibited in the monastery. Then the storm blew over and the interdict was lifted.

During these chaotic times it was impossible for the community to receive postulants, and since the great hardships had caused a number of deaths its ranks were diminishing. In 1816, as a means of procuring much needed revenues, the nuns opened both a boarding school and a day school for children of the village. Direction of these schools was entrusted to Dame Maximilienne Guillaume, a former Bernardine of Wauthier-Braine whose monastery had been destroyed.

In the meantime Dom Jerome Minsart, a former monk of Boneffe who had joined the diocese of Namur after his community had been dispersed, had begun to show great interest in the future of Soleilmont and wished to help the nuns give their life a contemplative orientation once more. Since repeated attempts to buy the abbey were fruitless and the nuns, as tenants, were not allowed to repair or alter the buildings, Dom Jerome bought the monastery of Colen and offered it to the community of Soleilmont so that they might make a fresh start. But the sisters were adamant in their desire to remain in their own monastery. Dame Maximilienne Guillaume, however, did accept the offer and founded a community at Colen. Without her, it was impossible to maintain the school at Soleilmont. The problem of poverty became more acute, and the sisters were growing old.

In 1824 Dom Jerome visited Soleilmont once again and spoke in glowing terms of the monastery of Colen, which was now flourishing. Again he tried to persuade the nuns to transfer there, and again the answer was a decided 'no'. The nuns preferred to hope. Five years later the abbey was sold again, this time to Augustin and Florenz Honorez of Mons. They, just like the previous owner, were unbending in their refusal to let the community buy back its original property. By 1836 only four religious remained: Dame Caroline Baar and Dame Catherine Bertinchamps, choir nuns; and Sr Augustine Delcampe and Sr Dorothy Benoît, laysisters. Sr Augustine was already over ninety and Sr Dorothy was eighty-two. These four steadfastly continued their monastic life as best they could in a house ravaged by dampness and neglect.

THE ABBEY IS REPURCHASED

At this moment, when every glimmer of hope seemed all but extinguished, Dame Caroline Baar tried once more to persuade Monsieur Florenz Honorez to permit her to repurchase the abbey. Very unexpectedly, he called her to Mons to settle the transaction, and on 8 December 1837, the church and monastic buildings, as well as part of the garden, once more became the property of the little community. The pastor of Gilly raised funds for the nuns, and benefactors appeared on the scene. Soon a complete restoration of the buildings was begun. Wishing to assure the subsistence of the community and to repopulate the novitiate, Dame Caroline asked Dame Maximilienne of Colen to permit two of her young nuns to come to Soleilmont for three years, so that the school might be reopened. New life arrived with the young sisters. When classes began in autumn there were twenty boarders and sixty day pupils. Before long, this number doubled. Three postulants received the habit in 1839, and by the next year there were four young professed sisters and four more new postulants. The community had resumed recitation of the Divine Office in choir, even though the Hours had to be adjusted somewhat because of the schoolchildren's schedule.

The school was undoubtedly the means of survival for Soleilmont, but little by little its needs began to take precedence over the practices of the monastic life. In the early 1880s the community made a serious effort to remedy the situation and return to a contemplative life. Canon Ignatius Van Spilbeeck, former prior of the Abbey of Tongerloo, was of great help to the nuns at this time as a guide. An important step toward achieving their goal was the closing of the day school in 1883–84. But there was still the boarding school, and the community found itself faced with a dilemma: either close the school and cut off the source of vocations, or maintain the school and bear its consequences for the monastic life. These consequences were already making themselves felt. If the monastery was going to maintain its school it would have to keep pace with other schools. Other educational institutions were, in fact, opening in the vicinity and entering into competition with the abbey school. Furthermore, great progress was being made in education. A decision was made which seemed inescapable if the community was to survive: the boarding school would be continued. When young nuns finished their novitiate they were sent out for higher studies, or for summer courses, so that they might be prepared for teaching positions. Trips and excursions were organized for the pupils. The life of the sisters lost its aspect of monastic solitude and silence.

AFFILIATION WITH THE CISTERCIAN STRICT OBSERVANCE

When the First World War came, the boarding school had to be closed. Dame Xavier Mathieu, who had been a novice in the 1880s when Canon Van Spilbeeck was trying to re-orient the nuns toward the contemplative life, headed the community. An excellent religious, she had studied at Louvain. While she was superior, chanting of the Divine Office was reintroduced, at least on feast days, and the observance of silence was restored. Then, with the encouragement of the community's chaplain, Fr Abel Brohee, Dame Xavier requested affiliation with the Cistercian Order of the Strict Observance. Shortly after the war, on 2 June 1919, Pope Benedict XV authorized the community to resume the contemplative life, and the General Chapter of 1922 approved the affiliation. The Abbot of Westmalle was designated as Father Immediate. It was a new beginning for this centuries-old community. A fervent regular life was restored and postulants arrived.

During World War II the community was able to remain in its monastery and, in spite of the deprivations which go with war, could maintain a normal monastic life. In June 1950, thirteen nuns were sent out to found the Flemish-speaking community of Our Lady of Nazareth at Brecht, not far from Antwerp.

Life went on peacefully in the little abbey in Gilly until Christmas night 1963. About 10:30, while the sisters were sleeping in the peace and joy of the feast of the Nativity of the Lord which they had just celebrated, flames suddenly broke out in one of the attics and quickly spread through the building. No lives were lost in this violent fire, fortunately, but in the morning all that remained of the abbey were bits of two wings. The sisters were offered hospitality by the religious of St Joseph's Hospital in Gilly. There they remained for three weeks, going each day to the abbey to remove the debris and make habitable once more what remained of the building. On 18 January 1964, the community moved back to Soleilmont, into the wing which Dame Anne Robert had built as an infirmary in the sixteenth century. The church, cloisters, and chapter room—all architectural treasures—were lost forever, as were also invaluable documents and works of art. Among these should be mentioned the 1239 Bull of Gregory IX, a stole which had belonged to St Bernard, and the famous painting of St Lutgard by Jouet.

For nine years the nuns lived amid the ruins, while plans were being made for their new monastery. Toward the end of 1973 they moved into the 'new' Soleilmont, situated at Fleurus in the ancient Soleilmont Wood which had been part of the abbey's domain before the Revolution. Several years later, paternity of the monastery was transferred from Westmalle to Scourmont.

From their former buildings dating from the thirteenth to eighteenth century, the nuns moved to a strikingly modern monastery designed with lines of cistercian simplicity by Frans Laurent. Several works of art salvaged from the fire have their place in the low white monastery clinging to a slope in a clearing in the Wood, blending the old with the new. This typifies the community itself which, while rooted in the rich heritage of the past, is turned toward the future. And in the new monastery, just as in the old, it is before Notre Dame de Rome that the cistercian nuns of Soleilmont sing the *Salve Regina* at the end of each day.

Abbaye N.-D. de la Paix
Chimay

APPENDIX

ABBESSES OF SOLEILMONT

1252: Aleyde
1366: Marguerite
 : Helwide de Lonvirval
 : Oda de Virsel

After the Reform at the beginning of the Fifteenth Century

1414–1438: Marie de Senzeilles
1438–1439: Catherine de Visé
1439–1461: Antoinette de Harby
1461–1474: Charlotte de Raesveld
1474–1496: Isabeau de Lannoy
1496–1515: Jehanne de Trazegnies
1515–1543: Agnès de Sautour
1543–1555: Isabelle de Henricourt
1555–1578: Anne Robert
1578–1583: Louise Heller
1583–1603: Madeleine Bulteau
1603–1639: Jacqueline Colnet
1639–1649: Anne Etienne
1649–1661: Marie de Burlen
1661–1694: Eugénie de la Halle
1694–1712: Isabelle Wolff
1712–1730: Josèphe Staignier
1730–1739: Humbeline de Bavay
1739–1766: Joseph Berger
1766–1775: Bernard Lévêque
1775–1805: Scholastica Daivier

After the French Revolution: Prioresses

1805–1814: Bernard Ducarme
1814–1819: Joséphine de la Charlerie
1819–1830: Marie Pierard
1830–1847: Caroline Baar
1848–1854: Stéphanie de Werpe
1854–1858: Marie Corbay
1858–1894: Xavier Glaesner
1894–1902: Alphonse Xhaufflaire
1902–1909: Bernard Richir
1909–1918: Xavier Mathieu
1918–1921: Marie Clément
1921–1927: Ignace Vermeulen

After Re-affiliation to the Order of Cîteaux: Abbesses

1927–1936: Gabrielle André
1936–1939: Scholastica Dal
1939–1945: Gabrielle André
1945–1950: Agnès Swevers
1950–   : Térèse Devos

NOTES

1. Galliot, *Histoire du Comté de Namur* (Liège, 1788) 4:313.
2. *Abbaye Cistercienne Notre-Dame de Soleilmont* [Booklet published by the Abbey, 1978] 4.
3. V. Barbier, *Histoire de l'Abbaye de Floreffe*, 2nd edition 1:76; 2:42. Berlière, in *Monasticon Belge*, gives a number of variants for the spelling: Soliamont, Solismons, Sorellimons, Soreaumont, Solyamont, Soliaulmont, Sorialmont, Soleaumont, Solealmont, Soleiaumont, etc.
4. *Gallia Christiana*, 3, Instr. X, col. 134; Galliot, *Histoire*, 5:412.
5. Charters of Soleilmont. A *bonnier* was a land measure equaling 122–42 *ares*. An *are* was ten meters square.
6. Bull of Gregory IX. cf. *Abbaye Cistercienne*, 4.
7. Octave Daumont, *Soleilmont, Abbaye Cistercienne du Pays de Charleroi*, (Charleroi-Paris, 1937) 26–27.
8. *Ibid.*, 42–43.
9. Dom Bruno Maréchal, *Histoire de la Fondation de l'Ancienne Abbaye de Soleilmont* (1726) [a manuscript in the archives of Soleilmont] p. 13.
10. Théophile Ploegaerts, *Les Moniales Cisterciennes dans l'ancien Roman-Pays du Brabant*, Part I (Bruxelles, 1925) p. XXI.
11. Maréchal, *Histoire*, 14.
12. Ploegaerts, *Les Moniales*, p. XXII.
13. Joseph Canivez, *L'Ordre de Cîteaux en Belgique des Origines (1132) au XXième Siècle*, (Chimay: Abbaye N.D. de Scourmont, 1926) 274.
14. Daumont, *Soleilmont*, 46.
15. *Ibid.*, 52.
16. *Ibid.*, 53–55.
17. Canivez, *L'Ordre*, 31.

18. Daumont, *Soleilmont*, 114.
19. *Ibid.*, 128–30.
20. *Ibid.*, 117.
21. *Ibid.*, 96–98.
22. *Ibid.*, 81. Jeanne-Catherine may have been a relative of Adrienne de Henry. Adrienne herself, who was thirty years old at the time of the 1639 election, was only twelve when Nicolas de Henry made this donation to the abbey.
23. *Abbaye Cistercienne*, 6.
24. Daumont, *Soleilmont*, 123.
25. *Ibid.*, 68.
26. *Ibid.*, 190.
27. *Abbaye Cistercienne*, 8.

EPILOGUE

Does St Bernard Have a Specific Message for Nuns?

Jean Leclercq

CONSIDERING ALL St Bernard did to found and fill monasteries for nuns, we may find it surprising that he wrote so little about them, for them, and to them. He wrote more frequently about, to, and for married women. This in itself is enough to prove that he gave consideration to women and their role in the society of his times.[1] He also gave an important place in his writings to the feminine as a symbol of God's action in the world and of humanity's return to God within the Church. Union with God expressed in bridal imagery is already found in the Old Testament, particularly in the *Song of Songs* and the wedding song which is Psalm 44 [Hebrew 45]. The theme is also used in the New Testament, from the Gospels through St Paul to the *Book of Revelation*. This was a theme greatly cherished by St Bernard, and it is interesting to ask how he dealt with it when addressing nuns.

THE MYSTERY OF THE COMMONPLACE

Bernard wrote only three letters to nuns, and they were short letters at that. In the first, written to a young nun, he preaches radical detachment and absolute fidelity to her new vocation.[2] We can easily picture the many young noblewomen who, in a burst of enthusiasm, followed brother, sister, uncle, sometimes even the whole family along the monastic path. Understandably enough, some young women—for example, the young Sophia to whom Bernard also wrote[3]—had tired of a castle life with nothing to interest them beyond a round of futile occupations. To enter a highly motivated community, sharing in the fervent zeal for converting a castle into a monastery or for building an abbey and cultivating the surrounding land, was activity calculated to stimulate their fervor. But very soon, here as in other areas of life, a stranger called Routine crept in, and the nuns began to feel the hardships, even the monotony, of their chosen life.

The anonymous nun to whom Bernard sent his Letter 114 seems to have been going through some such crisis. We do not know who she was; perhaps she was not one particular nun but every nun who finds herself in the spiritual state which Bernard was describing. This obscure and perhaps symbolic nun, who once lived an easy life surrounded with marks of respect in the family manor, now found herself with no consolation at all except that of God. Gently but frankly, Bernard went, as usual, straight to the point. The first sentence draws a contrast between heaven and earth, this valley of tears and the joyful city of God. It is this state of contrast in which the nun now finds herself, for she has left the valley of tears and found the joyful city of God where her only true happiness lies. Compared to this all the rest is sadness, sorrow, bitterness, ugliness; in a word, boredom. Then without further ado, Bernard asks a personal question in confidence:

> Tell me now, witness before me. Examine yourself; you know no one better than you know yourself. Well now, is it not simply that the Holy Spirit is crying out in your heart? Did not he persuade you of this truth himself even before I suggested it?

And with the sure skill of a true spiritual master, Bernard goes on to bring the nun back to the moment of her conversion, to the remembrance of her first decision and her first love. 'You renounced all that was of no worth among your natural gifts—age, respectability, beauty, noble birth—in order to take your delight in the realities of the inner life.' Once more, as always, Bernard appealed to interiority, the return to the heart, true self-knowledge.

Having recalled the lasting values of every monastic vocation, and having invited the nun to examine her conscience, the Abbot of Clairvaux, with no beating about the bush, brought his correspondent to acknowledge that she had slipped from this high level. He told her that she had been living according to her own law, belonging neither to God nor to the world, behaving in a worldly way under the religious habit. And so, he tells her, you now find yourself falling between two stools. This expression brings a smile to our lips, softening the severity of the scolding and the sadness of the situation. Even the world has rejected you. In short, Bernard says for the second time, you are dead. This is the fate of those who commit themselves and do not persevere, those whose outward life is at odds with their inner dispositions. We would sum up this state by saying of a nun that she does not put her heart into her life.

There is no doubt that this relentless analysis of a fidelity crisis describes the temptation which must have assailed many young men and women after the first period of fervor in the monastery. Is not every one of us called to make a second journey,[4] to go through a new conversion process and thus begin a new stage in life? This is a frequent, almost normal, situation and one which should cause no despair, for Christ is faithful forever. Bernard goes on to recall this to his nun correspondent:

> But look here! By God's mercy you have come to life again. You live to righteousness and no longer to sin, to Christ and no longer to the world. You must go on dying, but to yourself, to the world, and this will be a happy way for you to be truly living!
>
> Here you are then, back to your vow, to your profession, to the truth of your name as a nun. Finished now is the caricature you gave of yourself when you had saucy looks and haughty head, loud laughter and provocative gait, eccentric clothes and a wimple instead of a veil.

One may wonder whether this is a factual description of the nun to whom Bernard is writing. Did her spiritual journey pass through such contrasting stages? We do not know, but the fact that Bernard thought fit to write and publish this letter leads us to suppose that, not only was it possible, but that it actually did happen. He could hardly have been less disillusioned, more realistic and clear-sighted. Cloistered life has never been easy and pleasant for every nun at every stage of her life. Bernard found it necessary to remind us of this in a straightforward way, honest as he was with the young aristocrats who continued to flock to the monastery. It was urgent, he thought, to warn them of what to expect and to present every dimension of the monastic commitment.

But it was not Bernard's custom to end on a negative note, so he went on to write: 'Look here! By Christ's workings, all this is over and gone forever; interiority has come into its own again. It is the Holy Spirit who has brought this about in you.'

And then, with wonderful indulgence: 'There is an excuse for your recent fit of tepidity. The Holy Spirit who breathes where he will, when he will, had not yet breathed in you.' Thus our nun experienced what some today would call a renewal, and to be more exact, a charismatic renewal, a new and fiery outpouring of the Holy Spirit. 'See to it that this fire which has been kindled within your heart be not extinguished!'

This is the only fairly well-developed message in which Bernard sketches

the outlines of a spirituality for nuns. Actually, what he wrote applies equally
to monks. The important thing for both nuns and monks is expressed here by
Bernard in terms of interiority, the language of the heart. It is not feelings
which count, even strong feelings of love. What counts is fidelity.

Bernard wrote to another anonymous nun in the same vein.[5] The nun
was going through another sort of monastic crisis. She belonged to an urban
community, the benedictine abbey of Sainte-Marie in Troyes. But she aspired
after a poorer and more ascetic life where she would have fewer visitors and
greater peace. She wanted to be in the 'desert', either alone or with a few
sisters; surely this was the best way to be pleasing to God alone. Certainly
not! was Bernard's categorical answer. Solitude also has its dangers; life in
community offers certain safeguards—control, correction, holy emulation,
and mutual good example.

There is nothing 'mystical' in all this, nothing but good hard common
sense and acceptance of the ordinariness of things and people. To the factors
which are universally applicable when it comes to discernment, Bernard
added one that was specific to this nun's community. Saint Mary's of Troyes
had just gone through a renewal process; therefore each member of the
community was bound to give the best of herself to the others. The end of
this letter does no more than enlarge on the theme of attachment to one's
community. Gently, trying to help her see herself more clearly, Bernard
suggested some of the motives which might underlie the nun's desire. Was
it not precisely because the monastery was beginning to be more fervent
and more austere that she felt the need to separate? Bernard says that he
does not wish to decide on this question, for the nun has a spiritual mother
and sisters who are also trying to dissuade her. All that he can do is offer
some advice: 'Listen, my daughter, listen to the advice of fidelity. Whether
you are sinner or saint, do not leave the flock to which you belong.'

The third nun to whom Bernard wrote was an abbess, the most illustrious
mystic of her day. She was the first of those great prophetesses and vision-
aries of whom the following centuries were to give so many examples—
women who sometimes had such great influence on the Church and on the
men who governed it.[6] This was abbess Hildegard of Bingen and she was
having the first of her sensational revelations about people and realities
touching the christian mysteries. Hildegard and others were surprised at the
visions and wondered what confidence they should have in these revelations.
The abbess was a humble woman and so put the question to St Bernard.
Though he went twice through the Rhineland and passed near her monastery
at Bingen, he did not go out of his way to see her and get firsthand information. He contented himself with sending her one of the shortest notes he
ever wrote. It is only twelve lines long—so short that fifty years later, in the
circles where Hildegard had lived and where she was now venerated by

one and all, it was thought fitting to make the text longer than it had originally been.

The authentic letter is very restrained—a joust of humility between the
visionary and the man she had consulted. Bernard says that he is no more
than a sinner and he is surprised to see the confidence she has in him. Feeling,
however, that he cannot fail to repay the charity she has shown him, he is
moved to answer her questions. Then in a few brief words, he approved the
revelations. The reason he gave for his approval was that Hildegard was
humble. This humility was decisive for Bernard, since, according to St James,
'God only gives grace to the humble'. If Hildegard had received God's
grace, it was because she was humble and must remain so. 'So much for
what depends upon us, the only thing that we exhort you to do and beg you
to observe.' Bernard, the abbot of Clairvaux, charged with preparing the
Crusade and at the height of his fame, prestige, and influence, had nothing
to teach someone who was taught by the Holy Spirit. He commended to
her prayers himself and those close to him.

These three letters show us that each time Bernard wrote to a nun, even
when she was a mystic, he did not deal in rapture; his letters are moderate,
sober, and precise. He was not of the earth earthy, but he confined himself
within the limits of the ordinary. We might even be tempted to say that he
was humdrum. What he said to nuns applies to every man or woman living
in the Church. From this we conclude that Bernard had no special message
for nuns.

NUNS AS SHARERS IN THE CHRISTIAN HERITAGE

When we say that Bernard had no *special* message for nuns, does that
mean that he had no message at all for them? No! But they are to appropriate, without complacency or a sense of privilege, what is common to all the
members of the Church. Bernard's esteem for nuns was such that he did not
feel it necessary to set them on a pedestal or come to their defense as if they
had a right to some kind of monopoly. It was enough for their own joy and
that of other Christians that they should be members of the Church, and
even that they should be the Church itself, as is the case for 'all of us, we
who together are the Church'.[7]

In the first place, they may lay claim to the core of the christian mystery,
the reconciliation of humanity with God through Christ in the Holy Spirit.
This reconciliation has been expressed traditionally in the image of bridal
union with God, and Bernard proposes this way of life and this symbol to
all men and women. To young Sophia who, living in the world, could have
fallen victim to a search for the glory of worldly elegance—a danger which

lay in wait for idle and affluent nobility—Bernard penned an exhortation to remember that she is a bride of Christ, who will reveal his glory to her when the day comes for the everlasting embrace. Meanwhile she must remain faithful in her state of virginity. This fidelity is a personal union with some-one dwelling in her heart:

> Within you is he who is your joy, he who makes your joy, if at least you are to believe what has been written: 'Christ dwells by faith in your heart'. And elsewhere, 'All the glory of the king's daughter is within'.

The rest is only the logical consequence of bringing one's outer conduct into line with this inner, hidden mystery. This ideal was proposed to all without exception. St Paul taught the indwelling of Christ to the faithful of the Church at Ephesus and not only to one special social or ecclesiastical class.[8]

Bernard sent this basic message to Queen Melisenda at Jerusalem. The same dangers lay in wait for her, but hers were even greater because of her extremely high social rank and the temptation of abusing her royal power now that she was a widow. Bernard suggested the same remedy—union with 'Christ and Christ crucified', as St Paul wrote to all the faithful of the Church at Corinth.[9] Here, bridal union with Christ is presupposed without being expressly mentioned. It is evident that Melisenda now had Christ as her only spouse. He ruled her and it is in him that she must rule.

Bernard also wrote to married couples, to Simon and Adelaide, the duke and duchess of Lorraine.[10] In his introductory address Bernard expressed the customary wish in words so daring that they are difficult to translate: 'May they delight in one another in chaste and loving embrace, so that the sole love of Christ holds sway in each!' It would be difficult to combine in fewer words married love and total love for Christ. Husband and wife are, in the manner unique to their married state, specialists of bridal union with Christ.

Among Bernard's correspondence we find two private notes sent to 'Er-mengard, erstwhile countess of Brittany'.[11] Nowhere else in the whole of his works do we find Bernard giving vent to such affections as he shows to this friend. These notes are little masterpieces in the genre that we might call 'intimate letters', where the heart speaks without constraint. The word heart is repeatedly used, now applied to Bernard and now to Ermengard. These texts deserve careful analysis, but all we can do here is point out that we are attending one of those 'jousts of love' which abound in courtly litera-ture. The central theme is that of separated love, love from afar. Bernard writes to his friend saying that though they are far from each other they are closely united and that it is God's own finger, the Holy Spirit, who has en-graven this love on their hearts. Here Bernard plays with words which are assonant—*rara* and *caritas*. 'The rareness of our meetings is dear to me!' Then he gives his reasons, saying that such love is 'affection tested in charity', a truly christian love existing in each. Open-eyed and generous, this love is willing to accept the physical absence of the other.

This fiery language of the love of friendship can be transposed to the plane of the love relationship which every Christian should have with God. Love of this sort engages every capacity of human affectivity. It is love from afar, lived out in separation joyfully accepted in faith. Each partner in this love-match both gives and receives, and each helps the other to live out this giving and receiving. Such inner dispositions suggest a reciprocal and limitless love. It is the love of Christ's own heart for us in the Holy Spirit; and in this same Spirit Christ expects us to love him in return. This love makes us sharers of that divine love in the Father's heart which he has for us in his only Son and which he has made known to us through him. It is this same love which the Holy Spirit continues to engrave on our hearts: *Cor sponsi, cor Patris sui.*[12] Christ is the bridegroom, and his heart is the very heart of his heavenly Father.

Bernard did not develop the doctrinal implications of the two notes he wrote to Ermengard. But what has just been briefly sketched is set out at length in his works and in particular in the *Sermons on the Song of Songs*. These sermons were written at the request of a Carthusian, Bernard of Portes. St Bernard chose to compose his work in the form of a series of sermons, obliging himself to speak to an imaginary audience. In the rare circumstances in which he found it necessary to allude to this audience, he gives us to understand that they were composed for his own monks. But in fact he was quite aware that he was writing for a mixed public of both men and women. Consequently, we may confidently attest that, except for one or two details, all that he says applies equally to nuns as to monks.

MAN AND WOMAN IN THE ETERNAL DEPTHS OF THEIR EQUALITY

Need we ask then why Bernard has no special message for nuns? The truth of the matter is that he considered monks and nuns on an equal footing; both were members of the Church, equal in their capacity as children of God and human beings. In the Bible, God is presented under masculine and feminine symbols. His eternal Wisdom made flesh is like the woman of the Gospels who turns the whole house upside down to find the silver coin struck in her own image. Under the aspects of Truth and Mercy, and every other feminine attribute, he comes down to fallen humanity in order to restore it to its original truth and kindness.[14] Or again, God identifies himself with Peace, Righteousness, and Charity as with his 'sisters' and 'daughters'. These three kiss and bring lost humanity back 'into the joyous embraces of Peace, to sleep and rest in her bosom'.[15]

In another passage Bernard described God as a Father who has the compassion of a mother, as suggested by Isaiah 49:15.[16] His 'chambermaids'—*assistrices cubiculi*—and the 'princesses of his palace' are Hope, Prudence, and friend Temperance. God reveals himself under the feminine figure of Wisdom. But the most important figure, the queen of all, is Charity.[17] In one of his letters, Bernard spoke of Lady Charity.[18] In Parable Five, he called Charity one of God's three daughters, her sisters being Faith and Hope and her friend Piety.[19] A whole feminine world is imagined and symbolized in God as in all humans. There exists an order of things which lies beyond division or limitation because they are essential and universal. This means that they are found in the relationship of all that God is and all that he does with every human person. Christ is man, but he is so for men and women alike, with no exception.

Among humans, equality is absolute. Eve and Adam, even after the Fall, are still images of God, made free with a liberty that can never be taken from them. It is in this context that the affirmation of woman's independence must be placed: 'The sweetness, the delight, the attraction for the forbidden fruit is part of you, but it is not that which is most truly yours. That which belongs really to you is different and has another origin; it is eternal and comes from eternity'.[20] Both man and woman are able to behave tenderly. The most wonderful thing about Moses, for example, was his ability to take pity on a thankless people and to speak affectionately of them as parents do about the children to whom they have given birth. Moses was never angry. He sought nothing but his children's well-being and happiness. In a charming and moving parable we read:

> It is as if a rich man said to a poor woman, 'Come into my banqueting hall, but leave the little baby you have in your arms outside; he will disturb us with his crying'. What would she do? Would she not prefer to go hungry rather than leave her dear little treasure outside and eat alone in the rich man's house? And so Moses will not enter into the joy of his Lord without the rowdy and thankless people to whom he is bound by motherly affection. His heart aches with pain, but he prefers that to being separated from the people he loves.[21]

All that is greatest in a human being, all that is most noble and most like to God—precisely because it comes from him—is neither specifically masculine nor specifically feminine. The woman who poured out her ointment on the Lord's feet showed an immense capacity for devotion and fidelity, as she anticipated his hour of glory. Jesus gave this act of devotedness its full meaning as he did that of the women who followed him to the sepulchre and were the first to witness his resurrection.[22] Everyone can and should imitate their faith and love. Men too were privileged to show their attachment to the Lord. Both men and women are compared to those courtiers of the female suite in the *Song of Songs*, honoring the king in his palace.[23] Finally, every member of the Church can be a mother by giving birth spiritually to Christ in self and in others. Bernard applied to himself these words spoken by Jesus in John 16:21: 'A woman in travail is sad'. But afterwards the sorrow is wholly replaced by the joy of seeing Christ being formed in the offspring.[24]

In short, we may say that there is not a single aspect of the divine mystery and the divine work of salvation, not a single reality of the spiritual life which, according to St Bernard, is to be attributed solely to nuns and other christian women to the exclusion of monks and other christian men. Bernard did not deny that certain women in the Gospel showed a special love for the Lord, for example, Mary of Nazareth or Mary Magdalen.[25] But he always gave the reason for such special love. The former was exceptional, alone of her kind. The latter, on the other hand, was in the condition common to all humankind; she was a sinner. Because of this, and because she was at once loving and forgiven, she has become a universal archetype.

THE INDIVIDUAL AS BEARER OF THE UNIVERSAL CALL

Thus St Bernard had no reason to deliver a message for nuns which would differ from the message he had for every Christian, particularly those called to the monastic life. Bernard neither excluded nuns nor showed a preference for them. His attitude reflected his theology concerning the differentiated equality existing between men and women in their relationship to God. He did not even speak of a complementarity, which would only be another way of insisting on the difference between the sexes. He considered the mystery of the human condition as a whole. He ceaselessly taught humanity's essential unity in its beginning and its end, the totality of salvation in the Church. Every human existence comes from the Father and returns to him, through the saving work of Christ and under the guidance of the Holy Spirit.

It is on the basis of this christian anthropology, common to all members of the Church, that Bernard proposed to all, especially to those in the monastic state, a very demanding program. Bernard urged all without distinction to a generous and daily commitment to God in *ascesis* and the search for prayer, and a no less serious commitment to other people. When he wanted to be truly universal in his message, he spoke in the first person singular, saying 'I' with exacting honesty. He acknowledged his own temptations, his inclinations, his miseries and also his lofty gifts. He mentioned too his community and his own attachment to it.[26] 'Oh foolish man who believe that I am not you!' said a nineteenth-century french poet. The messages which go furthest, which fly over greatest distances and reach the greatest number of people, are the messages delivered as personal confidences—provided of course, that they are not motivated by a desire for self-display. Thomas Merton in our own day reached thousands, even millions, of people, most of whom had never lived a life similar to his. He succeeded in awakening the true self in each, by speaking of himself and of the things which God could do for others as he had for him. A twin gift is needed in order to steer this type of expression safely through dangerous waters. It can succeed only when it is undergirded with both talent and holiness. Bernard was a master in this literary genre, to the great joy and benefit of nuns and monks alike.

Clervaux

NOTES

1. On these subjects and the texts used here, I have given more detail in *St Bernard and Women*, forthcoming.
2. *Epistola* 114; *Sancti Bernardi Opera*; Edd. J. Leclercq and H.M. Rochais (Rome 1957–1977) 7:291–93. Further citations from St Bernard are from this edition.
3. *Ep.* 113.
4. Cf. Gerald O'Collins, *The Second Journey. Spiritual Awareness and the Mid-Life Crisis*, (New York, 1978).
5. *Ep.* 115; SBOp 7:294–95.
6. *Ep.* 366; SBOp 8:323–24.
7. *'singuli nos, qui simul Ecclesia sumus'.* SC 57:3; SBOp 2:121.
8. *Ep.* 113; SBOp 7:287–91.
9. *Ep.* 289; SBOp 8:205–6.
10. *Ep.* 119; SBOp 7:299–300.
11. *Epp.* 116–17; SBOp 7:296–97.
12. *SC* 62.5; SBOp 2:158.
13. *Gra* 32; SBOp 3:188.
14. *Ann* 1.6; SBOp 5:17.
15. *Ann* 1. 14; p. 29.
16. *Par* 1.6; SBOp 6/1:261–67. Par 1; SBOp 6/2:261–67.
17. *Ibid.*, 2; 6/2:267–73.
18. *Ep.* 14; SBOp 7:63.
19. *Par* 5; SBOp 62:282–85.
20. SC 82.4 SBOp 2:294.
21. SC 12.4 SBOp 1:62.
22. SC 12.7 SBOp 1:65.
23. SC 23.9 SBOp 1:144.
24. SC 29.6 SBOp 1:207.
25. In the book *Monks and Marriage in the Twelfth Century*, I have assembled texts.
26. In *Aspects of Monasticism* (CS 7) pp. 251–65: 'St Bernard and the Christian Experience', I have assembled texts. Others could also be quoted.

AFTERWORD

The Echo Within

WE HAVE LIKENED the women in this volume to distant echoes. There is another echo, another voice, if you will, which an authentic religious woman of any age hears, and hears as an inner experience. Insofar as she listens and responds to this inner echo, she can inspire us and share with us a new vision by which she re-expresses the dignity of womanhood. This echo is heard in the heart of every woman, and every man, if they will but listen. Sometimes hard to hear and difficult to interpret, sometimes clear and compelling, it can reverberate from a good or an evil source. In the monastic tradition there is a process which seeks to teach us to listen to these voices and to decide which is truly the spirit of God and speaks for our good. It is called 'discernment of spirits', and in our lives we are constantly being urged to discern the source of the echoes we hear.

In this volume we learn of women who have discerned a call to serve God by living as 'religious women'. What does this mean? Each would probably express the meaning it had for her in a uniquely personal way. Here I will briefly recall the experience of my own vocation and the meaning of this call, and then reflect on these issues, using examples from this volume.

After twenty-seven years in a contemplative cistercian monastery of the twentieth century, I am still discovering the meaning of a call which has revealed itself only bit by bit. I can remember at the age of twelve or thirteen seeing in a seventh grade history book a picture of a monk. Until then I had never heard of monks. They were described as people who lived in silence and did nothing but love God all day. I could not imagine what this meant, and that night, looking out my bedroom window at a clear, vast, star-studded sky, I pondered that somewhere under that sky were monks who did nothing but love God all day. Immediately I felt a premonition, an inner echo, that one day I too would be a monk. My response was immediate; I walked away from the window with one clear thought: 'No, I am *not* going to be a monk'. I had many plans for my future and I was not too young to realize what this choice would mean. And so for some nine years I went merrily along with very little thought of religious life and a great deal of thought about marriage, a family of my own, and a career in nursing. I was halfway through college and dating steadily when the echo sounded again. It came as a sudden and insistent call, a compelling attraction to God and his love. I found myself longing to express my love for him in the most complete way possible.[1] I was, literally, hit over the head. This impulse continued amid hesitations and doubts and very logical reasons why I should not listen. It continued amid complications and obstacles which gradually fell away. It continued amid the acute pain of leaving nursing and saying goodbye to close friends. It continued even during the final wrench of leaving a wonderful mom and dad and the companionship of four fun-loving brothers. No one but God could have done this to me. I didn't even like nuns; their lifestyle had always seemed cold and inhuman. My family was not a religious one and vocation to the religious life had never even been mentioned at home. Yet I have never regretted my choice or doubted that the call echoed God's loving will; nor have I ceased to marvel at the grace which has been my cistercian vocation, tailor-made for me.

The monastic life, as I was to learn, is a journey to purity of heart,[2] growth into our true self, the person God wishes us to be: it is union with him in love and it is his gift to *all* of us. It is to let God peel away all the illusions we cherish, to let him recreate us as new men and new women wholly attentive to that inner voice, the echo of his guiding Spirit. It is a long and laborious discernment. The barely heard whispers or the insistent inner voice must be experienced, listened to, and then questioned. Does it call to good or to selfishness, to growth of my true self or of my non-loving false self? In our epilogue article, Jean Leclercq describes, in the words of St Bernard's letters, the ups and downs of this interior adventure of constant conversion to 'truly seek God'. It is amid and by these very labors that we hear our summons to union with, and transformation in, Christ. The echo guides, invites, and touches our heart until ' . . . Christ prays to the Father in me, suffers in me, dies in me . . . sees through my eyes, listens through my ears, loves through my heart'.[3]

Is this call to union spoken only to religious? By no means. As Fr Leclercq again reminds us, this summons to union with God is given to 'all men and women without exception'. The 'religious woman', like the 'religious man', is a *sign* of every person's human-divine vocation; as she daily responds in freedom, faith, and hope to her inner call—her relationship of love with him who is calling, who is the Word spoken by the Father—deepens, her sense of oneness with him grows. Her words, actions and attitudes become Christ's words, actions, and attitudes; the union of human and divine centers and the true self emerges, a woman fulfilled and completed in God. Having left all to follow Christ and to respond to his call, she now finds her deepest sense of worth in listening to this voice within, aware that he is present at the center of her being as Father, Son, and Holy Spirit, ever speaking his will and love. This call can be lived in a religious lifestyle or in any lifestyle which expresses the deepest meaning of our gift of life.

It took many years of monastic living for me to begin to understand, much less to live, my call. When I began I did not know how to pray and knew next to nothing about 'the spiritual life' and the mystery of my inner echo. Yet the one thing I learned along the way was that God speaks to us wherever we are; his call reechoes as we change and grow.

The women we meet in this volume heard a call to be 'religious women'. Because *Distant Echoes* focusses mainly on the exterior life of nuns, few references to this interior call are to be found in it. But the call still reverberates in the lives of all these women and it gives heart and meaning to the records of their activities. Ann Warren introduces us to anchoresses 'whose heart the Holy Spirit moved to seek a desert place', who 'desired greatly . . . to lead a solitary life'. Dennis Devlin writes of Mary of Oignies, who heard the call through the text of St Luke's Gospel: 'whosoever will come after me, let him deny himself and take up his cross and follow me'. And, he adds, 'she made it her life to follow Christ'. Sharon Elkins quotes Gilbert of Sempringham as saying 'I found young women who, often instructed by us, wanted to aim without impediment for divine slavery, disregarding the cares of the world'. In these instances the promptings of the Spirit are fairly clear.[4]

But entry into the religious way of life may be, or may seem to be, brought about quite by chance or even by coercion. Mary Skinner's work suggests that frankish women may have had as little choice about entering the cloister as they did about entering marriage. As Ann Warren remarks, the ideal must always live within the real. Jo Ann McNamara points to some of these realities: Asella's father dedicated her virginity from childhood; Eustochium and Paula II, growing up in very protected circumstances, were greatly influenced by the holy desires of their mothers. She also reminds us realistically of 'tales of women in medieval convents where social status, dowry, and family influence were the major qualifications for entry into community'.

The call has been heard through seemingly chance circumstances and the response made, not in total freedom, but because of family expectations by a desire for refuge from marriage or calamity, or by social custom (as widows routinely entering convents at the death of their husbands). Are all these false vocations? Two factors interrelate here the need for discernment and the realization that God is God. He can speak to us in any situation.

Discernment in assessing the true motives of those wishing to enter religious life has been stressed from the sixth-century *Rule* of St Benedict to the instructions of present day canon law. The *Rule* says, 'try the spirits if they be of God'. Once a postulant has entered, 'a senior who knows how to gain souls for God shall be appointed to watch over him, minutely to examine his entire conduct, and to ascertain if he is truly seeking God and is zealous for the work of God, for obedience, and for humiliations.' Yet we know this goal of 'truly seeking God' is reached only by on-going conversion. The newly converted often does not seek God; he must come to learn to do so in the 'school of the Lord's service', and this loving God meets and accepts us where we are, calling us forward to follow him in purity of heart. The same is true of those entering religious life through chance or coercion. We trust that God accepts the social and religious conditions we create and works within them. The chance circumstance, the parental choice, may be his providential means of providing an environment in which the echo of his summons can be heard. Women or men choosing religious life from motives of frustration, immaturity, or selfishness have caused, and will certainly cause, difficulties and scandals, as will people entering marriage or remaining single for similar reasons. Yet someone who has begun in ignorance, or unwillingness, or from mixed motives can grow into the peace of a mature choice, to experience the conversion Benedict demands and truly to hear the distant echo of God's voice prompting and guiding her to an authentic response and choice. Gertrude the Great could be such an example. She was placed in the abbey in 1261 at the age of five, possibly as an orphan. While circumstances led her to the convent, we know from her writings that she deeply and deliberately chose her monastic life as she matured.[5] Her life and the life of each and every person is a sacred time, a sacred history—God intervening and guiding each moment.[6] 'Christ is the Lord of history that moves', wrote Thomas Merton. 'He not only holds the beginning and the end in his hands, but he is in history with us, walking ahead of us to where we are going.'[7]

The authentic religious woman is the woman who has lovingly and freely, whatever the circumstances that led her to it, bound herself to live this transformation into Christ. By word and by deed, she puts on his poverty, accepts chastity and professes obedience, letting the Holy Spirit speak to, and in, and through her. The meaning of her life can help us discern the meaning of our own womanhood and manhood drawing us towards a lifegiving union with God and with one another in love. As we study the medieval religious women in *Distant Echoes* and its sequels, *Peace Weavers* and *Hidden Springs*, may they speak to us of the human-divine free person who we are each meant to be; may they be, indeed. distant echoes of the voice which summons each of us to the joy and fullness of being for which we were uniquely created, inviting us to to listen and respond, at this very moment, to the echo of that voice within, the Holy Spirit.

Sister Lillian Thomas Shank ocso
Our Lady of the Mississippi Abbey
Dubuque, Iowa

NOTES

1. Each experience of vocation is unique. Some feel the call strongly and insistently, as was my experience; others experience confusion over both the reality of a call and its content, i.e. where and how to respond.

2. See Cassian, *Conferences*, 1.4ff.

3. William Johnston sj, *The Inner Eye of Love* (Harper and Row, 1978) 51.

4. We have in these examples three typical ways in which God's call is often heard: 1) The interior promptings of the heart; 2) The holy spiritual guide whose example and advice are means God uses to invoke an awareness of call and a response to that call; 3) The medium of God's word in scripture. These words are not just read but pierce inner depths inviting to a reponse. The classic example of this is St Antony's call in his *Life* by St Athanasius. In my own experience, the being 'hit over the head' was in reality a dynamic experience of the words of scripture 'You shall love the Lord your God with all your heart and soul and mind and strength'.

5. St Gertrude's total commitment in monastic life is seen in all her writings but see especially her 'Second Exercise-Spiritual Conversion' (p. 15–24) and her 'Fourth Exercise-Renewal of Monastic Profession' (p. 51–78) in *Exercises of Saint Gertrude*, translated by Mother Columba Hart osb [Newman Press, 1955].

6. See 'On Creation and History', Chapter Fourteen in *Personal Witness*, a biblical spirituality, by John J. Navone sj, for a biblical Old and New Testament interpretation of 'history' in our lives.

7. Thomas Merton, *He is Risen* (Argus Communications) pg. 5.

NOTES ON CONTRIBUTORS

ELIZABETH CONNOR is the superior of Abbaye Notre Dame de la Paix, Chimay, Belgium. A cistercian nun since 1953, she received her B.S. and M.A. degrees in the Classics Department of The John Hopkins University. She has been active in the Cistercian Law Commission since 1970, and serves as associate editor of the journal *Cistercian Studies*.

SHARON ELKINS has been assistant professor of historical theology and catholic studies in the Religion Department of Wellesley College since 1976. She also teaches church history at Pope John XXIII National Seminary for delayed vocations to the Roman Catholic priesthood. She holds a Ph.D. in the study of religion from Harvard University, and an M.T.S. from Harvard Divinity School. Currently she is completing a book manuscript entitled *Holy Women of Twelfth Century England*.

JO ANN McNAMARA is professor of history at Hunter College in New York City, a founding member of the Institute for Research in History and an active organizer of the Berkshire Conferences on the History of Women. Her research has led her in recent years from the Middle Ages to the early christian centuries. Her *A New Song: Celibate Women in the First Three Christian Centuries* is presently in press, and she is working on a sequel covering the fourth and fifth centuries as well as on a series of translations of the lives of Merovingian women saints.

JOHN A. NICHOLS, professor of history at Slippery Rock University in Pennsylvania, received his Ph.D in medieval history from Kent State University in 1974. He has published a number of articles on cistercian nuns in medieval England, among them 'The Internal Organization of English Cistercian Nunneries' *Citeaux* (1979) and 'Medieval English Cistercian Nunneries: Their Art and Physical Remains' *Mélanges Anselme Dimier* (1982). He is currently completing a book on the *Cistercian Nuns of Medieval England*.

PENNY SCHINE GOLD is assistant professor of history at Knox College in Galesburg, Illinois. She received her M.A. in history and Ph.D. in medieval studies from Stanford University. She has published articles on the iconography of the Virgin Mary and the canon law of marriage, and a book on *The Lady and The Virgin: Image, Attitude and Experience in Twelfth-Century France*.

SALLY THOMPSON is a research assistant at Westfield College, London.

After reading history at Cambridge University, she taught and worked in educational administration. With a grant from the Leverhulme Foundation, she is completing her Ph.D. thesis on English nunneries during the Middle Ages. She has published 'The Problem of Cistercian Nuns in the Twelfth and Early Thirteenth Centuries' in *Medieval Women* (1978).

ANN K. WARREN holds a lectureship in the department of history at Case Western Reserve University, where she also received both her M.A. and Ph.D. degrees. Her doctoral work on english anchorites is currently being prepared for publication. She has read a number of papers on women as anchorites and has an article forthcoming on that subject in the *Dumbarton Oaks Papers*.

JEAN LECLERCQ is a benedictine monk of the Abbaye Saint-Maur et Saint-Maurice, Clervaux, Luxembourg, and teaches medieval spirituality at the Gregorian University, Rome. A prodigious author of books and articles, he is perhaps best known for *The Love of Learning and the Desire for God* (1961), and for the critical edition of The Works of Bernard of Clairvaux. A listing of his publications to 1973 can be found in *Bernard of Clairvaux: Studies Presented to Dom Jean Leclercq* (Cistercian Publications).

COBURN V. GRAVES is professor of history at Kent State University. He received his A.B. at Boston University and his M.A. and Ph.D. at the University of Chicago. His publications on various aspects of medieval cistercian history have appeared in *Speculum, Mediaeval Studies, Analecta S.O.C.*, and *Studies in Medieval Culture*.

DENNIS DEVLIN received a Ph.D. from the University of Chicago and currently teaches and does administrative work at the Grand Valley State Colleges in Michigan. His scholarly work has centered on popular religious attitudes in the Late Middle Ages, much of it focusing on the role of women in the popular religious movement. He is also the coordinator of the Great Lakes History Conference which meets in Grand Rapids each spring.

SUSAN PINGREY MILLINGER is associate professor of history at Roanoke College in Salem, Virginia. She received her Ph.D. in medieval european history from the University of California, Berkeley in 1974. She is a frequent reader of papers on religious women at medieval conferences and has published 'Liturgical Devotion in the *Vita Oswaldi*' in *Literature, Liturgy and Legend in Anglo-Saxon and Carolingian History* (1979).

DOROTHY DE FERRANTI ABRAHAMSE received her B.A. from Mount Holyoke College and her M.A. and Ph.D. from the University of Michigan. Her special interests lie in the religious and social history of the middle Byzantine Empire (eighth-eleventh centuries), particularly its hagiographical tradition and the role of women in byzantine religion. She has studied byzantine hagiography as a source of information on childhood and magic, the changing image of the saint, and byzantine monasteries for women. She is currently working on a study of female sanctity in Byzantium, and lecturing in history at California State University at Long Beach.

JANE TIBBETTS SCHULENBURG, associate professor of history at the University of Wisconsin-Madison, Extension and Women's Studies, received her Ph.D. in medieval history from the University of Wisconsin in 1969. She has published several articles on medieval women, including, 'Sexism and the Celestial Gynaeceum: from 500-1200', *Journal of Medieval History* 4/2 (June, 1978) and 'Clio's European Daughters: Myopic Modes of Perception', in *The Prism of Sex*, edd. J. Sherman and E. Beck (1979). She is presently working on a book on the female religious experience ca. 500-1100.

MARY S. SKINNER is assistant professor of history and religion at Wheaton College, Norton, Massachusetts. She earned her B.A. from Bryn Mawr, her M.A. from Columbia and her Ph.D. in history from Syracuse in 1977. Her area of research is early medieval french families, and she has published 'Aristocratic Families: Founders and Reformers of Monasteries in the Touraine, 930-1030,' in *Benedictus: Studies in Honor of St Benedict of Nursia* (1981).

LILLIAN THOMAS SHANK is a cistercian nun of Our Lady of the Mississippi Abbey near Dubuque, Iowa. She first entered the Order at Mount St Mary Abbey in Wrentham, Massachusetts in 1956. In 1964, she went to a new cistercian foundation, near Dubuque. A graduate of Mount St Joseph College near Cincinnati, Ohio, she received an R.N. from Mount St Joseph Good Samaritan Hospital nursing program. She has taught monastic history for the past fourteen years and served her community as infirmarian, prioress, bookkeeper, manager of their candy business, candy cook, and tractor driver on the abbey farm.

INDEX OF PERSONS AND PLACES

Persons active before 1500 are listed under their given names.

289

The editors of Cistercian Publications are grateful to Dr John A. Nichols for preparing this index.

CISTERCIAN PUBLICATIONS INC.

TITLES LISTING

THE CISTERCIAN FATHERS SERIES

THE CISTERCIAN STUDIES SERIES

* Temporarily out of print   † Forthcoming

Temporarily out of print   † *Forthcoming*

Temporarily out of print   † *Forthcoming*